Systems
Management
of Operations

PRENTICE-HALL, INC.
Englewood Cliffs, N.J.

MARTIN K. STARR
Columbia University

Systems

Management

of Operations

Printed in the United States of America

13-881524-0

Library of Congress Catalog Card No: 73-143437

Current Printing (last digit):
10 9 8 7 6 5 4 3 2 1

Prentice-Hall International, Inc., *London*
Prentice-Hall of Australia, Pty. Ltd., *Sydney*
Prentice-Hall of Canada, Ltd., *Toronto*
Prentice-Hall of India Private Limited, *New Delhi*
Prentice-Hall of Japan, Inc., *Tokyo*

To My Sister

. . . Renée

The title, *Systems Management of Operations*, was chosen to emphasize that the subjects covered in the chapters of this book are highly dependent on each other. The dependencies differ according to the type of system that exists and the kinds of model that the manager decides to use.

Guidelines

These two aspects of systems (types of shop system and kinds of model) appear repeatedly. Thus, the *key* to using the text effectively is to recognize two major classification systems. The first, which is methodological, is regularly applied to the second, which is problem oriented.

I   Model Type: Methodology (Technique orientation)
    1.   Network theory and algorithms
    2.   Programming models with fully defined objectives and constraints
II Shop or Systems Type: (Problem orientation)
    1.   Flow shops
    2.   Job shops
    3.   Project systems

Technology and Methodology

It is well-known that operations combine to form three basically different classes of processing systems, namely, the *flow shop*, the *job shop*, and the *project*. Almost every industry has its share of all three kinds of process systems, although most accent one form more than another. When products (or services) achieve a high demand level, a flow shop can be used. Alternatively, a large *variety* of products can be generated by the job shop. *Combinations* of flow and job shop occur quite often because they can provide a balanced product-mix. Repair and maintenance operations characterize the job shop while R&D is a system of projects.

The operations manager knows it is essential that he be well-versed in *all* shop configurations. It is the mark of his professionalism that his methodological skills transfer easily between industries, e.g., from food to flight,

Preface

or from petro-chemical plants to custom tool and die makers. For this reason, management education stresses methodology.

The operations, themselves, are technological, involving physical transformations of input materials to output products and services. But technology, unlike methodology, is not readily transferable between industries. A machine shop manager does not easily manage a petroleum refinery, a telephone system manager will not find technological similarities between communication and canning.

Operations managers rely upon their technicians and engineers to deal with technology. We often hear about technological change causing a system to become obsolete. It is as true that methodological advances can render a system obsolete although we do not hear so much about this subject, perhaps because it is far more difficult to explain. While basic management principles do not change quickly, new techniques and improved methods for achieving management objectives have become available in a rapid succession. There is competitive advantage in being the first to use new approaches for controlling projects, scheduling job shop work, balancing the flow shop, controlling quality and managing inventory. Techniques for improved planning and control are being developed all the time. As a class of methods, they are particularly well-suited for dealing with large and difficult problems which require enormous amounts of detail to obtain useful solutions.

Text Objectives

No matter what the technology, the operations manager's job is filled with details that must be well-managed. That is what this book is all about. *Systems Management of Operations* is an up-to-date text in the operations (and production) management field. It presents important models and procedures, stressing *application* of mathematical programming. Further emphasis is placed on network theory and related algorithms. Thus, the importance of *branch and bounding* has been recognized. Accordingly the text develops the branch and bound technique with some patience and, hopefully, with clarity.

Management planning and control techniques now extend well beyond traditional production fields, encompassing operations of transport, logistics, communication, service systems, and public functions. The organization of the text was designed to present, as best as possible, the large amount of basic material that applies to *flow shops*, *job shops*, and *projects* in this broad sense of generalized operations. Toward that end, these text materials have benefited from instructional experience and testing in teaching.

Chapter Summary

Chapters 1 through 5 develop many of the fundamentals needed to study the three types of systems. In these chapters a logical flow of ideas enables the student to visualize the system as a network model having designed capacities for a specific set of facilities. In later chapters it is shown how the operations manager schedules work so as to best use these facilities. In turn, the operations manager also influences the design of network capacities based on expectations of work load for which forecasting is essential. Forecasting considerations are emphasized in Chapter 9, at a point where the basic models that apply to all three types of systems have been explored:

Chapter 6 treating line balance of the flow shop,
Chapters 7 and 8 dealing with project network methods,
Chapter 9 explaining methods of aggregate scheduling of the job shop.

In Chapter 10 various models that are variants of network and programming methods are introduced which are essential for the adequate management of the work load in a job shop. Chapter 11 explores the sequencing of operations through specific facilities. This discussion is a natural extension of the job shop material covered in Chapter 10; in addition, some sequencing considerations for the flow shop are given.

Chapters 12, 13 and 14, dealing with inventory, quality and facilities management fully reflect the operations manager's interrelations with marketing and finance. The facilities management chapter reports on the state of the art. Inventory and quality control models are covered in detail although each field requires far greater treatment for the specialist.

Operations management represents a synthesis of techniques; a blending of methodologies across a spectrum of problem types. Thus, in Chapter 15 on manpower management the notion is developed of a fair wage for a fair day's output using both classic and contemporary points of view.

Acknowledgments

I thank Professor Matthew F. Tuite for his insightful comments on the text. My treatment of aggregate scheduling (Chapter 9) benefited from my conversations with James P. Monahan of Columbia. Similarly, the approach taken to the subject of sequencing was clarified through discussions with David G. Dannenbring, also of Columbia and now at the University of North Carolina. I appreciate David's conscientious reading of the text. Also, I thank Jerrold P. Katz for his diligent help in preparing an especially strong teachers' manual for this text. And with gratitude, I note that Judith L. Dumas administered this project and typed the manuscript with grace and skill.

Fundamentals **1**

Configuration

of **2**

Operating Systems

The Structure

of **3**

Decision Models

Contents

Cost Models 4

The Product-Mix Problem and Linear Programming 5

Line Balancing the Flow Shop 6

Project Systems 7

Additional Project Systems Concepts 8

Aggregate Scheduling,

Forecasting, **9**

and Prediction

Shop Loading **10**

Sequencing

Operations **11**

Inventory
Management **12**

Quality
Management **13**

Facilities Management **14**

Manpower Management **15**

Bibliography

Systems

Management

of Operations

Models have always existed, an awareness that models have existed has been with us for several hundred years, but the recognition of model properties is just yesterday's achievement. This recognition of **properties** has made an enormous difference to the operations management field. In fact, such recognition created operations management as a field because the properties of models were found to be very general, so general, that all products (not just manufacturing products but industrial products in the broadest sense) and any services could be studied.

Fundamentals 1

Production is a word that describes materials changed by *tools*. *Operations* is a more general term describing the use of tools to achieve changes that are not limited to manufacturing operations on materials such as iron, aluminum, plastics, and petroleum. A rigid interpretation of what a tool is can mislead us.

Tools are not simply Cro-Magnon axes, nineteenth-century hammers, or even twentieth-century inventions such as complex lathes and numerically controlled milling machines. Jet planes, telephones, and radios can be considered as tools and so can hospital facilities, stocks and bonds, weapon systems and computers—software (programs) as well as hardware (machines). With each passing year, tools become more difficult to classify, as historians of technology will attest.[1] Major changes in our abilities to shape the materials of the environment have occurred and continue to occur. Still, we can agree to define tools as *controlled forces used to operate on the environment to bring about goal-oriented change.*

The last hundred years has witnessed a growth in the rate and volume of tool *use* that is astounding. This growth will continue, but tool forms and their uses will probably change markedly. Production and, more generally, operations managers will be the eyes, ears, and hands of such change. Also, they will be the minds that devise the changes to which they react.

The Problems of Operations Managers

Operations management is a *many-problem field*. In other words, the manager concerned with operations encounters one problem after another. These *many* problems arise because *many* operations must be accomplished

---

[1] Much insight can be gained from studying the exceptional literature that exists. For example, Charles Singer, E. J. Holmyard, and A. R. Hall, *The History of Technology* (in five volumes) (London: Oxford University Press, 1954).

to assure that the result of the operations is of agreed upon quantities, on schedule, with specific qualities and costs. Clearly, these operations create *many* problems, and it is not obvious how to treat such great variety. Seldom is the manager faced with one big problem for which one major strategy decision will suffice. Instead, he experiences cascades of interrelated problems. There is no one technique for solving problems at all levels simultaneously, and each company or institution is required to recognize its own unique cascades of problems.[2] In addition, problems generally shift quite rapidly over time for each organization.

The core of operations difficulties is that there are so many different problems encountered each day and so many reasonable arrangements (billions, trillions) for meeting quality, quantity, schedule, and cost with differing kinds of satisfaction. Every different solution has its own costs, delivery dates, changes in resource levels, contributions to profit, or other benefits. Even if the manager could calculate all the benefits of the different options, he would not have a guideline of which systems configuration to choose. Under these circumstances, getting an answer so that the system can operate is what operations management is all about. Clearly, the problems are excessive combinatorial richness, contradictory criteria for judging performance, and so many criteria that it is a big job to determine just what to do for each case.

This book begins by classifying problem types: *flow shop*, *project shop*, and *job shop* operations. These classes will be explained in great detail as we continue. They differentiate between fundamental types of processes. Each problem type has an associated set of reasonable approaches and a cascade of interrelated problems that can only be understood in terms of models which describe the system under study.

Models of Operations

By simplifying reality in a systematic and organized fashion, it is possible to study systems that are too complex to be understood by intuition. Then, for such systems we can diagnose errors to bring about useful remedial changes. The idea of a model is crucial to this reasoning, because a model is a simplified representation of reality. It is constructed in such a way as to explain the behavior of some but not all aspects of that reality. The reason that a model is employed is that it is always *less complex* than the actual situation in the real world. It must, however, be a good representation of those factors or dimensions that are strongly related to the systems objectives; otherwise, it will not be a useful model, and, therefore, it should not be used.

Model building in the production or operations management field fol-

[2] Hospitals, libraries, and governmental administrative offices, for example.

lows the above prescription. More successful models have been developed in production than in any other functional area, for production has the advantage of being visible, and its surrounding environments are less uncertain than those of marketing or finance. Without doubt, the production function is represented by the most complete set of planning, problem-solving, policy, control and decision-making models that exist in any organizational division of industry.

There are many kinds of models. *Normative* decision models determine what "ought" to be done. *Descriptive* models communicate some part of what "can" be done. *Isomorphic* models do not combine variables but simplify reality by ignoring certain variables, bounding them out of the system being studied, or treating them as uncontrollable environments. Characteristically, no attempt is made to find out how the system affects the environments, but the environments are assumed to affect the system in a probabilistic fashion. A *homomorphic* model simplifies an isomorphic model of reality by combining some of its variables. (For example, substitute z into the homomorphic model for any x or any y in the isomorphic one. Homomorphic modeling loses information, but it achieves great simplification for analysis.)

Models can be *concrete* or *abstract*. Examples of the concrete are scale models of airplanes used in wind tunnels to test their aerodynamic characteristics, scale models of ships observed in towing tanks, scale models of buildings employed by architects, and scaled prototypes of automobiles used by designers. We can apply the term abstract to such diverse models as maps, diagrams, blueprints, and organization charts. Analog computers represent a cross between the concrete and the abstract. They function by means of correspondence between the physical properties of the computer (such as heat flows, voltage changes and pressure gradients) and the variables and their relations in the system being modeled. Digital computers have no physical correspondence to the problem. Being entirely abstract, they use numerical operations that model the logic of what happens in the real (or analog) system.

Models can be classified as being primarily *qualitative* or *quantitative*. The organization chart is qualitative, while mathematical equations epitomize the quantitative approach. No matter what their form, models can be appropriate or misleading. Correspondence to reality is the main criterion for deciding whether or not a model is really applicable.

Mathematical Programming

Unification of the operations management field would be achieved if we could write out the entire system of equations to describe the effect of all relevant factors on the systems objectives. Such equations would have to contain many probability statements, but this in no way affects the fact that they could be written if one worked hard enough. The system of equations won't ever be written in complete, isomorphic detail, because one has to work too hard interrelating all the cascades of interdependent effects. All relevant variables that interact with each other must be captured in the equations to reflect the way things actually happen. The solution to such equations would determine the *optimal* course of action for the organization. If a *normative* solution of the model (saying what ought to be done) cannot be obtained, simulation of various *descriptive* solutions explaining how the system would behave (if such and such a set of conditions were assumed) could be used. In a homomorphic sense, this job has already been approached by means of simulations of plant operations to help design systems.

For the system of equations, we require that a function such as ϕ be maximized or minimized, subject to the constraints of the system.

$$\max \phi = f(x_1, x_2, x_3, \ldots, x_n)$$
$$\alpha \geq g(x_1, x_2, x_3, \ldots, x_n)$$
$$\beta \geq h(x_1, x_2, x_3, \ldots, x_n)$$
$$\cdot \qquad \cdot \quad \cdot \quad \cdot \quad \cdot$$
$$\cdot \qquad \cdot \quad \cdot \quad \cdot \quad \cdot$$
$$\cdot \qquad \cdot \quad \cdot \quad \cdot \quad \cdot$$
$$\gamma \geq k(x_1, x_2, x_3, \ldots, x_n)$$

This is an important way of stating managerial objectives. The manager cannot optimize his system's behavior with respect to all his objectives, so he chooses one of them, ϕ, as being the most important one. All other goal factors are treated as constraints. Thus, ϕ is the objective; $\alpha, \beta, \ldots, \gamma$ are the system's resource constraints. The x_j's are the various activities that can be employed to achieve the objectives. The use of these activities depletes the resources. The programming formulation that we are using here might appear to be quite similar to that of linear programming, which we will review in detail shortly. However, the functions $f, g, h, \ldots, k$ are not likely to be linear and usually will include probability terms unless we assume that they are determinate.

We should notice that only n types of activities are listed. This is a practical limit. Man, after all, has bounded rationality[3] and cannot conceive of everything that "might be." In theory, a set of production department equations, a set of enterprise equations, national equations, or world equations might be written. The theoretical possibilities are not challenged or altered by the scope of the undertaking. The practical limitations become formidable at a level below that of the size of most firms and, in many cases,

---

[3] The concept of bounded rationality, introduced by Herbert A. Simon, *Models of Man* (New York: John Wiley & Sons, Inc., 1957), p. 199.

at a level below that of even the production department's system. Nevertheless, we must structure our thinking in such a way as to parallel the underlying meaning that is implicit in the total system of equations. And we should note that many of the variables in the system are environmental, affecting our dependent (performance) variables in specific ways and being affected, in turn, in fashions unspecified by our models. It is only over time that these cause and effect links can make themselves felt.[4]

Transformation

Operations are *controlled* (goal-oriented) transformations. A piece of metal has a hole drilled or punched into it; film is developed; a man travels from New York to Los Angeles; a new pit in a mine is opened—all are examples of controlled transformation. Yet, not all transformation forces are controlled. Many acts of nature, for example, are not even predictable. Controlled change must often take place in an environment of uncertainty. (Even though the winds are uncertain, the navigator brings his ship or plane to berth.) The state of the system can be watched, and if one knows what to observe, corrective actions can be taken to remedy undesirable deviations of the system from its expected standards of performance. This reasoning has to do with control theory and control mechanisms that are essential to operations management. Every action produces chains of reactions occurring throughout the system in something like the firing of a network of nerves. The analogy is not a bad one; in fact, the operations system can be viewed as a very simplified nerve network with beneficial results.

Network Models

In studying operations, every attempt is made to reduce complications caused by indirect, dependent, and cascaded relations. Even so, the cooperative, coordinated efforts of many individuals having different functional relations is essential for the organization's benefit. Network models help to render an intelligent view of systems complicated because of size and number of interconnections. The system is perceived as a network being composed

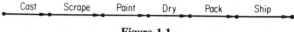

Figure 1.1

of many activities, each of which has a beginning and a completion. For example, Figure 1.1 illustrates a simple series of production activities. To

---

[4] For example, as regulation of pollution controls or law suits directed against inadequate product safety.

demonstrate the generality of networks, history can be portrayed in network form as shown in Figure 1.2.

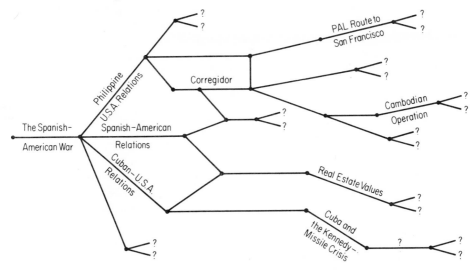

Figure 1.2

Production networks can be viewed as a set of facilities, represented by network nodes. Each node *provides service*, i.e., *specific transformations*. Units come to a network node to receive service. Thus, we have a provider of service and a user of that service. This is the underlying theme of transformation processes. To understand process control, it is essential that we classify the basic configurations that the transformation process can take, i.e., flow shop, job shop, and project shop. The process can be viewed as a single entity or as a number of individual units that are coordinated to act as a whole. Figure 1.3 shows a "big" system as a composite of many subsystems

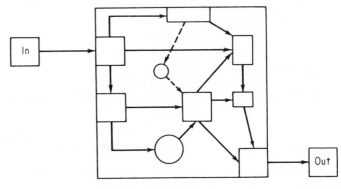

Figure 1.3

"The system" is a composite of subsystems.

contained within the total process. Each possible arrangement of components is a configuration in its own right. Such a model is conceptually applicable to a single individual or machine, a department of men or machines (see Figure 1.4), a division, the organization as a whole, or an entire industry.[5] In practice, every model is a sum of smaller models.

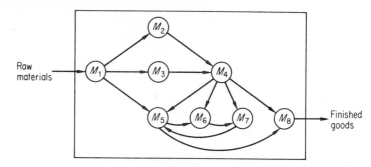

Figure 1.4

A system of interrelated machines, M_j.

Figure 1.5 depicts a flow of products through the transformation system of a three-product company. Each aggregation of individual input-output models produces a specific network configuration.

Certain network details can be highlighted to provide specific information to serve a need, often at the expense of other information that might be unnecessary in the intended context. For example, Figure 1.6 might be a flow of materials for some specific part of the production sequences of one of the products of Figure 1.5. Dimensional characteristics of the plant layout are lost, but the operational details of the process are magnified.

In all networks, some subgroup of nodes constitutes the model; the remainder of the network is the model's environment. Taken together, the model and its environment form the system (Figure 1.7). Measures of performance are restricted to the network sections bounded by the model, but the remainder of the network does affect the performance measures. What is the advantage of such a network model or, for that matter, a mathematical programming model or any model? The answer is that such models organize what happens in simple terms; they permit relevant issues to emerge, and often they allow solutions to be found for quite complex problems.

Systems

What part of the system is to be modeled? How does what is relevant get bounded into the model? What variables get considered and which ones

---

[5] To exemplify this, see industrial input-output analysis, pp. 446–450.

get left out? The answer is direct: All elements that affect performance measures must be included. If we are interested in evaluating racing speed, the thermodynamic factors of engine design interacting with body design and track and driver variables must be included in the racing model. So,

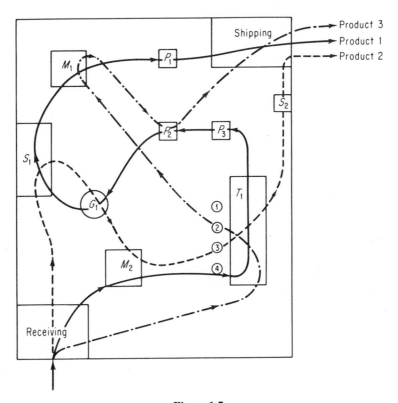

Figure 1.5

Flow process layout diagram for a system with multiple product-mix requirements.

we are bound by the rule that if it plays a real part in the problem, include it. Of course, if you can't see the "truth," you may settle for too small a system. Or if you think everything affects you, you may overdo model construction and bring it too close to reality to solve it. This wastes all your efforts. Or you may include wrong elements that invalidate your work. Troubles like this didn't stop systems analysts and engineers from getting Armstrong to the moon.

There are many possible ways of examining the same structure. The particular interpretation of a set of operations is dependent upon the specific perspective used. The modern management point of view cuts across departmental and divisional lines. Such an approach sharply diverges from the

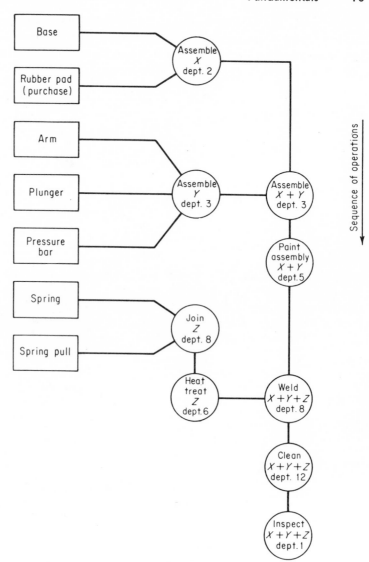

Figure 1.6

A "Gozinto" (goes into) chart for the finished assembly, $X + Y + Z$.

notion of a single functional area of management that can be isolated on an organization chart, as the one shown in Figure 1.8.

Most companies interpret the organization chart in a literal sense. They accept the concept of fixed organizational boundaries and the idea, bluntly stated, that each division should mind its own business. For example, in this framework, production people are expected to deal with technology, engi-

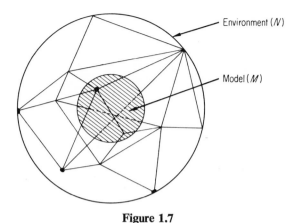

Figure 1.7

$M + N$ = the system.

neering, materials, equipment, and plant. Problems concerning product or service acceptance in the marketplace, price, distribution, promotion, and advertising are out-of-bounds. The operations department rejects "interference" from other divisions. This holds true for each division; a tradition that is at odds with modern management philosophy.

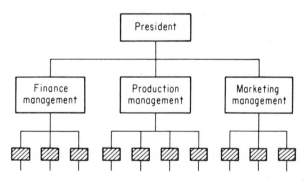

Figure 1.8

The static concept of organizational position.

Management today is aware that divisional decisions must include a realistic appraisal of factors that fall outside the *nominal* organizational boundaries. Furthermore, decisions and policies in one area affect the utility of decisions and policies in other areas. From this fact emerges the requirement that *boundaries must be redefined* according to the nature of the problem. (Figure 1.9 illustrates this requirement.) Arbitrary, traditional boundaries can inflict large penalties on the company. Faced with increasing competitive pressures, many organizations have recognized the need to realign divisional

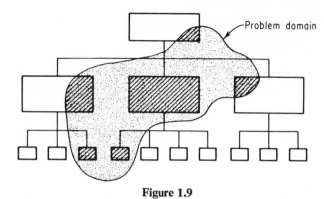

Figure 1.9

The boundary of a problem transcends traditional divisions.

viewpoints—to achieve integration and synthesis, a blend, a coming-together. In other words, they have accepted the systems philosophy to replace the older notion that sanctifies divisional boundaries.

The systems concept, as previously noted, operates on the premise that decisions must include all factors that are relevant to the problem, no matter how many organizational entities are involved.[6] Then, each division contributes in its own area of specialization to the resolution of the problem. Decisions of this kind are not made in an arbitrarily defined vacuum. Problems that are improperly bounded violate the systems concept, and this myopic approach to problem solving can produce severe penalties.

When the systems philosophy prevails, divisional points of view are reconciled and coordinated with the overall objectives of the company.[7] Why then should there ever be a unique operations management viewpoint in a company that accepts the systems philosophy? Seemingly, a single point of view would exist, namely, the company's point of view. Because each problem includes all relevant factors—no matter where they exist organizationally— then the company's objectives should prevail. Theoretically, this is true; realistically, many difficulties interpose themselves.

Input-Output Systems

When we concentrate on the network and look at any particular node— where one thing arrives and another leaves, where one operation starts when another is completed—an important analytic process is at work. Each

[6] The factors that are relevant to a great number of problems fall primarily within the jurisdiction of one particular organizational division. The divisional arrangement coincides, in these cases, with the systems boundaries.

[7] See the discussion of synthesis, Chapter 15, p. 474.

node represents an input-output system. Transformation is the foundation of input-output concepts. It is the function that relates the inputs (*I*) and the outputs (*O*). In mathematical terms, it is: $O = f(I)$, where transformation is equivalent to the function symbol, *f*. Graphically, we can represent this (Figure 1.10):

Figure 1.10

A group of input-output nodes can be gathered together and treated as a single node. This operation constitutes a *homomorphic* transformation of the larger network. On the other hand, by means of analysis, an iso-morphic system of interconnected operations can be broken down into a series of individual input-output models. This allows detailed study but raises questions of how the results of the study can be used to modify the total system (the problem of synthesis).

The operations that we have in mind *characterize* production systems in the factory—but they are not limited to manufacture. They apply equally well to supplying goods or services, transportation, communication, mining, office operations, hospital and library services, power plant, production and government and military systems. Operations management is applicable to all forms of transformations *organized* to meet specific objectives. As we proceed, our discussions will be concerned with: (1) the design; and (2) the use of *any* process or procedure that *transforms* a set of *input* elements into a goal-oriented set of *output* elements as shown in Figure 1.11 below. Each of these processes are nodes in their respective networks. Sometimes nodes represent massive homomorphic transformations, and at other times they are quite close to the basic operation units in reality.

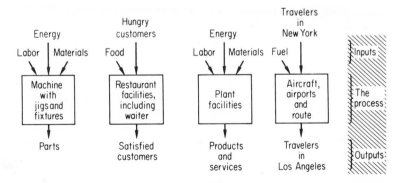

Figure 1.11

Some examples of input-output models.

Stochastic Input-Output Models

Queueing (or service) models justify the point of view that the production of goods is nothing more than a special case of providing transformation services. We class these queueing[8] models as *descriptive* models because they *do not provide* optimum solutions to a decision problem. They are problem-oriented models that can be used to explore the behavior of a given arrangement of facilities. Figure 1.12 shows the fundamental, single channel (one service facility) queueing system.

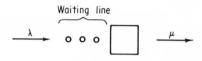

Figure 1.12

Single channel service system.

This stochastic[9] input-output model is the most general *prototype* of input-output analysis, i.e., the basic model of operations management. When the inputs arrive at regular, fixed intervals, and transformation takes place in a regular, fixed way, then we are dealing with a determinate input-output system. Usually, however, the input arrivals and the transformations are best described in terms of statistical distributions, which is why they are called stochastic input-output models. Clearly, the determinate form of the transformation model is simply a special case of the stochastic kind.

Figure 1.13 shows a multiple channel (*M* service facilities) queueing system, which adds an extra network dimension to our thinking. There are many strong mathematical models for dealing with the isomorphic realities of these multiple node systems. With *M*-channels, we have a more sophisticated version of an input-output model.

When the multiple channels are lumped together and treated as a single channel, as shown in Figure 1.14, a *homomorphic* transformation is involved. The *I-O* models we have considered reflect three facts:

1. The single channel representation for the total process is an oversimplification useful for conveying the character of the process but of no consequence when it comes to designing and controlling the real process. For this purpose a great deal more detail and explication is required.

[8] The word queue means a tail-like plait of hair worn behind; a pigtail. We use it in the sense of a waiting line.

[9] The term is generally applied to a process with random characteristics. The Greek root relates to aiming at a target, and in later use the word stochastic represented conjecture.

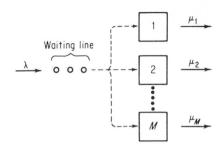

Figure 1.13

M-channel service system.

2. The categorization of facilities as being single or multiple channel is only a beginning. Many other important classes of differentiation exist and have to be considered.
3. To compare alternative process arrangements, it is essential that we develop relevant measures of effectiveness that can be used to evaluate the alternatives. In other words, there must be a sound basis for choosing one arrangement in preference to all others.

Knowledge of the structure of transformation models is fundamental to a nontrivial understanding of the process, which is composed of many queueing *modules* of operations. The modular characteristic of the process is such that many different arrangements are conceivable *but not equally desirable*. The utility of this viewpoint for the manager will depend on his comprehension of queueing systems analysis, which must be complete if he is to take meaningful observations.

Queueing models are concerned with the following generalized situations:

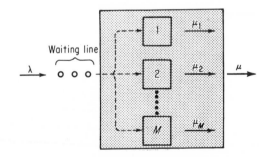

Figure 1.14

M-channel service system analyzed as a single channel service system.

1. The system provides a specific service under the jurisdiction of a manager. Service facilities might be composed of such diverse units as drill presses, milling machines, turret lathes, drop forges, plating tanks, airplane seats, hospital operating tables, supermarket checkout counters, tellers' windows, toll booths, shipping docks, airport runways, restaurant tables, telephone trunk lines, and machine repairmen.

2. Units arrive to receive the service. These can include materials to be machined or plated, travelers, patients, shoppers, customers, ships, airplanes, gourmets, gossipers, and machines that have broken down. The diversity of these applications is incredible.

3. There is an expected or average rate of servicing the units, for example, on the average, five units are serviced per day. We call this expected servicing rate μ. There is a distribution of servicing rates around a mean value. That is, sometimes more than five units are serviced per hour—at other times, less than five units receive service.

4. There is an expected rate of arrival of the units for servicing, for example, on the average, three units require service per day. We call this expected arrival rate λ. There is a distribution of arrival rates around a mean value.

5. *Because we are dealing with distributions*, a greater than average number of units can arrive for servicing. It is equally possible that a run of units will require longer than average servicing times. Under such circumstances a queue or waiting line can develop, even though the process has ample capacity and is capable of providing more service than is normally demanded, that is, $\mu > \lambda$. At other times, less than the expected number of units can arrive or shorter than average servicing times can occur. This produces idle time for service facilities. We have as a guide to the probable behavior of a single channel system the ratio $\rho = \lambda/\mu$. It is called the process utilization factor. We must also know or make assumptions about the shapes of the distributions around the expected values of λ and μ.

We shall first return to this basic model in Chapter 2; and later, additional use is made of it.

Outputs

How does an input-output process get started? Who defines the organization's outputs? Often, it is the marketplace. Financial considerations may dictate that a search be made for activities that will produce a satisfactory return on available capital. Extra capital is frequently a prime motivation for discovering new outputs. Diversification efforts produce similar results. Social and governmental forces can play a crucial role. The sales manager may learn that a competitor has introduced a new product or service that is receiving strong consumer acceptance. He suggests that his own management consider this new product or service possibility. New ideas come to the sales manager from a variety of sources operating in the marketplace. Frequently, a market survey will uncover a consumer need that is not being satisfied; or, a creative employee of the company may just "dream-up" an output that will achieve an economically satisfying level of demand.

The starting point can also be traced to input factors and to process factors. If a new material or a new energy source is developed, the discovery may suggest an output that was either overlooked or one that was previously technologically or economically unfeasible. Similarly, a technological process discovery can lead to a new design capable of shifting consumer demand from accustomed brands. Numerous cases are on record of where a process by-product is suddenly recognized as having marketable characteristics.[10]

Because of the *dynamic* character of the marketplace, new output opportunities are continually developing. A previously unwanted product or service can unexpectedly shift into a situation where it is in substantial demand. The converse is also true; an accepted product can begin to lose popularity. This can be traced to competitive activities, or to a shift in consumer wants. The workings of the marketplace and the financial motivations that lead to the search for new activities are continually interacting with the operations management area.

Process Efficiency

Outputs should have *greater value* than the *combined* costs of the inputs and the amortization charges for investment in the process. This is different from engineering expectations for physical systems where, because of friction and heat losses, the usable, physical output is less than the sum of the input energies. Thus, the *efficiency* of a process in engineering terms is:

$$\text{Physical Efficiency} = \frac{\text{Useful Output}}{\text{Input}} \leq 1$$

This condition would produce bankruptcy in the economic world. The efficiency of a production process, from the viewpoint of the physical system, is measurable in the above terms. At the same time, operations management is beholden to economic criteria. In economic systems, the efficiency must be greater than one, if a profit is to be made:

$$\text{Economic Efficiency} = \frac{\text{Revenue}}{\text{Costs}} \geq 1$$

[10] Serendipity, which is the *unexpected* occurrence of a fortunate situation, has recently become an important objective of managers. The term is nineteenth-century, but only in the last ten years have managers who deal with great complexity come to feel that certain approaches to their "veiled" problems might be more "lucky" than others. See footnote 3, page 53, for the derivation of this word.

It is not essential that as the engineering aspects of process efficiency increase so do their economic counterparts. Costs may decrease, but so may price and revenue decline. Operation managers must be able to understand both these engineering and economic points of view.

A *process* consists of investments representing *fixed costs*. These are costs that do not vary as a function of the output rates. What kind of costs are invariant to the number of operations that are required? A good deal of interpretation is possible in the assignment of costs to this fixed charge category. For example, depreciation allowances that result from age characteristics are invariant to the amount of use that equipment receives. Consequently, it would seem appropriate to include such depreciation expenses as part of the fixed cost category. On the other hand, depreciation that results from use would violate this concept. It is quite difficult to separate these charges. Another fixed cost might be municipal taxes that are independent of the company's revenue. Fixed power and light charges and basic insurance charges also belong in this cost category. For the most part, fixed costs arise as a result of investments in plant, facilities, and so on. Most of these are depreciated as a function of time and not as a function of output volume.

Inputs are defined as factors that produce *variable costs*. Such costs are paid out on a per-unit (of volume) basis. Direct labor and direct material costs are typical. They can be charged with relative ease to each unit of output; but variable costs also create certain anomalies. There are, for example, indirect labor charges that are associated with office work. Such costs are difficult to attribute directly to a particular unit of output or on a cost-per-piece basis. With some sense of vagueness, they are assigned to the category of overhead costs. Similarly, salaries paid to supervisory personnel fall outside specific definition. Irregular expenses are generally treated as fixed costs.

Basically, materials, labor, and energy constitute inputs. Plant, equipment, and facilities make up the process. In these terms, it is the inputs to the process over which management exercises most of its *day-to-day* control. Since the process has more inertia than do the inputs, it is harder to achieve a change in the process than in the inputs.

We gain something by looking at this discussion in another way. This concerns the interrelationships of management. Marketing management understands the way in which output produces revenue. Financial management is expert in fixed costs being responsible for determining the extent of investment in the process and their economic constraints on the system. These restraints affect what will be made and how it will be made. Operations management translates the objectives and constraints into terms of variable cost systems. It is hardly surprising that operations-oriented departments tend to think in terms of operating costs. Still, these stereotypes represent a narrow point of view.

Of major importance is the fact that a process is composed of a set of operations. Traditionally, it is held that if each operation were made as efficient as possible, then: (1) the set of operations known as the process would be most efficient; and (2) if the process were most efficient, then the economic value would be maximized because the costs would be minimized.

Modern operations management recognizes that both of the above points *may* be wrong. The field no longer concentrates attention on individual operations. Getting work done is still the core issue, but the manner of getting work done that is most compatible with the organization's objectives has been subjected to new criteria. We can say that *measures of effectiveness* are now being used in addition to *measures of efficiency*. Measures of efficiency are operations-oriented. Measures of effectiveness are process-oriented and systemic in nature.

Operations Management

The management of systems to process inputs, transforming them into outputs that have positive *value*, is the mission of operations management. The *coordination* of many activities is required, such as the time studies of industrial engineers, the hiring practices and wage systems of industrial relations and personnel, the demand forecasts of the sales and marketing department, and record generation of accountants and financial decisions of the controller. The picture changes, of course, according to the specific situation.

Our interest in management will be defined in terms of operating and designing the process (or alternatively, controlling and planning it). The organization must maintain inventories at required levels and control output quality and quantity according to standards. A variety of criteria exist to describe how well management is performing; for example, is it achieving minimum process costs, minimum total elapsed job-processing times, maximum capacity utilization, and maximum profit? Since obtaining one objective often precludes obtaining the others, the choice of appropriate objectives is related to the organization, its specific type of system, what methodology is available, and the values held by the managers. At one time, this was not considered an issue. All managers were said to have the same objectives and constraints. Probably, the statement still holds true for objectives but constraints seem to differ, and as will become apparent, the solutions to problems are highly sensitive to constraints.

Capacities and Flows

Aggregations of operations can be represented as graphs or networks consisting of transformation nodes $(n_1, n_2, \ldots, n_N)$ and directed arcs that are ordered pairs (n_i, n_j) having a directed path between them. The arcs serve as nodal inputs and outputs, as shown in Figure 1.15. The design of

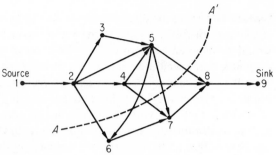

Figure 1.15

the system determines the specific capacities, c_{ij}, between the nodes of the directed paths. Planning regulates the actual flows, f_{ij}, so that $c_{ij} - f_{ij} \geq 0$. Process models frequently group nodes to partition the system into a smaller number of input-output units in order to reduce the complexity of the system being studied. For example, Figure 1.16 results from isolating nodes 1 and 9

Figure 1.16

after aggregating nodes on their respective sides of the cut AA' in Figure 1.15.[11] The Ford-Fulkerson algorithm provides a method for determining the maximal flow in a directed network.[12] Other approaches exist for determining the shortest and longest routes through a network. By analogy, these characteristics of network models (or their equivalents in matrix form) can be related to production volume, costs, and profits and, thereby, used to resolve operation management problems. Network configurations can differ significantly according to the type of operations system that is involved.

Deviations from planned flow patterns may be traced to chance variabilities caused by facility breakdowns, variations in worker performance, absenteeism, etc. But, in general, the overall process is designed to perform in a stable fashion, amenable to verification through statistical quality control methods. Additional variability often enters the system in the form of fluctuating demand and variable lead times for the delivery of materials that must be inventoried for use by the process. The essence of operation manage-

[11] A cut can be found that represents minimal flow capacity across a boundary that separates the source and sink of the network. This minimal cut establishes the maximal flow of the network. It is not hard to find the minimal cut for simple networks as illustrated by Problem 2 at the end of this chapter.

[12] See L. R. Ford and D. R. Fulkerson, *Flows in Networks* (Princeton, N.J.: Princeton University Press, 1962).

ment methodology is therefore directed toward rationalizing the complexity of alternative combinations for using raw materials, in-process inventories, and production capabilities to produce process flows that meet finished goods inventory requirements and consumer demands, in the best possible (optimal) fashion.

PROBLEMS

1. What would be the appropriate homomorphic representation of Figure 1.15 on p. 20 if the only change made is that the arrow 5-6 is reversed in direction? (NOTE: We shall discuss, at a later stage, the use of feedback to achieve operations control.) What other cut of the network can be found that allows the straightforward homomorphic transformation even though the direction of the arc 5-6 continues reversed?

2. Consider the networks of directed arcs and associated capacities shown in Figure 1.17 below:

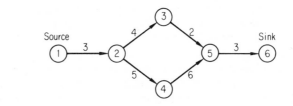

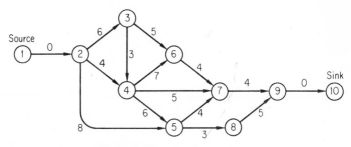

Figure 1.17

Determine the maximal flow from the source to the sink of these networks. (It may help to try various network cuts to determine the minimal cut-maximum flow characteristics of the networks.)

3. The Gamma Company determines that it can achieve savings by subcontracting its die-cast work. The die-casting department is to be closed down. The head of the die-cast department cannot be expected to view this decision in the same way that other company executives will see it. How can he identify with company objectives when his

services are about to be terminated? The manager of the production department may also resist this decision. His budget will be cut; his importance in the organizational hierarchy will be diminished. What kinds of problems are these, and what can be done about them?

4. The actual, thermodynamic efficiency of a combustion engine can never reach 100 per cent. But, if the utility of the engine to the user of the engine were also considered (in addition to the thermodynamic characteristics), why is it expected that the input-output efficiency will rise to be greater than 100 per cent?

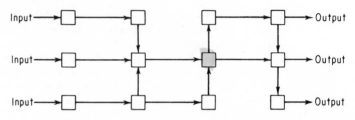

Figure 1.18

The failure of one mechanical component can produce the equivalence of failure in other mechanical components. There is only one mechanical unit in this diagram that when broken down will shut off the entire system.

5. Develop a network of historical events similar to the one drawn for Figure 1.2, p. 7. Use some period of history that interests you. (Note that as you interpret the meaning of various arcs and nodes in such a system, many questions arise which might not have occurred to you without the network model.) What quantitative meaning can you give to such a network?

6. Which node, when removed from the network, will stop the system? Explain why this node might be a bottleneck. How does this node illustrate the statement that systems units are interdependent?

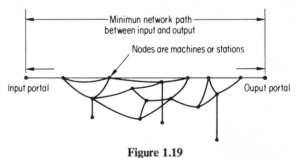

Figure 1.19

7. How can the string network illustrated in Figure 1.19 be used to determine maximum travel distance (or, say, profits) between any two network nodes? How does this string network qualify as an analog computer? (See p. 4.)

Information is the foundation upon which the operations management area is built. Long before this field was dominated by quantitative techniques, a class of information organizing devices was developed. It consisted of charts, tables, and, above all, graphics that brought together the necessary facts for scheduling, sequencing, and more generally controlling the multitude of operations that made up the process. Many of these chart and graph techniques are still in use. Often, even though a mathematical or computer analog exists that perfectly represents what the chartist is trying to achieve, the hand and eye approach is retained and used. Many times, these two different ways of assembling information are used in parallel because communication and understanding are far more easily achieved when a visual system represents purpose.

Each class of system has its own form of information. One of the most powerful ways of organizing the systems with which we will deal is in terms of how often the same operations are performed, how frequently the same sequences of operations are used, how many different kinds of operations there are, and how interrelated they are to each other. From such analysis, we obtain these classifications: flow shop system, project shop, and job shop. Queueing models often provide a good deal of insight concerning the operating characteristics of small network sectors.

Configuration

of 2

Operating Systems

Competent production and operations planning result in the construction of systems represented by networks with carefully designed capacity configurations. The directed flows of such networks satisfy consumer demands in an optimal fashion. But to achieve this objective requires many prior steps. Considerations of marketing, finance, technology, and so forth, produce highly differentiated network configurations, the major classes of which are flow systems, job shop systems, and project systems.

Classification

What distinguishes the different types of systems, and what relevance do these distinctions have for the manager?

The flow system is a relatively continuous process and, in general, the most efficient production configuration. Units receive service in a serial-type fashion. Since there is continuity, a lot of thought can go into the design of the flow system. Reasonable investments for studying and perfecting flow system operations can be substantial because the operation set-up costs are carried by a larger volume of items. In the flow shop, each item moves along as though carried by a conveyor (and, in a paced flow shop, a conveyor often is used). Mass production, as visualized in the automobile industry, is one form of flow shop; it is not, however, the only form. Perhaps the best definition of a flow system is simply to take literally the concept of flow whether it is the flow of work moving past process facilities or the facilities moving past stationary work. The serial production of flow shops encourages *division of labor* according to skills and operation specialization improving the efficiency, productivity and inventory levels of the system. Refineries and many chemical industries are based upon continuous flow systems. To a reasonable extent, commercial aircraft can be said to operate in a continuous (or relatively continuous) flow system. Some flow systems embody interrupted and changing flows. They are frequently called intermittent flow systems.

Project systems will be treated after flow shops. They possess many characteristics of flow shops and also of job shops. In some ways, a project

24

bridges these two fundamental systems. In other ways, it is uniquely its own special form of a system of operations. In particular, it is basically a one-shot affair. The operations in a project system are not repeated. There is no meaningful concern for volume of production since the project is a unique undertaking. Consider the Apollo moon shot as a good example of a project. When, and if, moon shots become a regular occurrence, the project system will give way to an intermittent flow system.

The job shop system is based upon batch-type processes. The batches of materials quite often are *made to order* on *general purpose* equipment. With such general purpose equipment, many different kinds of items can be made on the same facility. *Special purpose* equipment, most often found in the flow shop, is less flexible but usually more efficient for those jobs which it has been specially designed to do. Batch scheduling integrates the operations of the job shop system. It is not unusual that a job which is done will never be repeated again.

Configuration Factors

What forces lead to the selection of a particular configuration? In the first place, demand levels play a great part. If the demand for a given number of particular items is not large and not likely to be repeated again (i.e., static), we treat the order as a one-time situation. The job shop system is ideally suited when the need is for "make to order." With dynamic or continuous demand, it becomes reasonable to "make for stock," thereby gaining the advantages of the flow shop.

In the second place, the design of the product-mix, or whatever output the system produces, can influence the volume of standard or modular parts that are required. With high degrees of modularity[1] flow systems of operations can be set up even though no one output of the organization justifies the flow shop volumes. For example, say that the same motor unit appears in a variety of household appliances, none of which have sales that justify a flow system configuration. The modular motor aggregates demand permitting the use of the flow shop with its economic advantages.[2]

[1] See Martin K. Starr, "Modular Production—A New Concept," *Harvard Business Review*, 43: 6 (November–December, 1965) 131–142, and the discussion on p. 371.

[2] The trend toward modularity is reinforced by the consumer's demand for *maximum productive variety* (or maximum choice). To achieve this variety, capacities to design and manufacture parts that can be combined in numerous ways are required, as well as compatible managerial abilities. The drive toward productive variety is being forced by external factors, but it is made possible because of internal ones. We can state that:

1. The force for this change comes from the marketplace.
2. The means for change resides in:
   . . . methodology derived from the management sciences;

We may ask, how many different products are there, and what is their ABC dollar volume distribution? The ABC notion is an important one.[3] Few organizations have equal product volumes for all the products in the line. Normally, some are heavy and some light. Similarly, a few per cent of all beer drinkers account for a very large per cent of all beer that is drunk. The same reasoning applies to who flies the most miles, income distributions, etc. The key point here is that there may be economic justification to set up a flow shop for A-type items (Figure 2.1).

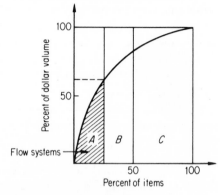

Figure 2.1

With the ABC format in mind, we can briefly reexamine the notion of modularity. How similar are the products in the line? With modularity, it is possible to discuss *parts* instead of *items* and to get an ABC distribution where the *x*-axis is: per cent of parts. Then given that a small enough number of items contribute a large enough part of the volume, we move toward the scale efficiencies of the flow shop by aggregating equivalent operations and providing for special purpose functions as, for example, in auto production.

Technological Constraints

What influence do technological considerations have on the system's configuration? Modularity means the same part number; to the engineer

---

    . . . technology derived from the physical sciences;
    . . . data processing ability obtained from electronic computers.

In other words, the consumer is demanding ever greater variety from which to choose. And new methodologies and technological achievements have developed within the production area that permit the consumer to force this issue.

[3] The ABC distribution follows a mathematical form known as the log-normal distribution (i.e., a normal distribution of logarithms), see Figure 2.1. A variety of curves can be drawn between (0, 0) and (100, 100) including the straight-line diagonal.

and operations manager it means the same technological sequence. Flow systems epitomize a well-developed set of operations constrained by technological sequence.

Thus, with m machines there are $m!$ technological orderings that are theoretically possible. In an $n \times m$ problem (n jobs) there can be $(m!)^n$ different possible arrangements (see Table 2.1[4]). Therefore, a reasonable designation of flow shop is as follows: all jobs follow the same machine sequence; and in the job shop system they do not. Of course, the notion of "all" should be changed to "enough," invoking the sense of the ABC distribution. Then, where there are two machines, A and B:

Table 2.1 There Are Eight Unique Orderings for Three Jobs

	1	2	3	4	5	6	7	8
Job 1	AB	AB	AB	AB	BA	BA	BA	BA
2	AB	AB	BA	BA	BA	BA	AB	AB
3	AB	BA	AB	BA	BA	AB	BA	AB
	Flow Shop	Job Shop			Flow Shop	Job Shop		

For the project system, $n = 1$. Therefore, only one of the rows in the table could apply, and the technological orderings of the project could be no greater than $m!$.

It should be noted that at each machine, the jobs can be ordered in $n!$ ways. Therefore with m machines there are theoretically $(n!)^m$ sequences of jobs through machines. For the case of 2 machines and 3 jobs, we generate

Table 2.2

There are 36 unique sequences	Machine	
	A	B
1	1 2 3	1 2 3
2	1 2 3	1 3 2
3	1 2 3	3 2 1
4	2 1 3	2 1 3
5	2 1 3	3 1 2
.	.	.
.	.	.
36	3 2 1	3 2 1

a table of 36 possibilities, as shown above in Table 2.2. Not all these sequences may be feasible, however, because of technological sequencing constraints.

[4] From Mahendra A. Bakshi and Sant Ram Arora, "The Sequencing Problem," *Management Science*, 16: 4 (December, 1969), B247–B263.

We can illustrate the flow system as a serial production operation and the job shop as a batch operation (Figure 2.2). The project is clearly seen as a hybrid of the two systems with the special property of being nonrepetitive.

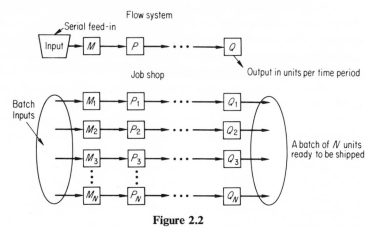

Figure 2.2

Systems Design

We have classified systems according to their structural characteristics as flow systems, project systems, and job shop systems. Additionally, we should note that all three of these types of systems differ markedly in their basic *design (capacity) considerations*. For the flow shop, a single product of high volume moves through the network. Keeping the entire network busy is a common objective. And, as we have indicated, variants of sufficiently *similar technology* often can be substituted for the single product, and the flow system can be maintained. The flow shop configuration permits fewer nodes to be designed for the network, and each node has greater input-output capacity than would be the case for job shop configurations.

Design considerations for the job shop are severe because the character of demand can shift over relatively short periods of time. However, because there are more nodes (skills and abilities) required for multiple products having *dissimilar technological* constraints, the allowable investment per node is smaller than for flow system networks. The assumptions for the job shop begin with a large, fixed set of nodes which can accommodate a variety of flows. One view of the problem is how to use the capacities of the nodes in the best possible fashion. While some idle capacity is expected, its cost is lower than for the highly specialized facilities of the flow shop.

The *operations (flow factors)* of each type of system will differ. We can think of the operations as specifying and controlling the flows, f_{ij}. Thus, the ratios, f_{ij}/c_{ij} must usually be closer to one for the flow system than for the job shop. Decision models can differ according to whether c_{ij} or f_{ij} or $(c_{ij} - f_{ij})$

is the variable under consideration. When c_{ij} is the variable, major systems design factors are under investigation. Network capacities can be altered, even in a flow shop, by hiring, shifting, and laying off workers. Machine investments—especially, special purpose facilities—are less adaptive. Flows are related to demands that are made on the capacity potentials of the facilities. If c_{ij}'s are specified, then operations are at issue; yet, different solutions will generally be obtained if f_{ij}'s are maximized or $(c_{ij} - f_{ij})$'s are minimized.

Project systems are used once; but the c_{ij}'s still command large investments because projects represent a significant effort with a large percentage of the organization's assets at stake. Again, technique is used to maximize project flows, usually with the intention of minimizing the completion date of the project subject to a given project budget.

Mixtures of flow systems, project systems, and job shop systems are common. For example, if a particular job in the job shop gets big enough (in investment), the resulting network closely parallels the project shop. If it gets big enough, in the number of parts to be made and run length, the resulting network might be considered to be an intermittent flow shop. Transportation, parcel post and mail deliveries would be fairly representative of an intermittent flow shop whereas auto production, refining operations and film processing represent a continuous flow shop. An additional factor of importance is whether the flows are determinate or stochastic (random). Most projects are treated as determinate, but troubles arise when this assumption is false. Indeterminancy in the flow system requires careful analytic treatment for capacity design, and elaborate control systems are not unusual.

Management Information Systems

The content and configuration of information for each kind of system will differ. Over the years information systems have developed that are compatible with the nature of the transformations with which the company is dealing.

Designing the system of operations begins with *technological* knowledge of what is to be done. In many cases, this relates to product outputs requested by marketing, since what is to be made is what marketing can sell. Therefore, *blueprints* are the starting point (Figure 2.3). Where many different products are called for on an intermittent basis (typical of a job shop), a great variety of blueprints are on file, and others are being created all the time. Flow process industries would have blueprints of process equipment, but outputs would generally be specified by chemical equations translated into "recipes" for producing food, fuel, and pharmaceutical outputs. The blueprints for transport industries involve distances, assigned routes, maintenance requirements, and so forth. The idea of "the blueprint stage" is simply to *fully* specify the

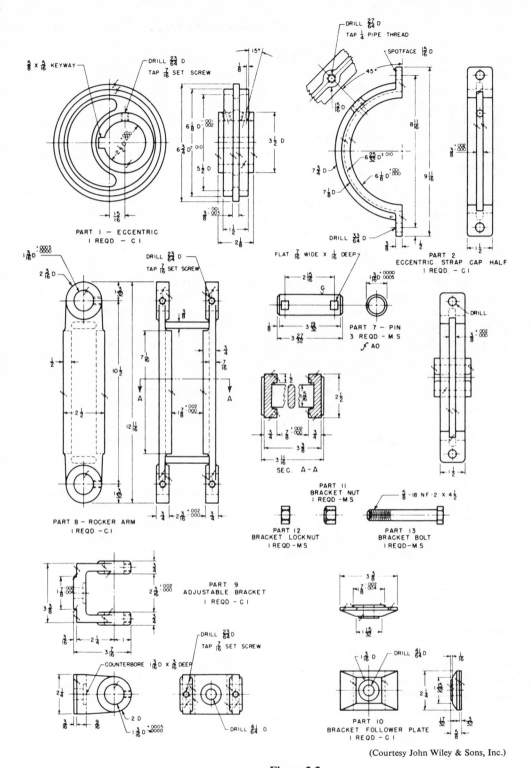

(Courtesy John Wiley & Sons, Inc.)

Figure 2.3

30

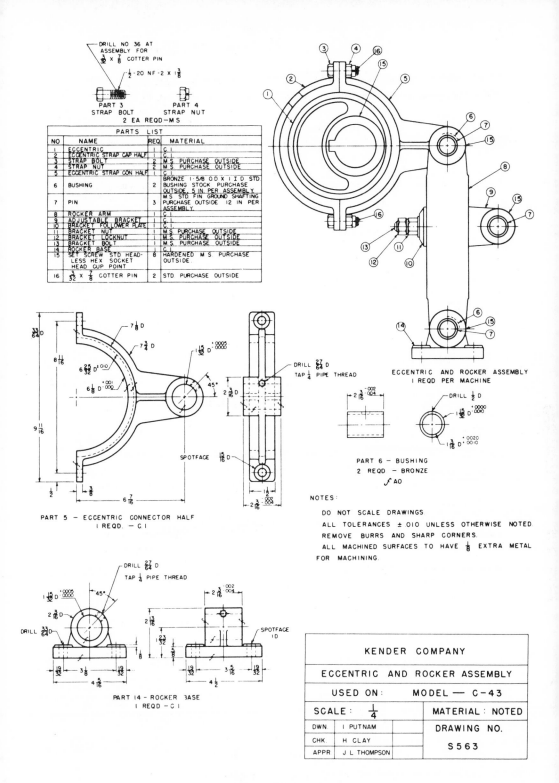

DRILL NO 36 AT ASSEMBLY FOR $\frac{3}{32} \times \frac{7}{8}$ COTTER PIN

$\frac{1}{2}$-20 NF-2 X 1$\frac{3}{8}$

PART 3 STRAP BOLT

PART 4 STRAP NUT

2 EA REQD—MS

PARTS LIST			
NO	NAME	REQ	MATERIAL
1	ECCENTRIC	1	C.I.
2	ECCENTRIC STRAP CAP HALF	1	C.I.
3	STRAP BOLT	2	M.S. PURCHASE OUTSIDE
4	STRAP NUT	2	M.S. PURCHASE OUTSIDE
5	ECCENTRIC STRAP CON HALF	1	C.I.
6	BUSHING	2	BRONZE 1-5/8 O D X 1 I D STD BUSHING STOCK PURCHASE OUTSIDE. 5 IN. PER ASSEMBLY
7	PIN	3	M.S. STD. FIN GROUND SHAFTING PURCHASE OUTSIDE 12 IN PER ASSEMBLY.
8	ROCKER ARM	1	C.I.
9	ADJUSTABLE BRACKET	1	C.I.
10	BRACKET FOLLOWER PLATE	1	C.I.
11	BRACKET NUT	1	M.S. PURCHASE OUTSIDE
12	BRACKET LOCKNUT	1	M.S. PURCHASE OUTSIDE
13	BRACKET BOLT	1	M.S. PURCHASE OUTSIDE
14	ROCKER BASE	1	C.I.
15	SET SCREW STD HEADLESS HEX SOCKET HEAD CUP POINT	8	HARDENED M S PURCHASE OUTSIDE.
16	$\frac{3}{32} \times \frac{7}{8}$ COTTER PIN	2	STD PURCHASE OUTSIDE

ECCENTRIC AND ROCKER ASSEMBLY
1 REQD PER MACHINE

DRILL $\frac{27}{64}$ D
TAP $\frac{1}{4}$ PIPE THREAD

PART 5 - ECCENTRIC CONNECTOR HALF
1 REQD. - C.I.

PART 6 - BUSHING
2 REQD - BRONZE
$\int$ AO

NOTES:

DO NOT SCALE DRAWINGS
ALL TOLERANCES ± .010 UNLESS OTHERWISE NOTED
REMOVE BURRS AND SHARP CORNERS.
ALL MACHINED SURFACES TO HAVE $\frac{1}{8}$ EXTRA METAL FOR MACHINING.

DRILL $\frac{27}{64}$ D
TAP $\frac{1}{4}$ PIPE THREAD

SPOTFACE 1 D

PART 14 - ROCKER BASE
1 REQD - C.I.

KENDER COMPANY	
ECCENTRIC AND ROCKER ASSEMBLY	
USED ON:	MODEL — C-43
SCALE: $\frac{1}{4}$	MATERIAL: NOTED
DWN I PUTNAM	DRAWING NO.
CHK H CLAY	S 563
APPR J L THOMPSON	

Figure 2.3 (cont.)

nature of the desired outputs so that nothing can be left to the imagination in how to achieve those outputs. Projects make use of blueprints and other means of specifying outputs as required by the project technology.

In conjunction with blueprints (and frequently shown on them) is the *bill of materials* (Figure 2.4). It specifies all the parts required to make a

Item ___Switch Z 33___   Sheet No.__1__ of __2__
Drawings__Z 1-Z 6___   Assembly_5HP MOTOR J_

Part No.	Part name	No./item	Material	Quantity/item	Cost/item	Remarks
CH 20	CASING	1	SF60	0. 25 lbs.	$0. 15	Cast, trim
SJ 64	DRIVE SPRG.	2	Sprg. St.	-----	$0. 08	Purchase
RH 82	1" ROD	3	1045 ST.	4 in.	$0. 05	Make
TJ 32	FITTING	1	Ti-6Al-4V	0. 10 lbs.	$0. 85	Forge, anneal

Figure 2.4

Bill of material.

finished component or item, detailing the number of parts per item and the quantities of materials required by each part. Those parts that are to be purchased are indicated. Projects and flow shops use the bill of materials in whatever form is likely to be most useful.

In a multi-product plant where several different items share parts, an *explosion chart* is used to identify the aggregation of part requirements. This chart is a compilation of bills of materials for items having common parts. It is a matrix of parts v. items used for exploding end-use demands into classes of similar activities (Figure 2.5). Thus:

		Item					Part Production Requirements
		1	2	3	4		
	A	2	1	0	0	. . .	R_A
Part	B	0	1	0	0	. . .	R_B
	C	0	1	1	0	. . .	R_C
	⋮	⋮	⋮	⋮	⋮	⋮	
	Demand	D_1	D_2	D_3	D_4		

Figure 2.5

With concentration on modular characteristics, the number of entries per row can be substantially increased; or, on the other hand, the number of rows required to support a given variety of items might be decreased. In the case of both make and buy decisions,[5] it is essential that total requirements reflecting part interdependencies for all items be known. The key is that *total* demands by parts—or by types of efforts in general—must be used as a basis for planning.

A *route sheet* (also called *operations* or *specifications sheet*) describes the processing steps, or operation sequences, required to make each part. Routing is broadly applicable to a variety of industries. For example, routing information must be determined by airlines for their planes or by mining engineers for their excavations. The route sheet often shows the order in which opera-

Part No. __CH/20__		Economic lot size __500__
Part name __CASING__		Process time/pce. __3.5 h__
Blueprint No._____		Set-up time __2 h__

Use for __Switch Z 33__	Quantity per __1__
__Switch Z 34__	__1__
__Sub-contract T. 102__	__50/mo.__

Material __SF 60__	Vendor __BQV__	
% scrap __10__	Weight __¼ lb. per__	Cost __$0.15 per__

Operation No.	Operation	Machine No.	Tool No.	Department
1	CAST	M235	DX 103	D6
2	TRIM	M81	DX 104	D8
3	DRILL(2)HOLES	M631-5	JigX103	D2
4	BROACH	M631-5	JigX1035	D2
5	TUMBLE	DR3 24	——	DR 3

Inspection ____✓____

Authorization ____✓____

Figure 2.6

Route sheet.

tions to complete the part are to be completed (Figure 2.6). Although routing frequently identifies specific facilities at which given operations will be performed, output scheduling is not involved because (clock) arrival times of

[5] See pp. 340–347, 352–356.

the jobs at the facilities are not indicated. Further, there is no specification of the work sequence for a variety of different parts at a given facility. Such assignments are usually made by the foreman or his dispatchers. When certain parts are to be purchased, the relevant information is maintained on stock cards, and this includes information about specific vendors, order quantities based on inventory analysis, price and quantity discount data, and expected lead times for deliveries.

When there are several technological sequencing options, a *precedence diagram* (or matrix) can be drawn up to clarify such flexibility (Figure 2.7a and b).

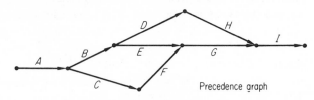

Precedence graph

Figure 2.7a

Precedence graph.

or in matrix form:

(Row is followed by column)

→	A	B	C	D	E	F	G	H	I
A	x	1	1	0	0	0	0	0	0
B	0	x	0	1	1	0	0	0	0
C	0	0	x	0	0	1	0	0	0
D	0	0	0	x	0	0	0	1	0
E	0	0	0	0	x	0	1	0	0
F	0	0	0	0	0	x	1	0	0
G	0	0	0	0	0	0	x	0	1
H	0	0	0	0	0	0	0	x	1
I	0	0	0	0	0	0	0	0	x

Figure 2.7b

Precedence Matrix

Precedence decisions play an important design role in determining major project network configurations. They are also critical for assigning job shop sequences in accord with technological constraints. And, as will be seen, the precedence diagram is particularly applicable to assembly and project shop operations. Precedence is, in a real sense, the blueprint of the flow shop.

Networks of each type are treated in different ways. The information system responds to the fundamental differences. For example, in the job shop, a series of *manufacturing orders* are closely related to routing sheets with the additional information specifying the number of each part to be made. The flow shop system, on the other hand, is designed to a specific productivity rate. Changes in this rate are major decisions; unlike the determination of job order size. Routing and precedence are so basic to both project and flow shops that they influence investments and engineering design. In the job shop, among the most critical functions are (1) scheduling production batches, (2) assigning work to facilities (called shoploading), and (3) sequencing operations at a facility. Some of these operations apply to the project shop and occasionally to the intermittent flow shop.

In the early 1900s, Henry L. Gantt developed a shoploading chart[6] to assist in the job shop assignment function. The chart depicts cumulative workload assigned to machine centers in calendar time. Gantt also developed a layout chart[7] which showed the actual plan of sequencing jobs at each facility. Even now, such charts continue to be used for comparing planned and actual accomplishments. Various kinds of loading and layout charts are available that enable control to be exercised over the production system and allow *expediting* to occur when there is schedule slippage. But the methods for planning production schedules, assigning work, and sequencing have improved greatly. Change can occur, however, because the operations manager never overlooks the fact that the flow shop possesses economic advantages as far as productivity and unit costs. If marketing can increase demand, the system can be moved closer toward the flow shop configuration; and if the production manager can encourage standardization and *modularity*, this also will allow the system to move toward flow shop configurations.

Basic Queueing Configuration

Before the requirements for operating a large system can be studied, the behavior of the basic input-output model of capacity must be understood (see pp. 12–19 in Chapter 1). In its simplest form, the capacity of a facility to provide service *exactly* matches the demand for that service. The demand (or

[6] See p. 268.
[7] See p. 57.

load) arrives at regular intervals, and the servicing times equal these arrival intervals. Since there is no variability, the only question that remains is what capacity should the facility have? Clearly, its capacity must exceed the demand; ideally, it would just equal it.

Now, however, introduce the notion of random irregularity in demand arrivals and/or variable servicing times. Then, even though the average arrival interval is exactly matched to the average service interval, two difficulties can arise. First, sometimes the facility is idle, because there have been no arrivals for an unusually long time and/or because the facility has had a *run* of remarkably short service times. Second, sometimes a *queue*, or waiting line develops, because there has been a cluster of arrivals and/or because a number of long service periods were required. Figure 1-12 illustrates a single channel stochastic input-output system. Figure 1-13 represents a multiple channel stochastic input-output system.

For the successful operation of such a random process, management must decide how much capacity is required, what type of facility will provide optimum service, how to arrange grouped facilities, and what resources might be shifted around to minimize both queues and idle times. To exemplify the complexity of queuing configurations, note that there are cases where the manager, instead of providing service, requires it from a subcontractor or vendor. Although there is relatively little control over the services provided by an outside organization, the manager can generally choose his source of supply from among several competing offers. Direct facility control offers the greatest opportunity for the application of queueing models. Nevertheless, the role of vendors and subcontractors can be built into the total design of the system.[8] Whatever the specific situation, some *measures of effectiveness*, such as the nine shown below, are required to evaluate the service capacity of the facility. Others can be found that are suited to particular situations.

1. The average number of units in a queue, L_q.
2. The average number of units in the system, L. (This includes the number in the queue and the number in service.)
3. The average waiting time or delay before service begins, $W_q = L_q/\lambda$.
4. The average time spent by a unit in the system, $W = L/\lambda$. (This total delay includes the delay before service begins and the time to complete service.)
5. The probability that *any* delay will occur, $p(n > M)$, where n equals the total number of units in the system, and M stands for the number of service facilities.
6. The probability that the total delay will be greater than some value of t, $p(W > t)$. (A comparable expression could be written for W_q.)

[8] An entire class of inventory models belong to the queueing model family. See for example, Martin K. Starr and David W. Miller, *Inventory Control: Theory and Practice* (Englewood Cliffs, N.J.: Prentice-Hall, Inc., 1962), pp. 146–150, 242–248.

7. The probability that all service facilities will be idle, p_0.

8. The expected per cent idle time of the total service facility, $\bar{I} = \dfrac{M}{M} p_0 +$ $\dfrac{(M-1)}{M} p_1 + \cdots + \dfrac{(M-n)}{M} p_n + \dfrac{(M-M)}{M} p_M$, where p_n equals the probability that n units will be in the system, both waiting and receiving service from M facilities.

9. The probability of turn-aways, resulting from insufficient waiting line accommodations, p_N, where $N - M$ represents the maximum number of units that can be stored or accommodated on the waiting line at any moment.

Having evaluated the characteristics of a process in terms of such measures of effectiveness, management can try to regulate the process' performance. Thus, management will control operations to the extent possible by:

1. Securing additional servicing facilities.
2. Rearranging existing service facilities; for example, take three clerks who perform specialized sequential operations on a purchase requisition and revise the job so that the clerks are specialized by types of purchase orders that are handled entirely by one person. In the same sense, preventive maintenance is a rearrangement of service functions used in place of, or in conjunction with, remedial maintenance.
3. Replacing existing service facilities with improved ones. This is partly a function of technological change and partly a function of aging and deterioration of facilities.
4. Establishing a system of priorities whereby certain units receive attention before others do.
5. Providing special service facilities for units having exceptionally long or short service times.

Classes of Models

Consideration of queueing models will be divided into five parts:

1. Sources of input.
2. Queue accommodations.
3. Queue discipline.
4. Service facilities.
5. Process load and process capacity.

Combinations of the five factors account for most of the important process variations that occur.

Sources of Input

When the number of elements that potentially can require service is very large in comparison to the number that actually do, then we can treat that number as though it were infinite. For example, the number of cars that *might* arrive at a toll booth is much larger than the number with reasonable arrival rates could possibly be. In contrast, some input populations are restricted in number so that the arrival of one unit significantly alters the probability that another unit will arrive. These are finite sources. For example, let the queue be the number of absentees in a secretarial pool consisting of ten secretaries. As another example, assume that six similar machines constitute the press shop department. We should distinguish between:

λ = The individual unit parameter, and

λ_n = The process parameter, where n = the number of units waiting for or receiving service in the system.[9]

Observations of breakdowns in the press shop when all machines are operating reveal that, on the average, 12 hours elapse between such breakdowns. This means that, on the average, one machine breaks down every 12 hours and $\lambda_n = 1/12$, where the unit of time in which λ is measured is hours.[10] Now, assume that four of the six machines are shut down because it is decided to subcontract some of the operations to a company with larger and faster presses. A new set of observations is made for the two remaining machines, and the average time between breakdowns is found to be 36 hours. Then, $\lambda_n = 1/36$, which is considerably smaller—a result with which our intuition concurs.[11] When there were six machines operating, the breakdown rate *per machine* was $1/12 \div 6 = 1/72$. This resulted in a *departmental* breakdown rate of $6 \times 1/72 = 1/12$, which was reported. With two machines operating, the departmental breakdown rate was $2 \times 1/72 = 1/36$. The value of λ_n cannot change appreciably when the source is either very large or infinite. Even with fairly large sources, λ_n would hardly be affected by the number of units that have left the population source to request service. On the other hand, when the source is finite, say of size S, the number of units that have left the source to request service will modify the process arrival rate. Thus, $\lambda_n = (S - n)\lambda$.

Models of Service Operations

To illustrate, the queueing formula

$$p_n = \frac{M!}{(M - n)!} \left(\frac{\lambda}{\mu}\right)^n p_0$$

[9] The same reasoning holds true for μ_n and μ where M = service rate .

[10] See the definitions in Chapter 1, pp. 14–16. When a finite source exists, λ must be described by λ_n, where n is the number of units in the system, and λ_n is a function of that number. For this case, $\lambda_n = \lambda_0 = S\lambda = 6(1/72) = 1/12$. Note that $n = 0$ because there are no breakdowns.

[11] Here, $\lambda_n = \lambda_0 = S\lambda = 2(1/72) = 1/36$.

can be used to describe a machine repair system where λ characterizes the breakdown rate of each machine (as an individual). Now, p_n is the probability of n machines being out-of-order; therefore, p_0 is the probability of no breakdowns. There are M machines and only one repairman, whose service rate is μ.

Let $M = 3$, $\lambda = 1$ per day and $\mu = 2$ per day. The following computations apply.

$$n = 0 \qquad p_o = \frac{3!}{3!} \left(\frac{1}{2}\right)^0 p_0 = 1.000 p_0$$

$$n = 1 \qquad p_1 = \frac{3!}{2!} \left(\frac{1}{2}\right)^1 p_0 = 1.500 p_0$$

$$n = 2 \qquad p_2 = \frac{3!}{1!} \left(\frac{1}{2}\right)^2 p_0 = 1.500 p_0$$

$$n = 3 \qquad p_3 = \frac{3!}{0!} \left(\frac{1}{2}\right)^3 p_0 = 0.750 p_0$$

$$\overline{\Sigma p_n} = 1.000 \qquad = \overline{4.750 p_0}$$

Therefore, $p_o = \dfrac{1.000}{4.750} = 0.21$; and $p_1 = p_2 = 0.32$, $p_3 = 0.15$. The same kind of calculations can be used, where S = the number of servicemen. Thus:

$$(0 \leq n \leq S) \quad p_n = \frac{M!}{(M-n)!n!} \left(\frac{\lambda}{\mu}\right)^n p_0$$

$$(S \leq n \leq M) \quad p_n = \frac{n!}{S! S^{n-S}} \cdot \frac{M!}{(M-n)!n!} \left(\frac{\lambda}{\mu}\right)^n p_0$$

and as before:

$$\sum_{n=0}^{n=M} \frac{p_n}{p_o} = 1/p_0$$

And, when M can be considered to be infinite:

$$(0 \leq n \leq S) \quad p_n = \frac{1}{n!} \left(\frac{\lambda}{\mu}\right)^n p_0$$

$$(S \leq n) \quad p_n = \frac{1}{S! S^{n-S}} \left(\frac{\lambda}{\mu}\right)^n p_0$$

and since $M = \infty$:

$$\sum_{n=0}^{n=\infty} \frac{p_n}{p_0} = \frac{1}{p_0}.$$

Queue Accommodations

A natural restriction on queue size exists if the storage facilities needed to accommodate a waiting line are limited. For example, the size of a doctor's waiting room provides a physical upper limit on queue length. Similarly, on a production line, the in-process inventory will be limited by the amount of storage space that can be made available between operations. Figure 2.8 depicts the fact that only an inventory limited to N items can be carried between operations A and B.

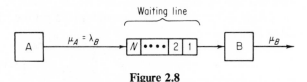

Figure 2.8

There is a limitation on the size of the in-process inventory between operations A and B.

We know that because of variability in both arrival and service rates a queue can form under even the most favorable process utilization ratio, ρ. When this queue has grown to size N, several different things can happen.[12] For example:

The $N + 1$ arrival is turned away—which could mean it is taken to an outside storage depot. In the case of a person arriving at the dentist's office when it is completely filled up, the individual becomes a self-motivated turn-away.

The $N + 1$ arrival does not leave the first service facility, A, but stays there until the queue in front of B can accept it. In this way, A is blocked for other service and forced to be idle. This is equivalent to shutting down operation A until the "bottleneck" is cleared up.

The design of the process must take these possibilities into account. It is unusual that a large in-process inventory can be tolerated. In some production lines no queue is permitted.[13] Our discussion begins to converge on such fundamental subjects as line-balancing, plant layout, and process design. Queueing service models express many of the basic relationships that unite the important elements of a system.

Queue Discipline

Further process control can be achieved by means of policies that regulate the behavior of units waiting for service. Briefly, here are some of the many possibilities.

---

[12] The appropriate equations are: $p_n = \rho^n p_0$; $p_0 = \dfrac{1 - \rho}{1 - \rho^{N+1}}$; $L = \sum\limits_{0}^{N} n p_n$; $W = L/\lambda$;

$L_q = \sum\limits_{1}^{N} (n - 1)p_n$; $W_q = L_q/\lambda$.

[13] Especially where the facilities are arranged for continuous production, that is, a flow shop exists.

1. *Priorities for Service.* If a power failure shuts down a large portion of a refinery, it is to be expected that all other repair work that is going on will be suspended until the cause of the power failure is detected and corrected. This is an example of a *preemptive priority*.[14] In this case, even units that are receiving service are returned to the waiting line because of the emergency. Situations also exist where service has to be completed before the priorities take effect. Frequently, different levels of priorities exist. Units in the waiting line are arranged in their order of importance, not in the order with which they arrive. A great number of different priority rules can be constructed that will achieve significantly different system performances.

2. *Service Granted on a Random Basis.* Often, as the number of units requiring service increases, and as the number of servers becomes large, a random selection is made from the waiting line. Telephone calls can be handled in this manner, where incoming calls, waiting for service, are selected at random to be given access to the trunk lines. In department stores, for better or worse, customers are awarded service on an "almost" random basis by salesgirls. In some systems it is difficult to know the correct order of arrival. To counteract customer illwill, numbered tickets are made available at the entry portal and service is assigned in this numerical order.

3. *Defection and Deflection.* For various reasons, arrivals may decide to leave the queue after they have joined it. This we call defection. They can return at a later time, or perhaps they will never be seen again. Anyone who has spent hours waiting on lines, searching for parking places, and bucking traffic will appreciate the range of goodwill penalties that the inability to defect creates. Many times, an individual observes the length of the waiting line and decides not to join it. This we call deflection. The individual may not ever return again. Although a penalty occurs, the manager may not even be aware of it. Observing and measuring defection can be difficult; it is almost impossible to pin down deflection. The design of the process and the environment in which it operates will determine the probabilities of defection and deflection from a waiting line. Where multiple channels exist, as in a bank, one might find himself hopping from service channel to service channel. Such defections to advance one's cause is termed *switching*.

4. *Entrance in Batches.* Some service facilities can render service only after a minimum number of arrivals has appeared.[15] A variant of this rule requires that a fixed number of units receive service at one time. Other rules

---

[14] As before, repairmen constitute the service facilities; arrivals are equipment failures. If preventive maintenance is used, then arrivals are admitted by appointment and according to a preplanned schedule. Emergencies are assigned preemptive priority.

[15] This can be coupled with a maximum number that signals that service *must* begin.

are based on minimum and maximum waiting times. A great variety of combinations can be found. With such production processes as tumbling or plating, a batch of items are processed together. Elevators provide service in batches, as do Broadway shows and merry-go-rounds. A production process that utilizes batch service will exhibit unique behaviors that no other process design can produce.

5. *First In—First Out.* Of all possible input disciplines, perhaps FIFO (First In—First Out) has received the most attention from methodologists. In this case, each unit enters service in the order of arrival. Even when many service facilities exist, a single queue forms, and when a service facility becomes available, the first on line enters. Although FIFO rules cover a great percentage of applications, many others exist that should not be overlooked, for example, LIFO (Last In—First Out).

Service Facilities

As has already been noted, we can differentiate between service facilities by the number and type of such facilities and by the way in which they are arranged. As was done in the classification of input sources, we can categorize the number of service facilities as being finite or infinite. Examples of infinite numbers of service facilities do not come readily to mind until we realize that the meaning of a service facility does not have to be literal. In other words, the life of radioactive particles, bacteria, and, in fact, the life of human beings can be considered as a service facility. Each life occupies a kind of metaphysical service channel. Birth is comparable to the arrival process, whereas death removes the unit from the service facility. Thus, the service time of the unit is equivalent to the unit's lifetime. We let T_S equal the mean servicing time, or life expectancy, of a unit, where $T_S = 1/\mu$. If we assume that the population in question is 200,000,000 and that the average life expectancy of a unit is seventy years, then, because the process average $\mu_n = n\mu$, we get:

$$T_S = \frac{1}{\mu} = \frac{n}{\mu_n} \quad \text{and} \quad \mu_n = \frac{200{,}000{,}000}{70} = 2{,}857{,}143$$

deaths per year, which is equivalent to almost 5.5 deaths per minute. This result would be precise only if the age composition of the population had reached a steady state, i.e., stabilized.

The birth and death process is a queueing-type model of long standing. Its characteristics are applicable to agricultural processes, the production of pharmaceuticals and antibiotics, the behavior of demographic systems, as well as machine failure and replacement studies. It can be used for a class of inventory problems where the demand for a part is an arrival. The part to be stocked is the facility in this case. The facility is busy if the part is out of stock. A waiting line of unfilled orders can develop. The number of channels is equivalent to the number of parts that are carried. An idle facility is a part that is in stock.[16] We see that literal interpretations of service facilities do not do justice to the scope of production problems that can be viewed in terms of queueing models.

With more than one service facility (that is, multiple channels), the facilities can be set up in either a parallel or series configuration. The arrangement decision (see Figure 2.9) is a major form of producing process control.[17]

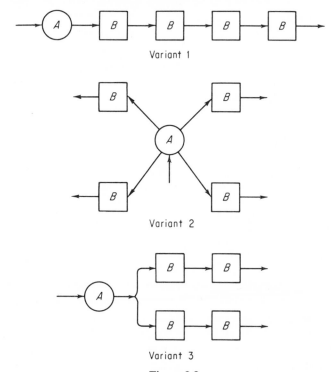

Figure 2.9

Alternative arrangements of facilities produce different systems' performances. Thus, three possible arrangements are shown with one A facility and four B facilities.

Another alternative in the design of service facilities is the choice of a fast facility to replace several slower facilities. To illustrate this case, when a machine breaks down, the entire repair crew can be used to fix it. As an alternative, each man on the team can be assigned a breakdown as it occurs. Under the latter procedure, part of the repair crew will be idle. Finally, a system for assigning the entire crew if there is only one breakdown, splitting

[16] This model is explained in detail in Martin K. Starr, David W. Miller, *Inventory Control: Theory and Practice* (Englewood Cliffs, N.J.: Prentice-Hall, Inc., 1962), pp. 146–150, 242–248.

[17] See pp. 400–404.

the crew in half for two breakdowns, dividing the crew in thirds for three breakdowns, and so on, can be utilized.

In the area of service arrangements, a variety of possibilities exist. Each situation is circumscribed by its own conditions. The ingenuity of the manager is called upon to recognize appropriate strategies. It should be amply clear by now why there cannot be any one, two, or even ten models that will take care of all possible variants of service systems. Ignoring some of the refinements already mentioned, we have considered the following number of basic variants.

Input sources:	Infinite, Finite	2
Queue accommodations:	Infinite, Finite	2
Queue discipline:	Random choice, Defection, Priorities by arrival order, Priorities by policy, Batch requirements	5
Service facilities:	Single and multiple channel; Arranged in parallel, and series	3

Consequently, there are 60 ($2 \times 2 \times 5 \times 3$) major varieties of service models that exist in the terms given above. When we consider the range of possibilities introduced by different possible input (arrival) and output (service) distributions, this number becomes infinite. Even when considering only five types of input distributions and five types of output distributions, the number of possibilities is multiplied by $5 \times 5 = 25$, yielding $25 \times 60 = 1500$ variations.

Process Load and Process Capacity

The load must be expressed as a rate. It is designated by the input, or arrival, parameter, λ. The average output potential of a process is a measure of the capacity of the system. It must also be expressed as a rate, viz., the service rate, μ. If there is a crux, or a core, to the subject of production process control, we have reached it now. Input and output rates can vary in many ways. Consequently, we must be able to describe and characterize both the input and output distributions as accurately as possible. Why is this the crux? Because the essence of queueing theory is embodied in the relationships of the input to the output. Therefore, we must know how to make proper observations of: (1) the intervals between arrivals to the process, that is, the intervals between inputs; and (2) the durations of service intervals, that is, the intervals between outputs.

There is no essential difference between input and output with respect to measurement or the derivation of the appropriate distribution. So we can equally well talk of one or the other. Measurements can be obtained in several ways. A simple procedure is to set up a system of continuous observation for some representative period of time.[18] The observations should be repeated

---

[18] An alternative method is to sample the system randomly over time. This approach can be formulated as an operation sampling problem.

over a number of days, weeks, or whatever period of time is required to give assurance that the inputs and outputs are not changing. In some cases, a statistical control chart[19] can be used to monitor the stability of the inputs and outputs. Then, a reasonable procedure might be:

Step 1. *Probability Density Distributions.* To obtain density distributions for arrivals, we can record the times of successive arrivals. Then, by subtracting successive times from each other, we obtain the intervals between arrivals. A hypothetical example of this is given in Table 2.2.

Table 2.2

Arrivals: Unit Number	Arrival Time	Interval Between Arrivals (Minutes)
1	8:05	—
2	8:10	5
3	8:22	12
4	8:23	1
5	8:34	11
6	8:41	7
.	.	.
.	.	.
.	.	.
$i-1$	t_{i-1}	.
i	t_i	$t_i - t_{i-1}$

To obtain density distributions for service times, we can record the servicing periods required by successive units. Thus, we obtain Table 2.3.

Table 2.3

Unit Number	Duration of Service (Minutes)
1	10
2	4
3	11
4	6
5	8
6	12
.	.
.	.
.	.
i	s_i

Using the interval between arrivals and the duration of service (in whatever time unit is appropriate), we proceed to obtain our distributions. To

[19] See Chapter 13, pp. 383–400.

form the probability density distributions, we count the frequency with which each interval size occurs. The frequencies are converted to probabilities in the usual manner. (See columns 1, 2, and 3 of Table 2.4.)

Table 2.4

1 Δt	2 Frequency	3 Probability	4 Cumulative Probability[20] $P(> \Delta t)$
0	0	.000	1.000
1	0	.000	1.000
2	1	.028	.972
3	2	.056	.916
4	3	.083	.833
5	4	.111	.722
6	5	.139	.583
7	6	.166	.417
8	5	.139	.278
9	4	.111	.167
10	3	.083	.084
11	2	.056	.028
12	1	.028	.000
	36	1.000	

[20] Δt = the interval between arrivals or the service duration intervals. Note that we accumulate probability from the bottom going up.

Step 2. *Cumulative Probability Distributions.* The distributions that we require should describe:

For inputs—the probability that an arrival interval is greater than Δt.
For outputs—the probability that the duration of a service interval is greater than Δt.

To achieve these results, we simply add the respective density distributions, starting with the largest intervals. (See column 4 of Table 2.4. For economy of space, only one hypothetical distribution is developed. It could apply to either arrivals or service durations, although for a real problem we would always need one distribution for the inputs and one for the outputs.)

Having obtained our cumulative distributions, we are now ready to examine each of them in terms of two important factors:

1. Are the input and output processes homogeneous (or stationary) over time? A rough criterion to use with respect to the time-homogeneity requirement would be that the distribution shapes, obtained in successive periods of time, are similar. In other words, the distribution of the first sample period as compared with that of the second sample period is essentially the same. These data can then be pooled. Although such a criterion lacks rigor, it can be of practical utility if used with care. A more satisfactory criterion is supplied by

statistical control theory. Comparatively little work has been done on the nonstationary problem, and we will not consider these cases in our discussion.

2. What are the shapes of the distributions? Figure 2.10 illustrates a number of theoretical distributions.

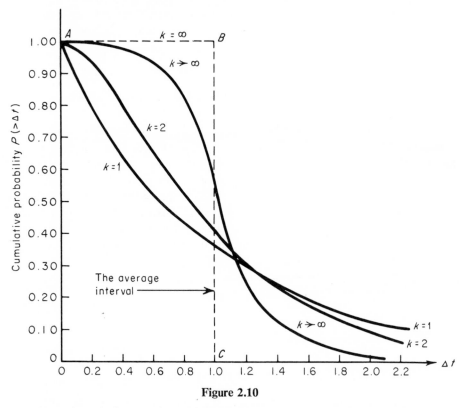

Figure 2.10

Some theoretical cumulative probability distributions; as the parameter k approaches infinity, the distribution takes on the shape, ABC.

Frequently, some member of this family of curves will provide a reasonably good approximation to the observed distribution. The curve marked $k = 1$, in the figure, is an *exponential distribution*. It is identified with the case of *pure randomness*. Pure randomness exists if there are no sequential patterns of long and short intervals. The exponential distribution is observed when the intervals between arrivals or the service intervals are entirely independent of the length of all previous intervals. In effect, the succession of intervals is the outcome of a random process. A process of this type is exemplified by the succession of heads and tails of a coin. The coin has no memory of prior outcomes. The output rates of a machine are usually of this type. On the other hand, here are some examples that would not satisfy this requirement: A pieceworker's rate increases with practice and decreases with fatigue, producing a cyclical pattern over the day; the speed of a machine increases as it heats up, and the temperature rises as a function of use; a maintenance crew always attempts to beat the servicing times of another crew; and, finally, the accident rate of an individual increases because of the psychological phenomenon of accident proneness. The lack of independence is more frequently associated with the man component in the system than with machines. We assume that an exponential distribution exists:

> For inputs—when the intervals between arrivals are known to be independent of each other; and
>
> For outputs—when the service durations are known to be independent of each other.

It is characteristic of the exponential distribution that the average interval is equal to the standard deviation of the distribution intervals, that is, $T_S = \sigma_S$. For the other distributions shown in the figure, the standard deviation is less than the expected value of the interval. Thus, as k gets larger, σ_S gets smaller. The value of σ_S approaches zero when k approaches infinity. This is the case of constant service time, or of scheduled arrivals. Many situations are reasonably well described by the $k = 1$ type distribution. Our discussion of queueing models in Chapter 6 for example, limits our attention to such cases, but we must not forego realization that process design involves an enormous variety of types of distributions, all of which must be properly treated for satisfactory control.

PROBLEMS

1. In the following list, the process configurations tend to be alike within each industry. What are those configurations, how do you explain their pervasiveness, and can you think of any significant exceptions?

   (a) machine tools   (f) aircraft manufacture
   (b) farming   (g) emerald settings
   (c) canning   (h) smoking pipes
   (d) commuter railroads   (i) cigarettes
   (e) telegraphy   (j) women's fashions

2. Discuss the nature of investments and operating costs in each type of system. In what way do these factors show up in the information systems that parallel the process configuration?

3. Why is the concept of modularity stressed in the text? Follow through with a reasoned argument as to how awareness of these notions can benefit the organization. Can you give any examples of organizations and institutions that do not presently use modularity that could benefit by doing so?

4. Explain what factors might account for the frequency with which the *ABC* effect is encountered. Can you write an equation having one parameter that can be changed, enabling the shape of the curve to go from a straight line (the diagonal), to a very skewed (rapidly rising) curve?

5. How many technological orderings are possible with five jobs and three machines? What approach might be used to represent these? How many flow shop configurations emerge? Now consider the order of processing jobs at the machines. How many theoretically possible sequences are there? In a real situation, how many of these might be feasible if a flow system exists with special purpose equipment?

6. If $\lambda/\mu = \frac{1}{4}$, $M = 5$ and $S = 1$ (see pp. 38–39), what would $\sum_{n=1}^{5} (n - 1)p_n$ equal? What does this figure represent?

   Now, let $M = \infty$, all other elements remaining as before. Derive $\sum_{n=1}^{\infty} (n - 1)p_n$.

7. There is discussion concerning whether two servicemen would provide a more economical situation for the job shop ($\lambda/\mu = \frac{1}{4}$; $M = 5$). If servicemen receive $200 per week, what machine downtime cost would leave the manager indifferent as to whether one or two servicemen were hired? Under the circumstances, are there any additional intangible factors that should be considered?

Decision models are a class of input-output models where controllable strategies and uncontrollable environments interact to produce a great number of **possible** outcomes. For a variety of reasons, it is not a simple matter to discover the one outcome you favor the most and then to make it happen exactly as you wish. But decision models help the manager to achieve the outcome he wants because they organize his problem area in a thoroughly operational way.

The Structure

of 3

Decision Models

Decisions about operations (no one of which may be critical) taken one after another, in the many problem systems of production, transport, communications, etc., determine the organization's success. The manager directs his system by recognizing his opportunities, specifying decision alternatives, and choosing among them. Decisions are also involved in planning major investments. These are design decisions that affect the nature of operations, whereas operating decisions determine what part of the given system's potential will be used.

Decision Structure

In its simplest form, a decision situation is composed of five basic elements. These are:

1. *Strategies* or plans for using *resources* S_i, $(i = 1, 2, \ldots, n)$; constructed of controllable variables;
2. *Environments*, N_j, $(j = 1, 2, \ldots, m)$ composed of noncontrollable variables;
3. *Outcomes* (O_{ij}) that are observations of results that occur when a specific strategy is employed and a particular environment exists;
4. *Predictions* (p_j) of the likelihood that each environment will occur; and
5. *The decision criterion* that dictates the way in which the information above will be used to select a strategy to follow.

Decision theory applies to all types of decision situations. Because we are concerned with designing and managing systems of operations, we must be prepared to discuss all the elements of the decision process.

Strategies

Given two strategies, A and B, the decision problem consists in selecting one of them. If that choice must be made *regularly*, it is most typically a short-term *control* situation. Infrequent comparisons that involve large investments

51

are usually *planning* situations. Planning decisions are characteristically saddled with multiple objectives. The manager will seldom possess the same degree of belief in what he knows about planning situations, as compared to what he knows about short-term, repetitive problems. With this in mind, we can explain decision theory so that it is compatible with the requirements of both types of situations.

Strategies are proposed courses of action that can be quite general or highly detailed to include all the elements required to convert an abstraction into a reality. There would be no need for a decision if only one course of action could be taken. Decision making is the process by which the selection is made, not the process by means of which the strategies are formulated. One or more measures of the performance or effectiveness of each strategy are required. The number of such measures is dependent upon the number of objectives. *Measures of effectiveness* are the only *formal* means of comparing alternatives. But, having chosen a strategy, one must still be able to implement it and monitor the results to make certain that they are consistent with expectations.

The word strategy was at one time exclusively a military term. It has, however, been widely accepted by present-day management. Strategy connotes the fact that competitors exist whose respective plans affect each other. Industry has become increasingly aware of the fact that competition exists on many levels. Each company competes not only with organizations that produce goods in their own product class but also with any product or service that siphons off funds that could have been spent on the company's product. Even in a theoretical, planned economy the same competitive factors operate. The consumer spends his money for clothing and shelter, thereby reducing his ability to buy food. The same applies to hard goods, entertainment, and luxury items; and such factors as government taxation and insurance are part of this overall competitive picture.

If the word strategy helps to keep awareness of the competitor in focus, then its use is more than justified. The design of a product, the composition of a product-line, the selection of equipment, the specification of quality standards, the kinds of materials that will be used, the design of the process, including plans for automation—all such considerations cannot be measured for effectiveness unless the behavior of competitors is taken into account. Since competitive behavior is not often explicitly represented in decision models concerning operations, it must be introduced as an extra, qualitative factor. The manager of operations seldom thinks in terms of "our strategies" and "their strategies." This is changing; the operations manager recognizes the role that he can play in the *design* of operations. He understands that he is *not only* responsible for creating strategies for his own company *but is also* responsible for helping to predict the range and effect of strategies that competing companies might use. The operations manager is under pressure to "keep things rolling." Preoccupation with his own company's strategies is so intense that he is likely to assume that marketing will be responsible for competitive behaviors. With new technologies, the view is unrealistic.

Strategic Innovation

Methodology has little to do with the *creation* of strategic alternatives. The development of strategies is partly in the technological and partly in the managerial domain. The nature of a specific problem determines the extent to which each participates. If the situation is primarily devoted to a technical problem, such as the construction of a blanking die[1] or the design of a new polymerization[2] procedure, then technological knowledge will predominate. On the other hand, if a new plant site must be selected or a guarantee policy developed, management's sense of the situation will determine the strategic alternatives.

The operations manager considers the *ability* to develop strategies of paramount importance. They must be developed before a decision can be made. How does this get done? Somehow, knowledge of technology and methodology fuses with principles of managing and with data about the company, vendors, and competitors. Rarely will several individuals create the same strategy to meet the same situation. Undoubtedly, this is due in part to their respective experiences, which necessarily differ. But other factors must also operate because one person alone can produce many alternatives. Until we are able to understand the nature of thinking and the characteristics of creativity we shall not be in a suitable position to explain the *innovation* of strategies. The enumeration of strategies by *imitation*, on the other hand, is not difficult to explain. In particular, for short-term planning a company desires to imitate some of its previous behaviors. The frequent alteration of accepted strategies can be costly. When one deals with longer-term situations, it is also reasonable to include strategies that are based on industry and company experience. So a degree of copying is neither unexpected nor undesirable. At the same time, opportunities for innovation always exist. If our company does not innovate, perhaps our competitors will. By luck, by serendipity,[3] by Jove and by genius, every now and then a brilliant strategy

---

[1] Blanking is the process of punching a piece of material from flat stock that will then undergo further operations.

[2] The chemical reaction whereby a number of molecules of the same or different kinds form a complex molecule of high molecular weight, called a high polymer, which has different physical properties from the original molecules.

[3] Serendipity: The gift of finding valuable or agreeable things not sought for; a word coined by Walpole in allusion to a tale, "The Three Princes of Serendip," who in their travels were always discovering by chance or by sagacity, things they did not seek. (*Webster's New International Dictionary*, 2nd ed, unabridged.)

Note that while serendipity includes luck, it implies some relationship between chance and sagacity.

appears. It is imperative that the decision system should be able to recognize this fact. It must also be able to sort through a set of possibilities that are quite conventional and to pick out the best of that lot. Perhaps the careful consideration of various strategic alternatives feeds inspiration and ultimately leads to a better set of strategic possibilities. This is the only way in which decision theory could affect the creative process. As previously noted, we can represent strategies by S_i, where i can take on any value 1 through n. Thus, if $n = 5$, we have five strategies. There are times when an infinite set of strategic possibilities exists, that is, $n = \infty$.

Environments

Environments, N_j, $j = 1, 2, \ldots, m$ (also called states of nature) are those factors in a situation that affect the expected results of a decision but that are not completely under the decision maker's control. Weather, political events, and the state of the economy are three examples.[4] More appropriate to the operations area are such environments as failure rates of equipment, price changes by vendors, new materials, technological process innovations, consumer demand levels, labor turnover rates, and absenteeism. We can represent environments by N_j, where j can take on any value 1 through m. There are times when it is empirically reasonable or mathematically convenient to allow m to equal infinity. In any case, a statistical distribution is the only possible description of which environment will prevail.[5]

Decisions Under One Environment

There is a *tendency* to look the other way, eliminating environmental differences, when a noncontrollable variable does not seem crucial. This is particularly true in dealing with operations. In many cases it is justified. Each specific case, however, must be judged on its own merits. When we are able to ignore environments we call this class of decision problem *decision making under certainty*, abbreviated as DMUC. Some typical examples are:

1. Machine loading problems in the job shop, that is, assigning various jobs to machines and sequencing and scheduling these jobs through the shop;

[4] An old German proverb states: "Time, women, and luck change with the blink of an eye."

[5] A different choice of strategies often can alter the situation by removing an environment. For example, by selecting different kinds of equipment, or by utilizing preventive maintenance—both of which are strategic elements—some control over failure rates is available. Similarly, salary level—a strategic variable—can alter turnover and absenteeism.

2. Determining an optimal product-mix for the intermittent flow shop or job shop;
3. Assigning men to jobs in a project system;
4. Deriving an optimal traffic plan for shipping goods from factories to warehouses;
5. Determining optimal production runs; that is, how many units to produce at one time, usually applicable to intermittent flow shops and job shops;
6. Line balancing, which is assigning flow shop operations to stations.

Although exceptions exist for each of the six situations listed above, the majority of actual cases fall into the DMUC category. However, the assumption of certainty must never be taken for granted.

Decisions Under Several Environments

A particular strategy and a specific environment produce a unique set of results each of which is called an outcome, O_{ij}. This is the outcome for the ith strategy and the jth environment. We observe, measure, and record only those results that are of interest. The management objectives determine what is interesting. For example, a certain product design, S_1, operating under a given set of environmental conditions, N_1, will fail after a stated number of hours; it may require a certain amount of maintenance; it can provide a measurable level of performance satisfaction. In addition, it produces a specific volume of sales; some number of returns will be experienced; a calculable portion of plant capacity will be used up; a given amount of materials, labor, and energy will be consumed; a certain contribution to profit will be made. These typify outcomes of different kinds. The table below

		Environments				
		N_1	N_2	N_3	N_4	N_5
	S_1	3	5	4	2	8
Product Designs	S_2	5	3	2	4	6
	S_3	4	4	4	4	4
	S_4	4	5	4	2	8

Table of Decision Outcomes

presents an example of a decision matrix where four designs are being evaluated under five different environmental use conditions with respect to one outcome objective. For this example, let us presume that the objective is to choose the design that promises the longest expected lifetime of use. The (4×5) matrix produces twenty cells or intersections. At each intersection an entry can be made that describes the expected lifetime of the particular design, operating under the specific conditions. These outcomes might be obtained by laboratory experimentation.

The generality of the decision matrix is apparent. In the general form that it is written, the strategy could equally well describe such diverse situations as the best way to lay out the plant; the choice of an optimal numbering system for a catalogue; or where to go on a vacation. The environments would describe relevant noncontrollable factors applicable to the case. For *each intersection* an outcome measure must be obtained that would adequately describe the objectives of the operation. If multiple objectives exist, multiple outcome entries would appear at each intersection.[6]

(DMUC) Decision Making Under Certainty

When only one environment is relevant, then we have DMUC. The decison matrix

$$N$$

S_1	6000
S_2	3000
S_3	4000
S_4	5000

is a typical, albeit limited, example. We search through the column of outcomes, O_{ij}. Depending upon our objective, we locate the outcome (or those outcomes) that most closely fit the bill. If the objective were to maximize the daily production flows f_{ij} (where i is the source and j is the sink), then strategy S_1 will be chosen. If the objective were to minimize idle capacity ($O_{ij} = c_{ij} - f_{ij}$, where i is the source and j is the sink) then S_2 would be chosen. In some cases, it is possible that an intermediate value, say for planned capacity, c_{ij}, is wanted. Plans S_3 or S_4 might satisfy this requirement. DMUC can present a problem when there are so many plans being considered that searching time and the expense of deriving all the necessary outcomes by brute force is prohibitive.

Let us consider several points. *Whoever must deal with problems at the operations level must be prepared to handle a great number of variants.* These are typically short-term decisons. They tend to be repeated many times over. Losses sustained by not getting the best possible configuration are minor for any one decision. But when repeated over and over again, such losses can mount up to very sizable sums of money. Therefore, it is reasonable for such cases that substantial investments be made in the *search process*.

The number of ways that jobs can be scheduled through a large plant are

---

[6] In Chapter 14, pp. 415–418, a method of treating multiple outcomes is discussed.

usually of the same order of magnitude as the number of electrons in the universe; yet this kind of decision must be made daily or weekly. A reasonably good plan could be found by a Gantt layout chart as shown in Figure 3.1.

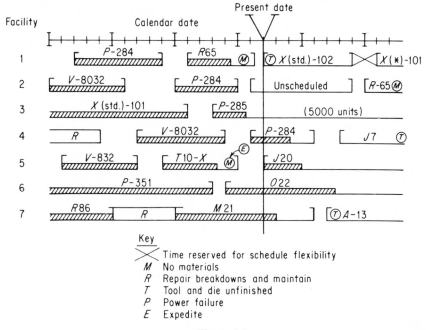

Figure 3.1

The Gantt layout chart (a reserved time planning system). Status: (1) job P-284 is ahead 1.5 days; (2) job J20 is ahead 3.0 days; (3) job O22 is ahead 5.5 days; (4) job M21 is ahead 1.0 day; (5) job R65 is 2 days short of completion—and 3 days late (M); (6) job P-285 is 1.5 days short and 1.5 days late (set-up time; will catch up); (7) job T10-X is 1.5 days short and about 4 days late (M) (E).

This is a trial-and-error type method. Linear programming[7] provides an analytical model for reaching decisions under certainty. When employed in conjunction with a computer, LP can be expected to quickly locate the theoretically *optimal* plan for the conditions that are stated. In practice, the actual choice may differ from the theoretically optimal plan simply because not all the relevant constraints are satisfactorily stated, or because the assumptions inherent in the model may not be perfectly fulfilled by reality.

In general, for this type of problem, linear programming will provide a better solution than the Gantt chart method. The savings may be realized in

[7] See Chapter 5.

two ways. First, use of the Gantt chart is very time-consuming and requires skill. There is the cost of developing the schedule and the penalty to be paid for the delay in achieving the schedule. For sizable search problems, linear programming is less expensive to use and will produce schedules in minutes. Second, if the situation has been properly described, then the analytic solution will be always as good or better than the trial and error result. Even if the net savings are as small as ten dollars a day, the company can save more than two thousand dollars a year. Generally, much greater savings than these will be realized.

We shall treat a number of techniques that are useful for resolving problems of DMUC; but of great importance is the warning: We can only use deterministic search techniques (such as linear programming) when certainty is a fair assumption. If probability distributions exist but are ignored, then great violence can be done to the system. In fact, if the single-state assumption is a poor one, then a Gantt chart procedure employed by an intelligent planner may provide better answers than some formal system incorrectly applied. If the single-state assumption is arrived at by cutting corners and ignoring or overlooking inherent variance in the system, then the degree of belief in the solution will be quite low.

(DMUR) Decision Making Under Risk

If two or more environments are relevant and if a high degree of believability can be placed on the forecasts with respect to the probability of occurrence of these environments, then decision making under risk (DMUR) exists. Let us say that each environment N_j has a probability p_j of occurring. Then the sum of all p_j's, taking into account every possible value for j, must be one. Mathematically we write:

$$\sum_{j=1}^{j=m} p_j = p_1 + p_2 + p_3 + p_4 + p_5 \ldots + p_j \ldots + p_m = 1.00$$

If there are five relevant environments, then $m = 5$. We note that DMUC can be a special case of DMUR, where the probabilities of all the environments, except one, would be very small.

Many short-term and some long-term problems can be tackled within the framework of DMUR. Long-term predictions are of dubious validity, and risk methods when used in this area must be taken with a "grain of salt." They can still be guides, however, particularly when an analysis of the sensitivity characteristics is used.[8] Both behavioral and physical types of problems are amenable to the methods of risk analysis. In general, however, the investigation of indeterminate physical systems produces a relatively high

[8] See pp. 95, 136, 351–352.

degree of accuracy, whereas the same type of risk study represents a rather crude approach to the behavioral phenomena. Some examples of problems that properly belong to systems of DMUR would be: machine breakdowns and process failures; frequency of rejects; distribution of delivery intervals (lead times); measures of worker productivity; and the analysis of relatively stable consumer demand systems. These same methods are not likely to be useful when an attempt is made to forecast events that will occur in the long-term future such as: long-term consumer demand for a new service; new product consumer demand (where the new product represents a substantial innovation and there is nothing comparable to utilize as a guide); speculative real estate ventures; developments in architectural style and available building materials; technological changes; stock market indexes; wage rate demands; union attitudes; and the state of the economy.

We know that when a problem conforms to the specifications of DMUR it is resolved by using *averages* or *expected values*. This satisfies the fact that over a period of time the ups and downs of the system will average out to produce the result given by the expected value. Because probabilities sum to one, the expected value will be given by the formula:

$$EV_i = \sum_{j=1}^{j=m} p_j O_{ij}$$

or: $p_1 O_{11} + p_2 O_{12} + p_3 O_{13} + p_4 O_{14} + p_5 O_{15} + \ldots + p_m O_{1m} =$ the expected value for the first strategy, and so on. Thus, we are saying that the average value of the ith strategy will be equal to the sum of the products of each row entry multiplied by its appropriate p_j.

Short-term systems with repetitive behaviors readily lend themselves to this form of analysis. In fact, the expected value criterion is totally applicable for any single decision when the estimated probabilities have a high degree of believability. This last statement may not be intuitively appealing, nevertheless, it is statistically correct. In any case, it is seldom a matter for discussion because in situations where a decision is to be rendered only once, it is unlikely that the predictions, if they can be obtained, possess the same degree of believability that applies to repetitive decision systems.

Forecasts and Predictions[9]

There is only one way that chance enters the decision system. That is, through the uncontrollable variables that characterize environments. Although we have no control or only partial control over these variables, we are not helpless. We may not be able to control the movement of the sun, but we do very well in predicting its positions. Many actions are predicated on the

[9] Also, see Chapter 9.

ability to foretell the future. Because we know what to expect from nature, we can choose an appropriate strategy. In effect, the ability to predict gives us a kind of control (call it *choice control*) *over outcomes*, even though we remain helpless with respect to controlling the environments.

Some predictions can be made with relative certainty; the time of sunrise and sunset are good examples. We can also make excellent predictions about the tides; but our ability to predict the weather is nothing to brag about. Generally, natural and physical phenomena can be predicted with greater precision than behavioral phenomena, which can be exceedingly difficult to handle. This generalization begins to map out the area of forecasts and prediction, but like most sweeping statements, it hardly does justice to the true state of affairs. Accordingly, let us attempt a further refinement. Large physical entities, which are assemblages of many small particles, tend to behave in a predictable fashion. Statements about the individual or relatively small groups of particles usually are subject to far more conjectural forecasts.

Where volition and human behavior are involved, the ability to make forecasts and predictions usually improves as the number of individuals included in the system increases. The behavior of a single individual is considered, by and large, to be unpredictable; but the behavior of a large group of individuals can be anticipated with some accuracy. If this were not true, sales forecasts would be absurd. In general, as the number of units grows larger, forecasts tend to improve. But we must be wary. Social and cultural factors tend to reduce the uncertainty of human behavior in certain areas so that an individual becomes almost totally predictable. At the same time, a complex set of group behaviors can interact with each other to produce almost impossible conditions for prediction. The stock market is a good example of this.

The manager must deal with both behavioral and physical systems. Forecasts and predictions are a necessary part of his job. Management, reflecting the scientific attitudes of the nineteenth century, began its practice without recognition of this fact. Just as science was forced to give way to indeterminism, so too was management. The change was gradual. It is not complete and is still taking place. The production function, unlike other organizational functions, is uniquely involved with both determinate and nondeterminate systems. Many technological problems fall into the class of physical phenomena. At this level, precise predictions can be made. On the other hand, workers tend to complicate life. In fact, for the production manager they have been a prime source of insecurity over the years. The production manager liked to think of men as though they were machines, not because he wished to strip them of their humanity, but because their unpredictable performances introduced the element of uncertainty into the manufacturing process. Other major sources of similar trouble were the consumer and the competitor. As long as demand was greater than supply and as long as competition was negligible, the consumer and the competitor could be ignored. When this was no longer so, the production manager was delighted to relegate the problems of consumer uncertainty and competitive maneuvers to a specialist in the area, viz., the marketing manager. The employee, however, remained in the production manager's bailiwick.[10]

Degree of predictability is not the only difficulty. First comes the problem of categorizing and enumerating the unique situations that are pertinent to the problem area. It is pointless to begin to estimate the likelihood that one or another situation will occur (i.e., forecast) until we know with some assurance how many different environments apply to a particular planning problem. When we combine these two facets, enumeration and then prediction, the real picture begins to emerge. There are those situations in which only one environment can occur no matter what strategy or plan is employed. This is equivalent to saying that all variables affecting the outcomes are under the manager's control.

The Decision Matrix

Assume that four different investment plans exist for a "new product" system. The strategy S_1 is labor intensive; S_4 is an automated system, with S_2 and S_3 representing mixtures of labor and computer-controlled machines. The objective is to minimize the payback period, i.e., the number of years to pay for the investment. The outcomes are measured as payback years.

If annual demand is fixed by contract, then a decision under certainty can be made. The outcome matrix consists of a single column, and for each strategy there is a calculated value, as shown below:

	N
S_1	$O_1 = 5$
S_2	$O_2 = 4$
S_3	$O_3 = 3$
S_4	$O_4 = 4$

Because only one environment (the contract) exists, no risk statements are required; and there is no need to forecast a set of environmental probabilities, i.e., $p(N) = 1.00$. Our visual search quickly reveals S_3 as the desired minimum.[11]

When we change the assumption of certainty, we acknowledge the

---

[10] Over a period of time this uncertainty is being removed by automation—not by solution of the existing problem. In other words, these problems become less pressing as they become obsolete.

[11] Ordinarily, however, the column is too long to search visually, and so superior search techniques, such as LP must be used.

existence of more than one environment. The possible environments are mutually exclusive (only one can occur at a time). It is essential to be able to identify *all* relevant environments and to derive the likelihood of occurrence for each environment, that is, the forecast. By adding these probabilities, we convert the outcome matrix to a decision matrix.

For our example, we will no longer assume that a contract exists; then, the demand level can vary. The matrix below describes such a situation, where outcomes continue to describe payback years.

| | Environment | | | | |
	N_1	N_2	N_3	N_4	N_5
Probabilities	0.1	0.2	0.1	0.4	0.2
S_1	3	7	4	8	5
S_2	4	5	5	6	4
S_3	5	3	4	5	3
S_4	6	1	3	7	4

If we believe in the forecast, the problem is resolved by using a decision model under risk. The expected values are:

$$EV(S_1) = 3(.1) + 7(.2) + 4(.1) + 8(.4) + 5(.2) = 6.3$$
$$EV(S_2) = 4(.1) + 5(.2) + 5(.1) + 6(.4) + 4(.2) = 5.1$$
$$EV(S_3) = 5(.1) + 3(.2) + 4(.1) + 5(.4) + 3(.2) = 4.1$$
$$EV(S_4) = 6(.1) + 1(.2) + 3(.1) + 7(.4) + 4(.2) = 4.7$$

The selection of S_3 is made because it promises a minimum value.

Stability of the System

How believable are these probabilities? We can have a high degree of confidence in our forecast if we know that the system that *underlies* the appearance of the environments is unchanging and that our estimates provide a good description of the relative frequencies with which the environments occur. Both of these conditions are required. We could have a very accurate description of what happened in the past, but the past may not be indicative of the future. Assuming that the fundamental conditions from whence the environments are derived remain unchanged, then we say that the system is *stable*. Stability is a vital concept for all management decision activities. The relevance of stability for short-term planning is critical; it is a basic assumption. Stability is much more likely to exist for a short rather than a long time interval. Statistical quality control, which we shall discuss in a later chapter, is one of the most powerful tools that the operations manager possesses because, when properly used, it can inform him of the fact that a once stable system is no longer so.

Decision Examples

A great variety of decision problems can be formulated in the simple terms that we have described. Here are a few examples:

Example 1. S_i We are concerned with plans to locate and develop a new plant in a foreign country. Our strategies represent the list of possible locations.

N_j We have essentially no control over the political and economic conditions that exist in each country. These environments might be described in terms of social stability, form of government, state of the economy, and education level of workers.

O_{ij} In this example, we might estimate a single outcome for each intersection, namely, profitability of the plan. (We should note, however, that multiple outcomes would result if we require outcome measures related to profitability after one year, five years, and ten years.)

Example 2. S_i The design of a supersonic transport (SST) is on the drawing board. The design can develop in a number of different ways. Only some of the major characteristics of the aircraft have been totally fixed at this point in the process.

N_j There are competitors' plans that are in various stages of development. Some of the designs are already built and flying.

O_{ij} We desire to estimate the *superiority or inferiority* of each of our company's possible designs as compared to each of the possible competitive designs—in terms of maneuverability, sonic boom, economy of operation, economy of maintenance, cost of development, landing characteristics, and so forth.

Example 3. S_i Our strategic alternatives represent several possible variations of a new antibiotic. None of these has been produced—even in test quantities. This is because each variant requires substantial investments before even limited quantities can be made available.

N_j Various types of users of the drug constitute the environments. Thus, we include diabetics, children with measles, elderly people with high blood pressure, and pregnant women.

O_{ij} Multiple outcomes must be estimated for the main effects and the side effects of each drug.

Example 4. S_i Several designs have been suggested for the control equipment required by the guidance system of a space probe.

N_j Environments must include estimates of the conditions of *outer space* including gravity level, temperature range, and so on. A proper description of each environment requires the specification of a particular combination of the various noncontrollable variables that would adequately describe outer space conditions.

O_{ij} The primary estimate concerns reliability. Cost in this case can be treated as a negligible factor.

Example 5. S_i A number of different machines can be used to perform a particular task. None of the machines has ever been built. When the decision is made, the selected machine must be custom built. The construction of any one machine is costly.

N_j The company can draw upon a labor group that possesses different levels of skill. This distribution might be specified in terms of the various skill levels presently available for the company operations.

O_{ij} Outcome estimates would be multiple and would include productivity, production rate, number of rejects, and various costs that are associated with set-up times, maintenance, and initial investment.

Outcomes

Outcome measures must be obtained that adequately describe the manager's objectives. Such outcomes are obtained in at least three basically different ways:

1. By means of estimates and guesses,
2. By observation and experimental results,
3. By a knowledge of relationships that have previously been hypothesized (a theory).

All three methods are commonly used by managers. In many cases combinations can be employed.

We are not discussing the criterion by which a choice is to be made between two or more alternatives. The decision criterion plays no part in the development of meaningful outcome measures. Outcomes relate only to what will happen when a particular strategy is used and when a specific environment has occurred.

As might be supposed, the use of estimates and guesses is prevalent in the long-range planning situation. Although estimates are employed in short-term planning and control systems, the other methods for obtaining outcomes are utilized with greater frequency. There is always room for error when estimates are supplied to describe outcomes. Mental gymnastics that defy description are required simply because they are totally internalized and part of the process of cerebral behavior—about which science knows almost nothing.

The phrase "mental gymnastics" is used because supposedly a mental image must be constructed from prior experiences to be representative of the situation that is presently being analyzed. Then, somehow, the estimator must be able to modify the complex parallel that he has built in his mind to obtain a reasonable fit with the situation that concerns him. That is why the *range of experience* of such an individual is important. Unless his mental library of experience is sufficiently great, he cannot be expected to recall from memory sufficiently good analogs.

A particular characteristic of long-range decisions is that the situations that must be examined are likely to be quite unique. Therefore, the ability to adapt, alter, interpolate, and extrapolate[12] supposes that some basic pattern of association can be determined. Our intention in this discussion has been to persuade the reader that the use of decision theory is not a mechanistic endeavor but that it is an exercise requiring great imagination and full use of knowledge and experience.

Each of the above decision problems is a unique system. Totally different technological backgrounds are required, and the managerial responsibilities differ markedly. But with respect to the basic pattern of the decision system we find a degree of homogeneity.

In order to bypass the *estimation stage* and supplement intuition concerning the values of outcomes with *experimental evidence*, an initial investment is required. The decision to study the problem on an experimental level represents a commitment of funds. For some of the examples previously listed, estimates may be exceedingly difficult to obtain. When the test conditions are almost as costly as the full commitment or when only a full commitment to a specific strategy would provide meaningful observations, the manager may be compelled to reach a decision on the basis of estimates. He cannot afford to obtain outcomes for every decision alternative.

Experimental methods are far more easily associated with short-term than with long-term systems. Even in a long-term situation, the decision maker can frequently find a way to hold back in the extent to which he commits himself. Thus, a pilot plant may be set up to test a new process; the plant may cost several millions of dollars. If the full scale investment had been made, the risk would have been multiplied many times; however, it was first necessary to have made a choice with respect to which alternative was to be tested. Thus, a "tentative" decision was made, subject to later reversal. This is a variant of the basic decision model, which belongs to the class of *sequential decision models*.

Similarly, a company will be forced to choose among many alternative plans for new products without having any experimental evidence available. Then, having reduced the size of the problem, it might be feasible to move a few selected product plans to the test market before making the major com-

[12] See pp. 250–251 for definitions.

mitment. Once a prototype, or model, has been constructed for each of several strategic possibilities, it is feasible to use the physical laboratory for tests of physical properties such as toxicity, strength of materials, and reliability. Behavioral outcomes can be obtained by societal experiments where a chosen sample of individuals is involved. Such experiments can be used to evaluate consumer responses, worker attitudes and abilities, vendor relationships, and community reactions. The essence of the experimental method is that a concrete form of the strategy must be developed.

Quite atypical of the long-term planning situation—but reasonably familiar to the domain of control system design—is the use of theory and hypothesis. This is the third way in which outcomes can be derived *by analytic means*, such as a mathematical equation or a set of logical postulates. The existence of a theory requires that the same type of situation or one that is closely analogous with respect to the relevant variables has been experienced before and formulated in an objective manner. In other words, a type of situation has been isolated for which a known pattern can explain all the variations that pertain to this situation. When this is true, the conditions must be rendered in explicit form, usually in mathematical symbolism. Because this kind of outcome derivation applies to a large segment of operations management problems, let us take a closer look at what is involved. We have to understand the fundamental nature of the relationships between strategies and environments.

A strategy may be representable in numerical terms if the controllable variables lend themselves to such characterization. The same applies to the noncontrollable variables that, when taken together, describe the states of nature. A mathematical function is used to relate these two kinds of variables and to derive the outcomes that they will produce. In mathematical terminology, outcomes are called *dependent variables*. The controllable and noncontrollable variables are called *independent variables*. We represent the outcomes by O_{ij}, where i is the particular strategy used and j is one of the environments that can occur.

$$O_{ij} = f(S_i, N_j)$$

The dependent variable O_{ij} is a function of the independent variables S_i and N_j. Now, of course, the *critical* question concerns the nature of the *actual function*. We require a *problem-solving* model. For example, a hypothetical relationship might be:

$$O_{ij} = S_i^2 - S_i N_j + N_j^3$$

We can see why it is necessary that the strategies and the environments be expressible in numerical terms. Alternative product or service plans do not easily lend themselves to such expression. Neither do plant location plans, process design plans, nor most other management *design* problems. On the other hand, engineering problems, inventory problems, and scheduling problems do fit this pattern. That is why, when we have moved from design to the operations level, a great number of situations can be resolved within a mathematical framework.

Let us consider another type of relationship that is found in several classes of operations management problems. It is of the form:

$$O_{ij} = \frac{aN_j}{S_i} + bS_i + c$$

We do not have to explain what these letter symbols mean in concrete terms. We know that each unique combination of a strategy and an environment produces an outcome according to this rule, where a, b, and c are specified constants[13] of the system. The company's objective is to find a minimum (or, in some cases, a maximum) value for the O_{ij}'s. We assume that by means of observation and experimentation the following values have been found for a, b, and c: $a = 20$, $b = 5$ and $c = 0$. This means that:

$$O_{ij} = \frac{20N_j}{S_i} + 5S_i$$

With no need for further specification, the outcome matrix can now be constructed:

		States of Nature, N_j				
		1	2	3	4	...
	1	25	45	65	85	...
	2	20	30	40	50	...
Strategies	3	21.7	28.3	35	41.7	...
S_i	4	25	30	35	40	...
	5	29	33	37	41	...
	.	.	.	.	.	
	.	.	.	.	.	
	.	.	.	.	.	

Thus, for example, when $i = 4$ and $j = 3$:

$$O_{43} = 20(3)/(4) + 5(4) + 0 = 35.$$

By using this simple mathematical expression, it is possible to construct the total decision matrix. Each value of S_i and each value of N_j produce a unique outcome. More often than not the equations are complex, but the nature of the method used is unchanged. The table we have constructed shows only integer values for the strategies and environments.[14] If this

---

[13] A constant is a system factor—under no one's control—that plays a part in determining the outcome. But it is fixed and invariant for all relevant situations.

[14] Such a condition would apply to cases where S_i might be the number of secretaries to be used in a workpool and N_j the number of reports to be typed by them in a week. Fractions of secretaries would be even more distasteful than fractions of reports.

restriction did not hold, then the matrix would be enormous because fractional values would exist for both types of independent variables.

We should note that with respect to each environment—that is, each column—a minimum value of O_{ij} occurs when a particular strategy is used. It isn't necessarily the same strategy that yields a minimum for each environment. Thus, the minimum value of the outcomes can occur with different levels of the strategic variable. (In the case of the third column, there is a tie, so either the third or fourth strategies can be used to produce a minimum.) As it happens, the equation that we have just used is typically associated with inventory problems where:

S_i is the ordering policy, specifying the number of units that would be purchased with each order or made with each production run;

N_j is the demand for this item, which is seldom controllable although to some extent advertising and promotion can affect it. By underproduction, we might also gain control, assuming that the demand is known to be at least equal to the chosen production volume. And contractual arrangements permit complete knowledge of demand and, therefore, assure control over the environment. In this case (demand being fixed and known) the problem becomes one of DMUC.

O_{ij} is the total cost of the ith inventory policy—given that the jth environment occurs.

There are three constant costs, a, b, and c, that apply to this system. We find that the term aN_j/S_i is a cost component that decreases with increasing levels of order or run size for any fixed level of N_j. If N_j is the number of units demanded per year and S_i is the number of units per order, then N_j/S_i has the dimensions

$$\left(\frac{\text{units}}{\text{year}}\right) \Big/ \left(\frac{\text{units}}{\text{order}}\right) = \left(\frac{\text{units}}{\text{year}}\right)\left(\frac{\text{order}}{\text{units}}\right) = \frac{\text{orders}}{\text{year}}$$

Therefore, if a is dimensioned as $\$/order$, then the term aN_j/S_i has the dimension of $\$/year$. The second term can be analyzed in the same way. For the inventory problem, it represents the cost of carrying inventory and carries the dimension of $\$/year$. The sum of these two kinds of costs yields the total cost per year.

When strategies and states of nature cannot be described in numerical terms or when no known or solvable mathematical relationship can be developed to describe outcomes, then the two methods of guess-estimating and experimentation would be used to build the outcome matrix. The use of a laboratory requires investment and, therefore, usually prevents experimentation on all possible plans. When major undertakings are being considered, parallel path problem solving (estimation backed up by experimentation) may become too costly to be feasible. Consequently, it is almost always necessary to begin the reduction process at the estimating level.

We can sum up by saying that outcomes are intersection values obtained by problem-solving models. The models can use mathematics, logic, experimentation, observation, and intuition. The outcomes are formulated to represent degrees of attainment of the management objectives.

(DMUU) Decision Making Under Uncertainty

Reviewing what we know about environments and their associated forecasts, some vital considerations are:

1. How many environments are relevant?
2. Are we able to identify all the relevant environments?
3. *Can we determine* the "true" frequencies of occurrence of these environments?
4. Are these frequencies fixed, that is, is the environmental (causal) system stable?

The third major class of decision problems concerns situations where the answers to the above questions are known to be unreliable. Such conditions cannot be categorized as DMUC or DMUR. The only alternative is DMUU because believability in what is known about environments is too low. It might appear to be the case that DMUU is the opposite of DMUC. This is not so. Because DMUC has only one state of nature with a likelihood of occurrence of one, the *opposite* of this would imply an unlimited number of states of nature, each of which has a near-zero probability of occurring. The implication is false. In any case, we would not know how to handle this opposite problem. Therefore, with decision making under uncertainty, we can only expect to enumerate a finite number of environments. The character of uncertainty is associated with the fact that we then acknowledge a total inability to estimate the likelihood of occurrence for each of these environments. In other words, we have no way of assigning the p_j values.

We have equated uncertainty with either an inability to make predictions or a low believability in such predictions. Furthermore, at least two environments are assumed to be relevant. The decision matrix shown below is intended to represent a problem in which three alternative processes are under consideration by the manager. Each process specifies a different arrangement of men and machines—sometimes called the man-machine interface problem.

	N_1	N_2
S_1	4.5	7.5
S_2	6.0	5.0
S_3	3.0	8.0

The states of nature express the fact that the cost of labor will either remain *constant* over a five-year period of time, called N_1, or the cost will *increase* over this period of time, called N_2. For realism, many more states of nature should be used in the analysis, including decreasing costs and specific divisions by the amounts of increase and decrease. Such elaboration would in no way improve the validity of what we are about to discuss. Management, we have hypothesized, is uncertain with respect to the five-year forecast for wage levels in its particular industry (an hypothesis that is not hard to believe).

The outcomes describe management's preferences for the alternative process designs, operating under the several environments. The decision maker's objective is to select the alternative that will maximize his preference.

Because management is uncertain, it cannot use selection methods normally employed for reaching decisions under *certainty* or under *risk*. What can be done? It is important to note that the company can employ a great number of different decision criteria—none of which can be called wrong. Thus:

Wald Criterion. According to the Wald decision rule, the manager should in turn inspect all the possible outcomes for each strategy. He selects the worst result that can occur for each strategy. The worst results are minimum values in this case because the objective is to maximize profit. Now, the strategy that produces the best minimum—therefore, the maximum minimum —value is chosen. Because this is the best of the worst, it is called the *maximin* criterion. The appropriate numbers for our example are shown below:

	N_1	N_2	Worst	
S_1	4.5	7.5	4.5	
S_2	6.0	5.0	5.0	(Best of the worst possibilities—*maximin*)
S_3	3.0	8.0	3.0	

Using Wald's decision rule, strategy S_2 should be selected. It promises the least objectionable result. The Wald criterion is associated with the behavior of a complete *pessimist*. It assumes that nature is not indifferent in the choice of an environment but hostile. A complete optimist, if such existed, would act in the reverse way. He would select the best outcome for each strategy and would then choose the one strategy that promised to provide the best result from among the best possibilities. This would be called a *maximax* result. The complete optimist would choose the third strategy. Thus:

	N_1	N_2	Best	
S_1	4.5	7.5	7.5	
S_2	6.0	5.0	6.0	
S_3	3.0	8.0	8.0	(Best of the best possibilities—*maximax*)

Savage Criterion. According to Savage,[15] when faced with uncertainty, the manager should try to *minimize his regret*. Savage defines regret as an *opportunity cost*. It is derived in the following way. First, assume that the environment, N_1, occurs. Then, if the manager had chosen S_2, he would have no regret. If, however, he had chosen the first strategy, S_1, then he would suffer a preference penalty of $6 - 4.5 = 1.5$ units; this provides a measure of his regret. If he had chosen S_3, he would suffer $6 - 3 = 3$ units of regret. The same thinking applies to the environment, N_2. It would also be used for any other environment, if it existed. The matrix that results from this regret transformation is shown below.

	N_1	N_2	Worst	
S_1	1.5	0.5	1.5	(Best of the worst possibilities—*minimax*)
S_2	0.0	3.0	3.0	
S_3	3.0	0.0	3.0	

Now, Savage states that it is appropriate to apply the Wald criterion to the regret matrix. Because we will always wish to minimize regret, we will choose the largest regret values for each row and then select the best of the rows that is associated with the smallest number. We see that the choice would be S_1.

Laplace-Bayes Criterion. Another way of resolving this problem is attributable to both Laplace and Bayes. The underlying rationale is known as the *principle of insufficient reason*. According to this principle, if the relative likelihoods for the various environments are *really* unknown, then we should act as though the probabilities for the environments were equally likely. Thus, with two environments, the probabilities would be divided into two equal halves. With three, the probabilities would be each one-third; with five, the probabilities would be each one-fifth. Using this decision rule, we determine the expected values for the three strategies in our example.

	N_1	N_2	EV_i	
	$\frac{1}{2}$	$\frac{1}{2}$		
S_1	4.5	7.5	6.0	(Best)
S_2	6.0	5.0	5.5	
S_3	3.0	8.0	5.5	

The Laplace-Bayes criterion finds that strategy S_1 is the best because it provides the largest expected value for preference.

Let us now recap our curious results and begin to examine the nature

[15] L. J. Savage, "The Theory of Statistical Decision," *Journal of the American Statistical Association*, 46, 253 (March 1951), 55–67.

of these decisions made under uncertain conditions. As might be supposed, the example was purposely chosen to indicate that different decision criteria are quite capable of producing differing solutions; yet, each criterion can be defended as being reasonable. But how can different solutions occur if the problem is analyzed rationally? The answer lies in the fact that each criterion is based upon a *rational policy*, but the various policies are not based on the same *value systems*. Policies, objectives, and attitudes interact in this domain, and there is no objective way to select one rational procedure in preference to all others.

We can understand this enigma by analyzing the significance of the Laplace-Bayes criterion. Figure 3.2 shows what would happen if we deviate

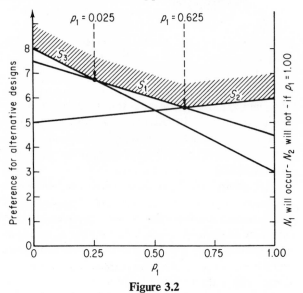

Figure 3.2

Attitudes impute probability judgments in spite of uncertainty (DMUU).

from the condition of equal likelihood associated with the principle of insufficient reason.[16] Let N_1 occur with the probability p_1 and N_2 with the probability $p_2 = (1 - p_1)$. The figure shows how the problem solution is altered as we change the value of p_1 from zero to one. The upper surface of this diagram is cross-hatched. It represents the maximum expected preference that can be obtained with different levels of probability for the environments. We see that when $p_1 \leq 0.250$ the S_3 segment is on top. Accordingly, S_3 would be chosen. When $0.625 \geq p_1 \geq 0.250$, then the S_1 strategy segment dominates

[16] We can present this *two*-dimensional diagram only when there are *two* states of nature. See also, Martin K. Starr, "A Discussion of Some Normative Criteria for Decision Making Under Uncertainty," *Industrial Management Review*, M.I.T. Journal, 8, 1 (Fall 1966), 71–78.

the situation. For all cases where $p_1 \geq 0.625$, strategy S_2 promises a maximum preference expectation.

One fact in particular emerges from this analysis. Namely, because the Wald criterion selected S_2, it imputes a value to p_1 of 0.625 or greater. A manager selecting S_2 is not really acting as though he were uncertain. On the contrary, his behavior indicates a belief (albeit hidden to him) that the environment, N_1, is more likely to occur than is N_2. We see that each criterion imputes particular values for the environments by the very act of selecting specific strategies. Thus, the pessimistic attitude is in some sense equivalent to the belief that N_2 is not as likely to occur as is N_1. The Waldian decision maker, as he selects S_2, is saying, in effect, "I am not really uncertain. My unconscious belief is that the state N_2 is less likely to occur than N_1." In general, any decision that deviates from the equally likely criterion implies that a decision policy has been chosen that embodies an attitude; and this attitude, in turn, implies that somehow *true* uncertainty does not exist.

Our analysis of DMUU reveals the fact that any choice imputes probabilities. Although the probabilities cannot be stated, measured, or explained, the manager acts as though he knows more about the system than he maintains. The fact that attitudes play such a crucial role is of real significance to all managerial analysis. An important question is: Which comes first, the attitude that imputes probabilities or the intuitive assessment of the probabilities that conditions attitude?

Problems involving uncertainty are not limited to long-term decision situations. A reasonable hypothesis might be that the Savage criterion of minimizing regret describes the way that consumers reach their purchasing decisions. In the same sense, consider the behavior of a worker who is about to be the subject of a time study. His strategic alternatives might be: to work at the normal rate; to work at a slower rate than usual; to work faster.[17] The environments can be:

N_1:   this is a routine time study.
N_2:   this is a special situation.

The worker might never know which environment describes the true state of affairs, but he is quite likely to have a predisposed attitudinal set. Equivalently, decisions must be made without sufficient information at all levels of management.

Decisions Made Under Partial Uncertainty

Mathematically more demanding (and intriguing) are those situations where risk conditions do not apply, but neither does the assumption of

---

[17] The motivation for working slower might be predicated on the basis of having a more favorable piece-rate set. The motivation for going faster might be to distinguish himself as a superior worker deserving a higher skill rating.

uncertainty. For example, the specific probabilities of the environments may be unknown, but the fact that a unimodal distribution is considered reasonable provides useful information. Similarly, all that may be known is that the probability distribution of the forecast is symmetrical. Nonparametric and distribution free methods of statistical analysis exist that add to the manager's ability to reach decisions.[18]

Decision Making Under Conflict

Another important class of decision model is concerned with competition. This is characteristic of military situations where weapon systems are evaluated in terms of their competitive efficiency. The nonmilitary importance of competitive decision systems is not less significant although less well-known. Usually, competition is treated as a marketing factor. Production interfaces with competition. The man who builds a better mousetrap is a successful production manager. If the world beats a path to his door, he must be prepared to supply this large market without losing the qualities of the mousetrap for which he is famous.

Competitive situations can be explained as a variant of the basic decision matrix formulation. Environments have been described as variables not under the manager's control; this also describes competitive strategies. Let us replace environments, N_j, with the strategies of the competitor, C_j. We now have a matrix that looks like this:

		Beta		
		C_1	C_2	C_3
Alpha	S_1	-1	0	$+3$
	S_2	-2	-3	$+3$
	S_3	-1	$+1$	-3

The characteristic of C_j is that although its variables are not under our manager's control, they are under some other manager's control.

The behavior of competitive systems has been analyzed and is known as game theory.[19] Games can be classified by the *number of opponents* that participate, the *relationships between these opponents*, and the *rules of the game*. Whenever there is conflict between companies, individuals, or between

---

[18] See, for example, M. K. Starr and D. W. Miller, *Inventory Control: Theory and Practice* (Englewood Cliffs, N.J.: Prentice-Hall, Inc., 1962), pp. 58–76, 152–62. Also, Sidney Siegel, *Nonparametric Statistics for the Behavioral Sciences* (New York: McGraw-Hill Book Co., Inc., 1956).

[19] J. Von Neumann and Oskar Morgenstern, *Theory of Games and Economic Behavior* (Princeton, N.J.: Princeton University Press, 1947).

departments, some form of game analysis can be applied. However, not all games can be mathematically formulated and be solved. One simple variant of game theory, amenable to solution under all circumstances, is the basic *two-person, zero-sum game.* There are only two opponents; the zero-sum condition requires that a gain by one player should be the other's loss. Thus, in the above matrix, which we shall assume represents Alpha winnings, the payoffs represent the amounts that Beta must pay to Alpha for each possible combination of Alpha and Beta strategies that might occur. Negative entries are Alpha losses and Beta gains. If Alpha plays strategy S_2 and Beta plays strategy C_3, then Alpha wins three points and Beta loses three points. This is a zero-sum game, which is not easy to find in real life.

However, with ingenuity, some systems can be transformed to meet this condition. For example, if a brand-share measure is used as the payoff measure, then what one company gains the other loses. If, on the other hand, the payoffs were written in terms of sales volume, then the zero-sum requirement would not be satisfied unless the total size of the market was constant over a period of time, which is rare. Usually, if both companies lower price, then more customers come into the marketplace to buy. The same kind of effect is expected if both companies intensify their advertising. In these cases, the zero-sum condition would be violated. For competitive situations between individuals, groups, departments, and divisions within a company, we can sometimes achieve the zero-sum condition by assuming that some constant element must be shared by the competitors, for example, responsibility, authority, or a share of the total budget. But, as soon as more than two competitors are involved, the two-person requirement cannot be satisfied. When more than two competitors are present, various kinds of *coalitions*, treaties, and agreements can develop and create special theoretic game situations.

Although game theory is an analytic model, nevertheless, it is possible to use qualitative factors to determine optimal strategic behaviors. Military planners have long made use of the game construction in this way for the purpose of choosing between major strategic alternatives. Examples of this can be found in the literature.[20]

To illustrate, consider the following example. Alpha and Beta manufacture typewriters. Alpha has developed a new typewriter that embodies a new patented principle. Management is studying the question of what to do with this new design. To keep the problem simple, only three possibilities will be considered.

S_1—Schedule heavy volume for the new product, and remove the present typewriters from the line to free production capacity;

---

[20] O. G. Haywood, Jr., "Military Decision and Game Theory," *Journal of the Operations Research Society of America*, 2, 4 (November, 1954), 365–85.

S_2—Introduce the new typewriter with low production volume, and maintain production of the present line of typewriters with unchanged volume;

S_3—Hold back on the new design until further production efficiencies can be introduced.

It is decided by Alpha's management that Beta—with full knowledge of the patented new design—has only three reasonable strategic choices.

C_1—Modernize the typewriters in their present line;

C_2—Keep the present line unchanged;

C_3—Attempt to develop a revolutionary new typewriter of their own on a *crash* program basis.

The Alpha Company managers prepare a payoff matrix. They must fill in the matrix with judgments concerning the way in which the situations described by the intersections, for example, S_1 and C_3, S_2 and C_1, will affect Alpha's long-term share of the market. Assume that after some discussion the following qualitative payoff matrix is developed and that there is general agreement among Alpha's executives with respect to the matrix evaluations.

	C_1	C_2	C_3
S_1	Good	Average	Good
S_2	Average	Excellent	Poor
S_3	Catastrophic	Good	Average

Let us say that a scale ranging from zero to six has been prepared where the values are interpreted as follows:

$$0 = \text{Catastrophic}$$
$$1 = \text{Very Poor}$$
$$2 = \text{Poor}$$
$$3 = \text{Average}$$
$$4 = \text{Good}$$
$$5 = \text{Very good}$$
$$6 = \text{Excellent}$$

The matrix is then loaded with the numbers that correspond to the qualitative judgments previously made.

		β_1 C_1	β_2 C_2	β_3 C_3
α_1	S_1	4	3	4
α_2	S_2	3	6	2
α_3	S_3	0	4	3

Using the game criterion employed when a rational opponent exists, Alpha looks across each of its strategic possibilities and picks out the worst possible results for each row (that is, the lowest number). These numbers are 3, 2, and 0. The best of the worst possible events, 3, called the maximin, can be obtained by using strategy one.

We observe that the Wald criterion, which was one variant of DMUU, is an absolute necessity in this case. There is no choice of a criterion to be made. *Only* the Wald *minimax* for one competitor and the *maximin* for the other can be used. The logic of the procedure we have used is based on the assumption that a zero-sum game exists. That is, if Alpha sees the relative goodness of four in the combination S_1C_1, then it is necessary that Beta would find a disadvantage of four (or minus four) when the combination occurs. Assuming that the managers of Alpha are considering this problem in terms of the effect of their decision on brand share, the zero-sum assumption would be legitimate. Numbers were used merely as an added convenience. We could have used words as well without bothering to translate them into scale values, i.e., a purely qualitative approach.

Let us now examine what Beta would do in this situation. Beta studies each of its columns, which are its strategic possibilities. Beta then chooses the worst possible result for each of its strategies. These are respectively four, six, and four. Because the payoff matrix is written for Alpha, it is necessary to remember that Beta would like to see numbers that are as small as possible. Therefore, the worst results for Beta are the largest numbers. Beta's decision criterion will be the minimax, that is, the best of the worst possibilities. The minimax solution in this case is either C_1 or C_3.

It will be observed that the minimax and maximin values are not identical. For Alpha the value of the game is three—for Beta it is four. When the *value* of the game, obtained in this minimax-maximin fashion is identical, then the opponents each use the *pure strategies* indicated by the criterion. When the value of the game for each player is an identical number, we say that the combination of strategies produces a *saddlepoint*. Alpha and Beta could do no better than to use this saddlepoint result. Frequently, however, the use of the Wald criterion does not produce identical results for both players. This is the situation in our example. We observe that Alpha obtains a different expected payoff with its pure strategy, S_1, than Beta obtains with its pure strategy, either C_1 or C_3. The fundamental theorem of game theory states that a saddlepoint can be found for these games by using what is called a *mixed strategy*. The saddlepoint represents an equilibrium condition that is optimal for both players. To mix strategies, each player randomly selects the strategy that he will employ, according to the previously determined probability of usage for each strategy that will produce a saddlepoint game. This will become clear as we proceed with our example.

We shall let the probabilities of using each pure strategy for Alpha be

α_1, α_2, and α_3, where the sum of the α's is equal to one, that is, $\Sigma \alpha_i = 1$. Similarly, for β we assign probabilities for each strategy of β_1, β_2, and β_3, where $\Sigma \beta_j = 1$. Now, a set of inequations and equations can be written to express the objectives of each player in terms of a measure v, where v is the value of the game. These equations are shown below.

1.	$4\alpha_1 + 3\alpha_2 + 0\alpha_3 \geq v$
2.	$3\alpha_1 + 6\alpha_2 + 4\alpha_3 \geq v$
3.	$4\alpha_1 + 2\alpha_2 + 3\alpha_3 \geq v$
4.	$\alpha_1 + \alpha_2 + \alpha_3 = 1.00$
5.	$4\beta_1 + 3\beta_2 + 4\beta_3 \leq v$
6.	$3\beta_1 + 6\beta_2 + 2\beta_3 \leq v$
7.	$0\beta_1 + 4\beta_2 + 3\beta_3 \leq v$
8.	$\beta_1 + \beta_2 + \beta_3 = 1.00$

The direction of the inequalities can be explained in the following way. Equations 1-3 express Alpha's desire to obtain a value for the game that will be at least equal to v. Equations 5-7 express Beta's desire to have the value of the payoff to Alpha be no greater than v. The fundamental theorem states that such a value v exists; it will be >3 and <4, in our example.

The equations can be solved in two ways. One is by using trial and error methods. There are eight equations and seven unknowns. Therefore, subsets of the equations would be solved until the right subset is found; thus, there is at least one subset that provides a solution that satisfies all eight equations. A simpler approach is to utilize linear programming. The mathematical statement for the conversion of the game into linear programming form is given in Chapter 5.

Let us consider the following payoff matrix, to illustrate dominance.

	C_1	C_2	C_3	C_4
S_1	-1	1	1	0
S_2	2	-2	2	3
S_3	3	3	-3	4
S_4	1	-3	1	-2
S_5	2	2	-3	5

In this case, Alpha would never use his fourth strategy because it is *dominated* by his second strategy. (That is, S_2 is better than S_4 in every case.) Once, *and only after* Alpha removes his fourth strategy, Beta finds that his fourth strategy is now dominated by his first strategy, and accordingly he removes C_4. Proceeding in this fashion the payoff matrix can be reduced to:

	C_1	C_2	C_3
S_1	-1	1	1
S_2	2	-2	2
S_3	3	3	-3

Complex sets of dominated strategies can result in large matrices. It is quite clear than an individual would be hard pressed to discover this network of relationships without formal assistance. By removing the dominated relationships, we have now reduced the size of the game to a 3 × 3.

To illustrate the nature of a relatively simple, nonzero competitive situation, let us examine the matrix below. Alpha and Beta have only two available

Matrix of dollar volume (in millions) per year

		Beta	
		Redesign	No change
Alpha	Redesign	2 / 2	5 / 1
	No change	1 / 5	3 / 3

Payoffs to Alpha 1

Payoffs to Beta   2

strategies, namely, redesign the product and do not change the product design. We see from the payoff matrix that if Alpha redesigns its product but Beta makes no change, then Alpha will make $5 million and Beta will make only $1 million. On the other hand, if Beta redesigns its product and Alpha makes no change, then Beta obtains $5 million and Alpha only $1 million. If both companies make no change they will each continue to net $3 million. On the other hand, if both proceed to redesign their products, their respective profits will be reduced to $2 million because of tooling costs and other investments.

What is each participant likely to do in this case? If Alpha and Beta compromise (at the possible expense of the consumer), they can each make $3 million. On the other hand, either Alpha or Beta or both may decide to take the chance that the other company will do nothing. Thinking that they can get the jump on the other; that they can increase their profits to $5 million, they will secretly prepare to intoduce a new design. (Even if a compromise agreement is reached, can Alpha trust Beta and vice versa?) It is in the effectiveness area that issues of this kind arise. Significant investments in research, plant, and equipment are at stake. The fact that the operations area of management is not directly related to the market and to competition does not alter the fact that the design of the production process is intensively involved with these factors.

PROBLEMS

1. Why is it particularly useful for production management to differentiate between decision making under certainty, risk, and uncertainty?
2. Solve the following decision problem for the various probability conditions that are specified.

	N_1	N_2	N_3	N_4	N_5
S_1	3	5	4	2	8
S_2	5	3	2	4	6
S_3	4	4	4	4	4
S_4	4	5	4	2	8

Outcomes are the *expected life* of the product.

	Values of p_j				
	N_1	N_2	N_3	N_4	N_5
Condition 1	0	1.00	0	0	0
Condition 2	0.20	0.30	0.50	0	0
Condition 3	0	0	0.30	0.30	0.40
Condition 4	0.20	0.20	0.20	0.20	0.20

Comment on the character of these various conditions and their effects on the results.

3. Develop the appropriate decision matrix for each of the problems below. This requires describing specific strategies and relevant environments. Load the cells of the matrix with reasonable estimates for the outcomes. Assign sensible forecast values. Solve the problem that you have designed. The generality of the decision matrix approach for resolving problems should become evident.

    I.   Strategies: A number of different equipment selection plans
        Environments: Equipment failure rates
          Outcomes: Measures of downtime
          Objective: Minimize downtime

    II.   Strategies: Various plant layout arrangements
        Environments: Varying demand levels for different items in the company's product-mix

Outcomes: Measures of bottlenecks and delay
Objective: Minimize delay

III.   Strategies: Different production materials, for example, various metals v. various plastics
Environments: Varying costs for these materials and different levels of consumer demand
Outcomes: Profit measures
Objective: Maximize profit

IV.   Strategies: Varying number of repairmen
Environments: Probabilities of machine breakdowns
Outcomes: Measures of the cost of downtime
Objective: Minimize cost

V.   Strategies: Different computer systems
Environments: Varying data loads on the department
Outcomes: Measures of the age of information
Objective: Minimize age of information in the system

VI.   Strategies: Different numbers of toll booths
Environments: Varying numbers of arrivals
Outcomes: Measures of customer waiting time
Objective: Minimize customer waiting time

VII.   Strategies: Various arrangements of supermarket checkout counters
Environments: Number of customers with small and large orders that come into the store
Outcomes: Measures of idle time of checkout clerks and customer waiting time
Objective: Minimize total cost of checkout clerks' idle time and waiting time of customers

VIII.   Strategies: Different catalogue numbering systems
Environments: Various users of the catalogue
Outcomes: Measure of errors in ordering
Objective: Minimize ordering errors

4. What factors would ordinarily be considered when a proposed plan calls for replacing a man with a machine? What criteria would apply to the decision?

5. Figure 3.3 presents three hypothetical functions.

   (a) $C_1 = f(n)$; C_1 = expected cost of creating n alternatives
   (b) $C_2 = f(n)$; C_2 = expected cost of choosing a single strategic alternative from among n possibilities
   (c) $R = f(n)$; R = expected reward when a best strategy is chosen from among n alternatives.

   (a) Working with the numerical values of the figure, how many alternatives would be desirable for a decision in this situation?
   (b) Although purely hypothetical, these concepts are important to the operations manager. Why?

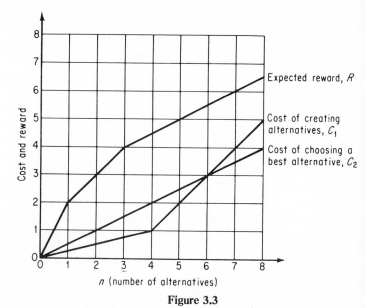

Figure 3.3

What is an optimal number of strategic alternatives (a hypothetical example).

The most difficult problems that managers face are those of measuring meaningfully so that the models they use can synthesize the various forms of information and thereby recommend a course of action to follow. Often models point out that there are other things to consider that may have been overlooked.

It is a remarkable fact that so many observations that the manager uses can be converted, theoretically and practically, into a single dimension of costs. For example, the weight of a package can be stated as a cost of "that much weight"—both in terms of product quantity and also the cost of transporting the package. We could go on and list many other factors that are important and find a cost equivalent expression for each of them.

The difficulty then arises: How does one find a numerical value that properly measures factors that are known to be related in an intangible fashion, such as dealer attitude cost implications, consumer responses to the costs of package appearance and pouring convenience, etc. In spite of this fundamental problem, a great deal can be done with cost models. This is particularly true because profits can be viewed as negative costs, once the marketplace is included as part of the system.

Cost

Models 4

All outputs of an input-output system can be categorized as either penalties or benefits. Each output measure can be regarded as *a* measure of the system's performance. Seldom does one measure suffice to describe the system, but cost is often regarded as a measure that comes close to doing this. Because the operations manager does not easily achieve synthesis with the total organization, he is particularly likely to work with cost measures rather than sales volume, share of market, or profit.

Fixed- and Variable-cost Systems

Management exercises *operating control* over the system in two different ways:

1. By determining the inputs with respect to input rates, cost, quality, and so on, the *variable costs* are controlled.
2. By altering the process (or procedure), that is, by rearranging the process elements, the *fixed systemic costs* are controlled.

Operation managers have thought in this way for many years, but they also found it convenient to consider revenues when possible. Thus:

1. Variable-cost systems—the major responsibility of operations management.
2. Fixed-cost systems—a design issue, dependent upon operations management decisions but fundamentally a responsibility of financial management.
3. Revenue—a major marketing responsibility.

Variable-cost systems have been touted as the major concern of production and operations managers. In recent years, it has become increasingly apparent that fixed-cost systems are responsive to the technological knowledge of operations managers. Revenue considerations, related to quality, cost and, therefore, price, product availability, and variety are both marketing

84

and production issues. In input-output terms, this can be illustrated as in Figure 4.1.

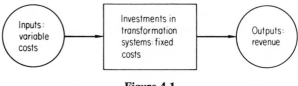

Figure 4.1

The Break-even Cost Model

To illustrate management's concern with these three factors we need only consider the application of the break-even chart, which is illustrated in Figure 4.2.

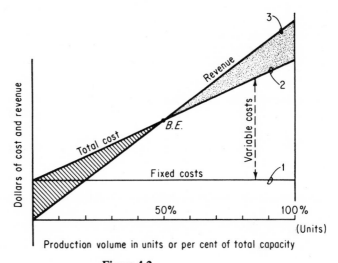

Figure 4.2

The break-even chart.

The chart, consisting of an ordinate (vertical-axis) and an abscissa (horizontal-axis), can be represented by conventional Cartesian coordinates. The ordinate presents a scale of dollars against which fixed costs, variable costs, and dollars of revenue can be measured. The abscissa can be dimensioned in terms of the production volume, that is, the number of units that are made by the company in a given period of time. It isn't difficult to translate this as a per cent of the total capacity that the company has available. All these dimensions will be found on Figure 4.2.

We observe that three lines have been marked on the chart. Line number one is a fixed-cost function. The fixed charges behave in the expected manner, that is, they do not change as a function of increased volume or increased utilization of capacity. Line two is a linear, monotonic[1] function that increases with increasing volume. In the real world, such linearity is neither expected nor obtained *perfectly*. Nevertheless, the assumption of linearity is not a major concession because linear relationships do *adequately* describe many situations. The operations field has, in the past, accepted this assumption for a great number of cases. The second line reflects the variable cost components that increase with additional volume. On the chart, variable costs do not begin at the zero level. Instead, they are added to fixed costs that exist even at zero production levels. Consequently, this second line is a total cost line, which results from the summation of fixed and variable costs. The triangular area lying between the fixed costs and total costs would then be the variable costs that are assigned to the production system.

For each unit of a particular item that we make, a certain amount of labor is required, and the necessary materials must be assembled and utilized to produce that unit. If materials that are used for one unit cost $.10, then the total material charges for one hundred units would be $10.00, and the total material charges for one thousand units would be $100.00. That is why this second function increases as we move to greater utilization of capacity. Recalling fixed-cost elements, we observe that only depreciation, which is applicable to machine utilization, would be included in the variable-cost section. Taxes that are levied on the basis of units produced or revenue obtained would also be appropriately included in the variable-cost class. Some power and light charges, heating charges, storage charges, and insurance charges are characterized by the definition of variable costs.

We have defined the total costs that are applicable to a company's operations. The categorization of fixed- and variable-cost charges fits conveniently with the assumption of an input-output system. The diagram can be translated into mathematical terms, but for purposes of communication with operations personnel, the break-even chart in its graphical form is a useful device. It is accepted and understood by operations managers to constitute an important bridge between modern and progressive practice and the old-time, traditional way of viewing decision making in the operations field.[2]

The third line shown in Figure 4.2 is a revenue line. It is also a monotonic function that increases with greater production volume. Here, too, we have a situation utilizing the assumption of linearity. But how long can this assumption hold? At some point, total revenue will not increase at the same

---

[1] Always increasing—never decreasing—and in this case at a constant rate because of the assumption of linearity. (Decreasing monotonic functions exist as well).

[2] The break-even chart was developed by Walter Rautenstrauch, an industrial engineer, in the 1930s. See W. Rautenstrauch and R. Villers, *The Economics of Industrial Management* (New York: Funk & Wagnalls Co., 1949).

rate, as the company manufactures greater and greater quantities of an item. The market for the item becomes saturated. The company must lower its price in order to obtain a greater share of the total market that is available.[3] A linear relationship is often used to describe revenue. This implies that the company is operating at a relatively low level in the total market so that "free competition" could adequately describe the situation.

The cross-hatched area between the total cost line and the revenue line represents loss to the company. This is the area to the left of the break-even point. The gray area represents profit to the company and lies to the right of this point. Therein lies the definition of the break-even point—no profit, no loss. The break-even point occurs at a given volume of production or a given utilization of plant capacity. Figure 4.3 shows the relationship of profit to production volume. The ordinate is measured as amount of profit.

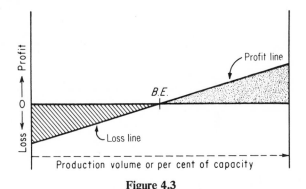

Figure 4.3

Profit versus production volume.

Two factors would have to be considered in reaching conclusions about any specific break-even situation. The first would be the position of the break-even point. The second would be the amount of profit on a marginal basis that is obtained for each additional unit of capacity that can be utilized. This is the slope of the line in Figure 4.3. In other words, if the profit/loss line shown in Figure 4.3 was rotated so that it had almost zero angle of slope, then little profit could be obtained as a result of increased utilization of plant capacity. As the slope of this line is increased by mechanically rotating it about the break-even point, then greater returns are obtained *once* demand exceeds the break-even point. At the same time, because of the linearity assumption, the

---

[3] Pricing problems are a mysterious and ill-defined area. Although we have generalized the effect of saturation as being correlated with price, this is not always the case. There are well-known instances where a company achieves a major market or at least increased revenue as a result of raising its price. Here we are dealing with the psychology of the consumer and the fact that a market may not exist for a low-price product because it does not carry sufficient prestige value to the consumer.

losses or penalties for operating *under* the break-even point also become proportionately greater as we move to the left from the break-even point. This is true in most actual situations.

Our second concern has to do with the position of the break-even point. If it is moved to the right, then the company must operate at a higher level of capacity before it is worthwhile for it to engage in business. Conversely, by reducing the value of the break-even point (moving it to the left) the pressure of this demand upon the company is decreased. But decisions can be complex with respect to these two criteria. Notice that in Figure 4.4 we have

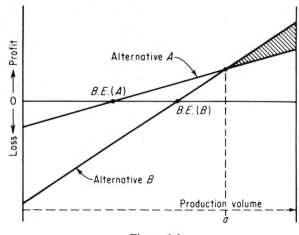

Figure 4.4

Profit versus production volume for alternative production configurations.

drawn two profit/loss lines. Each is presumably descriptive of a result obtained from different production configurations. Alternative A has a lower break-even point than alternative B making A more desirable than B *with respect to this criterion*. But the profit function B has greater marginal returns *once the break-even point has been reached*. B is preferred, therefore, with respect to this second criterion. If the company is able to operate at point a, then both alternatives yield equal profit. If we can operate at a volume in excess of point a, then alternative B is preferred. If we cannot, then our choice is for alternative A.

Algebraic Analysis of the Break-even Cost Model

It is straightforward to translate the break-even chart into its algebraic equivalent. Some individuals prefer the visual form, others prefer the mathematical statement, the choice being a matter of taste.

The symbols we will use are:

r = *Gross* revenue per time period T.

p = Price per unit (with the assumption that the market will absorb everything that can be made at the same price).

v = Number of units made in time period T (therefore, sales volume in time period T).

V = Total production capacity, (that is, maximum number of units that can be made in time period T operating at full capacity).

k = Fraction of total capacity that is utilized = v/V.

FC = Fixed costs per period T.

VC = Variable costs per unit of production.

TC = Total costs for period T.

PR = Total profit for period T.

The revenue line for period T is given by:

$$r = pv = pkV$$

The total cost line for period T is equal to:

$$TC = [FC + (VC)v] = [FC + (VC)kV]$$

Total profit for the interval T is (*in terms of volume*) then:

$$PR = (r - TC) = [(p - VC)v - FC]$$

(*and in terms of the utilization factor k*):

$$PR = (r - TC) = [(p - VC)kV - FC]$$

For example, let a one-year comparison be made of the alternative plans shown below ($T = 1$).

Decision Choice	Alternative 1 No Conveyer	Alternative 2 Install Conveyer
V	20,000 units per year	20,000 units per year
FC	$10,000 per year	$12,000 per year
VC	$0.50 per unit	$0.45 per unit
p	$2.00 per unit	$2.00 per unit
k	estimated at 0.90 for both alternatives when p = $2.00	

for alternative 1:

$$PR = (2 - 0.50)(0.90)(20,000) - 10,000 = \$17,000 \text{ per year}$$

for alternative 2:

$$PR = (2 - 0.45)(0.90)(20,000) - 12,000 = \$15,900 \text{ per year}$$

The break-even point is calculated by setting $PR = 0$, then

$$(p - VC)kV = FC$$

and

$$k(break\text{-}even\ point) = FC/(p - VC)V$$

For alternative 1:

$$k(break\text{-}even\ point) = 10{,}000/(1.5)(20{,}000) = 0.333$$

For alternative 2:

$$k(break\text{-}even\ point) = 12{,}000/(1.55)(20{,}000) = 0.387$$

NOTE: On the basis of profit for a k factor estimated at 0.90, we prefer alternative 1. It promises \$1,100 more profit than alternative 2. And, in terms of the break-even point, we prefer alternative 1 because it has a lower value. Since at full utilization of plant capacity, alternative 1 continues to be preferable to alternative 2, there is no doubt that we should select alternative 1, on the basis of this analysis.

In this next example, conflicting indicators appear in the cost model. (Let $T =$ three months or one quarter).

Decision Choice	Alternative 1 Machine A	Alternative 2 Machine B
V	5,000 units per quarter	5,000 units per quarter
FC	\$2500 per quarter	\$3500 per quarter
VC	\$0.50 per unit	\$0.10 per unit
p	\$2.00 per unit	\$2.00 per unit
k	0.60	0.60

We obtain: for alternative 1

$(k = 0.60)$: $PR = (2 - 0.50)(0.60)(5000) - 2500 = \$2{,}000$ per quarter;

for alternative 2

$(k = 0.60)$: $PR = (2 - 0.10)(0.60)(5000) - 3500 = \$2{,}200$ per quarter;

and for alternative 1

$(k = 1.00)$: $PR = (2 - 0.50)(1.00)(5000) - 2500 = \$5{,}000$ per quarter;

for alternative 2

$(k = 1.00)$: $PR = (2 - 0.10)(1.00)(5000) - 3500 = \$6{,}000$ per quarter.

Alternative 2 is preferred both at the point of estimated plant utilization (0.60) and at full utilization (1.00). But, the break-even points are:

for alternative 1:

$$k(break\text{-}even\ point) = 2500/(1.5)(5000) = 0.333$$

for alternative 2:

$$k(break\text{-}even\ point) = 3500/(1.9)(5000) = 0.368$$

Alternative 1 has a superior break-even point. It is clear that something else must be added to our analysis if it is to make sense. That something extra will be risk estimates associated with varying levels of plant utilization.

Risk Analysis and the Break-even Cost Model

Consider the kind of problem that exists for airlines when the volume of demand is not known with certainty. This operations management problem deals with actions required to move individuals from one place to another, in keeping with the expectations and needs of these individuals.

Suppose that Alpha Airlines needs to determine whether they should convert some of their aircraft to large airbuses. The company uses break-even

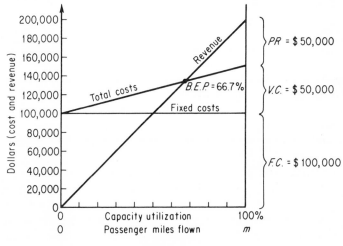

Figure 4.5

Break-even chart for present configuration of aircraft.

cost models. Figure 4.5 holds for the present configuration of planes; Figure 4.6 applies to the airbus configuration.

Comparing Figures 4.5 and 4.6, we note that the company presently has a lower investment in aircraft, but its variable costs of operating are relatively

high. Converting to airbuses substantially increases the fixed costs but succeeds in lowering the variable costs. Assuming that there are no surcharges
for the larger planes and that the same revenue line can be used for both
situations, we find that the present fleet achieves a lower break-even point

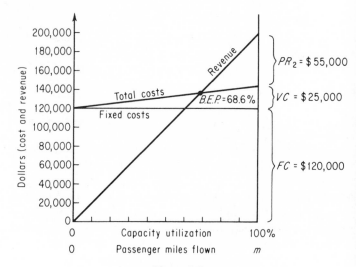

Figure 4.6

Break-even chart for airbus configuration.

than the proposed equipment.[4] This means that the actual "load factor" must
be higher for the conversion to be approved.

At the same time, we note that as compensation for this low break-even
point the airbuses produce higher marginal returns on profit. This means that
if Alpha Airlines is able to operate at higher passenger (and cargo) loads than
the break-even point, then a substantially greater profit can be obtained by
converting the fleet to these particular airbuses.

Something, however, is missing from this analysis. Either an estimate or
prediction of the *probable level of consumer demand* for seats and for aircraft
miles to be flown[5] or a forecast of the probability that each of the various
possible levels will be achieved is required. A different amount of profit is
associated with each level of demand. Therefore, we require a probability distribution to help us describe the relative likelihood that different amounts of
profit will be obtained.

Assume that a probability distribution can be determined to describe
the relative likelihoods that different profit levels will be achieved. Figure 4.7
combines the two break-even charts, Figures 4.5 and 4.6, and shows these

---

[4] Clearly, these are fictitious data since present "load factors" are below 5 per cent.
[5] Equivalent to an estimate of sales volume and utilized production capacity.

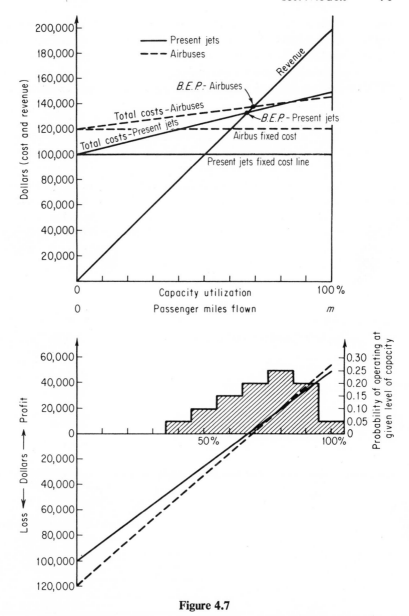

Figure 4.7

Risk analysis of the break-even cost model; present jets versus airbuses.

accompanied by a probability distribution. (The assumption is made that demand probabilities are independent of the type of plane that is flown—an assumption that may not stand up to reality.) We calculate the expected value of this irregular distribution to be equal to a load factor of about 73 per cent.

The distribution also has a standard deviation of approximately 16 per cent. A distribution such as this can be derived (when necessary) strictly by executive judgment.

Having this information on hand, we can now multiply each of the profit levels—including negative profit—by its respective probability of occurrence. Doing this for both alternatives, we derive an average or expected profit for both cases. By using a probability distribution, we have bypassed the need for a break-even point analysis. This is true because fundamental to the entire concept of the break-even cost point is the fact that managers have in mind an estimate of the likelihood that the company will operate below or above that point. Without this estimate in mind, the break-even point is meaningless. By using a statistical approach, we succeed in relating the two factors that previously were treated as separate components—namely, the position of the break-even point and the marginal rates of return. Based on this approach we have no difficulty in determining whether or not the company should convert to airbuses.

Decision Matrix of the Break-even Cost Model

When probability is included, break-even analysis turns out to be a standard decision problem under risk, whereas, in its traditional form it is equivalent to DMUU. Thus, it becomes the victim of the attitudes and values of management when employed in the manner that historical usage has assigned it.

Returning to the airline problem, assume that the outcomes and probabilities shown in the matrix below have a relatively high degree of believability.

Matrix of Outcomes (Measured in Thousands of Dollars)

p_k	0	0	0	0	.05	.10	.15	.20	.25	.20	.05	
k	0	0.10	0.20	0.30	0.40	0.50	0.60	0.70	0.80	0.90	1.00	EV_i
S_1	−100	−85.0	−70	−55.0	−40	−25.0	−10	+5.0	+20	+35.0	+50	+9.50*
S_2	−120	−102.5	−85	−67.5	−50	−32.5	−15	+2.5	+20	+37.5	+55	+7.75

p_k = likelihood of kth demand level occurring, where k = capacity utilization.

S_1 = present aircraft.

S_2 = airbus jet fleet.

Obtaining the expected value, we discover that the present aircraft will produce a higher level of profitability (denoted by *) than the airbuses. The method of DMUR removes the need for consideration of the break-even point or the marginal returns of profit.

As a further illustration, let us examine another set of likelihood estimates, p_k (all other values remain the same).

Matrix of Outcomes (Measured in Thousands of Dollars)

p_k	0	0	0	0	0	0	0	.20	.25	.20	.35	
k	0	0.10	0.20	0.30	0.40	0.50	0.60	0.70	0.80	0.90	1.00	EV_i
S_1	−100	−85.0	−70	−55.0	−40	−25.0	−10	+5.0	+20	+35.0	+50	+30.50
S_2	−120	−102.5	−85	−67.5	−50	−32.5	−15	+2.5	+20	+37.5	+55	+32.25*

Our result has shifted. Preference (shown by the *) now goes to airbuses. This is true in spite of the fact that the break-even points associated with both types of planes remain unchanged. We recognize that the increased marginal return rate of the airbuses has overwhelmed the break-even point advantage to be gained from the present type aircraft. The reason for this is that the second probability distribution is skewed to the right.

Sensitivity Analysis

Cost models lend themselves to sensitivity analysis, which consists of altering some of the estimates to see what happens to other measures of performance. For example, we might ask, How different must the original probability distribution for demand be to change the solution from S_1 (present fleet) to S_2 (airbuses)? Gradual changes (following specific patterns) made in the original distribution would help to answer this question. We know that there are circumstances where no matter what probability distribution holds, there will be no change in the solution (see Problem 5, pp. 115), i.e., the cost system is totally insensitive to the probability estimates. One often approximates nonlinear forms with linear substitutions. Sensitivity analysis can provide guidelines as to when this approximation is reasonable.

The Nonlinear Break-even Cost Model

It is apparent that the anticipated volume of operations is a critical factor in the system's design. If the market is such that at a certain price unlimited demand exists, then for these linear systems we would always operate as far to the right as our plant capacity permits. Of course, in reality at some point linearity ceases to be a reasonable description of the market's responses. Increased volume can only be obtained by a decrease in price or an increase in promotional and selling costs. These two situations are shown in Figures 4.8 and 4.9. The combination of effects is illustrated in Figure 4.10.

Each diagram is accompanied by a graph of the profit that can be obtained at different percentages of capacity utilization. We note there is a "best possible" point, at which the total profit is maximized. To achieve this level of capacity utilization requires cooperative effort on the part of all the manage-

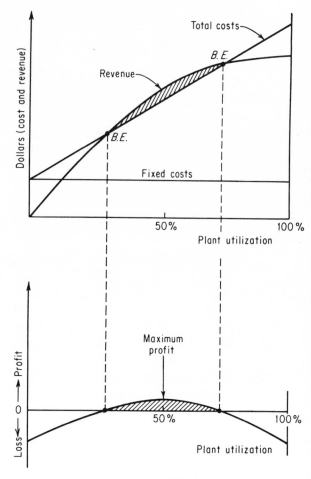

Figure 4.8

Break-even chart with the assumption of a decelerating revenue as the product price is lowered to achieve full plant utilization.

ment divisions. Financial management must provide funds to create and support the facilities necessary for the specified volume of production. The marketing department must be able to deliver the estimated number of customers and their sales at the price that is incorporated in the revenue line. And, of course, production must be able to deliver the goods in the required volume.

We see that production and operations management must help to determine a *configuration* (or design) *of production elements* that will yield a maximum profit. However, the problems of doing this are complicated far beyond anything that a break-even model can show. A danger of models is

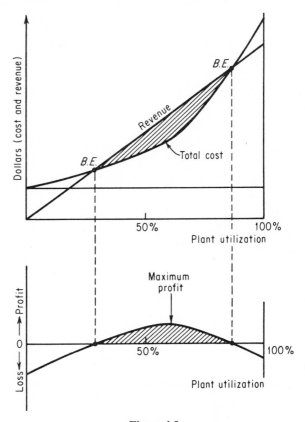

Figure 4.9

Break-even chart with the assumption of accelerating promotional costs required to achieve full plant utilization.

that many difficulties are represented in a simple fashion that belies the truth of the situation.

Even when recognized to be of nonlinear form, the break-even model represents only one product. For most companies, decisions must include the fact that a product-mix is involved. The line consists of a number of different items or services.[6] These must share resources including capital and manage-

[6] See Chapter 5 on the product-mix problem.

ment time. The break-even model is difficult to utilize when such additional complications are encountered. In addition, a specific period of time is embodied in each break-even analysis. If we assume that the company can sell five million units over a five-year period but only ten thousand in the first year, then a five-year break-even study may be quite appealing; whereas on the

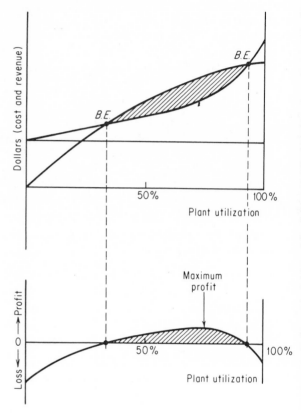

Figure 4.10

Break-even chart with both assumptions, that is, decelerating revenue and accelerating costs.

basis of a one-year analysis, the product would be rejected. But *cost estimates* applied to a five-year period might not be sufficiently believable to allow management to act on them. Further, *unexpected costs* can arise. For example, if the company overproduces, then overstock units could only be sold by reducing the price. If the unsold units are held in inventory, they will create *additional costs* such as storage, insurance, and carrying costs. For each nonlinear situation, some maximum profit (optimal) situation exists. The traditional break-even approach overlooks this vital characteristic of the problem.

The Utilities of Costs and Benefits

Utility is a term employed to describe the *real value* of cost and profit outcomes to the manager. Figure 4.11 shows relative rewards obtained from the two alternatives, A and B. We note that the reward scale is linear, i.e., an equal interval separates each million dollars of reward or penalty. Consequently, a four million dollar loss is considered to be exactly twice as much of a penalty as a two million dollar loss. Is this realistic? If not, what is wrong?

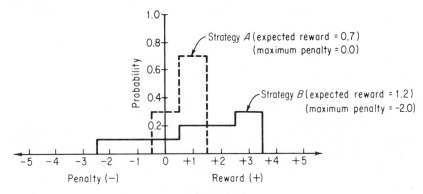

Figure 4.11

Two strategies on a linear scale. *A* is preferred to *B* on the basis of expected reward; *B* is preferred to *A* on the basis of maximum penalty.

At least two different things are wrong. Take the penalty side of the reward scale first. Suppose that A is chosen. Then a loss of up to two million dollars can occur. But what if the company will be totally ruined (bankrupt) if it experiences a loss greater than one million dollars? The importance of the penalty changes at the threshold level of one million dollars. A moment's thought tells us that the *undesirability* (disutility) of penalty increases at an accelerating rate as the ruin threshold is approached. Major losses in one area can curtail other profitable activities and destroy reserves that permit flexibility. Using a linear scale and the expected value criterion, the loss of four million dollars would be offset by a gain of four million dollars if their respective probabilities were held to be equal. The exact same result would occur if the offsetting losses and gains were only fifty dollars, which is not sensible.

Consider the direction of positive reward on the scale. Compare a one million dollar gain with a two million dollar gain; then compare a fifty million dollar gain with a fifty-one million dollar gain. In both cases, the superior reward is greater by one million dollars, but as to the percentage improvement, we have:

$$\frac{2-1}{1}(100) = 100 \text{ per cent} \quad \text{and} \quad \frac{51-50}{50}(100) = 2 \text{ per cent}$$

If the numbers were 100 and 101, the change would represent a 1 per cent improvement. The difference between one billion dollars plus one million dollars and just one billion is almost negligible. In estimating the value of rewards, there is a decelerating effect for a fixed increment of reward as it is added to increasing levels of reward.

One of the implications of what we are saying is that *companies of different sizes must necessarily evaluate costs and profits in uniquely different ways.* A company with assets of five million will perceive a reward of one million dollars as being a substantial gain, viz., $(100)(6-5)/5 = 20.0$ per cent. But a company capitalized at five hundred million might consider such a reward to be relatively insignificant, viz., $(100)(501-500)/500 = 0.20$ per cent.[7] The reward scale of Figure 4.11 is based on a *linear utility* function. This means that *the value or utility of a reward* is equivalent to the reward itself, shown by the straight line $V = R$ positioned at a forty-five degree angle in Figure 4.12. No ruin threshold can be applied to it. But the family of logarithmic curves possesses the characteristics we have been seeking. All these curves are assigned large negative values as their respective ruin thresholds are approached. The curves are differentiated by a parameter b. Three values of b are illustrated. We can consider this parameter to be a relative measure, indicating the size of a company's financial resources. Larger values of b represent greater assets. Correspondingly, disutility diminishes with greater assets (the ruin threshold moves to levels of greater loss). With greater assets, the utility of positive rewards diminishes.

Although these curves are purely hypothetical, they are conceptually important for understanding cost and benefit models. Companies having about the same level of assets can be expected to have similar but not identical utilities. Even within a single company, different individuals will assess utilities according to their own value systems. Many times, differences of opinion among a group of managers can be traced to discrepancies in their utilities.[8] Figure 4.13 portrays three managers who do not see "eye-to-eye" on the utilities of different profit and loss levels for their company. This is true in spite of the fact that a consensus exists about the ruin threshold and that zero

[7] These effects were noted by Daniel Bernouilli, a Swiss mathematician in 1730.
[8] When the situation is recognized, compromise is usually called for as the only immediate panacea. At the same time, it is indicative of a lack of rapport in the management team. More communication between executives, particularly when it is directed toward discussion of top-management policies, can usually help to homogenize the values held by individuals. But this can be effective only in the long run.

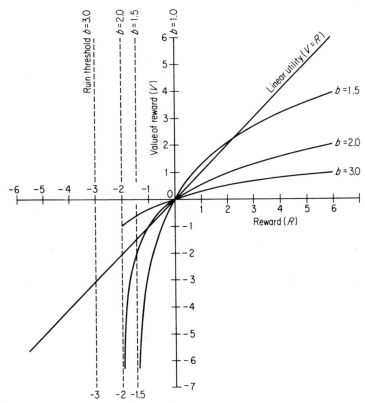

The non-linear relations are of the form $b^{V+1} - b = R$ or equivalently, $V = \left[\log_b (R+b) \right] - 1$

Figure 4.12

The utility, or value, of reward with linear and nonlinear assumptions. The parameter b represents levels of assets. For nonlinear cases, the ruin threshold is a function of b.

reward has zero value.[9] In fact, these executives are in close agreement about losses but in sharp disagreement about gains.

The transformation of outcomes to utilities is a management function. Operations and design decisions must include this basic factor. What is good for a large company might spell ruin for a small one. What is bad for a small company might be trivial for a large one. Such vital considerations are frequently bypassed, consciously ignored, or unconsciously overlooked.

[9] Actually, this is unreasonable. Zero reward is likely to be associated with negative value.

Let us presume that the manager's utilities can be expressed by the mathematical transform:[10]

$$\text{Value } (V) = [\log_3 (P \text{ profit } (PR) + 3)] - 1$$

This curve has already been drawn. It is identified by $b = 3$ in Figure 4.12.

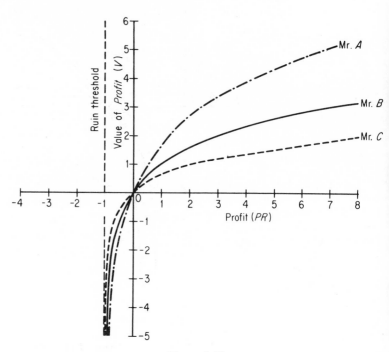

Figure 4.13

Three managers evaluate the utility of profit in different ways. (The utility transforms are determined by: $b^V - 1 = PR$, where the parameter b is now an expression of the manager's value system. Note that they all accept the same ruin threshold.

All that we must do is convert the reward scale of Figure 4.11 in accordance with these results, then calculate the *transformed expected values.*

[10] As expressed in Figure 4.12, this transform can also be written: $b^{V+1} - b = PR$, or specifically $3^{V+1} - 3 = PR$. We are dealing with a ternary (base three) logarithm. More familiar are Briggsian logs to the base 10, for example, $\log_{10} x$, called the *common* system. Or Napierian logs to the base e, for example, $\log_e x$, where $e = 2.7183 \ldots$ These are also called *hyperbolic* logs or *natural* logs. Particularly in connection with information theory, we come across binary (base two) logarithms, for example, $\log_2 x$.

For strategy A:

Reward	Utility Transform	Probability	Utility
+3	0.63	0.30	0.189
+2	0.47	0.20	0.094
+1	.0.26	0.20	0.052
0	0.00	0.10	0.000
−1	−0.37	0.10	−0.037
−2	−1.00	0.10	−0.100
		1.00	+0.198 = Expected Utility

Strategy B yields:

Reward	Utility Transform	Probability	Utility
+1	0.26	0.70	0.182
0	0.00	0.30	0.000
		1.00	+0.182 = Expected Utility

Necessary contingencies have been taken into account *if* the risk estimates are sound and the utility transform is accurate. But what if the $b = 2$ curve of Figure 4.12 was really a better description of the system? Computation will reveal that the expected utility of A would be minus infinity; an impossible choice. No wonder that under certain circumstances[11] we associate mixed feelings with what appears to be a sensible decision. If one could expose the complex pattern of the manager's judgments and intuitions, we may suppose that his uncertainty as to whether the utility transform would be properly described by $b = 2$ or $b = 3$ would lead him to decide on the safer, but less rewarding, alternative. Undoubtedly, we would also uncover the manager's quandary with respect to the believability of estimates.

The Costs of Foregone Opportunities

Throughout our work, we must keep clearly in mind the fact that *opportunity costs* play a major role in the development of useful models of operations.

---

[11] Especially when the decision problem is extremely *sensitive* to the accurate specification of factors that are characteristically surrounded by uncertainty.

By definition, opportunity costs represent the difference between the reward that would be obtained if the "best possible" alternative were chosen, and the reward that is obtained as a result of the alternative that is actually chosen.

Constraints produce opportunity costs. Unessential or irrelevant constraints lead to unnecessary opportunity costs. The fundamental structure of network models can be shown to parallel an opportunity cost reduction algorithm. In numerous places in the text, examples of such network models are developed.

A new product design that is selected from among a number of alternative designs will have zero opportunity cost if it is, in fact, the optimal design. It is not always possible to know when an opportunity cost has been incurred. The return on investment that might have been is not readily discernible, and few organizations spend the effort to examine how things might have turned out if they had acted quickly.

Standard Costs

The measure of variable costs often requires an estimate. For example, if the time to drill a hole of depth d is known for several depths, then when a job concerns depths not yet tested, the best estimate is derived by interpolation or extrapolation.[12]

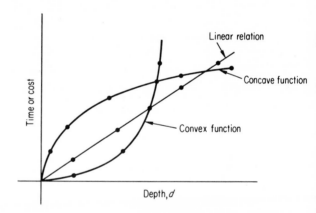

Figure 4.14

Figure 4.14 illustrates three regular functions for which only some of the points are sampled. The same principles can be widely applied to cost estimating.[13]

[12] See Chapter 9 on forecasting, pp. 250–251.
[13] Synthetic time standards, pp. 467–468, extend these ideas to a broader base.

Other Costs

Throughout the text, models of operations are developed that have performance measures that can also be transformed into costs. Profit, for example, can be treated as negative cost. Frequently, in linear programming formulations it is convenient to utilize this kind of transformation. Idle time, waste materials, and loss of brand share are convertible into cost terms. The distinction between fixed and variable costs must be maintained, however, if such dimensional conversions are to be useful. Overhead costs, which belong to a gray area of fixed costs composed of a variety of indirect expenses, are frequently overlooked in model building. Plainly, erroneous conclusions can be reached if the overhead is not properly assigned to each area and the models that are used by each area. *Sunk costs* are a particular kind of fixed cost. *They cannot be retrieved.* Again, a variety of operations models involve significant amounts of sunk costs, but this fact, which causes misleading conclusions, is not taken into account. As we proceed it will be necessary to define many additional costs. For example, in the area of inventory, it will be essential to define carrying costs, order costs, backorder costs, set-up costs, and so forth.[14] The broadest possible model of costs is one that allows the stream of organizational benefits and penalties to be related to each other over time.

Return on Investment (ROI)

No discussion of cost models would be complete if the notion of incoming and outgoing streams of funds were not discussed. These dynamic

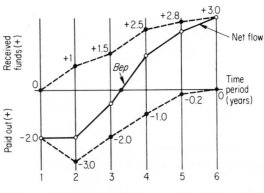

Figure 4.15

attributes of the input-output model are essential for many cost and benefit studies. Figure 4.15 represents a stream of funds received and another stream

[14] See pp. 337–340.

of funds paid out (over a six-year period of time). Net flow is also represented. Is the net flow curve a proper measure of the success of this system in generating benefits? Several points arise in attempting to answer this question. First, are the utilities for all the points on the net flow curve properly represented? Second, does the time that the break-even point occurs matter (here at about 3.3 years)?

Let us consider the second point. This break-even point only records that point in time where that period's inflow exactly equals that period's outflow. It would occur, for example, whenever the daily ledger balances, even though the project is deeply in debt. Therefore, our interest centers on cumulative records, that is, when does total cumulative receipts exactly balance total cumulative investments plus operating costs. Figure 4.16 is a redrawing of Figure 4.15 in these terms.

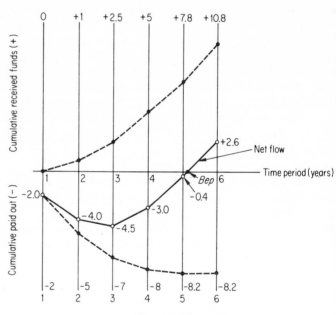

Figure 4.16

The cumulative break-even point occurs at 5+ years. This can be called the payback period. Many different standards and criteria exist for determining what a satisfactory payback period might be. The concept of the cost of money to the company always plays a major role.

Often, present worth calculations involving the cost of money must be introduced, because (in answer to our previous question) the utilities for all the points on the net flow curve are not properly represented. To understand this, let us compare two plans. In the first, we will build a plant. In the second, we will rent it. These two kinds of costs are not the same. Some method is required to compare costs that are incurred immediately or within a short period, such as buying, as compared to those that represent a stream of costs over a period of time, such as renting. Similarly, we require a way of comparing the income that will be obtained over a period of time from alternative product designs, where one product has an expected life of five years and another promises a smaller income stream but taken over a ten-year life. As another example, a process design change or an inventory study will produce different streams of savings over different periods of time.

For most systems, the length of time over which the monetary stream is reckoned will affect the conclusions that can be reached. A method of *discounting* is required to resolve the issue that has been raised. The premise upon which discounting is based is that a sum of money to be received at some future time has less value than the same sum of money owned at the present time. Essentially, this method provides for a comparison between an investment made in the present as compared to a stream of smaller payments made over a period of time. We can either derive the *present value* of the income stream, or we can determine what stream of money (perhaps borrowed from the bank) would be equivalent to the investment. In both cases, an interest rate and a planning horizon must be specified.

To illustrate, we shall assume that it is possible to buy a plant for $1,000,000. An alternative is also offered, namely, to rent at $80,000 per year. The question that must be answered is: How do these plans compare? First, we must obtain an estimate for the value of money. For example, 6 per cent per year might be the amount that could be obtained by investing a given sum of money in high grade stocks. The estimate of this interest rate will vary depending upon the size of the company, its growth potential, and capital requirements. We shall employ the 6 per cent rate, recognizing that each company must carefully determine their own appropriate rate of interest.

We ask the question: What is the present worth of an $80,000 per year income stream as a function of the length of the planning horizon that is employed? The formula for present worth (or present value) that we utilize is:

$$PW = N \sum_{n=0}^{n} \left(\frac{1}{1+r}\right)^n - N = N \sum_{n=1}^{n} \left(\frac{1}{1+r}\right)^n.$$

where:
PW = present worth
N = $80,000, the yearly rental value
r = interest rate, e.g., 6 per cent per year
n = the planning horizon of n years

This equation assumes that the first rental payment is made at the *end* of the period. Consequently, each dollar paid out costs us less than a full dollar, viz., $0.94. If we had that dollar at the beginning of the period, we could have invested it at 6 per cent per year. At the end of the year we would have $1.06, but we would only be required to pay out $1.00. The actual cost would be

$1.00 - 0.06 = \$0.94$. Thus, by deferring payment, we decrease the cost of such payments to us.[15] Every point of the net flow curve of Figure 4.16 would be recalculated to its present value. The position of the break-even point would change.

The following table shows the way in which present worth changes as a function of the planning horizon.[16]

n (years)	$\left(\dfrac{1}{1+0.06}\right)^n$	$\displaystyle\sum_{n=1}^{n}\left(\dfrac{1}{1+0.06}\right)^n$	$(80{,}000)\displaystyle\sum_{n=1}^{n}\left(\dfrac{1}{1+0.06}\right)^n$
1	0.943	0.943	75,440
2	0.890	1.833	146,640
3	0.840	2.673	213,840
4	0.792	3.465	277,200
5	0.747	4.212	336,960
6	0.705	4.917	393,360
7	0.665	5.582	446,560
8	0.627	6.209	496,720
9	0.592	6.801	544,080
10	0.558	7.359	588,720
11	0.527	7.886	630,880
12	0.497	8.383	670,640
13	0.469	8.852	708,160
14	0.442	9.294	743,520
15	0.417	9.711	776,880
16	0.394	10.105	808,400
17	0.371	10.476	838,080
18	0.350	10.826	866,080
19	0.331	11.157	892,560
20	0.312	11.469	917,520
21	0.294	11.763	941,040
22	0.278	12.041	963,280
23	0.262	12.303	984,240
24	0.247	12.550	1,004,000
25	0.233	12.783	1,022,640

We see that in the twenty-fourth year the income stream of $80,000 per year is equivalent to the purchase price of $1,000,000. Thus, it takes a period of about twenty-four years to balance the investment proposal. It is likely that the decision would be to rent because a planning period of twenty-four years is quite long, and up to that time it is less expensive to rent the

[15] If the payment is made at the beginning of the period, we would alter our formulas as follows (for $n + 1$ payments):

$$PW = N \sum_{n=0}^{n}\left(\frac{1}{1+r}\right)^n = N + N \sum_{n=1}^{n}\left(\frac{1}{1+r}\right)^n$$

[16] Tabled values are available for different interest rates and time periods. See, for example: R. S. Burington, *Handbook of Mathematical Tables and Formulas* (New York: McGraw-Hill Book Company, 1965).

facility. Carrying our thinking one step further, if an infinite planning horizon is utilized, then the series of payments has a convergent property that yields a measure of the value of the payment stream over this infinite time period. This is approximated by:

$$PW = \frac{N}{r} = \frac{\$80,000}{.06} = \$1,333,333$$

Thus, if an infinite planning horizon is used for the comparison between renting and buying, then it would be better to invest. Acknowledging that a variety of possibilities exist for choosing the span of the planning horizon, what factors underlie an appropriate choice?

The length of a planning horizon is frequently related to the computation of the payoff or payback period. This is the length of time required before an investment pays for itself, that is, before it begins to produce additional capital for the company. The computation of the payoff period (PP) is performed *without discounting*

$$PP = \text{Investment/Income per Time Period}$$

We see that a straight computation that ignores the discounting effect will indicate a shorter planning horizon than would be obtained if discounting were used. Thus, for example, if the investment required for a new product is $1,000,000 and it is expected to produce an income stream of $80,000 per year, the payoff period (without discounting) would be:

$$1,000,000/80,000 = 12.5 \text{ years}$$

However, when discounting is taken into consideration, we know that a period of twenty-four years would be required for the investment to pay for itself. Generally speaking, it is advisable to utilize discounting for such computations. But it must be pointed out that the planning horizon will be critically affected by the choice of interest rate that is charged. If a 4 per cent rate per year is used, then about eighteen years would be required to pay off the investment. If the rate is 2 per cent per year, then the result would be approximately fifteen years.

There is a variety of criteria that can be employed for long-term cost decisions. The choice depends upon the planning horizon that is being used. For example, we can state:

1. $\dfrac{\text{Annual Income Stream}}{\text{Investment}} \geq r$ (the annual interest rate)

2. or, $\dfrac{\text{Required Income Stream at Present Worth for } n \text{ Years}}{\text{Investment}} \geq 1$

3. or, $\dfrac{\text{Required Income Stream at Present Worth for Lifetime}}{\text{Investment}} \geq f, \ (f > 1)$

The first formulation is the *inverse* of the payoff period computation. It expresses the fact that the annual return on our investment must be equal to or greater than the interest rate that could be obtained by using an alternative investment. The planning horizon, in this case, is just one year.

The second formulation is based upon the selection of a period of time, n, to be the length of the planning horizon. For this planning horizon, we require that the break-even point will occur in the nth year.

The third formulation represents the number of times that we would like the income stream to pay for a given investment over its lifetime. Here, the planning horizon is infinite. Each of these criteria can result in different decisions. The differences must be interpreted as expressions of managerial values. For comparison of the different criteria, we can examine the following equations:

1.
$$\frac{\phi}{x_1 + x_2} \geq r$$

2.
$$\frac{\theta_n \phi}{x_1 + \theta_n x_2} \geq 1$$

3.
$$\frac{\Omega \phi}{x_1 + \Omega x_2} \geq f$$

ϕ = income per year
x_1 = fixed costs of investments
x_2 = variable, operating costs per year
θ_n = present value of \$1 paid at the end of each of n years
    = $[(1 + r)^n - 1]/r(1 + r)^n$
Ω = present value of \$1 assuming a lifetime income stream
    = $(1 + r)/r$
r = annual interest rate

Discounting is necessary to impose utility considerations on the value of costs and benefits that are anticipated For example, let us compare the alternative (materials handling) plans, A and B. The smallest common period for systems A and B will be six years since, during that period of time, system A will turn over twice, and system B will turn over three times. Then, using the discounting data given on pp. 108, for system A's two cycles we find:

End of Year	Plan A	Discounted Operating Costs	Total Discounted Cost	Average Cost Per Year
0	\$25,000 × 1.000 = \$25,000		\$25,000	
1		\$2000 × 0.943 = \$1886	26,886	\$26,886
2		2000 × 0.890 = 1780	28,666	14,333
3	\$25,000 × 0.840 = \$21,000	2000 × 0.840 = 1680	51,346	17,115
4		2000 × 0.792 = 1584	52,930	13,233
5		2000 × 0.747 = 1494	54,424	10,885
6		2000 × 0.705 = 1410	55,834	9,306

And for system B with three cycles we obtain:

End of Year	Plan B	Discounted Operating Costs	Total Discounted Cost	Average Cost Per Year
0	$20,000 × 1.000 = $20,000		$20,000	
1		$1000 × 0.943 = $943	20,943	$20,943
2	$20,000 × 0.890 = $17,800	1000 × 0.890 = 890	39,633	19,817
3		1000 × 0.840 = 840	40,473	13,491
4	$20,000 × 0.792 = $15,840	1000 × 0.792 = 792	57,035	14,259
5		1000 × 0.747 = 747	57,782	11,556
6		1000 × 0.705 = 705	58,487	9,748

We have discounted both investment sums and operating costs. Year by year these have been added together to give total discounted cost. We could make our comparison with these figures alone. At the end of six years, system A has accumulated total costs of $55,834, which is $2,653 less than system B's total. However, average costs are frequently used as the basis for comparison. These are the total costs divided by the number of years that the cost accumulation represents. Using either the total discounted costs or the average yearly determination of cost, we would select (materials handling) system A. It should be noted that when the facilities under consideration have different estimated service lives, then we must always use the smallest common cycle of these lifetimes.

The steps that have been followed are quite straightforward. System A requires an initial investment of $25,000. Because it is paid at the beginning of the first year, it is already at present value. At the end of the first year, $2000 has been paid out in operating costs. The $2000 is discounted to a value of $1886. In fact, the operating costs are paid out over the period of a year; therefore, a more accurate computation might be based on monthly operating charges that are appropriately discounted with the monthly discount factor. We observe that at the conclusion of the first year the average yearly costs for system A are $26,886. This is equal to the total costs for a one-year period of time. Next, we add the second year's operating costs, properly discounted, and again as though the total was incurred at the end of the second year. These amount to $1780. The second year's operating costs are then added to the previous year's total costs, giving a figure of $28,666. For average yearly costs—over a two-year period—we divide by two. This results in a figure of $14,333. We continue our computations in the same way until the total cycle period is covered. If the equipment has *salvage value* at the time it is replaced, then the appropriate amount, properly discounted, is subtracted from the total accumulated costs.

Throughout its history, production and operations management has been cost-oriented, just as marketing management has been sales-oriented.

These traditional points of view can be difficult to reconcile and coordinate. They seldom jibe with the *systems philosophy*, fostering divisional isolation. Modern management is moving rapidly beyond the constraining frontiers of exclusive attention to cost reduction or any other exclusive points of view that are coming to be recognized as mutually incompatible and deleterious. The operations management viewpoint is not static. It is merging with other divisional management viewpoints, and they are all coming closer together in the ultimate sense of framing a single, overall company viewpoint. But total unification—if it will ever be realized—is still a long way off.

An Appendix

The derivation of discounting formulas that are commonly used with dynamic cost models is presented below:

1. $$PW = \sum_{n=0}^{n} \left[\frac{N}{(1 + r)^n} \right] - N$$

where PW is the present value of an annuity of N paid each period for n periods, and r is the interest earned per period. This formulation is based on compound interest, where the saving is realized at the end of each period. We rewrite equation 1:

2. $$PW = N\left[1 + \frac{1}{1 + r} + \left(\frac{1}{1 + r} \right)^2 + \cdots + \left(\frac{1}{1 + r} \right)^n \right] - N$$

Let us first consider the case where $n = \infty$. Because the series is convergent, this will produce the limiting value of PW. We set $x = \frac{1}{1 + r}$, and, because $r > 0$, then $x < 1$. Thus,

3. $$PW = N[1 + x + x^2 + \cdots + x^\infty] - N$$
$$= N[x + x^2 + \cdots + x^\infty]$$

We use the following familiar series equivalence:

4. $$\sum_{n=0}^{n=\infty} x^n = [1 + x + x^2 + \cdots + x^\infty] = \frac{1}{1 - x}, \quad \text{where } x < 1$$

Then:

5. $$x \sum_{n=0}^{n=\infty} x^n = [x + x^2 + x^3 + \cdots + x^\infty] = \frac{x}{1 - x}$$

Thus, we can rewrite equation 3:

6. $$PW = N\left(\frac{x}{1 - x} \right) = N\left(\frac{\frac{1}{1 + r}}{1 - \frac{1}{1 + r}} \right) = \frac{N}{r}$$

We must now consider equation 1 where the upper limit is finite.

7.
$$PW = N[1 + x + x^2 + \cdots + x^n] - N$$

$$= N \sum_{0}^{n} x^n - N .$$

Using equation 4 and the modified series of equation 8 below, we derive equation 9.

8.
$$\sum_{n+1}^{\infty} x^n = [x^{n+1} + x^{n+2} + x^{n+3} + \cdots + x^\infty]$$

Dividing by x^{n+1}

$$\left(\frac{1}{x^{n+1}}\right) \sum_{n+1}^{\infty} x^n = [1 + x + x^2 + \cdots + x^\infty] = \frac{1}{1 - x}$$

Thus:

9.
$$\sum_{n+1}^{\infty} x^n = \frac{x^{n+1}}{1 - x}$$

Then:

$$\sum_{n=0}^{n=\infty} x^n - \sum_{n+1}^{\infty} x^n = \sum_{n=0}^{n} x^n$$

or:

10.
$$\frac{1}{1 - x} - \frac{x^{n+1}}{1 - x} = \frac{1 - x^{n+1}}{1 - x}$$

Therefore, we can write equation 7 in the following form:

11.
$$PW = N\left[\frac{1 - x^{n+1}}{1 - x} - 1\right] = N\left[\frac{x - x^{n+1}}{1 - x}\right]$$

Substituting for x:

12.
$$PW = N\left[\frac{\frac{1}{1+r} - \left(\frac{1}{1+r}\right)^{n+1}}{1 - \left(\frac{1}{1+r}\right)}\right] = N\left[\frac{(1+r)^n - 1}{(1+r)^n r}\right]$$

Solving for n, we find:

13.
$$n = \frac{\log N - \log [N - (PW)r]}{\log (1 + r)}$$

Therefore, when $PW = \$1,000,000$, we have:

$$n = \frac{\log 80,000 - \log [80,000 - (1,000,000)(0.06)]}{\log 1.06}$$

$$= 23.8 \text{ years}$$

which corresponds with our previous finding.

Problems

1. The Gamma Company has engaged a management consultant to analyze and improve its operations. His major recommendation is to totally conveyorize the production floor. This would, of course, represent a sizable investment to the Gamma Company. In order to determine whether or not the idea is feasible, a break-even analysis will be utilized. The situation is as follows: the cost of the conveyor will be $200,000 to be depreciated on a straight-line basis[17] over a ten-year period, that is, $20,000 per year. The reduction in operating cost is estimated at $0.25 per unit. Each unit sells for $2.00. The sales manager estimates that based on previous years the Gamma Company can expect to obtain a sales volume of 100,000 units—this represents 100 per cent of their capacity. Present yearly contribution to fixed costs is $100,000. Present variable cost rate is $0.50. Should the company install this conveyor?

2. The Omega Corporation is considering the advantages of automating a part of their production line. The company's financial statement is shown below:

Omega Corporation

Total Sales		$40,000,000
Direct Labor	$12,000,000	
Indirect Labor	2,000,000	
Direct Materials	8,000,000	
Depreciation	1,000,000	
Taxes	500,000	
Insurance	400,000	
Sales Costs	1,500,000	
Total Expenses		25,400,000
Net Profit		$14,600,000

The above report is based on the production and sale of 100,000 units. The production manager believes that with an additional investment of $5,000,000 he can reduce variable costs by 30 per cent. The same production volume would be maintained. Using a five-year, straight-line depreciation (that is, $1,000,000 per year), construct a break-even chart. If the company insists on a 20 per cent return on its investment, should they automate? (Discuss briefly your treatment of all costs.)

3. An economist of the Omega Corporation has determined that its revenue curve is not linear and is given by the following:

$$\text{Revenue} = 80,000,000(1 - 2^{-V/100,000})$$

[17] See pp. 437–438.

Using the data previously given, and assuming that full utilization of capacity permits a maximum production rate of 200,000 units per year, at what volume should Omega be operating without automation?

4. (a) List as many variable costs as you can.
    (b) List as many fixed costs as you can.
    (c) To what extent is accounting data available in various organizations with respect to such items?
    (d) What is overhead cost or burden? How should it be treated in a break-even analysis?

5. With regard to sensitivity analysis as applied to the probability estimates for a decision matrix of costs, under what circumstances would the cost system be totally insensitive to the probability estimates? How does the fact that $\Sigma_j\, p_j = 1$ affect the procedures for sensitivity analysis? Design a sensitivity analysis where the estimates being examined are the outcomes themselves.

6. Referring to Figure 4.13, p. 102, try to characterize each of the managers, Mr. A, Mr. B, and Mr. C by the kinds of companies and industries in which they are apt to be working. If they are in the same company, what organizational positions at what hierarchical levels are these gentlemen likely to hold? Assume that the profit axis is measured in millions of dollars. What would be your utilities for profits and what kind of ruin threshold would you set?

7. Apply discounting procedures with a 6 per cent interest base to the net flow information in Figure 4.16, p. 106. At what point in time does the break-even point occur? Prove that, if discounting had been used first on the inflows and then on the outflows, that the result would be the same as the one you just calculated. How much difference does it make whether the payments are assumed to be at the beginning or the end of each period?

8. Write a program for your computer to develop a table of present worth values where the value of r can be specified. Generate a table of values for $n = 1$ to 25 given that $r = .12$.

Linear programming (LP) is an input-output model.

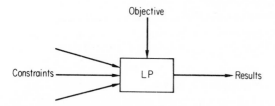

What it does can be viewed either in mathematical or network terms; one or the other approach has major advantages in specific cases. Each provides a different method of solution but the identical result. In this text, we shall examine as many as ten basically unique situations using LP terms. Above all, once the basic nature of LP is understood, it can be applied to a variety of different circumstances without difficulty.

A vital fact about LP is that it consists of the specification of one objective to be maximized or minimized and of a number of relevant constraints that are treated as subobjectives. There is a fundamental theorem in linear programming that the results cannot indicate more activities to be engaged in than the number of constraints.

The Product-Mix Problem and Linear Programming

5

Industrial organizations engage in one or more transformation activities. (For most companies, various sets of activities can be identified as those operations required to produce each product.) The product-line consists of such sets, which use up the resources that are available to the company. If there are many products, then the *job shop* system exists, with its own special resource configuration. When there are only a few products, or when the ABC distribution of products is really quite skewed so that only a few products dominate the use of assets and resources, then there is a flow shop configuration. Some in-between numbers of operations and resource patterns fit into the broad category of intermittent flow shops. Consider the fuel blending operations of a refinery. This has become a classic example of flow shop production with many variants being developed from a single basic process. That is, a great number of different fuel blends are produced from an ever-changing set of input resources (crudes) while the process remains essentially fixed.[1]

New Products and Services

New products, especially in the consumer goods fields, are reputed to have high failure rates.

As shown in Figure 5.1, the unsuccessful design does not achieve sufficient volume in a reasonable period of time, and so it is withdrawn. Many reasons can be given for this. Competitive actions, for example, can be decisively detrimental. The new product or service may not, under any circumstances, be acceptable in the marketplace. Even the lowest possible price can still be too great. Changes in the economy and other major, uncontrollable forces can produce chaotic conditions.

Still, in spite of the high, new product failure rate, the optimal strategy for a company may be to introduce many new products, knowing that a large percentage will fail. Although each new product has a relatively high likeli-

[1] Process parameters are altered while the processing functions are stable.

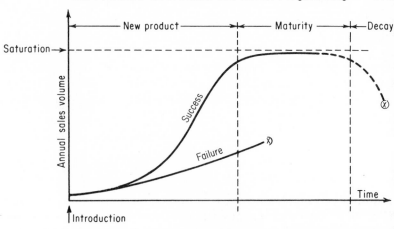

Figure 5.1

The morphology of products.

hood of failure, the one product that is a success is sufficient to more than pay for the whole program. This approach requires an operations management department that can cope with the great number of new products that are constantly being introduced. Numerous companies follow this pattern. Others take a quite different view. They utilize careful analysis for the introduction of a single product (or a few products), all of which have relatively high probabilities of success. The question of which is a better approach is a problem that synthesizes marketing, finance, and production issues. It may be subject to analysis, but a major stumbling block in answering the question lies in the inability to develop good estimates and forecasts for marketplace responses.

The main difference between products and services is ownership. Products can be purchased, stored, and consumed in a physical sense. Services cannot be stored, and as a general rule, the user does not try to establish ownership. Hotel rooms and commercial plane and train seats meet the latter criterion but not the former. Definition of services is confused by the diversity of services that can be offered. In any case, the differences between products and services that concern us are reflected by the type of production system that is required.

Product- or service-mix decisions will take into account the differences in resource constraints, objective fulfillment, and investment procedures that characterize the specific situation. It is usually stated that fabrication requires larger investments than do service functions. Such differentials exist, but they are not as extensive as one might at first suppose. Some service organizations have a greater investment in plant than do manufacturing organizations; for example, telephone and electric power utilities, hotels and restaurants, transportation facilities, and hospitals can require sizable investments. On the other hand, an employment agency or a travel agency can have minimum investments and almost no fixed assets. Each and every case has its own ramifications; and, given an appropriate point of view, they can be converted into situations that can be tackled by the concepts and approaches of product-mix analysis. The realization of this point is relatively new. With the development of linear programming, the generality of the product-mix problem was revealed in full scope.

Design of (Goods and Service) Systems

When an operating system exists (as an ongoing base), what starts re-design of the product-mix? *Financial* considerations can dictate that a search be made for new outputs that will produce a satisfactory return on investment (ROI). A balanced view of the *operations capability* of the total system changes according to resources on hand, per cent of process capacities utilized, and other *production* factors. At the same time, the question of marketability is obviously also critical. Triggered by competitive considerations, the *variety* of a balanced product-line is a factor leading to an extension of the existing product-line (i.e., specification of new outputs). Diversification objectives originating at a high management level also produce an intensive review of the entire present system. In other words, product-mix reasoning may proceed from any number of sources, ranging from process skills and production equipment to administrative know-how and unrealized distribution potentialities that the organization already possesses.

Product-Mix Problems

A company usually must determine its optimal product-mix within the framework of its limited resources. In general, the optimal mix is defined as that mix which will maximize the company's profit. For the determination of optimal mix, the financial, marketing, and production managers must pool their knowledge.

At a *global level*, the problem is one of maintaining the present situation, expanding existing product shares, and diversifying the product-line. The total mix of basic company activities (past, present, and especially future[2]) is considered. A *step below*, we find product-mix problems where a given set of resource facilities can be used in different ways. Another *step down*, we encounter the level of problems of variety where the questions asked concern

---

[2] The past influences the reservoir of skills, plus blueprints, tools, fixtures, and good-will. The present relates to the demand or load on the existing system's capacities, whereas the future presents opportunities to alter the system's capacities and the characteristics of the load as well.

the number of colors and styles that should be made for a particular item. We will consider the middle step, which is fundamental to sound operations management.

At the global, diversification level, a major issue is the extent to which an organization's assets are convertible. Where there is high resource convertibility, the company's planning can be very flexible. (The operations manager is generally quite broad with respect to the kind of technological system that he can manage effectively.) Concerning the bottom step, the variety problem is a special kind of "mix" problem. The same essential output is obtained from a specified set of resources. But, for sales promotion reasons that operate in terms of consumer psychology, the question is: How many variations on a theme should be developed? Variety interacts with the consumer's selection process to produce a greater sales volume than could otherwise be obtained. This is due, at least in part, to the fact that a varied offering can appeal to a greater number of larger specialized consumer segments. But variety costs money. There are more items to stock, more records to keep, more materials to buy (at lesser quantities so that discounts will be lower), and so on. There is an optimal level of variety. The product-mix method that we shall discuss can help to determine what this level should be.[3]

The Linear Programming Model

Within the product-mix problem class we find a number of situations well-suited for the linear programming type of analysis. For example, we have blending problems—the mix can be different petroleum crude stocks to be blended at the refinery; perfume blends, whiskey blends, and cattle and poultry feed mixtures. We also have straightforward manufacturing, product-mix problems that represent blends of a somewhat different kind, ranging from the intermittent flow shop through the "make to order" job shop.

The explanation of the linear programming technique is facilitated by employing an example. The situation can be kept manageable by considering the possibility of only a two-product line. We shall assume that the company makes only P_1 at the present time. Two departments are used. *First, the press shop blanks, draws, and forms the part.* Then the item is sent to *the second department where it is chrome plated.* The full capacity of the first department is utilized when ten units are made per day. On the other hand, only $83\frac{1}{3}$ per cent of the plating department's capacity is used. This, we may presume, results from the fact that the minimum plating tank capacity that could be purchased was capable of handling less than ten units per day. The next largest size could accommodate twelve units per day. The departmental capacities

---

[3] As a first approximation, the product-mix model can be used for both diversification and variety problems.

are the *resource constraints* in this linear programming problem. The item called P_1, returns a profit of $3.00 per unit.

The manager, wishing to get fuller utilization of his equipment, suggests that the company consider adding another product to the existing line. The new product, called P_2, is developed; a prototype is made; and the relevant costs and utilization factors are estimated. The marketing department feels that the new product should be sold at a lower price than P_1. In part, this is based on the fact that production figures indicate P_2 costs less to make. Assuming that only P_2 is made, twenty units could be made in the press shop with full equipment and manpower utilization, but only 12.5 of such units could be processed per day by the plating department. Thus, for P_2 production, the capacity of the plating tank is a limiting constraint. Meanwhile, *working together*, the managers agree that the per-unit profit of P_2 will amount to $2.00.

The above information is summarized in table form. These questions have to be answered: (1) Should P_2 be added to the line? (2) If so, how many units of P_2 should be made? (3) And, what is the optimal mix of P_1 and P_2?

	x_1 Units/Day P_1	x_2 Units/Day P_2	Restriction of Full Utilization
Department 1 (press shop)	10%/unit	5%/unit	100%
Department 2 (plating)	$8\frac{1}{3}$%/unit	8%/unit	100%
(Maximize) profit	$3.00/unit	$2.00/unit	

We read the table as follows:

$x_1 =$ The number of units of product-type P_1 that we will make per day.
$x_2 =$ The number of units of product-type P_2 that we will make per day.

Each unit of the P_1 type that is made uses up 10 per cent of the daily capacity of department 1 and $8\frac{1}{3}$ per cent of the daily capacity of department 2. Each unit of P_2 that is made consumes 5 per cent of the daily capacity of department 1 and 8 per cent of the daily capacity of department 2. If we make only P_1—as is presently done—we can produce a maximum of 10 units (department 1 is the *limiting resource*). If we make only P_2, we can produce a maximum of 12.5 units every day (department 2 is the *limiting resource*).

We should note at this point that if we could only make one or the other, then we would prefer to make P_1 because it promises a daily profit of $30.00, as compared to $25.00 for P_2. Although we can make more of P_2 than of P_1, we cannot make sufficiently more to counterbalance the fact that P_2 has a lower profit per unit. Neither making only P_1 nor only P_2 will provide full utilization of all plant facilities and resources.

Now, let us consider a mathematical product-mix analysis subject to these departmental constraints; our objective is to maximize profit. Because of the size of this problem, it is relatively easy for a manager to determine what should be done without recourse to linear programming. Various methods can be used to solve this problem. For example, algebraic, geometric, and matrix methods (such as the simplex algorithm) could be used. Normally, complex problems would be solved by means of the simplex method of linear programming. However, to understand what is involved in obtaining a solution, we will begin with a trial and error approach followed by a geometric resolution of the problem. (In turn, this will be followed by algebraic analysis and then by the simplex method.)

First, referring to the previous table, we construct the following inequations, representing the departmental capacity constraints.

$$10x_1 + 5x_2 \leq 100$$
$$8\tfrac{1}{3}x_1 + 8x_2 \leq 100$$

The objective is to maximize profit, that is, Maximize $[3x_1 + 2x_2]$. Furthermore, we can never produce negative quantities of a product, thus:

$$x_1 \geq 0, \quad x_2 \geq 0$$

These inequations fit the format of the linear programming model. They state the way in which each department's capacities will be utilized for different production schedules of P_1 and P_2. The inequations express the fact that it is impossible to utilize more than 100 per cent of any department's capacity. Thus, for example, if $x_1 = 10$, then department 1 is fully utilized. On the other hand, if $x_1 = 5$ and $x_2 = 5$, then only 75 per cent of the first department's capacity has been used up. We say that the remaining 25 per cent is departmental *slack*.[4]

Trial and Error Solutions

Plan	x_1	x_2	Department 1 Slack	Department 2 Slack	Profit
1	5	5	25%	18.3%	25
2	10	5	violation	violation	violation
3	5	10	0%	violation	violation
4	6	5	15%	10%	28
5	7.83	4.35	0%	0%	32.20

By substituting different values for x_1 and x_2 we can determine whether either departmental constraint has been violated and also what profit would result from such a plan. The table above shows a number of different com-

---

[4] As will be seen shortly, when using mathematical methods for solving linear programming problems we would appoint a slack variable to represent the departmental slack, for example, x_3. Then the inequation can be converted to an equation in the following way: $10x_1 + 5x_2 + x_3 = 100$.

binations of x_1 and x_2 values that might be tried. Several of the plans *violate* the departmental restrictions. Furthermore, for this particular set of trial and error plans, maximum profit is obtained with the fifth plan, which is a feasible product-mix strategy.

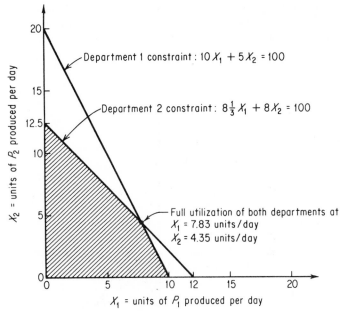

Figure 5.2

Feasible solution space for the product-mix problem.

Refer now to Figure 5.2. The two lines that cross each other within the first quadrant represent the two departmental constraints. Each line is appropriately labeled. It is simple enough to check and see that any combination of values for x_1 and x_2 that fall on a line produce 100 per cent utilization of whichever department that line describes. Thus, each line stands for the maximum utilization of the respective department. We should also note that for this case there is only one combination of x_1 and x_2 values that yields full utilization of both departments' capacities. It is the crosspoint. Let us ask a question at this stage but defer the answer until later.

Question: Does it follow automatically that any combination of x_1 and x_2 that fully utilizes all production capacity would be an optimal product-mix solution?

The area *under* each of the two lines is equivalent to the mathematical statement of an inequation that has the directional sense of *less than* ($<$). Thus, all points that fall in the first quadrant and meet the requirements of the constraints must lie *within the shaded area or on its perimeter*. We call this the *feasible solution space*. The first quadrant is specified by the *feasibility constraints*, $x_1 \geq 0$, $x_2 \geq 0$. Any combination of x_1 and x_2 that forms an allowable product-mix must be part of the shaded space.

Our stated purpose is to *maximize profit*. At least one point in the feasible solution space will achieve this result. It is unnecessary to use trial and error methods to determine which point will maximize the profit. We shall superimpose a family of profit lines on top of the previous figure. This is shown in Figure 5.3. Each of the parallel lines represents different combina-

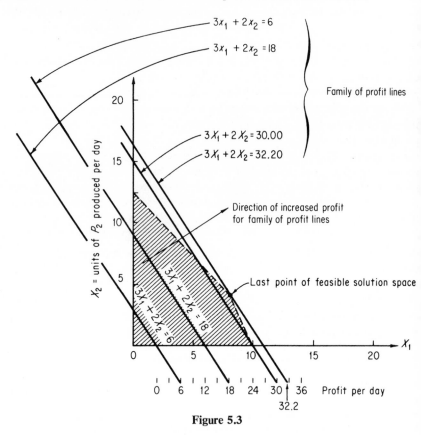

Figure 5.3

Family of profit lines superimposed on the feasible solution space.

tions of x_1 and x_2. All combinations of x_1 and x_2 that belong to any particular line produce only one specific level of profit. Thus, consider the line where profit equals eighteen. If we substitute any one pair of x_1 and x_2 values that falls along this line, that product-mix will produce a profit of $18.00. Furthermore, all the points that lie on this profit line of $18.00 fall within the feasible solution space.

If the line went through the vertex at the origin (0, 0), then profit would be zero. When hunting for an optimum solution, a starting point for beginning is often required. This "jumping-off point solution," called the first, feasible solution, is frequently chosen at the $(0, 0, \ldots, 0)$ origin for n-dimensional problems.

Figure 5.3 shows a profit line of value six in addition to the profit line of eighteen, previously discussed. Will it be possible to obtain even greater profit? Let us move to the profit line that is labeled $30.00. If we test the profit of each x_1, x_2 pair that falls on this line, we find that they all yield a profit of $30.00. In this case, however, it should be noted that part of this line does not fall within the feasible solution space, even though it is within the first quadrant. We know that those x_1, x_2 combinations that are outside the feasible space could not be used for the product-mix. Nevertheless, because some points do meet the departmental capacity constraints, a profit of $30.00 could be obtained. But this is still not the maximum possible profit.

As the profit lines move upward and toward the right, the profit level increases. We should, therefore, choose that member of the family of parallel profit lines that is the *last one to touch the feasible solution space* as the lines move upward. This is the line of maximum profit. For this example, it occurs at the intersection of the two department constraint lines. The production values for this solution are $x_1 = 7.83$ and $x_2 = 4.35$. With this solution, *there is no departmental slack for either department*. The profitability is $32.20 per day.[5]

Now, let us turn to the question that was previously posed but left unanswered. First, the solution just determined fully utilizes all departmental capacity. It is also optimal. However, what would the optimal product-mix be if the relative profitabilities of the different units in the product-mix were changed? Let us lower the profitability of the first product to $2.00 per unit and raise the profitability of the second item to $3.00 per unit. This produces a change in the solution, as is shown in Figure 5.4.

We observe that the optimal profit has increased to $37.50 per day. Also, department 2 is fully utilized, but department 1 is operating at $\frac{12.5}{20} = \frac{5}{8}$ of capacity. The point of full utilization for both departments is the crosspoint, and it can be achieved only at lower profit. So the myth that full use of capacity must be best for the company is revealed. It should also be noted that by altering the coefficients and observing the effects of such changes, a *sensitivity analysis* can be carried out (as was previously described, pp. 72, 95).

One additional point: a solution must occur at a vertex; and, therefore, as a special case, the solution can occur simultaneously at two adjacent vertices. When this happens, all points on the line that connects the vertices will also be optimal product-mix solutions. We can interpret the mathematical

---

[5] The values of x_1 and x_2 in this solution are fractional. If this violates the sense of the solution, then we must utilize the technique of *integer* programming. Frequently, it is quite satisfactory to round off fractional numbers so that a reasonable, discrete solution is obtained that is very close to optimal and that meets the system's constraints.

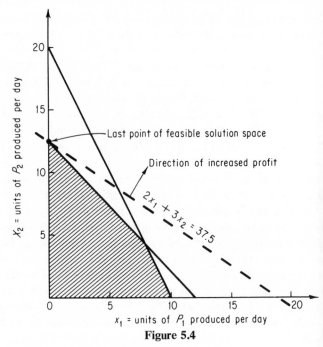

Figure 5.4

The optimal product-mix for the profit maximization problem changes when P_1 produces $2 of profit per unit and P_2 produces $3 of profit per unit. Thus: Maximize $2x_1 + 3x_2$. The solution is: produce 12.5 units of P_2 and no P_1; total profit = $37.50 per day.

basis for this effect; it is simply that the slopes of both the profit line and the constraint are identical. Further, if the problem is one of cost minimization, then the constraints are written as being equal to or greater than some value, i.e., $\geq$. The solution is obtained by determining the *last* possible cost line to leave the solution space as we move down and toward the left with our family of cost lines. It is apparent that the $(0, 0)$ jumping-off point used for profit maximization is not a vertex of this type of solution space. Therefore the way to begin a cost problem is to somehow find one of the vertices of the cost polygon. (This is shown in Figure 5.5.) Further, see pp. 137–138 for a discussion of the use of artificial variables, in this regard.

We can state some logical steps that underlie the solutions derived from linear programming.

1. Begin by selecting any vertex of the (complex) polyhedron that is formed when two or more products are involved. (The Cartesian coordinates of the geometric approach no longer apply when more than two types of products are to be mixed.) Obtain the measure of cost or profit at that vertex.

2. Find a test to determine whether an improvement in profit can be made by moving to another vertex. The mathematical form of the problem

lends itself easily to this step, as will be seen in the algebraic section that follows.

3. If improvement is possible, attempt to find the best possible change.
4. Make the indicated change by choosing another vertex and examining the solution's value.
5. Steps two through four are repeated until the test, in step two, reveals that no further improvement is possible.

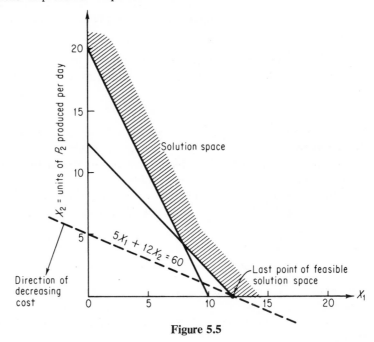

Figure 5.5

For cost minimization, the position of the feasible solution space is reversed and the optimum solution is associated with the last possible cost line to leave that space. Assume that P_1 costs \$5 per unit and P_2 cost \$12 per unit; then Minimize $0.5x_1 + 1.2x_2$. The solution is: produce 12 units of P_1 and no P_2; total cost = \$60 per day.

Linear programming is not a substitute for ingenious product design or creative new product engineering. The character of the ultimate product-mix is strictly a function of whatever products or services the manager was able to start with. If the various products that are competing for available capacity are individually excellent, then the product-mix will produce a large profit. Otherwise, the best that can be done may not be good enough.

Algebraic Formulation

There are m activities: $1, 2, \ldots j \ldots m$, and x_j is the level of the jth activity. Each activity level, x_j uses up different amounts of various resources. Thus: $a_{ij}x_j$ is the resource of the ith type required by activity j.

Example: Let j be a red nailpolish called Flaming Satin Red and x_j be the number of gallons of Flaming Satin Red nailpolish to be made. a_{ij} is pounds of burnt umber required per gallon of Flaming Satin Red nailpolish. Then, $a_{ij}x_j$ is the total number of pounds of burnt umber required when we decide to make x_j gallons of Flaming Satin Red nailpolish.

Let k be an orange nailpolish called Arabian Nights, which also uses burnt umber. If burnt umber is a scarce resource, then Arabian Nights and Flaming Satin Red must compete for it. We represent this as follows:

$$a_{ij}x_j + a_{ik}x_k \leq b_i$$

where b_i is the amount of burnt umber we have on hand.

Both nailpolishes use a fine sumac lacquer, of which there are b_2 cans on hand. Then,

$$a_{2j}x_j + a_{2k}x_k \leq b_2$$

Constraints can have many dimensions including amounts of machine capacity, manpower, material resources, power, etc. Restrictions also exist that specify that we cannot use less than a certain amount of the resource, for example, nutritive elements in a diet problem.

Each activity has a per unit cost or profit associated with it. Therefore, if cost, c_j, or if profit, π_j, yields total cost Z_c or total profit Z_π:

$$Z_c = c_1x_1 + c_2x_2 + \cdots + c_jx_j + \cdots c_mx_m$$

or

$$Z_\pi = \pi_1x_1 + \pi_jx_j + \cdots + \pi_mx_m$$

We want the value of Z_π maximized for profit and the value of Z_c minimized for cost.

The matrix methods (such as simplex) for resolving problems of the form:

$$a_{11}x_1 + a_{12}x_2 + \cdots + a_{1m}x_m \leq b_1$$
$$a_{21}x_1 + a_{22}x_2 + \cdots + a_{2m}x_m \leq b_2$$

$$\cdot \qquad \cdot \qquad \qquad \cdot \qquad \cdot$$
$$\cdot \qquad \cdot \qquad \qquad \cdot \qquad \cdot$$
$$\cdot \qquad \cdot \qquad \qquad \cdot \qquad \cdot$$

$$a_{n1}x_1 + a_{n2}x_2 + \cdots + a_{nm}x_m \leq b_n$$

$$\text{Maximize } Z_\pi = \pi x_1 + \pi_2x_2 + \cdots + \pi_mx_m$$

have their algebraic equivalents. These so closely parallel the matrix steps that a great deal can be learned about simplex by working out the algebraic solution.

Consider our previous example:

$$\begin{matrix} 10x_1 + 5x_2 \leq 100 \\ 8\frac{1}{3}x_1 + 8x_2 \leq 100 \end{matrix} \Bigg\} \; x_1, x_2 \geq 0 \text{ for feasibility.}$$

$$\text{Maximize } [z_\pi = 3x_1 + 2x_2]$$

The inequations can be rewritten as equations by creating two new variables x_3 and x_4, called slack variables (x_3, $x_4 \geq 0$ for feasibility). The $(0, 0)$ vertex is automatically the first feasible solution by making x_3 and x_4 *the* variables in the solution.[6] Thus, $x_3 = 100$ and $x_4 = 100$.

1. $10x_1 + 5x_2 + x_3 = 100$ *or* $x_3 = 100 - 10x_1 - 5x_2$

2. $8\frac{1}{3}x_1 + 8x_2 + x_4 = 100$ *or* $x_4 = 100 - 8\frac{1}{3}x_1 - 8x_2$

3. $Z_\pi = 3x_1 + 2x_2 + 0x_3$. Since $x_3 = 100$, $x_4 = 100$, $x_1 = 0$, $x_2 = 0$; the value of profit is zero.

In equation three, the profit coefficient of x_1 (equal to 3) is the largest one, so x_1 is put into the solution because it promises the greatest increase in profit, (based on unit values for x_j). If x_1 is set equal to 10, both equations are feasible; if x_1 is put equal to 12, equation one is violated. So, using 10, equation one becomes:

4. $x_1 = 10 - \frac{1}{2}x_2 - \frac{1}{10}x_3$. This x_1 relationship is substituted into equation two and the profit function, as well, giving equations five and six.

5. $x_4 = \dfrac{50}{3} + \dfrac{23}{6} x_2 + \dfrac{25}{30} x_3$

6. $Z_\pi = 3(10 - \frac{1}{2}x_2 - \frac{1}{10}x_3) + 2x_2 = 30 + \frac{1}{2}x_2 - \frac{3}{10}x_3$

Profit has now gone from 0 to 30. The coefficient of the x_2 variable in the profit function is positive; therefore, it can increase profit, so we introduce x_2. Either x_1 or x_4 (both presently in the solution) must be taken out of it, and the feasibility test will determine which one. Rewriting equation four ($x_2 = 20 - 2x_1 - \frac{1}{5}x_3$) and rewriting equation five ($x_2 = \frac{100}{23} + \frac{5}{23} x_3 - \frac{6}{23} x_4$). The latter (from five) is the limiting factor, so x_4 is removed. Then:

7. $x_2 = \dfrac{100}{23} + \dfrac{5}{23} x_3 - \dfrac{6}{23} x_4$

8. $x_1 = \dfrac{180}{23} - \dfrac{4.8}{23} x_3 + \dfrac{3}{23}x_4$

          (putting this relation for x_2 into equation four)

And the profit equation becomes:

9. $Z_\pi = 30 + \frac{1}{2} \left(\dfrac{100}{23} + \dfrac{5}{23} x_3 - \dfrac{6}{23} x_4 \right) - \dfrac{3}{10} x_3$

                 $= \dfrac{740}{23} - \dfrac{4.4}{23} x_3 - \dfrac{3}{23} x_4.$

---

[6] See pp. 138 for a discussion of the use of artificial variables to obtain a first feasible solution for cost minimization problems.

Since all profit coefficients are negative, the final solution has been achieved with $x_1 = \frac{180}{23}$, $x_2 = \frac{100}{23}$, and $Z_\pi = \frac{740}{23}$ —the same solution as was previously achieved geometrically.

Simplex Method

I.   Begin with a set of m inequations and n unknowns. Here, $m = 3$ and $n = 4$.

$$a_{11}x_1 + a_{12}x_2 + a_{13}x_3 + a_{14}x_4 \le b_1$$
$$a_{21}x_1 + a_{22}x_2 + a_{23}x_3 + a_{24}x_4 \le b_2$$
$$a_{31}x_1 + a_{32}x_2 + a_{33}x_3 + a_{34}x_4 \le b_3$$

II.   Appoint slack variables x_5, x_6, x_7. Since $m = 3$ there are three slack variables.

III.   Then, write the appropriate objective function. In this case, the objective is maximization. (We will treat c_j as being equivalent to π_j.)

Maximize:

$$[Z = c_1x_1 + c_2x_2 + c_3x_3 + c_4x_4 + (0)x_5 + (0)x_6 + (0)x_7]$$

IV.   Convert inequations to equations.

$$a_{11}x_1 + a_{12}x_2 + a_{13}x_3 + a_{14}x_4 + \quad x_5 + (0)x_6 + (0)x_7 = b_1$$
$$a_{21}x_1 + a_{22}x_2 + a_{23}x_3 + a_{24}x_4 + (0)x_5 + \quad x_6 + (0)x_7 = b_2$$
$$a_{31}x_1 + a_{32}x_2 + a_{33}x_3 + a_{34}x_4 + (0)x_5 + (0)x_6 + \quad x_7 = b_3$$

V.   Feasibility conditions include the slack variables, x_5, x_6 and x_7.

$$x_j \ge 0 \quad (j = 1, 2, 3, 4, 5, 6, 7)$$

VI.   Construct the first simplex tableau where the slack variables form the basis, listed as x_i.

ϕ_i	c_i	x_i	x_1	x_2	x_3	x_4	x_5	x_6	x_7	b_i
ϕ_5	0	x_5	a_{11}	a_{12}	a_{13}	a_{14}	1	0	0	b_1
ϕ_6	0	x_6	a_{21}	a_{22}	a_{23}	a_{24}	0	1	0	b_2
ϕ_7	0	x_7	a_{31}	a_{32}	a_{33}	a_{34}	0	0	1	b_3
		c_j	c_1	c_2	c_3	c_4	0	0	0	
		BFS_1	0	0	0	0	b_1	b_2	b_3	
		c_j^*	c_1^*	c_2^*	c_3^*	c_4^*	c_5^*	c_6^*	c_7^*	

There are three boxes in the simplex tableau: upper-right, upper-left, and bottom. The upper-right box contains all the assignments of the coefficients of the equations. This is just another way of writing the equations in IV. If we multiply each row coefficient by the column heading and then add their products, we derive the equations. For row one,

$$a_{11}x_1 + a_{12}x_2 + a_{13}x_3 + a_{14}x_4 + x_5 + (0)x_6 + (0)x_7 = b_1$$

The other boxes will be explained as we proceed to employ the simplex algorithm:

STEP 1:   Enter the appropriate values in the upper-right box.

STEP 2:   The row marked c_j (top row of the bottom box) is obtained directly from the coefficients of the objective function. In this case, if we multiply each row entry by the column heading and then add the products, we derive the objective function.

$$Z = c_1x_1 + c_2x_2 + c_3x_3 + c_4x_4 + (0)x_5 + (0)x_6 + (0)x_7$$

Since zero profit is associated with a slack variable, we have zero coefficients for x_5, x_6, and x_7.

STEP 3:   We derive the row marked BFS$_1$ (basic feasible solution number one, which is the second row of the bottom box.) There are always m columns representing the constraints that, when taken together, form an *identity* matrix (a square matrix, all elements being zero except the elements of the principal diagonal, which are all unity). For each diagonal element, enter the corresponding b_i value in the BFS row. Thus:

	x_5	x_6	x_7	
	1 ...	0 ...	0	$\leftarrow b_1$
	.			
	.			
	.			
	0	1 ...	0	$\leftarrow b_2$
	.	.		
	.	.		
	.	.		
	0	0	1	$\leftarrow b_3$
BFS	b_1	b_2	b_3	

All other entries in the BFS row are zero.

STEP 4:   The column marked x_i (upper-left box) contains the variables in the basis. They correspond to the unit elements of the principal diagonal.

Thus:

$$
\begin{array}{cccc}
x_i & x_5 & x_6 & x_7 \\
 & \downarrow & \downarrow & \downarrow \\
x_5 \leftarrow 1 & & 0 & 0 \\
 & & \cdot & \cdot \\
 & & \cdot & \cdot \\
 & & \cdot & \cdot \\
x_6 \leftarrow 0 & \cdots & 1 & 0 \\
 & & \cdot & \cdot \\
 & & \cdot & \cdot \\
 & & \cdot & \cdot \\
x_7 \leftarrow 0 & \cdots & 0 & \cdots & 1
\end{array}
$$

These are the same variables that have b_i values entered in the BFS row. At the outset, the x_i column lists the slack variables. This is always a convenient way to begin. The first basic feasible solution, BFS_1, will then be modified and new variables will replace the slack variables in the x_i column. At each stage the *variables* in the x_i column represent the activities or components of the *solution*. The corresponding b_i's are the activity levels of each variable.

STEP 5:   The column marked c_i (upper-left box) contains the coefficients of the objective function for the corresponding x_i variables. The same values appear in the c_j row under the appropriate column headings—in this case c_5, c_6, and c_7.

STEP 6:   Compute c_j^*, where $c_j^* = c_j - \sum_i [a_{ij}c_i]$

For our example:

$$
\begin{aligned}
c_1^* &= c_1 - a_{11}c_5 - a_{21}c_6 - a_{31}c_7 \\
c_2^* &= c_2 - a_{12}c_5 - a_{22}c_6 - a_{32}c_7 \\
&\quad\cdot \\
&\quad\cdot \\
&\quad\cdot \\
c_7^* &= c_7 - a_{17}c_5 - a_{27}c_6 - a_{37}c_7
\end{aligned}
$$

STEP 7:   Select the *largest positive* c_j^*. The variable heading that column is to be put into the next BFS.

STEP 8:   For that column, j^*, test:

$$
\phi_5 = b_1/a_{1j^*}, \quad \phi_6 = b_2/a_{2j^*}, \quad \phi_7 = b_3/a_{3j^*}
$$

Select the *smallest positive*, ϕ_i. The variable, x_i, is to be taken out and excluded from the next BFS.

STEP 9:   We have selected a column to put in and a row to take out. Take the coefficient at the intersection of this row and column. Divide all entries of that row—in the upper-right box—by the intersection value. For example, assume that a_{22} is the intersection value. Then our new row two will be:

$$\frac{a_{21}}{a_{22}}\left(\frac{a_{22}}{a_{22}} = 1\right) \quad \frac{a_{23}}{a_{22}} \quad \frac{a_{24}}{a_{22}} \quad \frac{0}{a_{22}} \quad \frac{1}{a_{22}} \quad \frac{0}{a_{22}} \quad \frac{b_2}{a_{22}}$$

We have in this way brought a 1 into the column of the variable to be put in.

STEP 10: We must next reduce all other entries in the column of j^* to zero. To do this for the first row, multiply all the row elements derived in Step 9 by a_{12}. Then subtract this *modified row from row one.*

$$a_{11} - \frac{a_{12}a_{21}}{a_{22}}, \quad 0, \quad a_{13} - \frac{a_{12}a_{23}}{a_{22}}, \quad \text{etc.}$$

Call this *new row one.* A zero appears in *new row one* in the column of the variable that is being put into the solution. Similarly, for row three, multiply the row elements derived in Step 9 by a_{32} and subtract this modified row from row three. Call this *new row three.*

STEP 11: We can now construct the tableau for BFS$_2$. Column x_i would be changed by substituting x_2 for x_6. All the entries are changed in the upper-right box. The old first row is replaced by the elements of the *new row one.* The *new second row* is the one derived in Step 9. The old third row is replaced by the *new row three.*

STEP 12: We can now complete all other assignments in the tableau using the rules as before. This is BFS$_2$.

Objective Z: At each step Z can be calculated by adding the products of $c_j \times$ BFS(j). Thus, for the first tableau:

$$Z_1 = (c_1 \times 0) + (c_2 \times 0) + (c_3 \times 0) + (c_4 \times 0)$$
$$+ (0 \times b_1) + (0 \times b_2) + (0 \times b_3) = 0$$

The optimal solution is reached when all c_j^* are equal to zero or take on negative values.

Let us work through the same numerical example that was used previously. The simplex tableau (VI) is as follows:

STEP 1:	ϕ_i	c_i	x_i	x_1	x_2	x_3	x_4	b_i
	ϕ_3	0	x_3	⑩	5	1	0	100
	ϕ_4	0	x_4	$8\frac{1}{3}$	8	0	1	100
			c_j	3	2	0	0	
			BFS$_1$	0	0	100	100	
			c_j^*	3	2	0	0	

STEP 2: $Z_1 = 3x_1 + 2x_2 + (0)x_3 + (0)x_4$

STEP 3, 4, 5, 6: Completed in Step 1.

STEP 7: The largest *positive* c_j^* is 3 for x_1. Put x_1 into the next BFS.

STEP 8: $\phi_3 = 100/10 = 10$, $\phi_4 = 100/8\frac{1}{3} = 12$. Therefore, x_3 being smallest is to be taken out.

STEP 9:   The coefficient at the intersection of x_3 and x_1 is 10. Therefore, the modified x_3 row is:

x_1	x_2	x_3	x_4	b_i
$8\frac{1}{3}$	$\frac{25}{6}$	$\frac{26}{30}$	0	$\frac{250}{3}$

STEP 10:   Subtraction is required:

x_1	x_2	x_3	x_4	b_i
$8\frac{1}{3}$	8	0	1	100
$-\,8\frac{1}{3}$	$\frac{25}{6}$	$\frac{25}{30}$	0	$\frac{250}{3}$
0	$\frac{23}{6}$	$-\frac{25}{30}$	1	$\frac{50}{3}$

STEP 11:   The new tableau is:

ϕ_i	c_i	x_i	x_1	x_2	x_3	x_4	b_i
ϕ_1	3	x_1	1	$\frac{1}{2}$	$\frac{1}{10}$	0	10
ϕ_4	0	x_4	0	$\frac{23}{6}$	$-\frac{25}{30}$	1	$\frac{50}{3}$
		c_j	3	2	0	0	
		BFS$_2$	10	0	0	$\frac{50}{3}$	
		c_j^*	0	$\frac{1}{2}$	$-\frac{3}{10}$	0	

STEP 12: $Z_2 = 30$; Steps 1′ through 6′ are already completed in the tableau.

STEP 7′:   Put in x_2 (with positive coefficient, $\frac{1}{2}$).

STEP 8′: $\phi_1 = 10/\frac{1}{2} = 20$, $\phi_4 = (50/3)/(23/6) = 100/23$. Therefore, take x_4 out.

STEP 9′:   The intersection coefficient of x_2 and x_4 is $23/6$. The modified row x_4 is:

x_1	x_2	x_3	x_4	b_i
0	1	$-\frac{5}{23}$	$\frac{6}{23}$	$\frac{100}{23}$

STEP 10′:   Multiply all row elements derived in step 9′ by $1/2$.

x_1	x_2	x_3	x_4	b_i
0	$\frac{1}{2}$	$-\frac{5}{46}$	$\frac{3}{23}$	$\frac{50}{23}$

and subtract:

1	$\frac{1}{2}$	$\frac{1}{10}$	0	10
$-\,(0$	$\frac{1}{2}$	$-\frac{5}{46}$	$\frac{3}{23}$	$\frac{50}{23})$
1	0	$-\frac{1}{115}$	$-\frac{3}{23}$	$\frac{180}{23}$

STEP 11′:   The new tableau is:

ϕ_i	c_i	x_i	x_1	x_2	x_3	x_4	b_i
ϕ_1	3	x_1	1	0	$-\frac{1}{115}$	$-\frac{3}{23}$	$\frac{180}{23}$
ϕ_2	2	x_2	0	1	$-\frac{5}{23}$	$\frac{6}{23}$	$\frac{100}{23}$
		c_j	3	2	0	0	
		BFS$_3$	$\frac{180}{23}$	$\frac{100}{23}$	0	0	
		c_j^*	0	0	$-\frac{53}{115}$	$-\frac{21}{23}$(STOP)	

STEP 12': $\quad Z_3 = 3\left(\dfrac{180}{23}\right) + 2\left(\dfrac{100}{23}\right) = \dfrac{740}{23}$

This is the same result as was previously obtained using the geometric approach and the algebraic method. Note that there are no $c_j^* > 0$.

We have only shown maximization procedures. If the problem requires minimization, then the dual form that will be discussed shortly can be maximized. Minimization procedures using the simplex are similar but not identical. Minimization frequently requires artificial variables because the slack variables carry minus signs. These points are discussed in the following section.

Some General Characteristics of LP

LP can be viewed as an input-output model. The analogy clearly requires the *synthesis* of many functions to be effective. For example, LP use needs detailed information regarding technological factors, market elasticities, and plant capacities: an exemplary combination of marketing, financial, economic, engineering, and other knowledge. Figure 5.6 portrays the input-output relations.

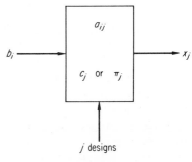

Figure 5.6

The process is capable of producing varying quantities of j different designs. There are i input resources, each of specific amounts, b_i. Output is specified for each j as x_j. Technological coefficients a_{ij} are the result of production abilities interacting with financial decisions. If the costs, c_j, are used, the problem is production oriented. If the unit profits, π_j, are employed, marketing is also responsible, since $\pi_j = r_j - c_j$, where r_j is the revenue of the jth design.

The *fundamental theorem of LP* is a major determinant of variety. The fundamental theorem states that the number of activities, j, in which the company engages will be no greater than the number of constraints that exist. Therefore, the size of the optimal product-mix increases as the market saturates (the function, r_j) or as the capacity to produce is exhausted on normal work time, so excessive unit costs occur (the function c_j). (See Figure 5.7.)

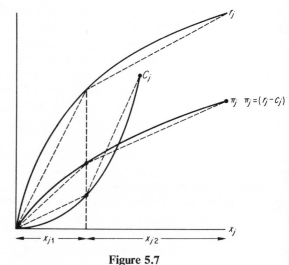

Figure 5.7

Profit π_j and revenue r_j curves are concave; cost curve is convex.

Partitioning can be used to treat these nonlinear situations. Two variables such as x_{j1} and x_{j2} are created. Since each must be bounded, i.e., $0 \leq x_{j1} < a$; $a \leq x_{j2}$, the result is that more constraints exist and therefore, in line with the fundamental theorem, more activities can be used. Note, if the profit curve is convex or if the cost curve is concave, partitioning cannot be used. See the use of LP in Chapter 8 to explain why this is so.[7]

As the programming iterations converge on a solution, discrete jumps from vertex point to vertex point of the convex set occur. Changes can only take place in this discrete way. This raises the question of how *sensitive* is the system to such hopping. Given a final solution, a small change in one of the estimates *might* cause the solution to hop to a highly different vertex. Since errors in estimates do not result in small, incremental errors, sensitivity analysis is often vital. What it means is that small changes are made in some of the estimates, and the problem is resolved in these terms. If the solution is stable, then the possibilities of erring in estimates is of no major concern. On the other hand, if the solution shifts easily, then it is important to discern which estimates seem most instrumental, how broad a range for these estimates can be tolerated, how believable these present estimates are, and how much additional information about them would cost.

[7] The reference is to pp. 224–226. This material can be studied for better understanding of the partitioning technique, at this point. However, in that case, a project shop situation is the basis of the example.

There are situations in which the value of Z will not change although an iteration has been completed. This will occur because as variables are moved in and out of the basis, several of the equations in the basis may temporarily lose their mutual independence. As a result, the number of independent variables in the basis of the LP solution is less than the number of constraints. The problem, called *degeneracy*, turns out to be purely computational. Degeneracy can always be remedied. Mention is made at a later point in the text of how to treat the occurrence of degeneracy when a network transportation algorithm is being used. For LP of the form we are discussing, further iteration will break the system out of its degenerate mode. If this does not occur soon enough, the dual transformation creates a new set of equations that have only the smallest chance of also being degenerate.

Let us briefly consider the dual here. An example of the use of the dual will be found on pp. 290–291. Dual variables (or shadow prices) assign value to resources that are fully utilized and no value to resources that are idle. The dual structure based on transforming x_j's to y_i's is shown below:

	x_1	x_2	
y_1	a_{11}	a_{12}	b_1
y_2	a_{21}	a_{22}	b_2
	π_1	π_2	

Primal Form: $a_{11}x_1 + a_{12}x_2 \leq b_1$
$a_{21}x_1 + a_{22}x_2 \leq b_2$
Max $\pi_1 x_1 + \pi_2 x_2$

Dual Form: $a_{11}y_1 + a_{21}y_2 \geq \pi_1$
$a_{12}y_1 + a_{22}y_2 \geq \pi_2$
Min $b_1 y_1 + b_2 y_2$

The dual variables y_1 and y_2 equal zero when their respective resources are not fully utilized. For each resource that is fully utilized, its dual variable will take on a positive value, the size of which indicates how much additional profit can be obtained by investing another dollar in that resource.[8]

Every primal matrix has a dual form. If the primal has M variables and N constraints, then the dual has N variables and M constraints. The primal tableau is $(M + N) \times N$. The dual tableau is $(N + M) \times M$. The difference (Size of Primal $-$ Size of Dual) is: $MN + N^2 - MN - M^2 = N^2 - M^2$. If $N \gg M$, i.e., there are many more constraints than variables, then the dual version requires much less computation. The dual also has advantages for the minimization problem which is often more complex to handle than the maximization problem because, in addition to slack variables, artificial variables are required. Thus:

---

[8] We can see why economists have found the dual variable intriguing, even before LP existed.

1. inequality:	$a_{11}x_1 + a_{12}x_2 + \ldots \geq b_1$
2. with slack variable S_1:	$a_{11}x_1 + a_{12}x_2 + \ldots - S_1 = b_1$
3. with slack variable S_1 and artificial variable A_1:	$a_{11}x_1 + a_{12}x_2 + \ldots - S_1 + A_1 = b_1$

It is essential to remove the artificial variables from the basis before any consideration is given to the cost coefficients in the objective function. This is quite readily done by finding any variable to put into the solution to replace the artificial variable so long as the feasibility conditions ($x_j \geq 0$ for all j) are maintained. Thereafter, the solution proceeds in the same way as it previously did. The dual form of a cost minimization problem obviates the need for introducing artificial variables.

The Extent to Which LP Can Be Utilized

The following situations lend themselves to LP analysis: (1) station design in line balancing; (2) project planning with respect to target date; (3) project planning in which cost is a relevant consideration; (4) aggregate scheduling where the work force can be varied; (5) transportation analysis that also can be applied to aggregate scheduling and shop loading; (6) product-mix determination (as previously described); (7) the trim problem as a special variant of production scheduling; (8) LP forms of shop loading; (9) job and plant layout; (10) input-output analysis to examine the interrelations of dependent subsidiaries; (11) game resolution using LP; (12) obtaining an optimum feed mixture at minimum cost.

Many of these situations are treated in the material that follows. In a number of cases, the network approach is more reasonable than mathematical programming. However, it is the broad applicability of the LP model that we wish to emphasize here.

LP Resolution of the Game

Instead of using trial and error to solve a set of game equations and inequations, the method of linear programming can be used.[9]

Consider the following payoff matrix, written for player x.

	y_1	y_2	y_3
x_1	3	5	5
x_2	6	2	6
x_3	7	7	1

[9] See pp. 57–78 in Chapter 3.

The appropriate equations (see pp. 74–78) are then:

1.	$3y_1 + 5y_2 + 5y_3 \leq v$
2.	$6y_1 + 2y_2 + 6y_3 \leq v$
3.	$7y_1 + 7y_2 + y_3 \leq v$
4.	$y_1 + y_2 + y_3 = 1.00$
5.	$3x_1 + 6x_2 + 7x_3 \geq v$
6.	$5x_1 + 2x_2 + 7x_3 \geq v$
7.	$5x_1 + 6x_2 + x_3 \geq v$
8.	$x_1 + x_2 + x_3 = 1.00$

We can solve this game for either y or x. We shall determine y's mixed strategy, using equations one, two, three, and four. The same procedure would apply to x, except that equations five, six, seven, and eight would be used, in the sense of the dual.

Let $Y_j = y_j/v$ and $V = 1/v$. Appoint slack variables, S_i. Then, we rewrite equations one through four in these terms:

$$3Y_1 + 5Y_2 + 5Y_3 + S_1 = 1$$
$$6Y_1 + 2Y_2 + 6Y_3 + S_2 = 1$$
$$7Y_1 + 7Y_2 + Y_3 + S_3 = 1$$

Maximize $V = [Y_1 + Y_2 + Y_3]$

$$Y_j \geq 0; \quad S_i \geq 0$$

The problem is now ready to be solved by a linear program. It should be noted that Max V = Min v. Thus, because the payoff matrix was written for player X, player Y's objective is to keep the expected payoff as small as possible. After the Y_j's are obtained, it is a straightforward matter to convert them into the y_j's required for the game's solution.

Environments

Many by-product and process effects are felt in the total system as the basic product materials are being transformed. Thus, in addition to producing a product-mix of acids, an odor is added to the air along with chemical impurities.[10] Material transformation from wood and rag to paper causes the stripping of forests and the pollution of rivers and air. The production of automobiles is simply a few steps removed in the sequential cascade of dependencies from the production of auto emissible fumes. All production transformations create profit beneficials and, at the same time, their environmental

---

[10] Unhealthy plant environments are not to be overlooked.

side effects. These are the responsibilities of the operations manager who knows that he is caught in a feedback loop where cause is effect and effect is cause. The environment affects the manager's decision and the manager's decisions affect the environment. The manager must be quite rational to know what to do about all this.

PROBLEMS

1. Before solving problem 2 below, estimate the length of time that you think it will take to complete it. Later, compare the actual time that it took to solve the problem with your estimate. Such a practice of estimating the times for completion of various projects and then comparing these estimates with the actual results can be useful, both as applied to yourself and others.

2. A greeting card manufacturer wishes to diversify his line. His designers have been experimenting with a new plastic material. It is available in thin sheets and lends itself to some unusual effects. The designers have come up with two alternative card designs—both of which appear to be totally acceptable. Because special equipment is required to print and cut this new material, the production manager wants to carefully consider the advantages of either card or the possibility of making both of them. The following data have been made available to him.

	Card A	*Card B*
Time to print one card on special machine	2.4 minutes	2.4 minutes
Time to cut and fold one card on special machine	4.8 minutes	1.6 minutes
Material required per card	80 square in.	240 square in.
Estimated profit per card	$0.70	$0.80

The company works a forty hour week and has 833 square feet of the material on hand and cannot obtain more in the near future. Assume no cutting waste and the requirement that the job be completed within one week. What product-mix should the production manager plan to use? Discuss your answer.

3. A paint manufacturer maintains an inventory of three basic dyes, D_i, $i = 1, 2, 3$. When mixed together in different proportions these produce standard colors, C_j, $j = 1, 2, 3, 4$. The profit per gallon for each color is known. The design of a fifth color using the same ingredients is suggested. The company estimates the profit per gallon for this new color. Should the new color design be included in the production schedule? What is the maximum profit associated with the solution?

How much of each inventory is consumed? Relevant data are given below:

	C_1	C_2	C_3	C_4	C_5	Pounds on hand
D_1	0.2	0.1	0.2	0	0.1	100
D_2	0	0.3	0	0.6	0	200
D_3	0.3	0.1	0.5	0	0.4	200
Profit per gallon	1	1	1.2	0.8	1	

Would the solution remain the same if 200 pounds of D_1 had been on hand?

4. For the linear programming problem illustrated in Figure 5.3, what profit equations describe the subset of lines that pass through the vertices of the feasible solution space?

5. Rewrite the problem used in the text (pp. 122–133) in its dual form. Solve the dual problem using the geometric approach, the algebraic approach, and then the simplex algorithm. Is the dual form an advantage here? Discuss.

The line balancing problem arises in the flow shop because jobs must be partitioned into equal work assignments to avoid idle time at specialized facilities. This is especially characteristic of labor-intensive systems, which explains why much line balancing work has been focused on assembly line balancing. In network terms, the nodes must be grouped into stations; the job flows cannot exceed station capacities and should be maximal, leaving minimum unused capacity.

Line Balancing
the Flow Shop

6

Care in planning the production process is most important for the continuous flow shop. It involves arranging facilities according to the given technological requirements of the products and forecasts of consumer demand levels. But there are degrees of continuity for the flow shop. They range from fully-automated, *paced-flow* systems (usually based on the mass production of items carried by a fixed-speed conveyer) to situations in which the demand for a group of similar items is continuous but varies in quantity over time. By similarity of items, we mean that essentially the same production routing and flow is required for each of the items that are run through the system in successive sequences.[1]

Progressive assembly or production line work is a synthetic function as illustrated in Figure 6.1.

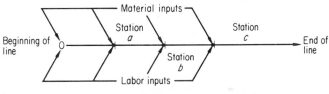

Figure 6.1

Sometimes an analytic production function is involved resulting in several flow systems. For example, see Figure 6.2, and note the cocoa bean flow diagram in Figure 6.3.

[1] See pp. 26–28 in Chapter 2.

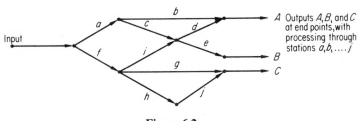

Figure 6.2

Analytic production function.

We see that in the case of the analytic system, the basic raw material is broken down, transformed, and decomposed into various products and by-products. Figure 6.3 pictures the flow of materials as exemplified by a typical analytic industry. In this case, the raw material is the cocoa bean. From the single basic raw material, four different products are derived, viz., cocoa butter bars, premium chocolate mix, regular chocolate mix, and cocoa. Flow charts of this type can be exceedingly helpful for process development of analytic systems. In synthetic operations, on the other hand, various materials and

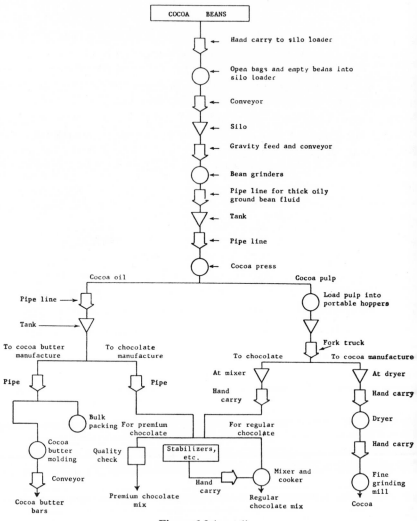

Figure 6.3 (part 1)

Chocolate manufacture—flow chart. [From Edward H. Bowman and Robert B. Fetter, *Analysis for Production and Operations Management*, 3rd. ed. (Homewood, Ill.: Richard D. Irwin, Inc., 1961), pp. 38–39.]

parts are fed into the main stream where they are joined together to form a basic unit. For example, Figure 6.4 shows an automobile assembly line. Each component is brought into the production line at the appropriate point, after which it loses its separate identity.

Synthetic processes lend themselves to flow systems; analytic processes tend toward job shop or intermittent flow shop configurations. Most processes *combine* both analytic and synthetic operations. This would even be true for the examples we have used. However, they can be distinguished as being *essentially* analytic or synthetic.

The stations through which materials flow generally have *special purpose facilities*, designed strictly for the limited, product-line under continuous

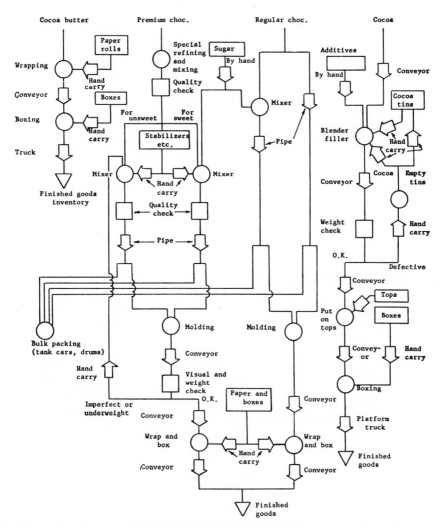

Figure 6.3 (cont., part 2)

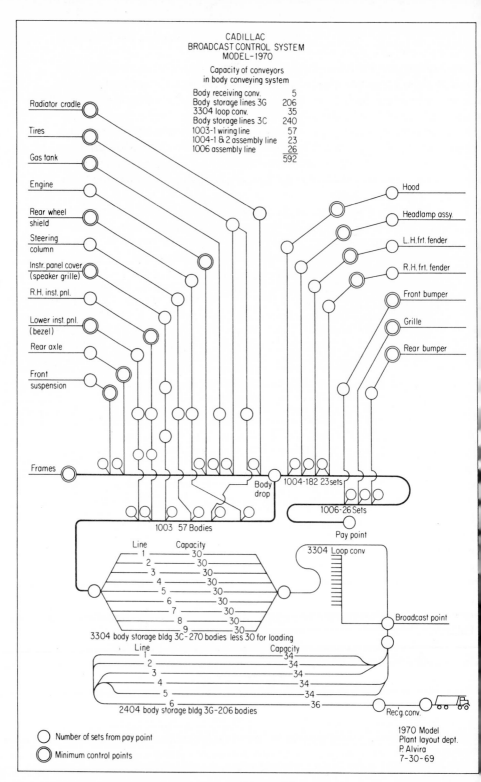

Figure 6.4

Cadillac broadcast system. (Courtesy Cadillac Motor Car Division, General Motors Corporation.)

flow. (Clearly, such configurations present different problems to the planner than do those comprised of *general purpose equipment* that can accommodate the many different operations of the job shop.) Serial production configurations involve successively differentiated steps (such as *a*, *b*, and *c* in Figure 6.1) based on their *division of labor*. This arrangement offers at least two advantages:

1. Items produced serially can be shipped continually, thereby reducing inventories; and
2. Specialization usually increases efficiency and the production rate.

> There is . . . the familiar economic principle that specialization implies trade and that neither without the other creates an ongoing process of economic development. If there was specialization without trade the tailor would starve and the farmer would go naked. On the other hand, of course, without specialization, trade itself cannot take place for there would be nothing to trade. It is one of Adam Smith's astonishingly acute perceptions that "the division of labor depends on the extent of the market." The division of labor, however, itself increases the extent of the market simply because we get specialization in traders and in trade itself, which facilitates further specialization in production, which facilitates further trade and so on in a magnificent process of disequilibrating feedback.[2]

The (generic) line balancing problem arises because jobs cannot easily be partitioned into equal work assignments with respect to the productive capabilities of people and facilities, neither of which work readily at the same rate. There is a matching problem. Design steps are needed to group sets of operations into *work stations*. We can design progressive assembly or process line functions in various ways. But, even the most automatic, *paced* flow system can be expected to change over time. Conversely, a large contract obtained by the job shop can be set up to approach the continuous, serial configuration of the flow shop. Some batching in serial transfers often occurs, e.g., a station completes two units at a time and then begins work on the next two. Assembly line operations have many of these serial flow characteristics (especially the paced-conveyer), which accounts for the fact that much of the literature has dealt with assembly line balancing rather than with generic line balancing, which subsumes assembly operations as a special class.

When demand permits, the continuous (or serial) flow shop, is used, because it is the most *efficient production configuration*. Extensive preplanning is required to achieve a successful design. Flow-shop systems are monitored to insure that they function as they were designed to operate. Less production-

[2] Kenneth E. Boulding, "The Specialist with a Universal Mind," *Management Science*, 14: 12 (August, 1968), B647–B653.

efficient, while being a greater producer of product diversity,[3] the job shop treats operations in batches. Each new job consists of a set of such batch-type operations. The movement of each of the batches must be planned for, bearing in mind that these jobs tend to interact with each other, *competing for facilities*. Repeated planning is costly. Consequently, the scope and precision of each job shop plan will necessarily be less than for continuous flow systems where a single, large planning investment is warranted by high production volume.

The Structure of Work Stations

There are various operations, $i = 1, 2, \ldots, k$, which are the smallest reasonable components into which the total job can be subdivided. The operations are to be grouped by work stations, $j = a, b, \ldots, n$. (Note that n counts the number of work stations.) Each operation can be assigned only once, but more than one operation can be assigned to a station, so $n \leq k$. There is a *cycle time*, C, which is the time the item may remain at each station. We can also interpret C, as follows. Let t_i $(i = 1, 2, \ldots, k)$ be the individual operation times. Then $\Sigma_i t_i$ is the minimum time required to process and assemble one unit, called the *total work content time*. The k operations are ordered by *precedence* relations (some combination of *synthetic* and *analytic* functions producing a list of *predecessors* and *successors*). Thus, if N units are to be made in a work period of T hours, we have $N/T = 1/C$, where the productive rate of the line is $1/C$, measured as items produced per unit time.

If we set s_j equal to the time assigned to the jth station for each item, i.e., the station time load per part, then $\Sigma_i t_i = \Sigma_j s_j$, and a reasonable objective of line balancing would be to: Minimize $\Sigma_j^n (C - s_j)$, for all j, $s_j \leq C$. This objective can be shown to be equivalent to minimizing n or C or nC.[4] It is also the same as minimizing the total idle time $\Sigma_j^n x_j$ as shown in Figure 6.5. We note that in a perfectly balanced (no idle time) flow shop, $s_A = s_B = \ldots$ $s_n = C$. Thus, for the equation, $\Sigma_i t_i / n = s_j + x_j$, in this case, all $x_j = 0$.

If the cycle time, C, is fixed by design, then the number of stations under perfect balance would be, $\Sigma_i t_i / C = n$. Such perfect balance may not be achievable because technological factors exist that do not let operations be so divided. Sometimes workers or facilities cannot be shifted between stations in such a way as to let all $x_j = 0$. These kind of restrictions often are referred to

---

[3] See pp. 370–372 where the concepts of variety are discussed. For more elaboration, also see, M. K. Starr, "Product Planning from the Top (Variety and Diversity)," *University of Illinois Bulletin*, 65: 144, Proceedings, *Systems: Research and Applications for Marketing* (July 26, 1968), pp. 71–77.

[4] Nick T. Thomopoulos, "Mixed Model Line Balancing with Smoothed Station Assignments," *Management Science*, 16: 9 (May, 1970), 593–603.

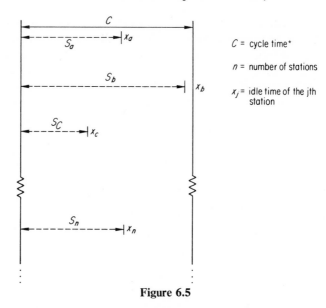

C = cycle time*

n = number of stations

x_j = idle time of the jth station

Figure 6.5

as *zoning* constraints. When perfect balance is not available, we measure the system's inefficiency by: $d = 100(nC - \Sigma_i t_i)/nC$. This equation for balance delay, d (see pp. 160–161) can be better understood by observing that $(nC - \Sigma_i t_i)/nC = (x_a + x_b + x_c + \ldots + x_n)/nC$.

It is evident that $t_{\max} \leq C \leq \Sigma_i t_i$ where $t_{\max}$ is the longest, indivisible operation, and if $C = \Sigma_i t_i$, there is only one station. For a given value of C, the optimal number of stations *must* be found as an *integer*, the *smallest* possible integer value of n. For example, assume that in Figure 6.6 the cycle time

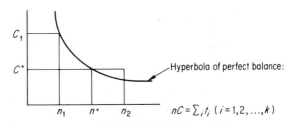

Hyperbola of perfect balance:

$$nC = \Sigma_i t_i \ (i = 1, 2, \ldots, k)$$

Figure 6.6

is given as C^*. The hyperbola of perfect balance requires n^* stations. This is not a practical solution if n^* is not an integer. Let n_2 be the *first* integer larger than n^*. Since $n_2 C^* > \Sigma_i t_i$, there is a cost of idle manpower and capacity in this n_2 decision. On the other hand, if $n_1 = n_2 - 1$, then $n_1 C^*$ is impossible because the work content is greater than the total station time provided, i.e., $\Sigma_i t_i > n_1 C^*$. The feasible alternative is $n_1 C_1$, which allows perfect balance but entails a cost of the lower productivity, $1/C^* - 1/C_1$.

The actual assignment of facilities to stations is not a simple matter. Salveson[5] provided one of the first analytic approaches to the problem. Later, Bowman suggested (as a theoretical possibility) an integer, linear programming solution that is based on an objective function that penalizes increasing the number of stations and adheres through precedence relations (see Figure 6.7) to technological and zoning constraints.[6] More elaborate procedures have also been suggested, but theory tends to dominate practice because the size of "real" problems is too large for the computational efforts required by those theoretical methods.[7]

LP Approach to Line Balancing

Consider the following network of ordered operations.

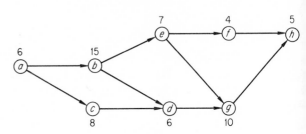

Figure 6.7

Set $C = 30$ minutes. There are j stations, $j = 1, 2, \ldots, n$ and i operations, $i = 1, 2, \ldots, k$ and then: from Figure 6.7 $(k = h)$ and $\overset{i=h}{\underset{i=a}{\Sigma}} t_i = 61$, so $n = \Sigma_i t_i / C = 61/30 = 2^+$ and therefore at least three stations are required. Perhaps, because of technological constraints or zoning restrictions, even more than three stations will be needed. No more than five are needed to satisfy precedences conditions. Question: How to prepare inputs in proper format to resolve this problem? We must express the following conditions:

1. No station overloading is allowed: $s_j \leq C$
2. All operations must be completed: $i = 1, 2, \ldots, k$
3. Precedence relations have to be followed: $\overset{h}{\underset{i}{\Sigma}} t_i > \overset{f}{\underset{i}{\Sigma}} t_i \ldots$ etc.

[5] M. E. Salveson, "The Assembly Line Balancing Problem," *Journal of Industrial Engineering*, VI: 3 (May–June, 1955), 18–25.

[6] See E. H. Bowman, "Assembly Line Balancing by Linear Programming," *Operations Research*, 8: 3 (May–June, 1960), 385–89.

[7] See for example, M. Held, R. M. Karp, and R. Shareshian, "Assembly Line Balancing—Dynamic Programming with Precedence Constraints," *Operations Research*, 11: 3 (May–June, 1963), 442–59.

4. No operations may be split between stations: On an assignment basis[8] this means that no two entries are permitted in the same row of the matrix (two entries *are permitted* in the same column).

Stations

j

		1	2	3	$\ldots$	n
	1	x				
Tasks i	2	x				
	3			x		
	$\vdots$					
	k				x	

5. Since the manager's preference is for a minimum number of stations, the objective will be to find the minimum necessary number of columns, n.

These conditions are mathematically representable as follows:

1. *No Overloading*

    The sum of operation times t_i that are assigned to a station j must be $\leq C$; thus for each station j, $\Sigma_i t_i X_{ij} \leq C$. Note: X_{ij} is valued at one if the ith task is assigned to the jth station, and at zero for no assignment (thus, an integer programming format is required).[9]

2. *All Operations Completed*

    $\sum_j^n X_{ij} = X_{i1} + X_{i2} + \ldots + X_{in} = 1$ that for $X_{ij} = 0$ or 1 states that the operation must be done at one of the stations. If zoning constraints apply to some operations, the appropriate value of X_{ij} is set equal to one and all other station alternatives necessarily are set equal to zero.

3. *Precedence Observed*

    In general, $X_{ij} \leq \sum_{j=1}^{j} X_{i-1,j} = X_{i-1,1} + X_{i-1,2} + \ldots X_{i-1,j}$

[8] An explanation of the assignment-type network algorithm is presented on pp. 269–278.

[9] See William J. Baumol, *Economic Theory and Operations Analysis*, 2nd ed. (Englewood Cliffs, N.J.: Prentice-Hall, Inc., 1965), pp. 154–62 for a clear discussion of the Gomory constraints. For the original work, see Ralph E. Gomory, "Outline of an Algorithm for Integer Solutions to Linear Programs," *Bulletin of the American Mathematical Society*, 64 (September, 1958), pp. 275–278.

Note, the $i - 1$st operation precedes the ith operation. If the $i - 1$st operation is assigned to any station up to the jth station, then a one exists in the sum so the ith operation can be assigned or not to the jth station. But, if the $i - 1$st operation has not been assigned to any station up to the jth station, the ith operation cannot be assigned. Such constraint relations must be written for each precedence relation that exists.

4. *No Operations Split*

This is the special requirement of integer programming where, in this case, $X_{ij} = 0$ or 1 The simplex method insures that $X_{ij} \geq 0$; the Gomory constraints[10] that X_{ij} is an integer; and from (2) above that this integer is either 0 or 1 The method of integer programming (a) reduces the feasible region so that only integer sets form possible solutions; (b) never excludes from the new feasible region an integer set that was originally feasible; (c) allows programming iterations to determine the optimal integer set.

5. *Minimum Number of Stations*

The optimal number of stations is $\Sigma_i t_i / C = n$, if this can be achieved. If it cannot, *assume* an upper limit to the number of stations needed, say $n + R$. Operations with no succeeding operations must be assigned increasingly larger penalties $(\alpha, \beta, \ldots \delta)$ as we go from $n + 1$ to $n + R$. In this case,

Minimize $Z = \alpha(t_h X_{h,n+1}) + \ldots + \beta(t_h X_{h,n+2}) + \ldots + \delta(t_h X_{h,n+R})$

To illustrate, let $\alpha = 1$, $\beta = t_h + 1$, $\delta = \beta(t_h + 1)$, etc. This pushes assignments to earlier positions and produces the optimal number of stations. For our example, it would probably be reasonable to let $R = 5$ or 6 depending on the amount of inflexibility that exists with respect to station design. Thus, R is an upper bound value chosen to represent more additional stations than are likely to be required. If R is set too low, an infeasible solution will result, until it's value is increased. (See p. 155.)

Bowman's model is too demanding for any large-scale problem. As a result, line-balancing heuristics have emerged as being of the greatest importance. In fact, the entire area of heuristic reasoning has received increasing attention resulting from the efforts of researchers to develop useful algorithms. Such work continues to expand because the early heuristics ignored many realistic requirements of the problem. For example, a paced line is not always used. Often, a line with controlled, variable speed exists. Also, little consideration has been given to those many situations where the t_i's are not determinate but random variables.

[10] See footnote nine above.

Heuristic Line Balancing Models

Heuristic comes from the Greek word, *heuriskein*, meaning to discover. The term has been used by Simon and Newell[11] to describe a particular approach to problem solving and to decision making. Heuristic models utilize logic and common sense derived by observation and introspection. These models replace classical mathematical ones when formal, analytic methods have little promise of ever being operational.

The essence of the heuristic approach is in the application of selective routines that reduce the size of a problem. Thus, for example, the production problem of assembly line balancing can be treated by reducing the total system to a series of simpler line balancing problems that can be studied analytically.[12] Another kind of reduction is used in which a relatively simple rule is applied repeatedly until all decisions that must be made have been made.

Looking at heuristic procedures in another way, sensible rules can be used to simulate the decision-making pattern of human beings as they would normally operate unaided in the system. The advantages of this approach are consistency, speed, endurance, and the ability to cope with more data and larger systems than is humanly possible. Once the basic decision-making pattern is developed, it can be expanded and applied to greater system segments. Accordingly, for situations that do not lend themselves to mathematical analysis, the heuristic approach is an attractive alternative. The key is to trace out and then embody the thinking process that an intelligent decision maker would use to resolve the specific type of problem. Heuristic models do not guarantee an optimal result. Instead, they are designed to produce relatively good strategies subject to specific constraints. For the line balancing problem, we will talk about a number of heuristics and illustrate one, in particular, so that all the above points will become evident.

Among its uses, heuristic models can test the decision maker's process of reasoning with respect to a great range of input conditions. A variety of situations can be analyzed in this way, once the appropriate logical model of connections has been constructed. Often, unsuspected system behaviors can be deduced. In addition, executives and employees can be trained to follow the heuristics of a successful pattern that has been previously established.

Heuristic models supplement the decision process. They represent a kind of nonfatiguing, all-persevering decision maker that is embodied in a machine to *imitate* the performance of a human being. The effort required to build and test a heuristic might not be justified for nonrepetitive decision problems; but it is well-suited to repetitive, complex situations that refuse to

[11] H. A. Simon and A. Newell, "Heuristic Problem Solving: The Next Advance in Operations Research," *Operations Research*, 6: 1 (January–February, 1958), 1–10.

[12] Fred M. Tonge, "Summary of a Heuristic Line Balancing Procedure," *Management Science*, 7: 1 (October, 1960), 21–39.

submit to straightforward mathematical analysis. The heuristic approach necessitates capturing some of the most relevant cognitive and inferential skills of the successful decision maker.

The formal study of heuristics represents something of a break with tradition. For many years, the notion that simplicity is a goal for scientific explanations of complex phenomena has been the motivating force in scientific achievement. In this sense, a concise mathematical statement meets the criterion of simplicity. This notion of simplicity can be traced to William of Ockham who, in the fourteenth century, proposed the Principle of Parsimony. Not at all facetiously, it has also been called Ockham's Razor. The underlying notion of this principle is that conclusions should be accepted that follow from the least number of propositions, assumptions, and steps of reasoning. From this "myth of simplicity," as it has been characterized by Mario Bunge,[13] has sprung reverence for so-called "elegant" mathematical solutions that are, in large part, praised for their succinctness. Similarly, astronomical theory has been deeply influenced by the notion of simplicity. Science today is still the heir to this tradition.

Whether useful or destructive for the physical sciences, the idea breaks down rapidly when applied to systems of many complex (especially behavioral) operations. Thus, one might say that *even if* the principle of parsimony operates on the machine side of the man-machine interface, it is hardly applicable on the man side. Heuristic models simplify, but they are not simple in the classic sense. They embody assumptions and convoluted reasoning as required. We recognize the fact that heuristic approximations might provide better solutions to complex problems than rigorous formal mathematics. In some of the operations areas, it seems especially clear that the tradition of the principle of parsimony works against us, not for us. With this in mind, let us turn to some specific line balancing considerations.

Kilbridge and Wester's Heuristic

Kilbridge and Wester[14] proposed a heuristic procedure that assigns a number to each operation describing how many predecessors it has. Then the first operations assigned to stations are those with the lowest predecessor numbers. Some further considerations also apply, but before describing them, let us set down a precedence diagram (Figure 6.8) that can be used to explain and demonstrate the heuristic.

The procedure for developing the precedence diagram is as follows. List in column I all operations that need not follow others. Then in column II,

[13] M. Bunge, *The Myth of Simplicity* (Englewood Cliffs, N.J.: Prentice-Hall, Inc., 1963).

[14] M. D. Kilbridge and L. Wester, "A Heuristic Model of Assembly Line Balancing," *Journal of Industrial Engineering*, 12: 4 (July–August, 1961), 292–98.

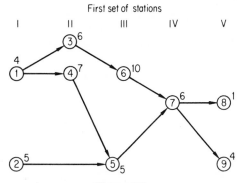

Figure 6.8

Precedence diagram.

list operations that must follow those in I. Continue to the other columns in the same way. Sequence is fully specified but column position is not. For example, operation 2 could be done as well in station II. Note also that the first basic feasible number of stations is determined by the longest chain of sequenced operations, not in time but in the number of operations. (Thus, in the prior LP model of Bowman, the upper limit $(n + R)$ for the number of stations can be determined.)

There exist many orderings that satisfy the precedence requirements. Intracolumn movement is totally free since these elements are mutually independent (not connected by arrows). Also, elements can be moved sidewise from their columns to positions to their right without disturbing the precedence restrictions. These kinds of flexibility are often called permutability of columns and lateral transferability.

To determine the cycle times, C, for which n is an integer, we write down +all primes of $\Sigma_i t_i$. (Prime numbers are integers that can only be factored into integers by one and themselves, i.e., 2, 3, 5, 7, ...) Then, all combinations of these primes that meet the condition: $t_{max} \leq C \leq \Sigma_i t_i$ are used to examine the permissible number of stations $n = \Sigma_i t_i / C$.

For our example, the total time is 48:

Operation	Total Time
1	4
2	5
3	6
4	7
5	5
6	10 (t_{max})
7	6
8	1
9	4
	48 = $\Sigma_i t_i$

The primes of 48 are: $2 \times 2 \times 3 \times 2 \times 2$. The constraints on cycle time are given by: $10 \le C \le 48$. Then, all possible combinations of the primes are classified as yielding feasible or infeasible cycle times.

Feasible cycle times	Infeasible cycle times	
$C_1 = 48$	$C_5 = 2 \times 2 \times 2$	$= 8$
$C_2 = 2 \times 2 \times 2 \times 3 = 24$	$C_6 = 2 \times 3$	$= 6$
$C_3 = 2 \times 2 \times 2 \times 2 = 16$	$C_7 = 2 \times 2$	$= 4$
$C_4 = 2 \times 2 \times 3 \quad = 12$	$C_8 = 2$	$= 2$

Arbitrarily, let us balance the $n = 3$ case (in Problem 5, p. 172, the line balancing result for $n = 2$ and $n = 4$ using the Kilbridge and Wester heuristic is requested).

The *first feasible* station design assignments are:

Columns	i	t_i	Column Sum	Cumulative Sum
I	1	4		
	2	5	9	9
II	3	6		
	4	7	13	22
III	5	5		
	6	10	15	37
IV	7	6	6	43
V	8	1		
	9	4	5	48

We count the number of predecessors for each operation (see Figure 6.8).

Operation	Number of Predecessors	t_i
1	0	4
2	0	5
3	1	6
4	1	7
5	3	5
6	2	10
7	6	6
8	7	1
9	7	4

On this basis we regroup. Column I operations are selected because they have the least number of predecessors. This means we first select operations 1 and 2. They have a total operation time of 9. Since $n = 3$, then $C = 16$, so we can introduce either operation 3 or operation 4 into station I.

Now, another rule applies. When there is a choice, choose first the longest operation times *that can be used*. Small operations are saved for ease of manipulation, at the end of the line. In this way the station is packed, i.e., $C - s_j$ is made as small as possible, and then station $j + 1$ can be studied next. Operation 4's time of 7 is larger than operation 3's time of 6. This gives a total time of 16. Station I is fully packed with no idle time.

Continuing in this way, we obtain three fully packed stations having no idle time.

Columns	i	t_i	Column Sum	Cumulative Sum
I	1	4		
	2	5		
	4	7	16	16
II	3	6		
	6	10	16	32
III	5	5		
	7	6		
	8	1		
	9	4	16	48

The precedence diagram can then be subdivided accordingly.

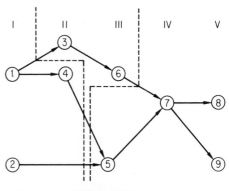

Figure 6.9

These three perfectly balanced stations can be used—if the technology permits (and this is probable because the precedence constraints have been observed), if facilities permit; and if operator movements permit. Realistically, taking other factors into account, there may still be better arrangements. If zone constraints do apply, operations can be separated into constrained zones to begin with and then assignments made for remaining operations. Optimal balance can be achieved in such simple examples as this one, but generally, we expect to do no more than satisfice—a good enough result is obtained to satisfy reasonable expectations.

(IGNORE)

Some Additional Heuristics

Another possible heuristic suggested by Helgeson and Birnie[15] is to make the next assignment to a station of an operation, i, whose *followers* have the *largest total time*, i.e., the sum t_i of all successors. They call their approach the Ranked Positional Weight Method. In the table below, each operation of our prior example (Figure 6.8) is associated with such a weight (the sum of all operations that follow it). The operations are then ranked by descending order of the weight measure.

Operation in Ranked Order	Weight	t_i	Station Cumulative Time	
1	39	4		
3	21	6		
2	16	5	15	
				I
4	16	7		
5	11	5	12	
				II
6	11	10		
7	5	6	16	
				III
8	0	1		
9	0	4	5	
				IV

Subject to the cycle time of sixteen, in the attempt to get three stations, operations are assigned that do not violate precedence or zoning constraints. When the total time for a station is exceeded, the attempt is made to find a feasible operation further down the list that can be included. This was not possible with station I. The heuristic requires that operations 1 and 3 be included as part of station I. Operations 2, 4, and 6 are the only ones that might then be included for completion without violating precedence. We could have operations 1, 3, and 4, but their total time is seventeen; for 1, 3, and 6, it is twenty.

[15] W. B. Helgeson and D. P. Birnie, "Assembly Line Balancing Using the Ranked Positional Weight Technique," *Journal of Industrial Engineering*, XII: 6 (November–December, 1961), 394–98.

This approach does not yield three stations but results in four stations operating under the cycle time of sixteen. The fourth station's unused capacity is particularly poor. Four stations might be used with a cycle time of twelve if a feasible station assignment can be found.

Tonge[16] describes a learning (reward and penalty) procedure that selects a heuristic randomly from a catalog of heuristics. The sequence of selections provides the basis for assigning operations to stations. When the selected heuristics produce improved solutions, they are rewarded by increasing the likelihood that they will be selected the next time. When they produce poorer solutions, a penalty is imposed that decreases such likelihoods. Among the set of heuristics employed to choose the next operation were:

A. longest operation time, t_i
B. largest number of immediate followers
C. operation i chosen at random.

In effect, the choice of heuristic is determined by $p(A)$, $p(B)$, and $p(C)$. These probabilities of choice sum to one, and initially, they are all equal, i.e., $\frac{1}{3}$. Then, according to the balance delay achieved by successive iterations, particular probabilities are increased as they appear to contribute to improved performance. Tonge concludes that this probabilistic approach results in fewer work stations than using any one individual heuristic alone or a purely random choice of operations. This approach may be particularly appealing for mixed model systems that must be line balanced.

Arcus randomly generated feasible sequences using probability assignments based on precedence, zoning, and feasibility relations. In addition, he used heuristic weighting to improve his results. The computer program generates one thousand sequences and the one that is chosen requires the minimum number of stations.[17] Obviously, there is reasonable expectation that a number of alternative configurations will require the same minimum number of stations, so there is additional leeway for interpretation. All these heuristics attempt to organize those operations that are free to move, recognizing that some operations cannot move because they are constrained by the partial ordering determined by precedence relations.[18]

[16] Fred M. Tonge, "Assembly Line Balancing Using Probabilistic Combinations of Heuristics," *Management Science*, 11: 7 (May, 1965), 727–35.

[17] It is reported that the generation of one thousand sequences for a system of seventy operations on an IBM 7090 required 30 minutes. A. L. Arcus, "Comsoal: A Computer Method of Sequencing Operations for Assembly Lines," see Elwood S. Buffa, ed., *Readings in Production and Operations Management* (New York: John Wiley & Sons, Inc., 1966), pp. 336–60.

[18] For summary coverage of line balancing approaches see: E. J. Ignall, "A Review of Assembly Line Balancing," *Journal of Industrial Engineering*, 16: 4 (July–August, 1965), 244–54.

Balance Delay and Optimal Cost Balance

In the literature, the term *balance delay* measured by the percentage: $d = 100(nC - \Sigma_i t_i)/nC$ is often used, where $nC \geq \Sigma_i t_i$ is essential; $\Sigma_i t_i/C = n$ when perfect balance is achieved and $d = 0$.

Actually, many costs are involved and a more systems-oriented view would suggest that a function such as total cost for different station arrangements $T(n, C)$, be minimized, where n must assume integer values.

$$T(n, C) = K_1(nC - \Sigma\, t_i) + K_2(C - C^*) + K_3(n - n^*)$$

Figure 6.10 will help us to interpret this equation.

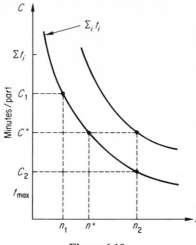

Figure 6.10

The hyperbola of perfect balance is labeled $\Sigma_i t_i$. Assume that C^* has been specified as the required cycle time but that n^* may not be an integer. Then, we could move to n_2 and hope that a realistic station balance could be achieved there. Or, it might be necessary to try $n_2 + 1$, etc. An alternative is to increase cycle time by moving to the next lowest integer number of stations, in this case, n_1. If the n_2 configuration can be designed, then there is the cost:

$n_2 C^* > \Sigma_i t_i$: the cost of idle capacity or of slower work, taxed at the rate K_1

An n_2 design may have higher manpower and facility costs, so we include the term

$n_2 - n^*$: with the cost coefficient K_3.

The alternative n_1C_1 configuration entails the cost:

$C_1 - C^*$: which arises because of lower productivity than specified
and is penalized by K_2. There is also a saving since $n_1 < n^*$.

This view is far more demanding than a simple request for minimum balance delay or for minimum n. It should also be noted that K_1 may be divided into a series of costs applicable to each station, that is,

$$K_1'(C - s_1) + K_1''(C - s_2) + \ldots$$

Because $t_{max} \leq C \leq \Sigma_i t_i$, cycle times such as C_1 and C_2, with integers n_1 and n_2, must be chosen to fall within the allowable range. The costs for *all* integer configurations might be obtained and compared. But, the point to bear in mind is that with many operations whatever heuristic algorithm is used will tend to reduce balance delay. As more stations are added, productivity will increase. More demanding routines must be developed based on shorter cycle times. The quality of the items being worked on can deteriorate under such circumstances.

Perfect Balance and the Stochastic Problem

In reality, no manager would wish to approach too closely the state of perfect balance. After all, the t_i's are seldom entirely fixed but are random variables. The more that human effort is involved on the line, the more this statement applies. Thus, the quantity $(C - s_j) = x_j$ is purposely maintained larger than zero so that the cycle time will not be exceeded. With a paced line, exceeding the cycle time means that the conveyer must be stopped and all $n - 1$ stations will be idle waiting for the other stations to catch up; or the part can be removed from the line creating a queue; or a special worker can be assigned who can shift from station to station to provide extra help where needed. Each situation has its own characteristics that determine what might be the best thing to do. And, even with a semi-paced line, similar problems arise.

As a rule of thumb, managers frequently load their stations within 90 per cent of their full utilization. This provides a degree of leeway for rest and changing pace. Also, it takes some of the pressure off the worker that a zero balance delay system incurs. The resulting product quality is improved, and the costs of inspection rejects is decreased. The total cost concept should include the additional terms related to costs of exceeding cycle times when this occurrence is a possibility. We should not overlook the fact that the line-balancing problem refers to the way in which machines and human components of a production line are matched with respect to their characteristic production rates. The machines can be counted upon for relatively deterministic t_i's whereas the human operators of the system have significant variability.

Queueing Aspects of Line Balancing

Let us now consider what happens when stochastic behavior characterizes the t_i's (i.e., the operation times are statistically distributed). This is not unusual.

If the station assignments are not properly designed, serious bottlenecks can develop, resulting in an extremely inefficient operation. Machine breakdowns can stop the entire line and cause a backing up of in-process inventories. There is only so much storage space between stations. A complete study of equipment characteristics is required. Line balancing can be handled by simulating *through-put*[19] in the system, taking account of all the random factors that can affect the process. Such simulations can be well worth the time and effort required if a large process investment is being tested. The second approach is to utilize the mathematical and statistical models derived from queueing theory.

Let us consider a production line where only two facilities, A and B, are involved. The technological sequence will be fixed: A first, B second. For example, A might be *drill hole* and B might be *ream hole;* A can be *make bumper* and B can be *attach bumper to chassis;* or A might be *prepare invoice* whereas B might be *mail invoice.* Technological constraints help to limit the size of the problem, but there are usually ample opportunities for arranging the facilities in alternative ways. We shall assume that facility A has an expected production output rate of eight units per hour. This in turn describes the expected load on facility B, which has an assumed process rate of ten units per hour. Furthermore, we shall not restrict the in-process inventory accommodations between the A and B production stages. Figure 6.11 depicts this arrangement.

Figure 6.11

Although B's capacity is greater than A's, a queue can develop. This might occur if A speeds up while B remains constant at the expected value. It could also be that a queue of in-process inventory develops because B slows down while A performs according to expectation. If both events occur

[19] These are the flows of information, materials, energy, and all resources that are used by the transformation process. For an example of how simulation is used, see pp. 170–171.

simultaneously, then the resultant queue can be quite formidable. The average number of units in the queue would be:[20]

$$L_q = \rho^2/(1 - \rho) \quad \text{where } \rho = \lambda/\mu = 8/10$$

Then:

$$L_q = 0.64/0.20 = 3.20$$

We can also determine the probability distribution $\{p_n\}$, where p_n equals the probability that a total of n units is in the system. Some units would be waiting for service[21] from process B, the remaining unit being served by B. When $n = 0$, facility B is idle. When $n = 1$, facility B is working and the in-process inventory is zero. When $n = 2$, one unit is waiting for B, and so forth. We know:[22]

$$p_n = (1 - \rho)\rho^n$$

Then, we can prepare the following table for facility B.

n	p_n		Probability Density	Cumulative Probability
0	$p_0 = (1 - \rho)$	$= 0.2000$		0.2000
1	$p_1 = (1 - \rho)\rho^1$	$= 0.1600$		0.3600
2	$p_2 = (1 - \rho)\rho^2$	$= 0.1280$		0.4880
3	$p_3 = (1 - \rho)\rho^3$	$= 0.1024$		0.5904
4	$p_4 = (1 - \rho)\rho^4$	$= 0.0819$		0.6723
5	$p_5 = (1 - \rho)\rho^5$	$= 0.0655$		0.7378
6	$p_6 = (1 - \rho)\rho^6$	$= 0.0524$		0.7902
7	$p_7 = (1 - \rho)\rho^7$	$= 0.0419$		0.8321
8	$p_8 = (1 - \rho)\rho^8$	$= 0.0336$		0.8657
9	$p_9 = (1 - \rho)\rho^9$	$= 0.0268$		0.8925
10	$p_{10} = (1 - \rho)\rho^{10}$	$= 0.0215$		0.9140
.	.		.	.
.	.		.	.
.	.		.	.
n	etc.		etc.	etc.

[20] This relationship applies when:

1. There is an infinite source;
2. There are infinite accommodations for a waiting line;
3. Service is granted on a FIFO (first-in, first-out) basis;
4. There is a single service channel; and
5. The arrival and service distributions are both exponential.

[21] These units comprise the in-process inventory.

[22] The same conditions hold as were listed in footnote 20. For these and other queueing formulations see: P. M. Morse, *Queues, Inventories and Maintenance* (New York: John Wiley & Sons, Inc., 1958); D. R. Cox and W. L. Smith, *Queues* (London: Methuen & Co., 1961); T. L. Saaty, *Elements of Queueing Theory* (New York: McGraw-Hill Book Co., Inc., 1961).

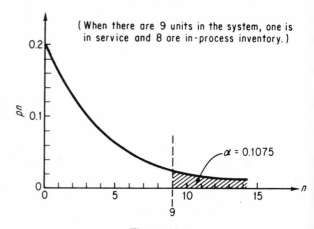

Figure 6.12

Probability density distribution for $\rho = 0.8$.

Figure 6.12 depicts the resulting probability distribution that n units are in the system. The area under the curve between zero and any value of n gives the probability that n or less units will be in the system. The remaining area is the probability that the *queue length* will exceed some designated value of $n - 1$. We have called this tail area α. Thus, the probability that the in-process inventory will exceed eight units is 0.1075, or about 11 per cent of the time. Figure 6.13 illustrates this same point in terms of the cumulative proba-

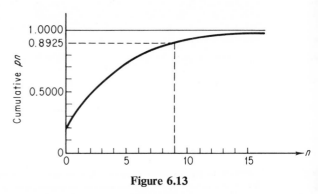

Figure 6.13

Cumulative probability distribution for $\rho = 0.8$.

bility distribution. The probability (0.8925) that eight or less units will constitute in-process inventory could have been read directly from the column of cumulative probabilities in the table.

When there are n units in this single channel system, one unit is being serviced. Therefore, the queue length is $n - 1$, which for the above example is equal to eight with a probability, $\alpha = 0.1075$. Many other performance characteristics of this system are also apparent. Facility B will be idle 20 per cent of the time. We know this from the fact that $p_0 = 0.20$. Facility B's output will be $(1 - p_0)\mu = (0.80)(10) = 8$ units per hour.

The line-balancing problem assumes real meaning when the production manager begins to associate costs and value with the system's performance characteristics. Thus, for example, he might assemble the following information:

Output Value: $4.00 per unit
Materials Cost: $1.00 per unit
Cost of Facility A:[23] $3.00 per hour
Cost of Facility B:[24] $5.00 per hour
Storage Cost: $0.20 per unit per hour

Then, the value of this arrangement, called Case I, would be:

Net value ($/hr.) = Total output value − Total input costs
$$= \text{(Output value)} (1 - p_0)\mu - \text{(Materials cost)} (1 - p_0)\mu$$
$$- \text{(Storage cost)} (L_q) - \text{Cost of facilities}$$
$$= \$4.00(8) - [\$1.00(8) + \$0.20(3.2) + \$3.00 + \$5.00]$$
$$= \$32.00 - \$16.64 = \$15.36 \text{ per hour.}$$

Now, the production manager has various arrangements that he would like to test so that he can achieve the best possible balance of his facilities. Let us assume that he is interested in the two alternatives listed below and pictured in Figure 6.14.

Case II: Facility A is as before. Two smaller B-type facilities having the same combined output as the large B facility will be used; these are called B_1. The cost of the two B_1's is the same as that of one B. The expected output rate of each B_1 is five units per hour. The output from A will be directed to a single waiting line. The relevant equations[25] and results for two service channels are:

$$\rho = \lambda/M\mu = 8/(2)(5) = 0.80$$

$$p_0 = \frac{1}{1 + \dfrac{\lambda}{\mu} + \left(\dfrac{\mu}{2\mu - \lambda}\right)\left(\dfrac{\lambda}{\mu}\right)^2} = \frac{1}{9}$$

[23] The cost factors of the facilities would be straightforward to compute if the facilities are salaried individuals; for machines and man-machine combinations, an approximate cost figure can still be found.

[24] *Ibid.*

[25] All conditions are the same as before, except that a multiple service channel exists. For derivation of these equations, as well as others, refer to sources listed in footnote 22.

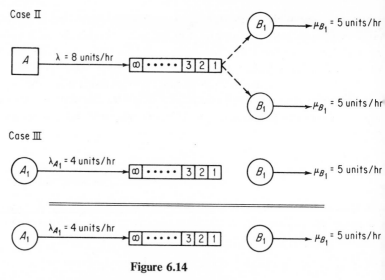

Figure 6.14

Service systems: Cases II and III.

$$p_1 = \frac{\lambda}{\mu} p_o = \frac{8}{5}\left(\frac{1}{9}\right) = \frac{8}{45}$$

$$L_q = \frac{\lambda^3 p_o}{\mu(2\mu - \lambda)^2} = \frac{128}{45} = 2.8$$

The expected output of this system is ten units per hour, $100(1 - 1/9 - 8/45) = 71$ per cent of the time; five units per hour, 18 per cent of the time; and zero output for the remaining 11 per cent of the time,[26] that is,

Expected output $= 10(0.71) + 5(0.18) + 0(0.11) = 8$ units per hour[27]
Then,

Net value ($/hr.) $= \$4.00(8) - [\$1.00(8) + \$0.20(2.8) + \$3.00 + \$5.00]$
$= \$32.00 - \$16.56 = \$15.44$ per hour

Therefore, the Case II arrangement is preferred to the original balance design of Case I.

Case III: Two smaller A-type facilities having the same combined output as the large A facility will be used; these are called A_1. The combined cost of the A_1's is \$0.50 less per hour than that of one A. No crossover is allowed between channels. That is, one A_1 is paired with one B_1 and is not permitted to supply

---

[26] We have zero output when $n = 0$; thus $p_o = 1/9 \cong 0.11$. The output is five units per hour when $n = 1$; $p_1 = 8/45 \cong 0.18$. When $n > 1$, the output is ten units per hour.
[27] It comes as no surprise that the expected output is equal to the expected input because the process' capacity exceeds the expected load.

the other B_1. The relevant equations are the same as those used for Case I.
For *each* A_1/B_1 pair:

$$\rho = \tfrac{4}{5} = 0.80$$
$$L_q = 3.2$$
$$p_o = 0.20$$

Expected Output $= (1 - p_o)\mu = 0.80(5) = 4$ units per hour[28]

Then, for the total system:

Net value (\$/hr.) $= \$4.00(8) - [\$1.00(8) + \$0.20(6.4) + \$2.50 +_{j}\$5.00]$
$= \$32.00 - \$16.78 = \$15.22$ per hour

In spite of the fact that the two A_1's cost less than the single A facility, Case I
is preferred to Case III. The arrangement of Case II is still better, however.
Presumably, the Case II design would be chosen unless still other alternatives
existed.[29]

Now, let us follow a simple industrial process with r stages and storage
space between to smooth through-put. Figure 6.15 below illustrates a pair of
stages, i.e., $r = 2$; ($\lambda =$ input rate, $\mu =$ output rate).

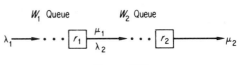

Figure 6.15

As one useful, extreme case, assume that the first server is nearly always busy,
then λ_2 very nearly equals μ_1. In other words, the input rate to r_2 is equivalent
to the output rate of r_1. When ρ_1 that equals λ_1/μ_1 is less than one, we know
that r_1's performance is amenable to straightforward queueing analysis.[30] If
$\rho_2 = \lambda_2/\mu_2 > 1$, then the queue length between r_1 and r_2 will grow to infinity.
Thus, r_2 represents a bottleneck where through-put backs up; *prior stages slow
down or stop.* Similarly, when $\rho_1 = \lambda_1/\mu_1$ approaches the value of 1, r_1 can be
viewed as a bottleneck in the system because of the extensive delay an arriving
unit must experience.

Now, consider what happens when the λ for any stage approaches zero.
It means that $\rho \to 0$ for that stage, which must then be idle a great percentage
of the time. Such a situation could occur when a preceding facility breaks
down. Without the in-process inventories that it normally produces, all

---

[28] *Ibid.*, footnote 27.

[29] Other alternatives might also have been tried if none of the designs yielded a
satisfactory measure of value.

[30] In the sense that an infinite waiting line does not form at W_1.

succeeding stages will be idled or shut down. Thus, if r_1 is often idle (alternatively stated, waiting is rare at r_1), then p_0 for facility r_1 must be substantial; p_1 will be large, but p_2, p_3, etc., will be close to zero and, therefore, negligible. Note the effect of this in the following formulation, which attempts to calculate an average value for λ_2 based on r_1's performance. $\lambda_2 = (0)p_0 + \mu_1(p_1 + p_2 + \ldots + p_\infty) = (0)p_0 + \mu_1 p_1 + \mu_1(0)$. If the r_1 stage is idle *most* of the time, then p_0 is almost one, and this result decreases λ_2 significantly in relation to μ_1. But, where a waiting line at W_1 occurs with regularity, λ_2 is close to μ_1. A fast machine at the r_1 stage might be idle a great deal of the time and yet, if matched with a much slower machine at the r_2 stage, produce a large W_2 queue.

The system is defined by the λ input rate and the successive processing rates, $\mu_1, \mu_2, \ldots$. Under *equilibrium conditions* (an average performance over the long run, called the *steady state*), each stage can be treated as having the same input rate, λ, as the initial stage. This is an important finding for which a strong proof can be obtained in mathematical terms. Let us examine the probability considerations in a two-stage system.

Let $p(n_1, n_2)$ = equilibrium probability that *total* occupancy is simultaneously n_1 and n_2. The equilibrium relations would be:

$n_1, n_2 > 0$ $(\lambda + \mu_1 + \mu_2)p(n_1, n_2) = \lambda p(n_1 - 1, n_2) + \mu_1 p(n_1 + 1, n_2 - 1)$
$$+ \mu_2 p(n_1, n_2 + 1)$$

$n_1 = 0, n_2 > 0$ $(\lambda + \mu_2)p(0, n_2)$ $= \mu_1 p(1, n_2 - 1) + \mu_2 p(0, n_2 + 1)$

$n_1 > 0, n_2 = 0$ $(\lambda + \mu_1)p(n_1, 0)$ $= \lambda p(n_1 - 1, 0) + \mu_2 p(n_1, 1)$

$n_1 = n_2 = 0$ $\lambda p(0, 0)$ $= \mu_2 p(0, 1)$

solve, subject to:

$$\sum_{n_1, n_2} p(n_1, n_2) \quad = 1.00$$

then $p(n_1, n_2) = (1 - \rho_1)(1 - \rho_2)(\rho_1)^{n_1}(\rho_2)^{n_2}$

For example, if $\rho_1 = 0.6$, $\rho_2 = 0.4$, we derive:

$p(0, 0) = 0.240$ $p(2, 1)\ = 0.144 \times 0.240 = 0.0346$
$p(1, 0) = 0.144$ $p(2, 2)\ = 0.144 \times 0.096 = 0.0138$
$p(0, 1) = 0.096$ $p(0, 2)\ = 0.400 \times 0.096 = 0.0348$
$p(1, 1) = 0.240 \times 0.240 = 0.0576$ $p(1, 2)\ = 0.240 \times 0.096 = 0.0230$
$p(2, 0) = 0.144 \times 0.600 = 0.0864$ $p(n_1, n_2) = $ etc.

From the equation for $p(n_1, n_2)$ we observe that an equivalent form would be derived from two *independent single channel stages*,[31] $p(n_1)p(n_2)$ where $p(n) = (1 - \rho)\rho^n$. Also, we note that each of the stages of such a system at steady state can be treated as having the same input, λ; therefore, $\rho_j = \lambda/\mu_j (j = 1, 2)$.

[31] See p. 163.

For *combinations of stages* in series and parallel (involving multiple servers at each stage), the occupancy formulation would be:[32]

$$p(n_1, n_2, n_3, \ldots n_j \ldots, n_r) = p(0) \prod_{j=1}^{r} \nu(n_j); \quad \begin{cases} \nu(n_j) = \rho_j^{n_i}/n_j! \, ; \, n_j \leq M_j \\[2mm] \quad\quad = M_j^{a_j}\rho_j^{n_i}/M_j! \, ; \, n_j \geq M_j \\[2mm] \quad a_j = M_j - n_j; \, \rho_j = \lambda/\mu_j \end{cases}$$

$$p(0) = \prod_{j=1}^{r} \left\{ \frac{1}{\sum\limits_{n_j=0}^{\infty} \nu(n_j)} \right\}$$

with r stages having M_j channels at each stage, and at each jth stage, $\rho_j = \dfrac{\lambda}{\mu_j}$; the value of μ_j applies to each one of the M stations in the jth stage.

Using Jackson's formulation, a sample problem has been worked out with the hypothetical parametric values shown in Figure 6.16 below:

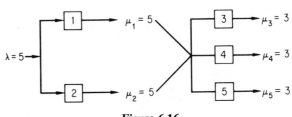

Figure 6.16

The results we have obtained seem reasonable. It is worth noting that this system has quite a high probability of being entirely idle (0.344). There is a small probability of a second stage queue (0.002 + 0.001) and a relatively large probability of a first stage queue.

		STAGE 2			
		0	1	2	3	4
	0	.344	.191	.053	.010	.002
	1	.172	.095	.026	.005	.001
STAGE 1	2	.043	.024	.007	.001	—
	3	.011	.006	.002	—	—
	4	.003	.001	—	—	—

We reiterate the assumption that is made: Within each stage, every server has an *identically distributed exponential service distribution* with a common value

[32] From J. R. Jackson, "Networks of Waiting Lines," *Operations Research*, 5: 4 (August, 1957), 518–21.

of "mu," so the model makes no provision for different capabilities within a stage.

The station design of the system determines the number of stations and their characteristics, $M_j \rho_j$. A well-balanced system with all *single channels* would be one where $p(1, 1, 1, \ldots)$ has a very large value. In the case of multiple servers, the goal would be $p(M_1, M_2, M_3, \ldots, M_r)$. Since small in-process inventories could be tolerated, some higher occupancy probabilities might also be permitted to have large values.

It might be reasonable to balance a system using the heuristic approaches previously described for deterministic t_i's. No one knows which of these might do better, but research on such questions is going on. No matter which heuristic is used, there is always the possibility that the variances of the t_i's will be large enough so that the line will have to be stopped, or one of the other approaches for treated violations of cycle time would be used in a cost analysis. Simulation of the system would normally lead to improvements in balance. But improvement would be obtained faster if it were known heuristically whether there should be high variance and low variance stations or homogeneous mixtures of variances instead. The high variance stations would be human worker groupings, and the low variance stations would be machine dominated stations. Workers at their individual machines might approximate homogeneous groupings. To exemplify the simulation approach, consider two machines A and B arranged in series. Machine A's output is Machine B's input. Assume that A's output is described by the following distribution:

Output Rate	Arrival Interval	Probability	Monte Carlo Number
2 units/min.	0.500 minutes	0.10	00–09
3 units/min.	0.333 minutes	0.50	10–59
4 units/min.	0.250 minutes	0.30	60–89
5 units/min.	0.200 minutes	0.10	90–99

Assume that B's output is described by the following distribution:

Output Rate	Service Duration	Probability	Monte Carlo Number
2 units/min.	0.500 minutes	0.10	00–09
3 units/min.	0.333 minutes	0.30	10–39
4 units/min.	0.250 minutes	0.50	40–89
5 units/min.	0.200 minutes	0.10	90–99

Monte Carlo numbers have been assigned. Then, the simulation consists of choosing successive pairs of random numbers and matching these against the input and output Monte Carlo numbers. The first random number indicates the interval until the next arrival; the second random number tells how long service will take. When a sufficient sample has been drawn, the waiting-line pattern, machine idle time, and other relevant measures of effectiveness of this facility arrangement can be derived. Thus:

Sample Number	Random Numbers	Arrival Interval	Arrival Time	Service Duration	Completion Time
			0.000		
1	05,62	0.500	0.500	0.250	0.750
2	16,44	0.333	0.833	0.250	1.083

Machine B has been idle from 0.750 until 0.833 = 0.083 minutes.

3	83,38	0.250	1.083	0.333	1.416
4	54,96	0.333	1.416	0.200	1.616
5	29,08	0.333	1.749	0.500	2.249

Machine B has been idle from 1.616 until 1.749 = 0.133 minutes.

6	71,57	0.250	1.999		

Machine B is busy so arrival must wait from 1.999 until 2.249. Therefore, at least one unit will be on the waiting line for 0.250 minutes.

7	91,92	0.200	2.199		

A second unit joins the waiting line at 2.199. Therefore, one unit waits from 1.999 until 2.199; then two units wait until 2.249. The random number 57 in the sixth sample indicates a service duration of 0.250. Thus, the sixth arrival begins its service at 2.249, as follows:

6			2.249	0.250	2.499

The seventh arrival waits from 2.199 until 2.499. The random number 92 indicates a service duration of 0.200. Thus:

7			2.499	0.200	2.699
8	03,83	0.500	2.699	0.250	2.949

The system is cleared of waiting units. Up to this time, Machine B has been idle 0.216 minutes; the waiting line has been occupied by a single unit for 0.450 minutes; and by two units for 0.050 minutes.

PROBLEMS

1. Draw a precedence diagram for the flow system in Figure 6.3 representing chocolate manufacture. Since the system is highly complex, it would be useful to analyze only a portion of it.

2. Explain how the flow shop offers the advantages of the division of labor, and present some explanation of why specialization increases efficiency and production rates.

3. A job consists of steps $i = 1, 2, \ldots i, \ldots N$, arranged in some feasible order. Each step takes $t_1, t_2, \ldots t_i, \ldots t_N$, respectively. This is illustrated in diagram I below.

If these steps can be grouped somehow into station systems such as indicated in diagram **II** below:

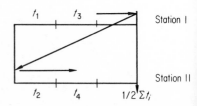

then, twice as many units can be produced each day.

Since two Type I setups in parallel could also double production, we could have either configuration A or B as shown below:

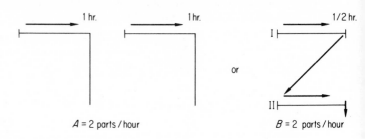

It is necessary to explain what the basic advantages are for each of these approaches to a system of operations.

4. Where a sequence of operation times sum to 6243 sec. and it has been requested that a productivity rate of approximately 10 parts per hour be obtained, examine the nature of station design recognizing the necessity for an integer number of stations. Allow for the fact that reasonable flexibility should be expected in the specification of cycle time.

5. Balance the line for the example in the text, pp. 155–158, for the cases where the number of stations are equal to 2 and 4 using the algorithm of Kilbridge and Wester.

6. What is the probability that a first stage queue will exist for the example that is worked out in the text in connection with Figure 6.15 where $\rho_1 = 0.6$ and $\rho_2 = 0.4$.

Building a ship or setting up a factory is a project.

Question: When will each Apollo mission cease being an individual project and become, instead, a transportation system to the moon?

Question: How does modular building construction practice alleviate project pressures?

Question: When is it reasonable to combine the technologies of flow shop-made walls and floors with job shop assembly methods for constructing buildings?

Question: Given the choice, would you prefer to be working in a flow shop, a job shop, or a project shop?

Question: If you are going to work in a flow shop, why should you care to learn about job shops and project shops?

Question: Do you think the stock market should reward a conglomerate that aggregates flow shops, job shops, and project shops?

The project shop can be viewed as an input-output system where resources and techniques are transformed into the ship, plant, or building that was the project's goal.

Project
Systems 7

Among a variety of individuals' behaviors and life styles, some are more suitable than others for working happily within a flow shop, a job shop, or a project shop. The demands upon the individual are as specialized as the opportunities for accomplishment. In choosing a career, one should bear in mind the fact that transfers between companies dealing in different products, or between functional areas such as production, marketing, and finance are accomplished more readily than transfers between these different types of operations networks.

Still, for analytic purposes, similarities exist that are as important as the differences. For example, the project can be compared to a flow shop which is going to be used only once, i.e., a non-repetitive flow shop. Thinking this way, leads us to emphasize the desirability of (station) balancing the project operations. Similar balance considerations would not be economically reasonable for the job shop; they are for the *project* because of its *investment level*. A job shop, on the other hand, which normally has many small projects that are scheduled to be in process simultaneously, moves closer to being a project shop when *one* particular order, which probably will never be repeated, dominates all others. The network characteristics are similar enough for all three classes of production activities to be intriguing, but sufficiently dissimilar to warrant different planning and control methods.

The Nature of Project Planning

We shall not return again to the flow shop with the same dedication and intensity. The major flow shop problem has been stated in Chapter 6. Now, turning to the project shop, we recognize that some projects are longer term than others. In general, longterm considerations apply to the design of transformation systems for which large investments have been made. Short-term models apply to the design and operation of requisite control systems.

Much of what is done in project planning is dependent upon the most basic levels of methodology—data collection and its simple classification. At the same time, judgment, intuition, know-how, and managerial art play a vital role. Each project has its own characteristic mixture. Every project *requires multiple predictions* of future environments. What will happen in the future is recognized to be conditonal upon the stream of events that precedes the point in time of the project. Great difficulties exist in achieving meaningful predictions; so little is known about making predictions that are successful.[1] The severity of this problem increases as the planning horizon (i.e., interval to project completion) moves further into the future. As the planning interval to project completion decreases, the precision of our predictions improves immensely. Figure 7.1 depicts the way in which the believability of a predic-

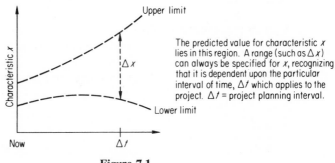

The predicted value for characteristic x lies in this region. A range (such as Δx) can always be specified for x, recognizing that it is dependent upon the particular interval of time, Δt which applies to the project. Δt = project planning interval.

Figure 7.1

A prediction regarding the value of Δx after an interval of time Δt is to be made. If the degree of belief in the prediction is to remain constant, then the limits that define Δx generally will move apart at an accelerating rate.

tion deteriorates as the planning interval increases. Decision-making methods (such as those described in Chapter 4) *can* be used for long-term situations, *but* the degree of belief in their results is another matter. We can unequivocally state that when decision-making methodology is employed for long-term project planning, it means something different to management than when it is being used to resolve short-term problems.

Long-term projects can be so long-term that they deal with the creation and development of a totally new enterprise. They can also treat the diversification and growth of an on-going organization. Accurate anticipation of technological changes is often critical in either case. The viable enterprise will continually assess its productive position with respect to organization, plant facilities, process, product-line, distribution system, technology, and methodology. Whether starting out from scratch or encouraging growth and the diversification of an existent organization, it is widely recognized that only through systems planning can acceptable long-range synthesis be achieved for the project. The following steps are usually basic:

[1] See pp. 249–252 for discussion of the prediction problem.

1. Create a project planning group.
2. State the objectives of the project.
3. Enumerate *everything* that must be done to achieve the project objectives.
4. Sequence the activities listed above.
5. Allocate such resources as materials, equipment, and manpower to each of the proposed project's activities on a *first-pass* basis that is acknowledged to be subject to later revision.
6. Estimate the time and cost required to accomplish each activity and to achieve the objectives of the project.
7. Revise the plan until an acceptable total plan is evolved.
8. Develop an organization that can implement, monitor, and control the project plan.[2]

Using this procedure requires that parts of the project be examined in detail; for example, the research and development (R & D) phase for new product and service development; questions of patentability; design of the project's environment, including plant selection and layout; and the society's reception of the project in both contemporary and "eventual" terms.

Degree of Project Repetition

Project decisions result in actions that are almost never repeated under similar circumstances.[3] Thus, the question of plant location, although it is under regular review should not, by its nature, result in a rapid succession of relocations. The decision to move a plant to a new geographic area is a major commitment that is best described as a *project*. Planning a project will usually encompass long periods of time. When a step is accomplished or a stage completed, it is unlikely to be repeated ever again in the same form. We can say that such planning problems are open-ended. Contrast this with the decision to place an order for materials that are used to make a high-volume item. This kind of decision is made repeatedly. Similarly, scheduling jobs on various machines is a daily or weekly proposition for many companies even though the jobs may continually differ. We can call these last examples closed-cycle planning, which in some ways is almost synonymous with short-term planning. Thus, developing the first spaceship bound for Alpha Centauri is a project, long-term and nonrepetitive; manufacturing these rockets in

---

[2] It should be noted that this is a different kind of monitoring and controlling operation than is required for repetitive situations, such as inventory, quality, and schedule control.

[3] When repeated, they are usually widely separated in time, but time is, after all, a relative matter. In an unstable system, long-term project planning conditions can occur in an interval of days or weeks; in a stable system, short-term project considerations can apply over a period of years.

quantities requires the design of a production system that involves short-term planning and repetitive decisions.

Degree of Project Reversibility

Degree of reversibility is another issue of importance. By the very nature of long-term problems, large investments are required. This means that a mistake can be serious. A company can be competitively crippled or rendered bankrupt. There exist *ruin thresholds* in long-term planning situations where a single decision can push the company across a threshold from which there is no return.[4] Short-cycle decisions, if repeated over and over again, can also result in ruin when the decision repeatedly imposes even a small penalty on the company that continually accrues. But generally, corrective action can be taken so that a new and better decision is substituted for the old one. If it is noticed that rejects, customer returns, back orders, machine idle time, set-up costs, or absenteeism are increasing, steps can be taken to correct these weaknesses long before any one-way doors are passed. Nonreversibility or minor degrees of reversibility characterize long-term planning and distinguish it from the short-term cases.

We can see why the type of methodology employed for long-term projects and short-term operations would be different. Complex methodology lends itself to repetitive decision situations. This is true because repetition in a reasonably stable system provides historical evidence that can be used for forecasting and predicting future events. Also, gradual changes can be introduced because penalties accumulate over a period of time. Experience and judgment, when fed with sufficient relevant information, are more likely to be effective than formal methodologies in the long-term situation where problems tend to be unique and lacking in specific precedence.

What can methodology do for long-term project planning?

1. It can categorize and summarize a mass of information so that it is most useful to the project leader.
2. It can organize the problem area, making all relevant variables explicit so that administrators can communicate with each other about the project.
3. It can be used to produce long-term predictions, especially about critical contingencies.
4. It can be used to structure projects so that details will not be forgotten; actions will be taken in appropriate sequence, intelligent allocations of resources will be made, and control over the development of the project will be insured.

---

[4] The likelihood of reaching such ruin thresholds, given different long-term plans, can be evaluated using simulation.

5. Alternative project strategies can be *tested* by various methods to determine how sensitive a particular strategy is to the relative accuracy of predictions and estimates.

With respect to point two above, long-term decisions are frequently founded upon nothing more than opinion. If differences of opinion exist, the *reasons* for the differences are vital. The reasons may be expressible only in qualitative terms. This in no way permits an executive group to dismiss differences of opinion or to superficially analyze the bases for disagreement. Such reasons are exceedingly difficult to uncover when complex problems are treated. Almost without exception, systematic explication is an absolute necessity.

Belief in the predictions mentioned in point three will tend to be of a low order. Nevertheless, they can be useful as a guide. There is a preference for strategies that promise greater flexibility. That is, other things being equal, decisions that permit corrective actions to be taken at a future date are preferred to decisions that cannot be compromised once they are made. A strategy that can produce a catastrophic outcome—although with very small likelihood—will be avoided, even though it has a higher expected value. This is because the disutility for irreversibility or ruin is likely to outweigh any usual outcome measures. There is also a preference for decisions that promise a reasonably good expected outcome, across a broad spectrum of likelihood conditions. This is so, as compared to decisions that produce an exceptionally good expected outcome across a narrow band of likelihood estimates, where the remaining possibilities are relatively undesirable.

The Gantt Project Planning Chart

Project planning is a most critical function in the life of the organization. A serious error can lead to the destruction of the enterprise. It is, therefore, not surprising that a great deal of effort has been expended on the part of both theoretical and practical workers to define and develop methods that can adequately treat the kinds of problems involved in projects.

One of the oldest methods for coping with the problem of project planning was developed by Henry L. Gantt.[5] It is known as the Gantt Project Planning Chart. The problems that Gantt and production people of his time were faced with had considerably less complexity than the problems that we face today. For his time and the requirements posed by the situation and the environment, the Gantt method was usually sufficient. Today, Gantt's trial and error method provides a means of organizing our thinking, but it does not satisfy the need for approaching optimality in our solutions. Furthermore, this method requires great amounts of trial and error time to handle problems

[5] (1861–1919).

that have an average level of complexity. Except for relatively small operations, the Gantt project planning approach is disappearing, but it has not been forgotten because the methods that Gantt developed form the fundamental basis for developing far more elaborate computer-driven project planning programs. Figure 7.2 pictures the Gantt Project Planning Chart.

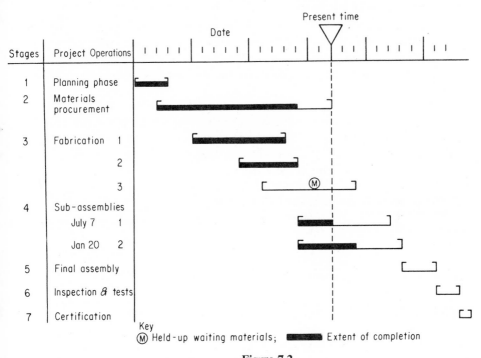

Figure 7.2

The Gantt project planning chart.

The intentions of the approach are two-fold. First, to set down—a priori—the steps, stages, or phases of work that must be followed in order to bring to fruition a nonrepeating, complex systems type of project. Second, to enable the production planner to monitor the way in which the steps of the plan are being carried through, that is, to track the status of the project over a period of time. These two purposes permeate all planning. They can be translated as: (1) making of the plan; and (2) carrying the plan to completion.

Implicit, however, is a third intention or purpose. In all projects there are *technological sequences* that constrain the arrangement of steps with which a project shall be accomplished. Sometimes (rarely) there is no constraint whatever on the arrangement to be used. Usually, the sequence of steps to be taken will be determined at the discretion of the project planner who takes into account the technological restrictions. *From the set of all sensible arrangements we would like to find the best arrangement.* Furthermore, it is quite apparent that certain steps can be accomplished faster or slower, depending upon the number of men who are employed, the kinds of facilities that are used, and so on. The way in which resources are allocated to the various steps of a project will determine how long it takes to accomplish each phase and how much it will cost. Taken together, both of these points spell out the fact that for any given project there is at least one best sequence to be followed and one best allocation of resources to the various stages with respect to a specific set of objectives. The Gantt method requires that the intuition and good judgment of the planner be responsible for approximating such an optimal project plan.

We see from Figure 7.2 that project planning begins by listing the required stages or jobs that are the component building blocks of the project. These must be completed in some specific successive order. The first of these stages is generally a mental process, which we have called the planning phase. Therefore, the construction of the chart itself represents a preplan. In the actual planning phase, adjustments are made to the basic set of steps; the order in which they are to be used; the allocation of resources to each step; and the estimated times for completing each job. As a general rule, we require materials, plant, facilities, labor, power, and so forth. Once these steps have been completed, the planning process moves on to the detailed level of utilizing resources and facilities in order to produce the chosen end result. Elapsed time to complete all the steps is usually considered to be of major consequence. That is where the second purpose of the Gantt chart appears. Running along the top of the chart is a time scale. This time scale can represent a sequence of days, weeks, or months. On the other hand, calendar dates can be associated with the time scale so that it represents a particular point in time. The former approach is useful when estimates of total time involved are required and when the starting point in real time is unknown: for example, if capital has to be raised to finance the project, but no one can estimate when the necessary monetary assets will be acquired. Plans will be launched at the completion of financing, but, since that date cannot be set, only abstract time can be used.

Usually, estimates are supplied for all steps in the process, representing a commitment to a particular pattern for the allocation of resources. When a starting date is specified, calendar time can be used for the time scale. When actual or real time is employed, then it is convenient to use the project plan as a check or control over what is happening so that revisions in the basic plans can be developed as required. Remember, at least in today's world, there are penalties that occur as a result of delays and as a result of poor integration of the planning elements. We cannot afford to have a press shop staffed and waiting with all the necessary tools and dies at their disposal while the research laboratory is still determining the proper materials to be used. Opportunity costs such as these can occur in many different ways.

The left-hand column that lists all the stages is, in fact, the *operational routine* that is required for the design of our system.[6] It is the system's plan. If we make a mistake here we may cost ourselves out of business. It is also essential to bear in mind that a competitor may have a system plan very similar or even destructive to ours. If his is without error; or if he meets his objectives on time and we do not; or if he is able to achieve the completion of various steps in less time than it takes us; or if he is a better planner than we are and finds ways to run various steps in parallel while we sequence them, it is quite likely that we will suffer many penalties as a result of our inadequacies.

Figure 7.2 indicates that a number of the steps can be operated upon simultaneously. To recognize this fact we observe that a number of operations frequently are intersected by any given time line. Often, some fraction of a job must be completed before the next step can begin. Sometimes stages can begin simultaneously. This is all in the project plan, but what about the actuality? The darkened portion of each activity box represents the per cent completion of that operation at a particular point in time. With succeeding days, the dark portion is lengthened until at completion the box is filled. Thus, we have a running record of accomplishments. The course of true anything never runs smoothly. Unexpected situations can arise and these difficulties may delay certain phases of the project. Typically, while some things lag, others spurt, and so some phases are ahead of schedule and others are behind. Project planning is both an a priori and an on-going operation. Constant refinement with new data is called for. Regular review is needed in order to adjust and up-date the running record of accomplishment. In rare instances a new project sequence must be developed because of difficulties that arise. It will be noted that in Figure 7.2 an arrow appears at a particular date on the time scale. That arrow is moved along on a daily or weekly basis, according to the actual date of the review period. In effect it says this is today. We look down at each of the stages and see that the dark bars indicate how much of the job has been completed. Some stages lag; others are ahead of schedule. One has not even begun although according to the plan it should have.

Project Completions and Complexity

At the time of the building of the pyramids some foresight had to be exercised. The project methods that were used have been lost to us, but there

---

[6] This may be the construction of a building, the development of a new product, or the publication of a book, magazine, or catalogue. Some companies, it can be seen, are designed to produce projects.

is no doubt that some planning device was utilized. To begin with, the idea of the project (building a pyramid) was conceived. Then, in logical order, the builders had to specify where to build, what materials to use, what labor would be required at each stage, that is, select the site, clear it, bring in the necessary materials, and then construct the pyramid. If the plan were to be carried through efficiently, then each of the phases would have to dovetail with the others. Otherwise, at various stages, materials might be lacking, or adequate manpower would be missing. The logistics of the problem were enormous. Materials had to be carried from great distances, and at these far away locations quarrying operations had to be set up. Work gangs, therefore, were required at the quarries to transport these giant blocks and, finally, at the building site to construct the pyramid. It is evident that many of these operations coexisted in time, so a general administration was required to see to it that the total operation was properly integrated.

The construction of the pyramids represents an example of the elements involved in planning. But present day systems require coordination and dovetailing to an even greater degree. In the first place, many more factors are involved and second, time losses are now of extreme importance. It is true that if the construction teams on the site of the pyramids were not supplied with sufficient building materials, a penalty was suffered. Enormous quantities of food had to be transported to these locations in order to keep the indentured slaves alive. This effort taxed the resources of the Egyptian kingdoms. However, there was no competition and no legal contracts with penalties to be paid if a job were not completed at a stated time.

Time has become critical in project planning. We recognize that the ability to reach the marketplace as quickly as possible with a new product or service can be a major influence on its success or failure. Excessive planning periods pose the threat of producing an obsolete product if project development takes too long. In the aircraft industry and in the computer field, for example, delay in carrying out a major plan can produce catastrophic results. Figure 7.3 portrays a four-year period to achieve a new car introduction. About two years before public introduction, the major characteristics of the auto design are finalized. If the target date is not met, serious competitive consequences generally can be expected to result.

We have reviewed many elements of project planning using the Gantt chart. We see that it is an effective way of keeping track of what *has* happened in terms of what we thought *should have* happened. It is also an appropriate control and accounting device. But what is lacking? The answer is that there is no suitable way of using the Gantt chart to determine how resources might have been allocated in a superior fashion. For example, if manpower had been shifted from stage five to stage four in Figure 7.2, it might have been possible to accomplish stage four in a shorter period of time. Correspondingly, stage five would have taken longer. Is this better? Another possibility would be to

TIMING SCHEDULE FOR A NEW CAR

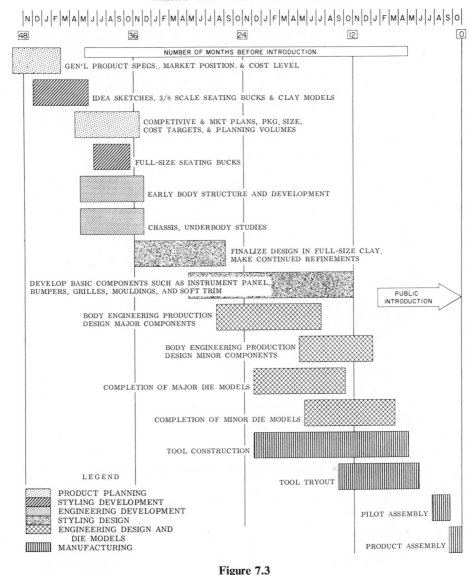

Figure 7.3

Project planning chart for new car introduction. (Courtesy Chrysler Corporation.)

plan certain delays in the system in order to minimize overall delay. We have not succeeded in associating costs with the various phases nor with the overall project planning. Problems that are amenable to the Gantt method cannot possess the kind and degree of complexities of series and parallel operations that are familiar in many present-day project management situations.

Network Methods

The weaknesses of the Gantt Project Planning Chart provided the focus for significant developments in the planning of long-term projects. A method was required that would permit optimal or near-optimal project sequences and utilization of resources. An appropriate methodology was found in the area of *network analysis*. Starting about 1957, a number of different approaches were undertaken at different locations and for different reasons. The reassuring thing about these efforts is the fact that in spite of a variety of names that emerged to label each system, they all turned out to be fundamentally alike. A rash of acronyms, such as those that follow, began to appear in literature devoted to the long-term planning area.

> PERT—Program Evaluation Research Task[7]
> CPM—Critical Path Method
> PRISM—Program Reliability Information System for Management
> PEP—Program Evaluation Procedure
> IMPACT—Integrated Management Planning and Control Technique
> SCANS—Scheduling and Control by Automated Network Systems

The differences between the approaches arise primarily as a consequence of the original job for which the method was developed.[8] All share in common the notion of a critical path, and it is for this reason that we have chosen to call this section critical path methods (CPM's). It is the only sensible choice of a name if the descriptive power of a name is of consequence. As for the remaining labels, PERT is the most familiar of all the above to managers, and we will, therefore, discuss the PERT variant of critical path methods.

Three steps are required to utilize these network analytic tools.

1. All the elements, jobs, steps, tasks, activities, and so on that are required to bring the project to fruition must be detailed.
2. A sequencing order must be determined that is based on technological and administrative dependencies. In other words, all necessary sequential constraints must be made explicit in terms of *precedence*.

---

[7] Later, the name was changed to Program Evaluation and Review Technique.

[8] PERT was developed by the U.S. Navy Special Projects Office in conjunction with Booz, Allen, and Hamilton. It was one of the first of the network methods and was used for the Polaris project.

CPM was developed by James Kelly and Morgan Walker in conjunction with E. I. duPont de Nemours and Company and Remington Rand at about the same time as PERT. CPM was used to plan the construction of a plant. Various distinctions are attributed to each of these methods and to others as well, but the similarities are far more important and will be accented by us in assessing the capabilities of project network methods in general.

3. The time (and cost) to perform each task, activity, and so on must be
    estimated.

Milestones and Precedence

When all this information has been assembled, a PERT network can be
constructed. Figure 7.4 presents an example of such a network. Activities are
arranged in sequential order with technological precedence constraints being
followed by other less rigid requirements.

PROPULSION FLOW CHART

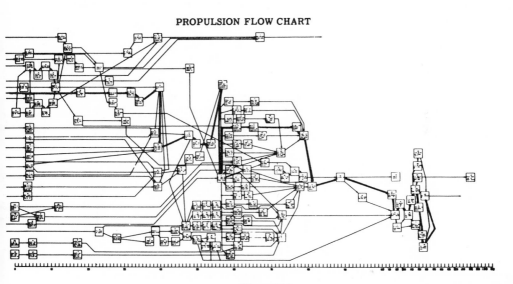

Figure 7.4

An example of a complex PERT network. [From R. A. Niemann and R. N. Learn, "Mechanization of the PERT System on NORC," *Technical Memorandum No. K-19/59, U.S.
Naval Weapons Laboratory* (Washington, D.C.: U.S. Government Printing Office, 1960].

Detail is essential for the success of the CPM's. Activities cannot be overlooked without adversely affecting the project. Various estimates are required
for each activity, with the result that for normally complex projects, a gigantic
amount of information is generated. Fortunately, computer programs have
been developed for treating this great detail of network systems.

The project is composed of an ordered series of activities (represented
as arcs) that are not repeated. As each arc of the project graph is completed,
it is *removed* from the network. The same kind of network changes apply to
the job shop, but in the job shop, new arcs are also being added constantly,
whereas the number of project network arcs eventually goes to zero. Unlike

continuous flow systems, such as a refinery, the project starts and stops; and because of the large asset base involved in one run through, project accomplishments are viewed as being independent of the rest of the system. Because the investment in project activities is usually large, project network methods have been developed and are used to achieve a kind of (station) balance for the system as well as a method for direct project schedule control. We must note that, at best, these network methods have only an indirect influence on project design.

The Gantt Project Layout Chart was a forerunner of present network models. Figure 7.5 shows how the Gantt-type chart converts to the precedence structure of a project network. The usual Gantt chart has been modified by the inclusion of milestone events to signify dependencies between the starting and stopping of activities.

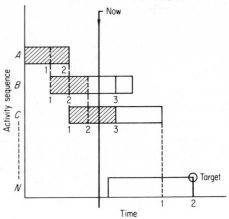

Gantt-type layout chart with milestone indicators

(Numbers under bars are milestone events which trigger the release of other activities.)

Milestone precedence chart

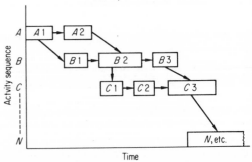

Figure 7.5

The shaded areas of the bars show actual completions. We note that activity
B requires expediting,[9] *C* is ahead. Perhaps some manpower could be traded
from *C* to *B*. As we shall show, similar schedule controls have been developed
for precedence networks. On the Gantt chart, milestone events such as *A1* and
A2 can be represented by separating the activity elements into new rows. These
milestones are important when they signify that the start of a new stage is
dependent upon the completion of prior ones. The fundamental weakness of
the Gantt chart is that it lacks clear-cut precedence dependency information.
The precedence network reveals all such dependencies, whereas the interpretation of Gantt chart dependencies is ambiguous.

Activities on Arcs and Nodes

The first step in all project planning is to list the necessary activities; the
second step is to fully describe precedence relations of predecessors and successors. The directed graph can be drawn in two ways: *first* (the more usual)
place activities on arcs (we can abbreviate AOA), then the network nodes
represent events of both completion and starting; *second*, put activities on
nodes (called AON). The variants are shown in Figure 7.6.

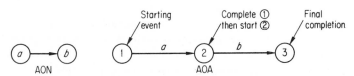

Two activities, *a* and *b*, where *a* is directly followed by *b*.
The start of *a* is 1; the completion of *b* is 3.

Figure 7.6

Each approach has its advantages. With AON it is easier to represent network
precedence dependencies. Dummies (described below) are not required. If
AOA is used, the perception of time can be more direct (i.e., related to the
length of the activity arc). Further, the AOA network format emphasizes
completion events as nodes (milestones for multiple activities), and this approach has advantages for schedule control. AOA is the most familiar network form, employed by both PERT and CPM, thereby paralleling most
network algorithms programmed for computers.

In planning a project, some activities go through a cycle of steps and
then repeat themselves many times at increasing levels of detail. Cycles of
activities would also be characteristic of control system functions. Cycles are

---

[9] This now well-known term "expedite" was first used by Henry Kaiser in connection
with the critical ship-building schedules of World War II.

not permitted in these networks. All project networks are *extensive*—no looping back is allowed. As shown in Figure 7.7 below, the sequence—test, repair, test—must be structured as Test 1 → Repair → Test 2, etc.

Consider the cycle:

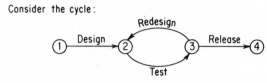

this must be treated as follows:

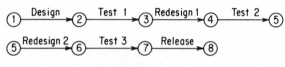

Figure 7.7

PERT networks must be developed in extensive form.

AOA Networks

We observe many different arrangements of activities and events. Some are arranged in series, meaning that the first activity must be finished before the succeeding one can begin. In other cases, several arrows emanate from a single event circle. These activities can parallel each other. Whenever materials, parts, subassemblies, or particular procedures come together for a new activity, an event circle must be used to signify that the previous activity has been completed. Proceeding in this way it is not difficult, although it may be tedious, to lay out the relevant network of activities and events.

Estimates of Time

Having listed project activities and sequenced them according to precedence relationships, estimates of how long it will take to complete an activity are needed. Ultimately, we want to find out the earliest possible date that the project can be completed. A popular method is to employ three estimates of the Beta frequency distribution (shown in Figure 7.8) as follows: an optimistic estimate, a; a pessimistic estimate, b; and an estimate of what is most likely, m. The three estimates are combined to yield an expected activity time (t_e). An *approximation* of the expected value of a Beta distribution is $t_e = \frac{1}{6}(a + b) + \frac{2}{3}(m)$. The variance of the Beta distribution is *approximated* by $\sigma^2 = [\frac{1}{6}(b - a)]^2$.

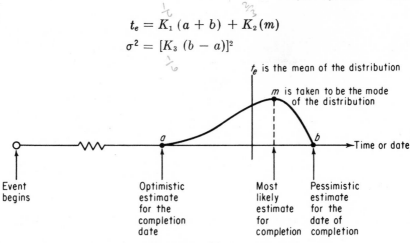

$$t_e = K_1 (a + b) + K_2 (m)$$
$$\sigma^2 = [K_3 (b - a)]^2$$

t_e is the mean of the distribution

m is taken to be the mode of the distribution

Time or date

| Event begins | Optimistic estimate for the completion date | Most likely estimate for completion | Pessimistic estimate for the date of completion |

Figure 7.8

A possible distribution for the elapsed time estimates. (There is no assurance that the three estimates a, m, and b fall at these positions on the time scale of the distribution.) For the Beta distribution, estimates for K_1 and K_3 of $\frac{1}{6}$, and K_2 of $\frac{2}{3}$ are often used.

The use of the Beta at least satisfies the need for a unimodal distribution (single peak) that does not have to be symmetrical and that has positive valued, finite end points. There are many who prefer a single estimate for the expected time. Similarly, variance can be estimated directly.

Dummy Activities

If two or more nodes have the same input arcs and the same output arcs, then using AOA procedures, it will be impossible to distinguish between the nodes (Figure 7.9).

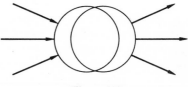

Figure 7.9

A dummy activity, which takes zero time, resolves this problem as shown in Figure 7.10.

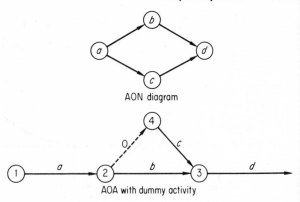

AON diagram

AOA with dummy activity

Figure 7.10

When two or more activities have some, but not all, their inputs in common, as in Figure 7.11,

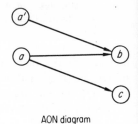

AON diagram

Figure 7.11

the use of a dummy resolves the problem of representation. See Figure 7.12.

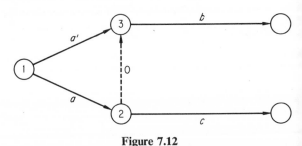

Figure 7.12

Critical Path

The critical path is the longest total time route through the network. Therefore, it defines the earliest possible time for project completion. There is at least one continuous path from the beginning to the end of the network, the sum of whose activity estimates is greatest. Network methods are designed to identify this longest time route through the system that is called the critical path. This is not easy to accomplish without an efficient computing algorithm (and usually a large computer) because of the size and complexity of most present-day projects.

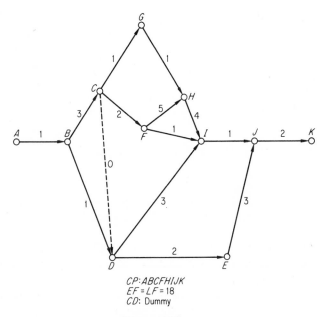

CP: ABCFHIJK
EF = LF = 18
CD: Dummy

Figure 7.13

In Figure 7.13, the critical path is *ABCFHIJK*. With this knowledge we determine that the completion time for the project is eighteen time units. (We note that a dummy activity, CD, associated with a zero time is used to signify that activities starting at node *D* may not begin until both *BC* and *BD* are completed.) In theory, it is easy to find the critical path, but in fact, a large project network poses great computational burdens.[10] A means of tracking all possible total paths is required. Ford-Fulkerson algorithms to determine maximum flow and longest network routes as well as linear programming routines have been programmed for a variety of computer systems.[11] The character of the algorithmic approach frequently used is revealed by the following discussion.

Obtain a cumulative total (Σt_e) for each node in the network moving

---

[10] Often, the total network is partitioned along the critical path into subsets at varying levels of aggregation for control purposes. These are called summary levels.

[11] See pp. 222–224.

along from one activity to the next according to indicated precedence relations. At each node, derive an early finish value, EF (also called T_E). This
cumulative total gives the earliest expected clock time at which each activity
can be completed. Note: when a node is reached through several arcs carrying
different cumulative EF values, accept the largest value of EF. See Figure 7.14.

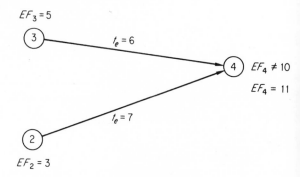

Figure 7.14

All further accumulation uses this largest number. Upon reaching the last
node in the network, the final EF value represents project completion. If several end nodes exist, the one having the largest EF value determines project
completion. That EF value measures maximum cumulative time and, therefore, sets the earliest possible finish time for the project.

The critical path can now be found by inspection. It is that set of activities for which $\Sigma t_e = \text{Max } EF$. But such tracing is, at best, an awkward procedure, especially for machine computation. So, instead, we work backward
in the network from the maximum completion time.[12] Another benefit of this
backward calculation is that it enables us to measure project *slack*. Slack is
the leeway (in time) afforded on noncritical paths. In other words, slack is the
amount of time that estimates along a specific network path can slip without
delaying the completion time of the project. From the max completion time
(Max EF) we subtract all t_e values leading into that node. This gives late
finish times, LF (also called T_L), which is the latest possible completion time
for an activity without its changing the project completion time. When two
or more arcs converge on a single node in backward movement, accept the
smallest value of LF and continue from there on with that number. See Figure
7.15. Now, at each node, LF minus EF measures slack or $(T_L - T_e)$. *Those
nodes where the difference is zero are on the critical path.*

[12] See the linear programming solution pp. 222–224.

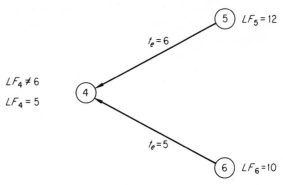

Figure 7.15

The Effect of Variance on Project Completion

Our understanding of maximum completion time can be augmented by a stochastic interpretation if a summed variance measure is used. Often the assumption is made that the activities are independent so that $\sigma^2{}_{\text{project}} = \Sigma \sigma^2{}_{\text{activities}}$ is allowed. The sum of the variances of a number of consecutive estimates of sequenced *independent* activities measures the variance of the total sequence. For example, if three estimates, t_{e_1}, t_{e_2}, and t_{e_3}, are made, each of them having a particular variance measure σ_1^2, σ_2^2, σ_3^2, then the variance of the sum of these estimates is given by $\sigma_1^2 + \sigma_2^2 + \sigma_3^2$. This relationship is depicted in

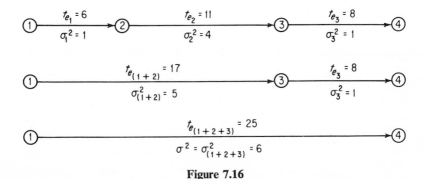

Figure 7.16

The variance, σ^2, of combined estimates is equal to the sum of the variances of the individual estimates of *independent* activities.

Figure 7.16. Also, a series of Beta distributions for individual activities tend to combine to form a Normal distribution for the sum of the individual activities. Thus, project completion time is an expected value of Max $\overline{EF}$

with variance $\Sigma_i \sigma_i^2$. Using Normal tables, probability statements can be made such as, there is 99 per cent probability that the project will be completed before some time t.

A Critical Path Example

The steps previously described are shown in Figure 7.17.

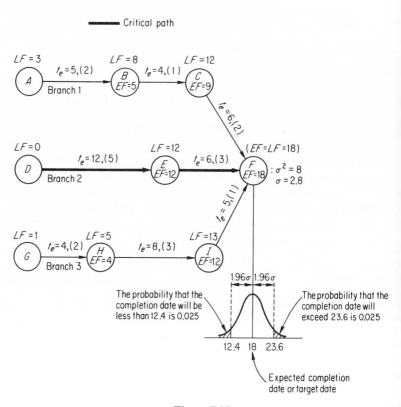

Figure 7.17

An abstract PERT network with hypothetical estimates supplied for t_{e_i} and σ_i^2. (The variance is shown within parenthesis.)

The last node in the network (called F) represents project completion. It bears a value that is the measure of the maximum cumulative time required to perform the longest time sequence of activities in the network. Examination of Figure 7.17 will show that the middle path dominates the cumulative total that has been carried forward. This branch requires the longest elapsed time for completion and is called the *critical path* of the system. Starting with the largest *EF*, which resulted from the middle path, we now move backward through the network. Successively, we subtract from each previously accepted *LF* value all expected elapsed activity times, t_e, that immediately precede it in the network. These values, called *LF*, are assigned to the event nodes that precede their respective activities. The difference, $LF - EF$ (or $T_L - T_E$) can now be obtained for each event node. It describes the amount of *slack* that exists at each node. As expected, at every node of the critical path, which, by definition dominates the system, $LF - EF = 0$. In general, a path has as much slack as the time required to complete that path is *less* than the time required to complete the project stages that make up the critical path. For our example, the top path has the most slack, and the third path has a small amount.

This finding is not trivial. It would be wasteful to do any expediting on either the first or third branches. The critical path cannot be allowed to slip. Therefore, the major emphasis of project control should be assigned to the critical path. This network system is called PERT/TIME. Time is the fundamental dimension of the planners' objectives. With this in mind, the variance measure can now be used even though this measure is not a mathematically rigorous one. We sum the variances, proceeding along the critical path. Thus, for the final event, which signals completion of the job, we can obtain not only the expected time for project completion but also an estimate of the variance around this expected value. Figure 7.17 above shows a distribution with both tails cut off at the 1.96σ limit. Each tail contains the probabilities of an event occurring approximately twenty-five out of one thousand times.[13] The upper tail contains long completion dates. The lower tail contains short completion dates. Thus, moving 1.96 standard deviations in either direction gives us a range of times for job completion within which there is a 95 per cent probability that the actual completion date will fall. Stated another way, we have determined an earliest and latest project completion date using a 1.96-sigma criterion. The computations can be handled in tabular form as in Table 7.1.

[13] Assuming that a Normal distribution applies, we would have:

Number of Standard Deviations for the Specification of the Range	Probability that the Actual Time Falls Within the Specified Range
1.00σ	68.0%
1.64σ	90.0%
1.96σ	95.0%
3.00σ	99.8%

Table 7.1   Computations Associated with PERT Network (in the general form utilized for computer systems)

Event	EF	LF	Slack (LF − EF)	Cumulative Variance
F	18	18	0	8
C	9	12	3	3
I	12	13	1	5
E	12	12	0	5
B	5	8	3	2
H	4	5	1	2
G	0	1	1	0
D	0	0	0	0
A	0	3	3	0

PROBLEMS

1. The Delta Company manufactures a full line of cosmetics. A competitor has recently brought out a new form of hair spray that shows every sign of sweeping the market and destroying Delta's position in the market. The sales manager asks the production manager what the shortest possible time would be for Delta to reach the market with a new product packed in a new container. The production manager sets down the following PERT structure:

Activity	Initial Event	Terminal Event	Duration
Design product	1	2	
Design package	1	3	
Test market package	3	5	
Distribute to dealers	5	6	
Order package materials	3	4	
Fabricate package	4	5	
Order materials for product	2	4	
Test market product	2	7	
Fabricate product	4	7	
Package product	7	5	

(a) Construct the PERT diagram.

(b) Estimate the durations that you think might apply in a reasonable way.

(c) Determine the critical path.

(d) Neither the sales manager nor the production manager are satisfied with the way the project is designed, but the production manager insists that because of the pressure of time the company will be forced to follow this plan. In what ways does this plan violate good practice?

(e) By trading-off resources would it be possible to reduce your critical path time?

2. In the example above, it was suggested that a reasonable method be employed for estimating the durations of activities. Now, employ the parameters of the Beta distribution. Discuss the relevancy of this latter approach in terms of the comparison between your first estimates and these new ones.

3. Draw up an appropriate PERT diagram for a football play.

4. Draw up an appropriate PERT diagram for moving a piano.

5. Draw up an appropriate PERT diagram for dictating a letter.

6. Draw up an appropriate PERT diagram for having a group of three people solve the following problem as rapidly as possible with full accuracy:

$$\frac{(10.314)^4}{(6.501)^2} + \frac{(3.241)^3}{(1.008)^5}$$

7. For the Gantt-type chart shown in Figure 7.18, construct the appropriate PERT network.

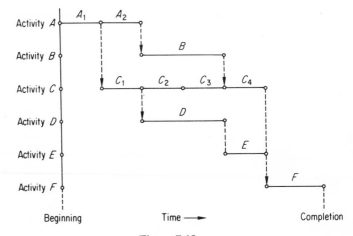

Figure 7.18

8. Find the critical path for the network in Figure 7.19, and use the variance measures (shown in brackets along each arc) to determine the earliest and latest project completion date with a three-sigma criterion.

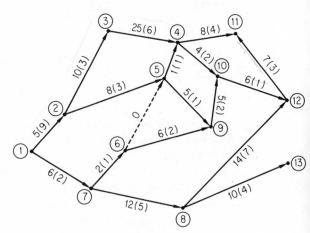

Figure 7.19

Time is critical in project planning, but cost is seldom to be ignored. Most often reallocations of manpower can succeed in improving the project target date, its upper variance limit, and the distribution of slack potentials in the network. Many considerations turn out to offer additional degrees of freedom.

Additional
Project 8
Systems Concepts

The existence of slack can be interpreted to imply that a better arrangement of resource utilization might be found. Any alteration of the project network that reduces the length of the critical path would decrease the amount of slack that has been observed in other paths of the network.

Trading-off Resources

A reasonable approach would be: (1) to obtain and employ *new resources* toward this end, and (2) to *shift resources*, wherever possible, from the paths having the largest amount of slack to the critical path. The first possibility should only be considered after the second possibility has been studied. There is no point investing additional funds before the present investment level has been brought as close to full efficiency as it can be.

Considering the second alternative, let us assume that the length of time it takes to complete each activity is linear in relation to the number of men employed on the job. We shall assume that the skills required are totally interchangeable between operations. We could then bring the entire network into better balance by shifting manpower resources from slack branches to the critical path. This has been done for the network in Figure 8.1, and the results are shown in Figure 8.2.

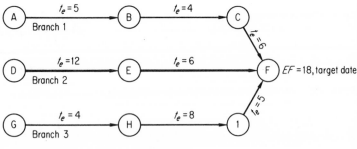

Figure 8.1

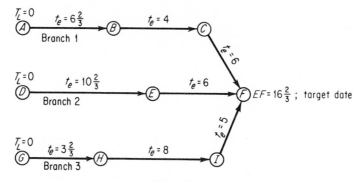

Figure 8.2

A perfectly balanced PERT network is achieved by trading off resources. We have permitted the resources to be fractioned and have used the following balancing equations: (1) for the first and second branches, $15 + x = 18 - k_1x$; (2) for the first and third branches, $15 + x = 17 - k_2x$; (3) where $k_1 + k_2 = 1$; (4) then: $x = 5/3$, $k_1 = 4/5$, $k_2 = 1/5$; (5) and x = the amount of time added to the first branch, k_1x = the amount of time subtracted from the second branch, k_2x = the amount of time subtracted from the third branch. All branches are critical paths—there is no slack in the system. The target date has been improved by $1\frac{1}{3}$ time units.

Shifting Critical Paths

MacCrimmon and Ryavec have shown that variability in the network can cause critical path estimates to be in grave error.[1] This is because any critical path can have competition from relatively "near-critical" competitors. Large t_e variance associated with relatively independent parallel paths can create serious alternative critical path potentials. Then, estimates of project completion dates can be off by a significant percentage. Network simulation can be used to illustrate this characteristic quite readily.

We shall describe the simulation procedure applied to the project network presented in Figure 8.3.

[1] K. R. MacCrimmon and C. A. Ryavec, "An Analytic Study of the PERT Assumptions," *Operations Research*, 12: 1 (January–February, 1964), 16–37. Also, A. R. Klingel, Jr., "Bias in PERT Project Completion Time Calculations for a Real Network," *Management Science*, 13: 4 (December, 1966), B194–B201.

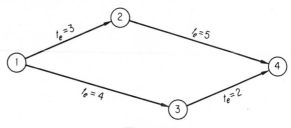

Figure 8.3

The critical path is 1, 2, 4 with $EF = LF = 8$. But, arcs 1-2 and 1-3 have t_e's that are random variables distributed as follows:

	Arc 1-2			Arc 1-3	
t_e	Prob (t_e)	M.C.	t_e	Prob (t_e)	M.C.
2	0.05	00-04	2	0.20	00-19
3	0.90	05-94	3	0.10	20-29
4	0.05	95-99	4	0.40	30-69
	1.00		5	0.10	70-79
			6	0.20	80-99
				1.00	

The Monte Carlo numbers (M.C.) are allocated in the exact proportions of the probability values of the distributions. Random numbers (which by definition favor no one number over another) are then drawn and matched against the assigned Monte Carlo numbers. See Table 8.1. In Figure 8.4, the random numbers (RN) result in one reverse—and one tie—of the critical path.

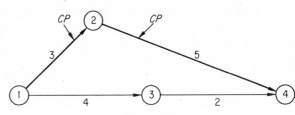

Figure 8.4

	M.C. Numbers		M.C. Numbers		M.C. Numbers		M.C. Numbers
t_e	1-2	t_e	2-4	t_e	1-3	t_e	3-4
2	00-04	2		2	00-19	2	00-99
3	05-94	3		3	20-29	3	
4	95-99	4		4	30-69	4	
5		5	00-99	5	70-79	5	
6		6		6	80-99	6	

Table 8.1   Table of Random Numbers

63854	69664	11034	00172	84723	35206	45956	32311	97825	68517
96268	11860	83699	38631	90045	69696	48572	05917	51905	10052
03550	59144	59468	37984	77892	89766	86489	46619	50263	91136
22188	81205	99699	84260	19693	36701	43233	62719	53117	71153
63759	61429	14043	49095	84746	22018	19014	76781	61086	90216
55006	17765	15013	77707	54317	48862	53823	52905	70754	68212
81972	45644	12600	01951	72166	52682	97598	11955	73018	23528
06344	50136	33122	31794	86423	58037	36065	32190	31367	96007
92363	99784	94169	03652	80824	33407	40837	97749	18364	72666
96083	16943	89916	55159	62184	86208	09764	20244	88388	98675
92993	10747	08985	44999	36785	65035	65933	77378	92339	96454
95083	70292	50394	61044	65591	09774	16216	63561	59751	78771
77308	60721	96057	86031	83148	34970	30892	53489	44999	18021
11913	49624	28510	27311	61586	28576	43092	69971	44220	80410
70648	47484	05095	92335	55299	27161	64486	71307	85883	69610
92771	99203	37786	81142	44271	36433	31726	74879	89348	76886
78816	20975	13043	55921	82774	62745	48338	88348	61211	88074
79934	35392	56097	87613	94627	63622	08110	16611	88599	02890
64698	83376	87524	36897	17215	74339	69856	43622	22567	11518
44212	12995	03581	37618	94851	63020	65348	55857	91742	79508
82292	00204	00579	70630	37136	50922	83387	15014	51838	81760
08692	87237	87879	01629	72184	33853	95144	67943	19345	03469
67927	76855	50702	78555	97442	78809	40575	79714	06201	34576
62167	94213	52971	85974	68067	78814	40103	70759	92129	46716
45828	45441	74220	84157	23241	49332	23646	09390	13032	51569
01164	35307	26526	80335	58090	85871	07205	31749	40571	51755
29283	31581	04359	45538	41435	61103	32428	94042	39971	63678
19868	49978	81699	84904	50163	22625	07845	71308	00859	87984
14294	93587	55960	23149	07370	65065	06580	46285	07884	83928
77410	52195	29459	23032	83242	89938	40510	27252	55565	64714
36580	06921	35675	81645	60479	71035	99380	59759	42161	93440
07780	18093	31258	78156	07871	20369	53947	08534	39433	57216
07548	08454	36674	46255	80541	42903	37366	21164	97516	66181
22023	60448	69344	44260	90570	01632	21002	24413	04671	05665
20827	37210	57797	34660	32510	71558	78228	42304	77197	79168
47802	79270	48805	59480	88092	11441	96016	76091	51832	94442
76730	86591	18978	25479	77684	88439	35112	26052	57112	91653
26439	02903	20935	76297	15290	84688	74002	09467	41111	19194
32927	83426	07848	59327	44422	53372	27823	25417	27150	21750
51484	05286	77103	47284	05578	88774	15293	50740	07932	87633
45142	96804	92834	26886	70002	96643	36008	02239	93563	66429
12760	96106	89348	76127	17058	37181	74001	43869	28377	80923
15564	38648	02147	03894	97787	35234	44302	41672	12408	90168
71051	34941	55384	70709	11646	30269	60154	28276	48153	23122
42742	08817	82579	19505	26344	94116	86230	49139	32644	36545
59474	97752	77124	79579	65448	87700	54002	81411	57988	57437
12581	18211	61713	73962	87212	55624	85675	33961	63272	17587
00278	75089	20673	37438	92361	47941	62056	94104	45502	79159
59317	31861	62559	30925	23055	70922	47195	29827	68065	95409
59220	42448	70881	33687	53575	54599	69525	76424	98778	10459
00670	32157	15877	87120	13857	23979	38922	62421	03043	19602

RN	t_e 1-2	RN	t_e 2-4	Σ	RN	t_e 1-3	RN	t_e 3-4	Σ	Results
63	3		5	8	84	6		2	8	Tie CP's
85	3		5	8	72	5		2	7	✓
46	3		5	8	33	4		2	6	✓
96	4		5	9	52	4		2	6	✓
64	3		5	8	06	2		2	4	✓
11	3		5	8	45	4		2	6	✓
03	2		5	7	95	6		2	8	Reverse CP
40	3		5	8	63	4		2	6	✓
01	2		5	7	23	3		2	5	✓
72	3		5	8	11	2		2	4	✓
Avg	2.9		5			4		2		

(✓ means CP unchanged)

Another PERT Network Simulation

As another illustration with some additional factors added, the performance of the network in Figure 8.5 with variable t_e's is simulated.

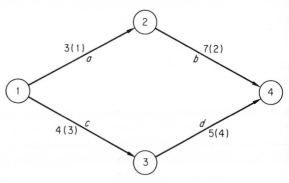

Figure 8.5

The standard deviation is shown in parenthesis. In this case, let us use random normal numbers. Such random numbers are based on the fact that a cumulative normal distribution can be drawn (Figure 8.6) and analyzed to provide a table of normal random numbers (Table 8.2). There are one hundred equal divisions on the *y*-axis, and each has an equal likelihood of being drawn by random numbers, 00-99.

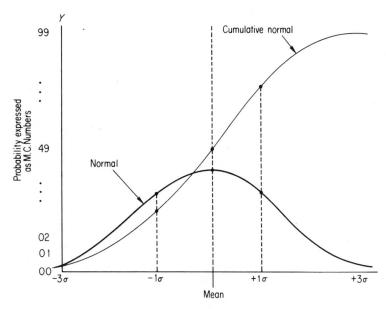

Figure 8.6

To understand the use of this figure, note that 68 per cent of the numbers on the *y*-axis must lie between $\pm 1\sigma$. Therefore, when we draw a *random number*, we read a value of $\pm k\sigma$, and it is $\pm k$ that we are sampling. Table 8.2 has made the conversion from random numbers to random normal numbers for us.[2] It should be noted that a figure, such as Figure 8.6, can be constructed for any form of distribution. Correspondingly, a table, such as Table 8.2 can be constructed for any distribution.

Say that the numbers are drawn as follows, using Figure 8.6.[3]

[2] From C. W. Churchman, R. L. Ackoff, and E. L. Arnoff, *Introduction to Operations Research* (New York: John Wiley & Sons, Inc., 1957), p. 181.

[3] This number is read from Figure 8.6. For the equivalent, using Table 8.2, assume that the top rows of the table are:

	(1)	(2)	(3)	(4)	(5)	(6)	(7)
1.	0.460	−0.170	−0.800	1.750	−1.640	−0.360	0.170
2.	1.000	. . . etc.					

Table 8.2   Random Normal Numbers*

$$\mu = 0, \sigma = 1$$

	(1)	(2)	(3)	(4)	(5)	(6)	(7)
1	0.464	0.137	2.455	−0.323	−0.068	0.296	−0.288
2	0.060	−2.526	−0.531	−1.940	0.513	−1.558	0.187
3	1.486	−0.354	−0.634	0.697	0.926	1.375	0.785
4	1.022	−0.472	1.279	3.521	0.571	−1.851	0.194
5	1.394	−0.555	0.046	0.321	2.945	1.974	−0.258
6	0.906	−0.513	−0.525	0.595	0.881	−0.934	1.579
7	1.179	−1.055	0.007	0.769	0.971	0.712	1.090
8	−1.501	−0.488	−0.162	−0.138	1.033	0.203	0.448
9	−0.690	0.756	−1.618	−0.445	−0.511	−2.051	−0.457
10	1.372	0.225	0.378	0.761	0.181	−0.736	0.960
11	−0.482	1.677	−0.057	−1.229	−0.186	0.856	−0.491
12	−1.376	−0.150	1.356	−0.561	−0.256	0.212	0.219
13	−1.010	0.598	−0.918	1.598	0.065	0.415	−0.169
14	−0.005	−0.899	0.012	−0.725	1.117	−0.121	−0.096
15	1.393	−1.163	−0.911	1.231	−0.199	−0.216	1.239
16	−1.787	−0.261	1.237	1.046	−0.508	−1.630	−0.146
17	−0.105	−0.357	−1.381	0.360	−0.992	−0.116	−1.698
18	−1.339	1.827	−0.959	0.424	0.969	−1.141	−1.041
19	1.041	0.535	0.731	1.377	0.983	−1.330	1.620
20	0.279	−2.056	0.717	−0.873	−1.096	−1.396	1.047
21	−1.805	−2.008	−1.633	0.542	0.250	0.166	0.032
22	−1.186	1.180	1.114	0.882	1.265	−0.202	0.151
23	0.658	−1.141	1.151	−1.210	−0.927	0.425	0.290
24	−0.439	0.358	−1.939	0.891	−0.227	0.602	0.973
25	1.398	−0.230	0.385	−0.649	−0.577	0.237	−0.289
26	0.199	0.208	−1.083	−0.219	−0.291	1.221	1.119
27	0.159	0.272	−0.313	0.084	−2.828	−0.439	−0.792
28	2.273	0.606	0.606	−0.747	0.247	1.291	0.063
29	0.041	−0.307	0.121	0.790	−0.584	0.541	0.484
30	−1.132	−2.098	0.921	0.145	0.446	−2.661	1.045
31	0.768	0.079	−1.473	0.034	−2.127	0.665	0.084
32	0.375	−1.658	−0.851	0.234	−0.656	0.340	−0.086
33	−0.513	−0.344	0.210	−0.736	1.041	0.008	0.427
34	0.292	−0.521	1.266	−1.206	−0.899	0.110	−0.528
35	1.026	2.990	−0.574	−0.491	−1.114	1.297	−1.433
36	−1.334	1.278	−0.568	−0.109	−0.515	−0.566	2.923
37	−0.287	−0.144	−0.254	0.574	−0.451	−1.181	−1.190
38	0.161	−0.886	−0.921	−0.509	1.410	−0.518	0.192
39	−1.346	0.193	−1.202	0.394	−1.045	0.843	0.942
40	1.250	−0.199	−0.288	1.810	1.378	0.584	1.216

* This table is reproduced in part from a table of the RAND Corporation.

	RN	k of kσ (see footnote [3])	Applied to Activity	σ	Value	Branch Completion Time
1st set	68	+0.46	a	1	3 + 0.46 = 3.46	
	43	−0.17	b	2	7 − 0.34 = 6.66	10.12
	21	−0.80	c	3	4 − 2.40 = 1.60	
	96	+1.75	d	4	5 + 7.00 = 12.00	13.60 (CP)
2nd set	05	−1.64	a	1	3 − 1.64 = 1.36	
	36	−0.36	b	2	7 − 0.72 = 6.28	7.64
	57	+0.17	c	3	4 + 0.51 = 4.51	
	84	+1.00	d	4	5 + 4.00 = 9.00	13.51 (CP)
	.					
	.					
	.					
	etc.					

So the bottom path cd of Figure 8.5, which is not on the critical path ab, has turned out to be significantly greater than critical in both trials.

MacCrimmon and Ryavec examined the behavior of PERT networks which have random variables for the operation times.[4] They found that under certain conditions the critical path based on estimates of the mean would readily shift to other paths. Accordingly, the project manager is well-advised to be skeptical about formal statements concerning critical paths. Among other things, they reported that, if one network path is clearly longer than any other path, the critical path calculation will be correct most of the time. But, when various paths exist that are roughly of the same length, with few common activity arcs, then shifts can occur; so the critical path is identified incorrectly a great percentage of the time. At the same time, the more slack that each noncritical path has, the smaller will be the error. It is also evident that a critical path having minimum variance will be overthrown often by noncritical paths having large variance. When there are many parallel paths, the errors in identifying the critical path will increase especially when the paths do not share a large number of common activities.

As a result of the considerations described above, many project managers have begun to use the notion of a *critical activity* rather than that of a critical path. This is particularly applicable when the conventional critical path is unlikely to contain a majority of the most critical activities. Further, it is unreasonable to assume that all successive events in the project network are independent. Especially for technical reasons, this assumption is unacceptable. When difficulties arise because an engineering principle does not apply at a specific arc ij, then this engineering problem is likely to get transferred to successive arcs in the network. Psychological dependencies can pro-

[4] MacCrimmon and Rayavec, *op. cit.*

duce similar dependency problems—the contagiousness of slow downs, low morale spreading pervasively, etc. Simulation can take this into account and represent it, if the dependency effects are known. (For example, by choosing one random number for both a and b and another random number for c and d, a specific kind of dependency is represented.)

Using Monte Carlo procedures, different activities will appear on the *shifting* critical paths of a system. A *criticality index* can be defined as the percentage of time that an activity appears on the critical path. An activity with a zero index presents no problem, nor does one that rates at, say, 90 per cent. But what about an arc ij that registers at 60 per cent? How much attention should be paid to that arc?

PERT/COST

The use of the critical path method has been extended in a number of different ways. Of interest to project planners, in addition to the time objective, is the desire to maximize the quality of the work or the performance characteristics of the system. Perhaps the most significant additional objective is to minimize cost, and relationships of cost and time have received considerable investigation. Various time-cost systems have been developed, and others are being developed to attempt to resolve this problem, which we recognize as one of conflicting multiple objectives. The PERT/COST system starts in the same way as does PERT/TIME. We construct the representative network of activities and events. We shall use the hypothetical network shown in Figure 8.7.

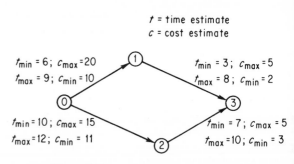

t = time estimate
c = cost estimate

$t_{min} = 6$; $c_{max} = 20$
$t_{max} = 9$; $c_{min} = 10$

$t_{min} = 3$; $c_{max} = 5$
$t_{max} = 8$; $c_{min} = 2$

$t_{min} = 10$; $c_{max} = 15$
$t_{max} = 12$; $c_{min} = 11$

$t_{min} = 7$; $c_{max} = 5$
$t_{max} = 10$; $c_{min} = 3$

Figure 8.7

A PERT/COST network with hypothetical data. For minimum cost, 0-2-3 is the critical path, with $EF = 22$ and cost $= 14$. The slack for 0-1-3 is $LF - EF = 5$. Assume that EF must be not greater than 20. The best COST/TIME ratio applying to the critical path is associated with activity 2-3 (see Figure 8.8). Making the required change, we obtain: $t_{23} = 8$; $c_{23} = 4\frac{1}{3}$. This gives 0-2-3 as the critical path with $EF = 20$ and cost $= 15\frac{1}{3}$. The slack for 0-1-3 is $LF - EF = 3$.

In this case we must develop at least two different estimates for each branch. These are: (1) a minimum time estimate and its cost; and (2) a minimum cost estimate and its time.

Figure 8.8 shows the way in which COST/TIME factors might be related for all activities of a network.

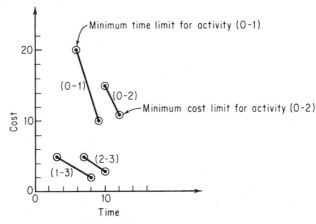

Figure 8.8

Some representative COST/TIME relationships where the weak assumption is made that linearity prevails over the specified range. The end points are assumed to be limits.

First, the minimum cost estimate is used for each activity, and the critical path is determined for those data. The result will then be a completion date that is based upon minimum cost requirements for completing the project. This completion date and the length of time required to complete the project under minimum cost conditions may be too great to be tolerated. Accordingly, alternative times, requiring greater costs, can then be substituted for chosen minimum cost activities along the critical path.

In this way, the critical path can be shortened until such time that: (1) another path becomes critical; or (2) a satisfactory compromise with the original critical path is achieved. As a rule of thumb, we make compromises for those activities along the critical path where the ratio of increasing costs for the activity with respect to decreasing time for the activity is smallest. As a reasonable trade-off rule, we select that *critical path activity* where: Δ COST/Δ TIME is smallest; then the next biggest ratio is used; and so on until a satisfactory compromise between time and cost is achieved. This means that the first change that is made promises the greatest decrease in time for the cost of achieving this decrease. We must note that the problems of critical path shifting based on the variance measures (as previously discussed) are not considered by this approach and, therefore, this approach cannot be entirely satisfactory. With attention to such problems, the PERT/COST method can be modified to meet the particular requirements of a given project. It is not presented as an optimizing technique. Instead, it is a logical attempt to utilize reasonable trade-offs between cost and time—where they count—in order to obtain an approximation to an optimal result.

Designing the Systems Output

Let us refer to the PERT charts, Figures 8.9, 8.10, and 8.11. Although these present a totally hypothetical model of a production plan, nevertheless, they give a fair representation of what must be accomplished and provide a likely sequence of steps to be followed. The plan lends itself to three divisions that are useful although arbitrary. The first can be called product and service development, which includes both research and development (R & D). The second division might be termed the process development stage. The third division is the actualization phase of the plan leading to the inception of production operations.

New product or service development starts with a collection of ideas; some are chosen for further study (Activities 0-1). Various ways of converting ideas into applications are investigated in the laboratory (Activities 1-2.) Promising alternatives must then be checked for factors such as their production feasibility—in a technological sense—production costs, financing requirements, and possible prices and qualities related to marketability. In addition, the human factors concerned with both product and process are considered from various points of view, including safety (Activities 2-3). From the alternatives, one or more possibilities are selected for further study because of encouraging evaluations. Product design is begun in earnest (Activities 3-4). At event 4, a basic decision is reached concerning the product or service design. This begins the developmental phase. Only occasionally do we return to research for help and guidance (Activity 4-5).

Product development requires product engineering (Activities 4-B), which includes further cost specification, the beginning of intensive market research (Activity 4-A), and the inception of plant and facilities specification (Activities 4-C). At this point we reach a boundary between product and process development. It is not that the product development phase is finished; rather, it is integrated with the further specification of the process.

Service development requires many of the same steps. Administrative outputs, for example, should be designed and checked in various ways to verify that they are serving the intended market—before the office process is installed. A steamship line must design its output, that is, how much cargo, how many passengers, what kind of cargo, and what kind of service to passengers. How else can the process be designed? The facilities must be developed so that they can provide the a priori specified services.

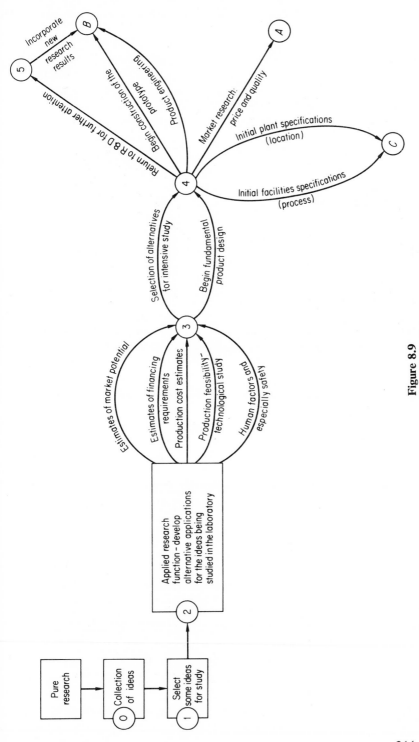

Figure 8.9

Model PERT network for the design of a production system:
Phase I—Product and service development.

211

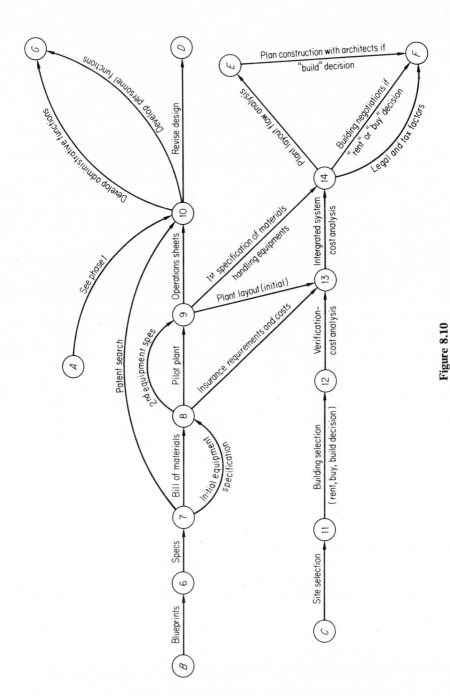

Figure 8.10

Model PERT network for the design of a production system:
Phase II—Process development.

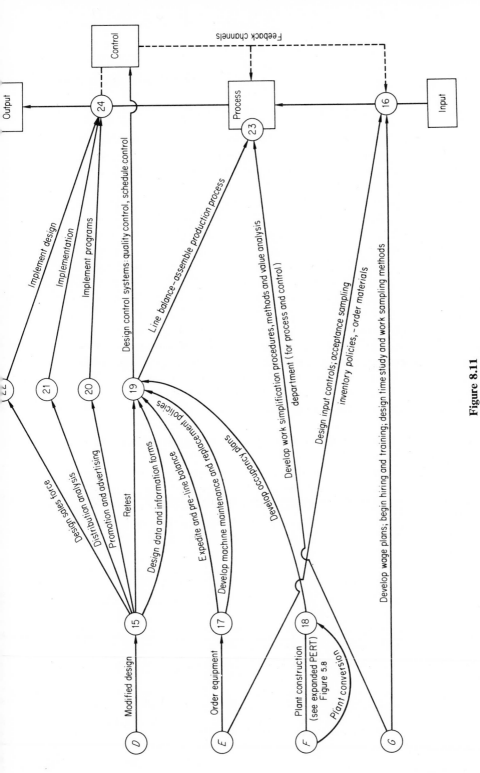

Figure 8.11

Model PERT network for the design of a production system:
Phase III—Actualization.

213

Research and Development (R & D)

Pure research[5] is a generator of ideas. There are many other ways that ideas come into being, but pure research findings are equivalent to *new* knowledge. Thus, they form a base from which creative thinking can be launched. There is no substitute for this foundation. Pure research is the "launching pad" for applied research. The laboratory efforts of applied research are devoted to exploiting pure research results. On the whole, only large companies can afford to engage in substantial amounts of pure research. The investments are large, the risks are significant, and the payoff is usually many years away. At the same time, when the payoff is realized, it is frequently very substantial.

Pure research allocations by industrial firms in the U.S.A. represent a small per cent of the total funds allocated for industrial research and development. The percentage is small because applied research, with relatively immediate commercial advantages, is the major preoccupation of industry. Although this orientation provides short-term benefits, in the long run it results in economic loss because important opportunities are lost.

After pure research comes applied research and then development. As we move in sequence through these phases, a greater amount of management participation is required. Usually, very close coordination is expected during the development phase. We can literally define "development" by this involvement with the management of operations.

R & D is a function of such critical importance to management that we must achieve familiarity with it. Every idea forces its own demands in terms of time, money, and talent required to bring it to fruition. Understanding laboratory work is not a requirement, but laboratory procedures are the technological components of the system. We should also note that R & D is applicable to both the service and product function. For example, hospital procedures should be under constant reevaluation; information retrieval is an area of research that is profoundly affecting library procedures; telephone facilities are a matter of social concern.

Some ideas work out; others will not. All R & D work does not succeed. Presumably, if talented people are employed in research, a greater chance of success exists. But it is not easy to define what constitutes talent. The use of psychological tests has shown no sign of pinpointing the requisite characteristics for ingenuity and creativity. However, as we proceed along the path from pure research to applied research and then to development, the kind of creativity that is required becomes less difficult to discuss. Also, the

[5] The best definition of "pure" research is that it is not "applied," that is, it has no immediate or obvious utility for increasing man's comfort or providing physical satisfactions or increasing his control over the environment. Pure research can, therefore, be equated to the pursuit of knowledge for the sake of knowledge.

ability to predict the time and effort that will be required to complete a project improves. Accordingly, it is easier to prepare development budgets than pure research budgets. Budget appropriation and control for R & D is one of the most difficult decision areas in an organization. Because the outcome of pure research is essentially unknowable beforehand, the question of how much to allocate to which projects is not answered by trivial viewpoints. The intangible elements dissipate as we move toward and through development stages.

R & D estimates of time and cost are crucial matters. It has been found that schedules of time and cost for applied research and development are subject to a "slippage factor." Figure 8.12 compares proposed and actual results for the length of time required to complete a project—in terms of manpower engaged on the project. Generally, this pattern holds; the amount of manpower *scheduled* to be used increases over a given period of time, then remains fairly constant at a plateau, and ultimately falls off quite sharply when the job is near completion. Unfortunately, actual results seldom conform to the planned schedule. It takes significantly longer to complete the job than had originally been anticipated, and it takes more manpower. The interesting thing about this is that *positive* slippage almost always occurs, and characteristically, it is somewhere in the neighborhood of 50 per cent. Comparable slippage occurs for cost estimates.

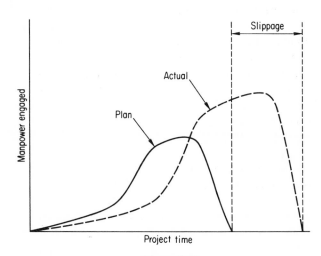

Figure 8.12

Typical manpower build-up and phasing out project.

One would think that knowledge of the characteristic slippage rate would allow project managers to make necessary allowance for both time and cost slippage in their estimates and, in this way, formulate an exact estimate of the actual time and cost required to complete the project. In other words, project estimates could be automatically increased by some known percentage to give modified predictions. Experience has shown, however, that the modified predictions will not be met. The actual results will slip by approximately the same percentage as before, but this time the slippage must be applied to the modified predictions. Consequently, self-deception doesn't work. The project manager ends up with a worse situation than if he had left well enough alone, because the actual time to complete the job is increased. The uniformity of slippage appears to confirm the fact that *fundamental behavioral factors* are involved.

There is one possibility for dealing with this situation, although under many circumstances it is difficult to achieve. Separate the planning and estimating functions from the research and development teams so that the latter are unaware of the fact that a modified prediction has been made. Under these circumstances it should be possible for the planners to match predictions with actual results. For example, an estimate of two months is made to complete a particular job, although management is, in fact, planning the project on the basis of a three-month period. If habitual slippage of 50 per cent operates, then the job should be completed in three months, and the *"hidden schedule"* will be met all along the line.

This procedure has built-in dangers. Should the research and development team guess or sense that management has a "hidden schedule," then the three-month period might slip to a 4.5-month period. If they believe that management had allowed for this when it had not, then double slippage might occur. We must recognize that slippage is not usually the result of a conscious process. Once research and development teams begin to doubt the intentions and honesty of project management and come to feel that they are victims of a *bluff*, then confidence in management deteriorates, causing a severe reduction in the team's effectiveness.

To further explain why slippage occurs, it is useful to consider project phases. At the beginning of a project, the desire to excel in fulfilling the project's requirements causes project personnel to take many more steps than they would permit at a later point when the pressure of a completion date is upon them. As time to achieve completion grows shorter, the project participants dispense with frills and special investigations. They begin, too late, to follow the original schedule. Finally, a crash program may have to be undertaken.

Recent work by Norden[6] indicates that the development function does give rise to certain patterns of cycles that are relatively independent of the nature of the project. These results make it appear likely that manpower re-

[6] Peter V, Norden, "Resource Usage and Network Planning Techniques," *Operations Research in Research and Development*, Burton V. Dean, ed. (New York: John Wiley & Sons, Inc., 1963), pp. 149–69. Also, see an up-dated version of this material in "Useful Tools for Project Management," *Management of Production*, M. K. Starr, ed. (Middlesex, England: Penguin Books, 1970), pp. 71–101.

quirements, time, and costs can be forecast with reasonable precision. Norden has found that five basic subcycles underlie most development projects.[7] These are shown in Figure 8.13.

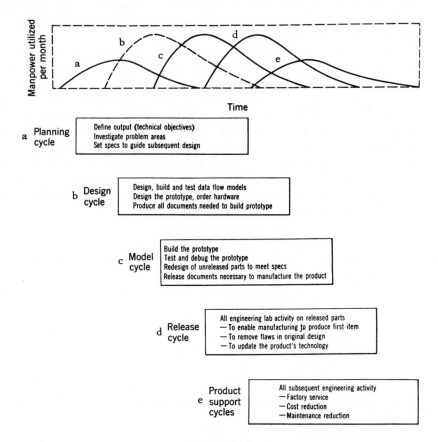

Figure 8.13

Typical manpower pattern of an engineering project. From: Peter V. Norden, "Resource Usage and Network Planning Techniques," *Operations Research in Research and Development*, Burton V. Dean, ed. (New York: John Wiley & Sons, Inc, 1963)., p. 160.

[7] In the life-cycle model, curves are fitted to successive cycles of project components. Norden has explained that the cycles do not depend on the work content of the project but seem to be a function of the way that engineers undertake technological development problems. Each cycle appears to be well-described by:

$$y' = 2Kate^{-at^2}$$

where y' = manpower utilized each time period,

K = total cumulative manpower utilized by the end of the project,

a = shape parameter (governing time to peak manpower),

t = elapsed time from start of *cycle*.

Also, see Chapter 15, pp. 472–473.

The productivity of indirect labor (such as clerical, administrative, and supervisory positions) is difficult to define and measure, but it is almost impossible to measure the productive output of a research and development team. Yet, this is a crucial measurement because of the large and increasing quantities of money that are being spent on research. Consequently, even a theoretical analysis would be helpful.

Let us define productivity as some number of units of project accomplishment per period of time. Underlying this definition is the belief that research tasks can be divided into units of accomplishment. Generally, we would like to maximize the productivity of the research team so that the job can be completed in the minimum possible time. To do this, we must utilize an appropriate number of research workers. But at the same time, there is a basic objective to complete the project at minimum cost. Thinking in these terms, an interesting result has been observed. Namely, the most efficient team size with respect to cost will frequently require a smaller group of research workers than would be needed for maximum group productivity. In other words, group size for minimum cost is smaller than for minimum completion time of the project.

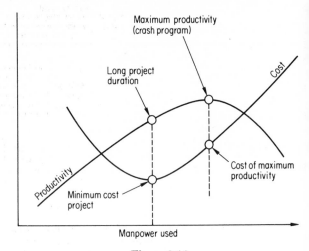

Figure 8.14

Cost and productivity relations underlying project cost/time analysis.

Figure 8.14 illustrates the point. The abscissa represents the number of workers engaged on the project. The ordinate is measured in two ways: productivity and cost. As stated, minimum cost occurs before the point of maximum productivity is reached. Cost is determined by the number of workers engaged on the project and the time required to complete the job. Thus, if we have two men earning $12,000 per year and it takes them six months to complete the job, then the total cost of the project is $12,000. On the other hand, if four men are employed, each earning $12,000 per year, and it takes them four months to complete the job, then the cost of doing this job is $16,000. Assume that one man requires eighteen months at a cost of $18,000. Minimum cost occurs with two workers.

How is productivity affected? Because the four-man group finishes the project in four months, it must be higher on the productivity curve than the two-man group. Let us assume that the four-man group produces the maximum number of accomplishments per hour. This is the team size that can finish the job first. More or less than four men will have a somewhat lower overall team productivity. With a little reflection, it is obvious that two men would be likely to have something more than half the productivity of four men. So, for our specific example, the four-man team can accomplish the job in the minimum amount of time but at a higher total cost as compared to the two-man team.

Which result do we want? If our objective is to minimize time, then four men are indicated. If our objective is to strike some efficient balance between the cost of doing the job and the time for completion, something less than the maximum productivity group size is indicated. A mathematical demonstration of the relations of minimum cost and minimum time for R & D project groups follows.

1. Assume that the project is divisible into A units, for example, units of per cent completion. Then $A = 100$ accomplishment units per project.
2. Let P_M = the number of accomplishments per day with M team members; that is, the daily productivity of M workers.
3. Then, let T_M = the total number of days required to complete the project with M workers; and $T_M = A/P_M = 100/P_M$ days per project.
4. We assume a simple productivity function:

$$P_M = f(M) = aM - bM^2 - e$$

where, in general $a \gg b \gg e > 0$ (condition Ω).

5. Maximum P_M is equivalent to minimum T_M; this occurs when $M_T = a/2b$. Thus: $dP_M/dM = a - 2bM = 0$.
6. Now, let the total cost of the project with M team members be C_M, and

$$C_M = kMT_M$$

(k is the wage rate in dollars per man-day).

7. Then, $C_M = 100kM/P_M = (100kM)/(aM - bM^2 - e)$.
8. C_M will be minimized when:

$$\frac{dC_M}{dM} = \frac{kAP_M - \dfrac{dP_M}{dM}(kMA)}{(P_M)^2} = 0$$

from which it will be found that min C_M occurs when: $M_C = \pm\sqrt{e/b}$.

9. Then, $M_C < M_T$, when $\pm\sqrt{e/b} < a/2b$, or $e < a^2/4b$, or $4be < a^2$.
10. This holds most of the time because of condition Ω.

This result is exceedingly important when we are dealing with sizable R & D allocations. Frequently, on government contracts, great urgency is attached to the program, and the objective is—first and foremost—to obtain maximum productivity and, thereby, minimize the total time to accomplish the job. There is a natural tendency to overestimate manpower requirements. The result of this can be quite misleading. We note that productivity drops off when more than an optimal number of individuals are involved on the job. This can be explained in a number of ways, including use of the old adage: "Too many cooks spoil the broth." For those who prefer a logical explanation: Productivity falls off above a certain group size because of communication and supervision problems. The number of information links that tie a group together increases as the square of the number of individuals working on the job. Organizational hierarchy and communication channels will reduce this number somewhat. But, in general, if an individual is added to a group of n members, then n new links are added to the information net. Thus, with an n-man team, there are $n(n - 1)/2$ information links. For example, with three individuals we have $3(2)/2$, or 3, information links. Now, adding one individual to the group, we have $4(3)/2$ equals 6 information links. The additional individual has increased the number of communication channels by three. Let us take this one step further and add another person to the group of four. We now have $5(4)/2$ equals ten communication channels—an increase of four.[8]

Overstaffing is a consequence of many basic urges of management. It is only natural to think that a "massive" effort can produce results faster than a minimum cost effort. As we have seen, it is frequently true that minimum cost will not coincide with minimum completion time. But the "massive" effort is likely to overshoot the mark and result in both project delay and additional costs. Our discussion should signal care when preparing research and development budgets. Further, in synchronizing development programs with production, greater forecast accuracy can be obtained if attention is paid to the relationships of time and cost. When preparing estimates for the PERT analysis, the above points should be kept in mind.

Let us briefly examine what can happen if management overestimates manpower requirements. Assume that a group size is chosen that is somewhat larger than would be required for maximum productivity. As a result of this choice, project costs will be greater than was expected and the job takes longer than the minimum time. The result is a bit paradoxical. The manager of development believes that he has underestimated manpower requirements. He attributes the additional cost to the additional time required to complete the

---

[8] It will be noted that we have divided by two, thus treating all two-way communication channels as though they were one. The factor of two is not critical. What is significant is the existence of an n^2 term in the formulation. Thus, the number of communication channels increases as the square of the number of individuals participating in the group.

project. The next time that a similar job must be undertaken on a tight schedule he employs even more people. This pushes the results even further to the right on our curve in Figure 8.14. Productivity is even lower; a longer time is required to accomplish the job; and costs are greater than ever. Instead of correcting his error, the manager is led further astray.

Cost and time estimates are predicated on historical records. Thus, over time, the budgets increase. More and more manpower is allocated to each job. We see that a form of Parkinson's Law[9] is in operation. Parkinson observed that work expands to fill up time available for its completion, which is another way of saying that people create work that would not otherwise be done. Then, when available man-hours are fully committed, we require more people to handle the new jobs that have been created. The process is self-perpetuating. When we couple this with the productivity paradox that we have just described, we can understand why many organizations have experienced great difficulties in controlling expenditures on large projects. Let us, therefore, try to sum up some basic rules that apply to the management of R & D programs.

1. The project objectives must be clearly stated. They should be reduced to the simplest possible terms. Unless this knowledge is shared by all participants, the R & D effort is bound to encounter many reverses. Much time will be spent finding out what everyone is trying to do.

2. Expertise is required to outline the steps of the program or project, which is supposed to deliver the specified results. Accurate time and cost estimates are essential. The slippage problem cannot be overlooked.

3. Duplication should be eliminated. However, under some circumstances *parallel path* research is warranted. Namely:

a. If a major conflict of ideas exists and there is great urgency to achieve the objectives, then it is sometimes reasonable to allow two or more groups to work independently on the different approaches. Preplanned evaluation procedures should exist so that as soon as it is possible the project can be trimmed back to a single path.

b. At the very inception of a program—during what might be called the paper and pencil, exploratory stage—parallel path research is frequently warranted and can be encouraged. All possible approaches should be considered and evaluated before large commitments of funds have been made.

c. We previously mentioned urgency. Let us now be more specific. When the risk of failure is high, for example, survival is at stake, or when the payoff incentive is sufficiently great with respect to the costs of achieving it, then parallel path research and development can be justified for as long a period of time as is deemed necessary to achieve the objectives.

d. In almost all other cases, duplication should be avoided.

[9] C. N. Parkinson, *Parkinson's Law* (New York: Houghton Mifflin Company, 1957).

4. R & D management in close liaison with line management should carefully evaluate the steps and phasing of the program. An optimum organization should be set up to handle the transitions between phases.

5. One person should be responsible for all major technical decisions. He must understand the nature of the problem, both the technological and the production constraints. Multiple decision makers tend to produce chaotic conditions.

These factors provide a basis for coordinating research, development, and the production function. Each situation has its own unique circumstances. Each deserves its own special treatment. Nevertheless, some generalizations apply and to the extent that it was possible, we have outlined these considerations.

Using LP to Find the Critical Path[10]

For analyzing and controlling large projects, a variety of PERT-type computer programs exist. After the network activities are designed and the time estimates supplied, either network or LP methodology can be used to identify the critical path and the existence and location of slack. Since we have discussed (in the previous chapter) the network approach due to Ford and Fulkerson, it will be profitable now to examine the LP method even though it is seldom the preferred approach.

For simplicity, we will use the symbols: $X_i = EF_i$ and $Y_i = LF_i$. There will be $i = 1, 2, \ldots, m$ event nodes signaling the start or completion of an activity, i.e., a *milestone*. In this application of LP, our objective is to minimize X_m. (We can let $X_1 = 0$ although this is not essential.) The relevant constraints are the set of $X_j \geq X_i + t_{ij}$ for all ij activity arcs. The nature of this constraint is to force the proper ranked ordering of the nodes. The objective of a minimum value for the last node will insure that it is the earliest possible completion time, given the preceding ranked ordering of the nodes. Thus, in Figure 8.15, the EF_i's are shown in boxes. These values are forced by the constraints:

	Route 1, 2, 4, 5	EF_i	Route 1, 2, 3, 5	EF_i	Route 1, 3, 5	EF_i
CONSTRAINTS:	$X_2 - X_1 \geq 2,$	2;	$X_2 - X_1 \geq 2,$	2;	$X_3 - X_1 \geq 1,$	1
	$X_4 - X_2 \geq 2,$	4;	$X_3 - X_2 \geq 3,$	5;	$X_5 - X_3 \geq 4,$	5
	$X_5 - X_4 \geq 3,$	7;	$X_5 - X_3 \geq 4,$	9;		

The constraints along Route 1, 2, 3, 5 specify that the minimum value for

[10] For a complete explanation of LP applications see J. D. Wiest and F. K. Levy, *A Management Guide to PERT/CPM* (Englewood Cliffs, N.J.: Prentice-Hall, Inc., 1969), pp. 68–73.

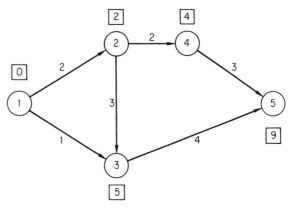

Figure 8.15

X_m is 9. These are the dominating constraints. Because we minimize (X_m), the total is pushed to nine (the smallest feasible solution). For example, if our network had consisted of only the three nodes 1, 2, and 3, then X_m would have been five at node three. In this particular case, the answers can be derived by observation, but generally, networks are far too complex to be resolved in this way. (Wiest and Levy reported that programs exist for solving networks with over two thousand arcs and one thousand nodes.)

The late occurrence times LF_i or Y_i are obtained for each node, using the same kind of constraints as before, namely: $Y_j - Y_i \geq t_{ij}$. But in this backward moving analysis we wish to minimize $mY_m - \overset{m-1}{\underset{1}{\Sigma}} Y_i$. Consider the network in Figure 8.15. We know that the previously derived value of X_m must equal Y_m; therefore, $mY_m = 5 \times 9 = 45$. Now, let us turn to $\overset{m-1}{\underset{1}{\Sigma}} Y_i$. The sum of the constraints up to $m - 1$ for the Route 1, 2, 3, 5 are $2 + 5 = 7$. The $\overset{m-1}{\underset{1}{\Sigma}} Y_i$ for Route 1, 2, 4, 5 is $2 + 4 = 6$, and for Route 1, 3, 5, it is 1.

Then, for each route, the value of $mY_m - \overset{m-1}{\underset{i}{\Sigma}} Y_i$ is given below.

$$
\begin{aligned}
&\text{Route 1, 2, 4, 5} && 45 - 6 = 39 \\
&\text{Route 1, 2, 3, 5} && 45 - 7 = 38 \text{ (CP)} \\
&\text{Route 1, 3, 5} && 45 - 1 = 44
\end{aligned}
$$

The node labeling for LF_i is specified by Route 1, 2, 3, 5, which is the desired minimum; it is also the critical path. Thus, the values of $Y_5 = 9$, $Y_3 = 5$, $Y_2 = 2$, and $Y_1 = 0$ are evident. As for Y_4, it must be equal to six because $EF_4 = Y_m - t_{45} = 9 - 3 = 6$. The critical path slack of zero and other paths' slack values are directly obtained from $LF_i - EF_i$ or:

$$Y_1 - X_1 = 0 - 0 = 0$$
$$Y_2 - X_2 = 2 - 2 = 0$$
$$Y_3 - X_3 = 5 - 5 = 0$$
$$Y_4 - X_4 = 6 - 4 = 2$$
$$Y_5 - X_5 = 9 - 9 = 0$$

The critical path must lie along the zero path; node four can slip by two without affecting the target date of the project.

Using LP for PERT/COST Analysis[11]

As we have explained, although t_e or t_{ij} (the estimated length of the directed arc between node i and node j) often is given as a single estimate, it is always known that t_{ij} can be changed, except in rare instances, by altering the cost allocation. In general, $t_{ij} = f(c_{ij})$ but frequently, we hypothesize that a *linear* relationship exists; thus: $c_{ij} = a_{ij} - b_{ij}t_{ij}$. The symbols are best explained by consulting Figure 8.16.

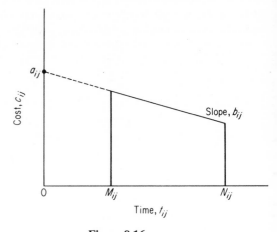

Figure 8.16

We let t_{ij} fall between N_{ij}, which is *normal time*, and M_{ij}, which is *crash time*, i.e., Constraint 1: $M_{ij} \leq t_{ij} \leq N_{ij}$. The total cost of the project is $\Sigma\Sigma c_{ij} = TC$, and, therefore, $TC = \Sigma\Sigma(a_{ij} - b_{ij}t_{ij})$. The objective is to minimize TC, which clearly is equivalent to Maximize $\Sigma\Sigma b_{ij}t_{ij}$. Then, additional constraints are required. Not unexpectedly, the same type of LP constraints as we previously encountered apply, i.e., Constraints 2: $X_j - X_i \geq t_{ij}$.

---

[11] *Ibid.*, pp. 74–75.

A project interval, T, that is feasible must be set—it can be achieved if all activities along the critical path are "crashed." If T is set too tightly, then there will be no room for trade-offs, and only one solution, every activity crashed, will prevail. This is hardly the intent of the study. Therefore, it is expected that T can be satisfied even when some of the activities are not "crashed." The problem is resolved by determining how much to spend on each activity so that $X_m - X_1 \leq T$, at *minimum cost*. (As before, X_1 is usually taken to be zero.) Different values of T can be tested and the associated value of minimum TC noted as a means of agreeing upon an acceptable interval, T. This LP problem is described by Wiest and Levy as large and requiring a considerable amount of computer time to solve. They state that it is often more efficient to solve such problems using network flow theory.

It is easy to extend the LP format to the nonlinear case of monotonic convex COST/TIME relations.

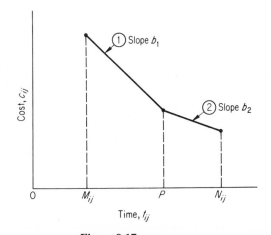

Figure 8.17

A monotonic, convex cost function.

These convex curves can be partitioned with linear approximations, as shown in Figure 8.17, where the partition occurs at point P. Here, two variables emerge (t_{ij1} and t_{ij2}) where there had been only one before (t_{ij}). If the curve had been approximated with three linear segments, there would have been three variables. The first new variable is constrained by $M_{ij} \leq t_{ij1} \leq P$ *and the* second by $0 \leq t_{ij2} \leq N_{ij} - P$. Note that because of its time-cost slope, t_{ij2} cannot be put into the LP solution as an active variable with positive values until t_{ij1} has been fully utilized (up to the amount P). This selection sequence must occur because $b_1 > b_2$ and, therefore, $b_1 t_{ij1}$ will be put into the solution before $b_2 t_{ij2}$, given the objective, Maximize $\ldots + b_1 t_{ij1} + b_2 t_{ij2} + \ldots$. The constraints must also be modified to include: $X_j - X_i \geq t_{ij1} + t_{ij2}$ and $t_{ijk} \geq 0$, for all k partitions of each ij.

When nonconvex cost functions exist, as in Figure 8.18, integer programming may be used to find optimal, time-cost trade-offs. We note that a

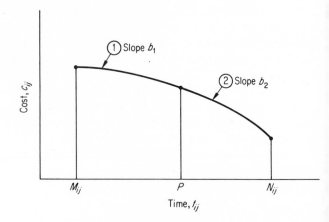

Figure 8.18

Monotonic concave function.

concave cost function has $b_1 < b_2$; therefore, t_{ij2} will be put into the solution first, if we proceed as we previously did. This result is impossible because the time along arc ij cannot start at (say $P = 3$ hours) without the prior time (of 0 to 3) having first been assigned.

Job Shop Projects

A special class of project control exists that warrants attention. For example, when sufficient stress is placed upon a particular project in the *job shop* but it does not deserve the kind of treatment that critical path models provide, then the line of balance technique (LOB) may be in order.[12] As in critical path analysis, this approach begins with a network of milestone events. The LOB network uses the completion or delivery of readily identifiable work components as these events. Project activities occur between the numbered nodes one through six in Figure 8.19. The operations that involve processing and assembly are associated with time estimates for completion. At each node an inventory of in-process parts must be available. The LOB will tell whether as of a particular date that inventory is sufficient to meet contract obligations for each type of event that the project includes.

A graph of cumulative production (inventory and shipments) as

[12] In 1941, G. Fouch at the Goodyear Company developed the LOB procedures. They were employed by the U.S. Navy during World War II and extensively since that time.

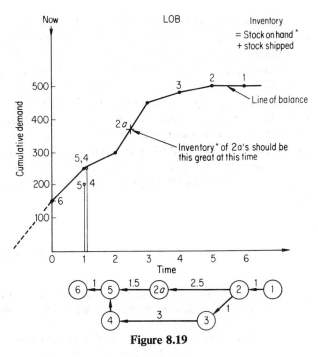

Figure 8.19

promised by contract is drawn with respect to calendar time. It should be
noted that these are *end-product* units so—if two parts are needed in a unit—

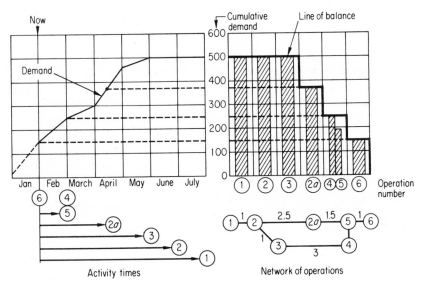

Figure 8.20

Line of balance.

that fact must be taken into account by doubling the required inventory at that point. Present time is located on the graph (NOW) and with it is associated the final event node of the network (6 in this case). All other network nodes are measured from that node (6) and located at their proper place in time. Where the time line of each event node intersects the cumulative shipment curve is the appropriate point on the line of balance that establishes required inventory for that point in time. In other words, the LOB describes the part or work demands that should have been satisfied for each stage in the project. The Figure 8.19 shows that exactly the right amount of stage 4 work is on hand but that stage 5 work has fallen below the requirements. A more conventional LOB diagram of this same situation is shown in Figure 8.20.

PROBLEMS

1. Design an appropriate PERT network for a steamship company that is about to change its accustomed routes so that containerization can be emphasized.

2. Assuming that linear trade-off functions apply, balance the network in Figure 8.21 so that both paths are critical.

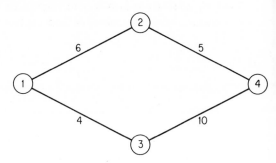

Figure 8.21

3. The variances for the network in Figure 8.21 are

Arc	Variance
1-2	4
1-3	3
2-4	5
3-4	4

and Normal distributions are assumed to exist. Simulate the critical path and develop indexes of criticality for each activity arc.

4. Explore the crash behavior of the network described below, assuming that the present plan calls for using only normal times. The following data relate cost and time. Now assume that speed is considered important, and the cost of the project can be doubled.

	Normal		Crash	
Arc	Time	Cost	Time	Cost
1-2	4	60	2	300
1-3	3	50	2	100
2-4	5	100	2	350
3-4	4	80	2	120

5. The network of operations for a job shop project is illustrated in Figure 8.22.

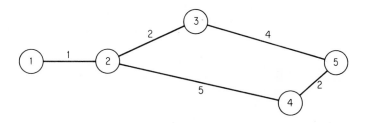

Figure 8.22

Network of operations.

The indicated times for producing lots of one hundred units are given in weeks. Deliveries of one hundred unit lots were to be made each week for ten weeks beginning eight weeks after the order had been received. It is now twelve weeks after the receipt of the order, and deliveries have been on schedule. Prepare the LOB analysis against which in-process inventories can be compared.

Aggregate scheduling represents an important technical approach that has significance for both flow shop and job shop systems. Various methods exist including numerical optimization using quadratic cost functions. There is a linear programming application, a transportation algorithm, and a simplification of the transportation method.

But aggregate scheduling gains much of its utility from the characteristics of predicting aggregate phenomena. The methodology of aggregate scheduling is entirely dependent on a full understanding of forecasting and prediction. So some effort is made in this chapter to explore what is known about forecasting but, in particular, prediction.

Aggregate Scheduling, Forecasting, and Prediction 9

Flow shops—paced and intermittent—and the job shop require many different methodological approaches for their planning and control. There is, however, a quite powerful approach that represents a homomorphic transformation of the complex system, which is applicable to both flow and job shops. It exists in the form of *aggregation* of both inputs and outputs, i.e., across a variety of different (input) facilities and (output) jobs. The aggregate is treated as one job made by one facility operating under several different modes, e.g., regular and overtime production. The organization's facilities are used to satisfy varying demand levels over time. Demands for different output are aggregated by considering them all to be demand for the output capacity of the facility.

In Figure 9.1, we portray seasonal demand for several different items and transform these into an aggregate demand for our production facilities. The aggregate production schedule over time is called, P_t.

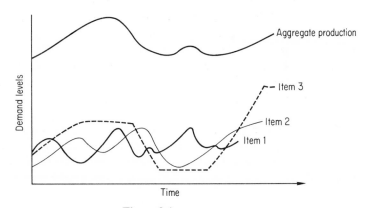

Figure 9.1

The facilities and especially the organization's work force can vary overtime. We will call the work force level at time t, W_t. An additional variable that we usually wish to control over time is the inventory level, I_t. Therefore, given

231

a "good" prediction of aggregate demand S_t over time, the problem to solve is: How should we vary P_t, W_t, and I_t so as to optimize the systems performance? Clearly, if the demand predictions are unreliable, then the aggregate method of scheduling is meaningless.

Two strategies suggest themselves. First, vary W_t so that P_t matches the demand S_t as closely as possible. In Figure 9.2, this is pattern B. Second, do

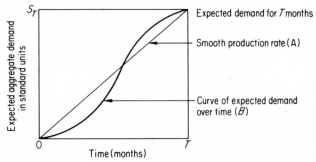

Figure 9.2

not vary the work force, thereby keeping P_t constant over time, i.e., $P_t = P$ for all t. In Figure 9.2, this is pattern A. The latter strategy permits a fixed-paced flow shop to exist where only a single technological sequence need be followed. In a job shop system, there are certain costs that disappear but other costs that increase when pattern A is followed.

Consider the obvious opposing costs. When the production rate over time, P_t, is smooth, then hiring, training, and other work force adjustment costs such as overtime go to zero. When P_t varies with S_t, work force adjustment costs rise. This increase could represent the costs of a constant size work force engaged in overtime or a fluctuating work force size, with or without overtime. Further, when P_t is constant, then demand fluctuations produce inventory costs for both over- and understocks. The extent of these costs depends on the demand fluctuation. If production rates match demand rates, then inventory-type costs trend toward zero. Figure 9.3 illustrates these opposing costs.

In such a system, there is a total cost, composed of inventory costs and work force adjustment costs, that reaches a minimum value for some combination of production rate tracking demand rate. One of the most significant models for determining optimum P_t's is described below.

The HMMS Model with Some Quadratic Costs

Production requirements for many items can be expressed in aggregate figures using *standard processing hours*. By such means, a transformation of production terms occurs, which enables both job and flow shop schedules to

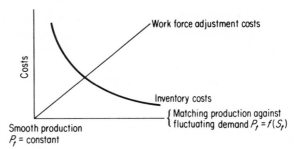

Figure 9.3

The x-axis represents the degree to which production rates match demand rates.

be developed in equivalent fashion. Specifically, if demand on the shop is not constant over time, then two options exist: first, to use smooth production over the period (say T months); or second, to regulate the production rate over time. The decision in favor of smooth production often is based on the notion of producing for stock, whereas irregular production occurs when producing to order. In this sense, the specific situation (flow or job shop) underlies the costs, which rational analysis converts into a production rate decision.

Production can be geared to the expected demand rate (option B), in which case there are no costs for overstock and understock, but there are costs for changing the rate of production—hiring, laying-off workers, training and so forth. The smooth production of option A eliminates the latter, work force costs but suffers the former, inventory costs. Option B for the flow shop also necessitates reevaluation of station design. In the case of the job shop, station redesign is a continual fact of life, so aggregate planning permits the basic costs of work force changes to be balanced against inventory costs.

Preparing forecasts of the expected demand over time is of great relevance. Various methods exist that include moving averages, exponential smoothing, regression and autocorrelation analysis.[1] We shall examine forecasting and prediction methods in some detail in this chapter. Once the existence of a reasonable time series of demands is assumed, the problem becomes one of balancing costs to provide an optimal work pattern. Work done by Holt, Modigliani, Muth, and Simon (in a paint factory) has provided an important aggregate scheduling model.[2] They examined all relevant costs (hiring, layoff, overtime, set-up, back ordering, and inventory carrying costs) using both linear and quadratic cost functions as required to provide adequate approximations of the cost systems. Their predictions of sales were based on

[1] For an excellent overall treatment of such methods see R. G. Brown, *Smoothing, Forecasting, and Prediction of Discrete Time Series* (Englewood Cliffs, N.J.: Prentice-Hall, Inc., 1963).

[2] C. C. Holt, F. Modigliani, J. F. Muth, and H. A. Simon, *Planning Production Inventories and Work Force* (Englewood Cliffs, N.J.: Prentice-Hall, Inc., 1960).

a method of moving averages, which we shall cover shortly. The authors explain that the paint factory experienced significant fluctuations in demand, and although large inventories were maintained, outages occurred frequently. As a result, sales were lost or else overtime and hiring costs were incurred. Worker morale was low and efficiency poor as workers stretched out their jobs during demand downturns.

"HMMS" built a mathematical model that involved minimizing a quadratic total cost equation:

$$\text{Minimize } \sum_{t=1}^{T} C_t \text{ where } C_t = C_1 W_t + C_2 (W_t - W_{t-1})^2 + C_3 (P_t - C_4 W_t)^2$$

$$+ C_5 P_t - C_6 W_t + C_7 (I_t - C_8 - C_9 S_t)^2$$

subject to the inventory constraint:

$$I_{t-1} + P_t - S_t = I_t$$

The variables are identified as follows:

$C_1 =$ costs related to payroll, i.e., absolute size of the work force.
$C_2 =$ hiring and layoff costs, in terms of work force *changes*.
$C_3, C_4, C_5, C_6 =$ different kinds of overtime costs.
$C_7, C_8, C_9 =$ different kinds of inventory costs.
$S_t =$ demand forecast for period t.
$I_t =$ on hand inventory minus back orders at the end of period t.
$P_t =$ the *aggregate* production rate in period t.
$W_t =$ the size of the work force for period t.

It is clear that we are dealing with a deterministic formulation of the aggregate scheduling problem. A search technique is required to find the optimum values for P_t and W_t. Consequently, the derivatives of the functions are set equal to zero to obtain the minimum cost. Since the costs were of no higher order than quadratic, linear decision rules of the following form resulted:

$$P_t = \sum_{t}^{T} \lambda_t S_t + k_1 W_{t-1} + k_2 - k_3 I_{t-1}$$

$$W_t = k_4 W_{t-1} + k_5 - k_6 I_{t-1} + \sum_{t}^{T} \alpha_t S_t$$

The coefficients λ_t and α_t take on particular values for specific industrial situations, remaining fairly stable as long as reasonably similar circumstances prevail.[3]

Figure 9.4 sheds a great deal of light on the construction of the cost functions.

[3] Results reported for the paint factory:

t	1	2	3	4	5	6	7	8	9	10	11	12
λ_t	.458	.233	.111	.046	.014	−.001	−.007	−.008	−.008	−.007	−.005	−.004
α_t	.010	.009	.007	.005	.004	.003	.002	.002	.001	.001	.001	.000

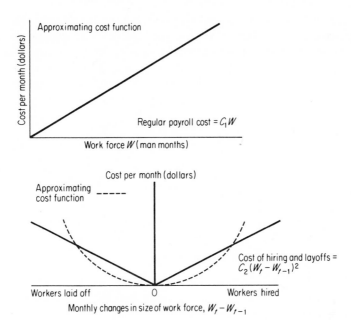

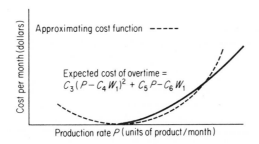

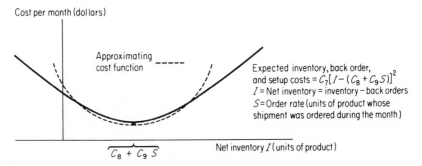

Figure 9.4

Hypothetical cost behavior as a function of planning variables. (From Charles C. Holt, Franco Modigliani, and Herbert A. Simon, "A Linear Decision Rule for Production and Employment Scheduling," *Management Science* 2: 1 (October 1955).

We expect our solution to represent some combination of changing production rates, changing work force size, varying degrees of overtime utilization, and fluctuating inventory levels. Figure 9.5 captures some of the aspects of this system's interrelatedness.

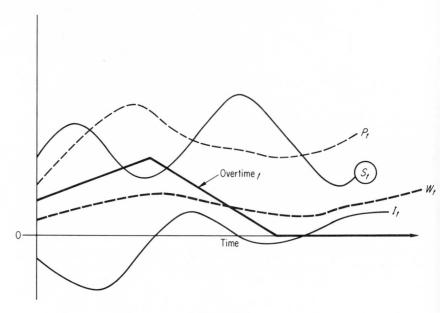

Figure 9.5

The aggregate scheduling problem requires period by period solutions that will optimize the total system, recognizing interperiod dependencies.

Note, for example, what happens to $W_{t-1} - W_t$ when the rule $P_t = S_t$ is followed (where it is assumed that each worker can produce ten units in every period):

t	S_t	P_t	I_t	$\sum_t I_t$	W_t	$W_{t-1} - W_t$
1	420	420	0	0	42	——
2	360	360	0	0	36	−6
3	390	390	0	0	39	+3
4	350	350	0	0	35	−4
5	420	420	0	0	42	+7
6	350	350	0	0	35	−7

In this second case, the work force is maintained at constant level so inventory fluctuates:

t	S_t	P_t	W_t	$W_{t-1} - W_t$	I_t	$\sum_t I_t$
1	420	400	40	0	−20	−20
2	360	400	40	0	+40	+20
3	390	400	40	0	+10	+30
4	350	400	40	0	+50	+80
5	420	400	40	0	−20	+60
6	350	400	40	0	+50	+110

In the usual case, combinations of these effects will be experienced.

The Equation System

We can easily write the equations to describe a three-period or quarter relationship:

$$
\begin{aligned}
TC = {}& [C_1W_1 + C_1W_2 + C_1W_3] \\
& + [C_2(W_1 - W_0)^2 + C_2(W_2 - W_1)^2 + C_2(W_3 - W_2)^2] \\
& + [C_3(P_1 - C_4W_1)^2 + C_3(P_2 - C_4W_2)^2 + C_3(P_3 - C_4W_3)^2] \\
& + [C_5P_1 + C_5P_2 + C_5P_3] - [C_6W_1 - C_6W_2 - C_6W_3] \\
& + [C_7(I_1 - C_8 - C_9S_1)^2 + C_7(I_2 - C_8 - C_9S_2)^2 + C_7(I_3 - C_8 - C_9S_3)^2]
\end{aligned}
$$

It is readily seen how much more demanding the equivalent expression would be for a year.

By setting partial derivatives equal to zero, a set of equations can be obtained for $W_1, W_2, \ldots$, etc., and for $P_1, P_2, \ldots$, etc. These will be linear with coefficients of similar form to those previously shown as λ_t and α_t. We recognize that different results will be obtained depending upon how we set T, the length of the planning horizon, and how often we update the coefficients, α_t and λ_t. It is evident that the ability to predict ahead a given number of periods, k, often begins to deteriorate as k gets relatively large. Therefore, the proper use of such a model requires validation of the planning horizon and the updating intervals. HMMS did validate their model; sales records for six prior years were studied. Performance under the model's linear rules was simulated and showed great improvements (lower process and freight costs, smaller inventories, higher sales, and numerous intangible gains).

The Linear Programming Approach to Aggregate Scheduling

A number of practitioners have suggested the use of LP for aggregate scheduling.[4] Generally, the objective function to be minimized is total cost.

[4] J. F. Magee and D. M. Boodman, *Production Planning and Inventory Control* (New York: McGraw-Hill Book Co., Inc., 1967), pp. 369–73. Also, see A. Kaufmann, *Methods*

Here such cost is treated as being reasonably well-represented by a linear function consisting of some combination of payroll, hiring, layoff, overtime, and inventory costs. Constraints are set on the availability of regular and overtime production capacity, the amount of capacity that can be added or removed, and restrictions on inventories that are in line with meeting demand (with or without back ordering).

Standard units are required to achieve comparability of inputs and outputs in aggregation. The standard unit will be given in terms of manhours required.[5] Say there are $i = 1, 2, \ldots k$ planning periods, and that:

$d(i) = $ *predicted* demand in period i.
$p(i) = $ actual regular production in period i; maximum regular production is $p_{max}(i)$.
$y(i) = $ actual overtime production in period i; maximum overtime production is $y_{max}(i)$.
$b = $ overtime cost per unit.
$c = $ inventory carrying charge per period.
$a' = $ cost of adding one extra unit of production capacity.[6]
$a'' = $ cost of removing one unit of production capacity.[7]
$u(i) = $ units of added capacity in period i.
$v(i) = $ units of subtracted capacity in period i.
$r = $ overtime units that can be produced for each added unit of regular production capacity.

The linear program can be understood by studying the following description of constraints and program objective.

Constraints on regular production

$$p(1) \leq p_{max}(1) + u(1) - v(1)$$
$$p(2) \leq p_{max}(2) + \sum_{1}^{2} [u(i) - v(i)]$$
$$\cdot$$
$$\cdot$$
$$\cdot$$
$$p(k) \leq p_{max}(k) + \sum_{1}^{k} [u(i) - v(i)]$$

---

and Models of Operations Research (Englewood Cliffs, N.J.: Prentice-Hall, Inc., 1963), pp. 40–44. And, F. Hanssmann and S. W. Hess, "A Linear Programming Approach to Production and Employment Scheduling," *Management Technology*, 1: 1 (January, 1960), 46–51.

[5] We are presenting a modified version of the Magee and Boodman model, previously referenced.

[6] These can be either machine or manpower changes.

[7] *Ibid.*

Constraints on overtime production

$$y(1) \leq y_{\max}(1) + r[u(1) - v(1)]$$
$$y(2) \leq y_{\max}(2) + r \sum_{1}^{2} [u(i) - v(i)]$$

.

.

.

$$y(k) \leq y_{\max}(k) + r \sum_{1}^{k} [u(i) - v(i)]$$

Inventory restrictions ($I_0 = 0$, meaning an initial inventory of zero)

$$p(1) + y(1) \geq d(1) \text{ (because demands must be met)}$$
$$\sum_{1}^{2} p(i) + \sum_{1}^{2} y(i) \geq \sum_{1}^{2} d(i)$$

.

.

.

$$\sum_{1}^{k} p(i) + \sum_{1}^{k} y(i) \geq \sum_{1}^{k} d(i)$$

Constraints on capacity changes

$$u(1) \geq p(1) - p(0) \quad \text{or} \quad v(1) \geq p(0) - p(1)$$
$$u(2) \geq p(2) - p(1) \quad \text{or} \quad v(2) \geq p(1) - p(2)$$

.

.

.

$$u(k) \geq p(k) - p(k-1) \quad \text{or} \quad v(k) \geq p(k-1) - p(k)$$

The objective function (minimize)

$$\text{Total cost} = a' \sum_{1}^{k} u(i) + a'' \sum_{1}^{k} v(i)$$
$$+ b \sum_{1}^{k} y(i) + c \left[\sum_{i=1}^{k} \sum_{j=1}^{i} \{p(j) + y(j) - d(j)\} \right]$$

These equations suffice to solve the scheduling problem within the LP assumptions. This is a convenient approach, but we should not lose sight of the fact that some simpler approaches exist as well. E. Bowman formulated a transportation algorithm that is highly efficient for aggregate scheduling with hand computation.[8] J. W. Gavett developed a dynamic programming

---

[8] Original citation is E. H. Bowman, "Production Scheduling by the Transportation Method of Linear Programming," *Operations Research*, 4: 1 (February 1956), 100–103. Further discussion will be found in E. H. Bowman and R. B. Fetter, *Analysis for Production and Operations Management*, 3rd ed. (Homewood, Ill.: Richard D. Irwin, 1967), pp. 134–36.

approach to the same problem.[9] Simulation has also been applied to test various schedules in a stochastic demand environment.

Using network properties of the transportation model, it is possible to solve quite large scheduling problems. Many forms of scheduling problems lend themselves to reasonable representation using the transportation model. In addition, this class of model has many other uses, so it is worthwhile becoming familiar with how the model is set up and how it is solved.

The basic idea of the transportation model is that it allocates a supply of resources to users of those resources in such a way as to find a pattern of allocation that minimizes costs or maximizes profits. Each source, shipper, or producer can split its allocations between users. And the output of several sources can be assigned to a single user. These relations are reflected in the matrix below where the cost of shipping one unit from a particular producer (P_i) to a specific consumer (C_j) is stated as c_{ij}.

		Consumers							
		C_1	C_2	C_3	...	C_j	...	C_m	Supply
	P_1	c_{11}	c_{12}	c_{13}		c_{1j}		c_{1m}	s_1
	P_2	c_{21}	c_{22}	c_{23}		c_{2j}		c_{2m}	s_2
Producers	P_3	c_{31}	c_{32}	c_{33}		c_{3j}		c_{3m}	s_3
	$\vdots$								$\vdots$
	P_i	c_{i1}	c_{i2}	c_{i3}		c_{ij}		c_{im}	s_i
	$\vdots$								$\vdots$
	P_n	c_{n1}	c_{n2}	c_{n3}		c_{nj}		c_{nm}	s_n
Demand		d_1	d_2	d_3	...	d_j	...	d_m	

[9] J. W. Gavett, *Production and Operations Management* (New York: Harcourt, Brace & World, Inc., 1968), pp. 459–63.

Constraints on producers' supplies (in a given time period) are indicated by s_i values and consumers' demands are shown by d_j's.[10]

First, let us consider a 2×2 transportation matrix, with the given values for supplies and demands for the period and unit costs of allocation as shown.

	C_1	C_2	Supply
P_1	4	6	600
P_2	2	5	400
Demand	300	700	1000

The minimum cost allocations can be determined by, *first*, finding any feasible allocation pattern (i.e., a pattern that properly matches supply and demand totals); *second*, by examining the effects of making changes in that pattern; *third*, making changes that assure improvement; and, *fourth*, stopping when no further improvement can be obtained. The similarity to linear programming rules is hardly accidental. Transportation models can always be solved by either LP or network methods.

As an example of a "jumping-off" point solution, assume the following:

	C_1	C_2	Supply
P_1	4 100	6 500	600
P_2	2 200	5 200	400
Demand	300	700	1000

The *first* requirement is met. For the second condition, we must study four options:

1. If an additional unit is assigned to P_1C_1, thus: $\begin{smallmatrix}101 & 499\\199 & 201\end{smallmatrix}$, the cost changes are $+4 - 2 + 5 - 6 = +1$. Therefore, to make this change would increase costs by one dollar for each extra unit assigned to P_1C_1, so we will not make such changes in the allocation pattern.
2. If an additional unit is assigned to P_2C_2, the same result occurs as we have just described.

[10] The reader's attention is directed to pp. 418–423 in Chapter 14, where the *classic* "distribution" form of the transportation model is used for plant location decisions.

$$\begin{array}{cc} 99 & 501 \end{array}$$

3. If an additional unit is assigned to P_2C_1, thus: $\begin{array}{cc} 201 & 199 \end{array}$, the cost changes are $+6 - 4 + 2 - 5 = -1$. Therefore, we wish to make this change, assigning as many units as possible to P_2C_2 because each unit so reassigned saves one dollar. How many units can be moved to P_2C_2? We can move

$$600$$

100 units, thus: $\begin{array}{cc} 300 & 100 \end{array}$.

4. It will be found that the same reasoning applies to P_1C_2; each unit so reassigned saves one dollar, and the maximum number of units that can be assigned to P_1C_2 is 300 ... (actually an identity with point three above).

Thus, the optimal assignment for this 2×2 problem has been easily determined. The network method we have been employing is called the "stepping stone" procedure.

For larger problems, several obvious questions present themselves, namely: (1) How do we quickly derive a jumping-off solution? (2) How can the patterns of reassignment be rapidly evaluated? (3) How do we determine the maximum amount that can be reassigned? Let us consider each of these questions, in turn, using a larger numerical example as a basis for discussion.

	C_1	C_2	C_3	Supply
P_1	4 50	6	3	50
P_2	2 50	5 110	8	160
P_3	7	3 190	2 60	250
P_4	4	5	6 140	140
Demand	100	300	200	600

Starting in the upper-left-hand corner, as many units are assigned to P_1C_1 as is *allowed* by whichever constraint dominates, i.e., the row constraint of 50 or the column constraint of 100. In this case, it is the row constraint, so 50 units are entered at P_1C_1, but the C_1 column still has 50 units of unfilled demand. These can be assigned at P_2C_1; however, all of P_2's supply is not yet assigned. In fact, 110 units can be assigned at P_2C_2, which leaves 190 units of C_2's demand to handle. Continuing in this way, we complete the total matrix of assignments. The procedure we are using is called the *Northwest Corner Method*. It will always satisfy the requirement for an initial, feasible solution but so would a procedure that starts at any corner. Whatever method is used to obtain an initial, feasible solution, it must produce $M + N - 1$ assignments given a matrix with M rows and N columns.[11] This number, which meets the specifications of the fundamental theorem of linear programming, does not only apply to initial solutions; it applies to all intermediate solutions and the final and optimal solution as well.

For question two, the net cost of all assignments that have not been made must be determined. Consider the possibility of assigning units to P_1C_2. The stepping stone configuration is as follows:

Put In	Unit Cost	Take Out	Unit Cost
P_1C_2	+6	P_1C_1	−4
P_2C_1	+2	P_2C_2	−5
	+8		−9

The net change is a saving of one dollar. Next, consider assigning one unit to P_1C_3.

Put In	Unit Cost	Take Out	Unit Cost
P_1C_3	+3	P_1C_1	−4
P_2C_1	+2	P_2C_2	−5
P_3C_2	+3	P_3C_3	−2
	+8		−11

The net change is a saving of three dollars. This change would be made rather than the previous one, which promises a saving of only one dollar. Still, we must evaluate the remaining possibilities for assignments. These are all shown within circles in the matrix below.

First iteration

	C_1	C_2	C_3	Supply
	4	6	3	
P_1	50	(−1)	(−3)	50
	2	5	8	
P_2	50	110	(+4)	160
	7	3	2	
P_3	(+7)	190	60	250
	4	5	6	
P_4	(0)	(−2)	140	140
Demand	100	300	200	600

[11] There is an exception that results in less than $M + N - 1$ assignments, called the state of degeneracy. See pp. 247–248 concerning the nature of degeneracy and what should be done about it.

The total cost is $(50 \times 4) + (50 \times 2) + (110 \times 5) + (190 \times 3) + (60 \times 2) + (140 \times 6) = 2380$. The best marginal change is -3, and it indicates that assignments should be made to P_1C_3. Before we proceed to question three, however, let us note one more stepping pattern. To evaluate an assignment at P_4C_1, we must assign a unit to P_4C_1, remove a unit from P_4C_3, assign a unit to P_3C_3, remove a unit from P_3C_2, assign a unit to P_2C_2, and remove a unit from P_2C_1. In all cases, the stepping pattern must leave the supplies and demands fully satisfied. The fundamental basis of all stepping patterns is that a horizontal step must allow a vertical step to be taken from it and then again horizontal and vertical movements can be made until closure is achieved. Thus, for example, two possible patterns are shown in the figure below.

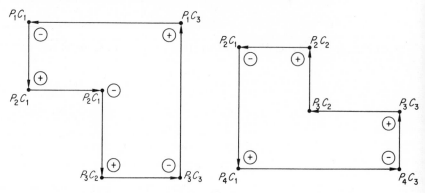

323g

The network on the left details (for the first iteration matrix, above) the necessary moves for assigning one unit to P_1C_3; the one on the right shows a similar assignment to P_4C_1. Once this network is determined, plus and minus signs can be added to show the increases and decreases in cost caused by such assignment. Starting with the cell to be assigned, alternate plus and minus costs can be entered as shown in the diagram. In this manner, the marginal costs of an assignment can be determined easily. For example, the marginal cost of assigning one unit to P_1C_3 would be equal to $+c_{13} - c_{11} + c_{21} - c_{22} + c_{32} - c_{33}$.

Referring to question three, how many units can be entered at P_1C_3? The stepping pattern for unit changes must now be examined in terms of how many units are presently assigned to each "take out" position (indicated by negative signs in the network). The smallest such number is the answer. Otherwise, some assignments would become negative, which violates the feasibility condition. Thus, for P_1C_2, no more than fifty units (at P_1C_1) can be reassigned; at P_1C_3, fifty units is again the maximum number; at P_3C_1, fifty units now at P_2C_1 dominate the reassignments; at P_4C_1, fifty units; at P_4C_2, 140 units at P_4C_3 is the minimum number.

We are now ready to make the reassignment to P_1C_3. Then we must go through all the steps again, reassigning until all evaluations of nonassigned cells indicate that no further improvement is possible. This is done below:

Second iteration

	C_1	C_2	C_3	Supply
	4	6	3	
P_1	(+3)	(+2)	50	50
	2	5	8	
P_2	100	60	(+4)	160
	7	3	2	
P_3	(+7)	240	10	250
	4	5	6	
P_4	(0)	(−2)	140	140
Demand	100	300	200	600

Total cost = 2230

The indicated change is to make an assignment of as many units as possible (140) to P_4C_2. Thus:

Third iteration

	C_1	C_2	C_3	Supply
	4	6	3	
P_1	(+3)	(+2)	50	50
	2	5	8	
P_2	100	60	(+4)	160
	7	3	2	
P_3	(+7)	100	150	250
	4	5	6	
P_4	(+2)	140	(+2)	140
Demand	100	300	200	600

Total cost = 1950

This is the final solution; there is none better. Had a zero appeared in the circled evaluations, this would have signified that alternatives existed. It would be up to the operations manager to decide which of the minimum cost alternatives he preferred.

We note that our final solution has six assignments, thus, it meets the condition $M + N - 1 = 4 + 3 - 1 = 6$. Later (see pp. 420–423), we shall show that when supply and demand are not equal, that a dummy slack variable (having *all* zero unit costs) can be created to take care of this situation. The dummy, whether it be needed for the rows or columns, is not simply a computational convenience; it has decision-making significance for the manager. Lastly, if we wish to use the transportation model to achieve profit maximization rather than cost minimization, the rule concerning which new assignment is preferred is reversed. The largest possible plus-valued marginal evaluation is chosen to be entered in the network. The procedure stops when all evaluations are negative. The significance of the transportation model is hard to miss. It does not require a square matrix (where each job can be assigned to only one machine); the solutions are relatively easy to obtain by hand computation. On the other hand, it is linear, since unit costs or profits are not able to be changed as a function of volume; and since each matrix applies to a specific period, no allowance is made for interdependencies over time.

Now, let us examine the Bowman transportation algorithm for aggregate scheduling. The matrix he suggests is as follows:

	Sales Periods					
	1	2	3	Final Inv.	Slack	Supply
Initial Inv.	0	c	$2c$	$3c$	0	I_0
Regular 1	r	$r+c$	$r+2c$	$r+3c$	0	R_1
Overtime 1	v	$v+c$	$v+2c$	$v+3c$	0	O_1
Regular 2	x	r	$r+c$	$r+2c$	0	R_2
Overtime 2	x	v	$v+c$	$v+2c$	0	O_2
Regular 3	x	x	r	$r+c$	0	R_3
Overtime 3	x	x	v	$v+c$	0	O_3
Demand	D_1	D_2	D_3	I_f	S	Grand total

where c = carrying cost per unit for the interval of time.
          r = production cost per unit.
          v = overtime cost per unit.
          I_0 = initial inventory.
          I_f = final inventory.

The regular transportation method is used for solution. It should be noted that in this matrix backorders are prohibited (by x).

Later (pp. 278–279) we will show how the transportation problem can be set up in LP terms.

Let us examine a simple two period problem where $c = \$100(.01) = \$1.00$; $r = \$100$; $v = \$120$; $I_0 = 100$; and $I_f = 50$. The matrix with the appropriate supplies, demands, and costs entered is shown below.[12]

	1	2	I_f	Slack	Supply
I_0	[0] 100	[1]	[2]	[0]	100
R_1	[100] 300	[101] ϵ	[102]	[0]	300
O_1	[120]	[121] 200	[122]	[0]	200
R_2	x	[100] 300	[101] ϵ	[0]	300
O_2	x	[120]	[121] 50	[0] 150	200
Demand	400	500	50	150	1100

Bishop's Simplification

George Bishop[13] noted that any stepping stone pattern inside the matrix (i.e., ignoring the slack column) produced a zero change. For example:

	$2c$	$3c$	
	-1	$+1$	$+r + 5c$
	[$r + 2c$]	[$r + 3c$]	$= \dfrac{-r - 5c}{0}$
	$+1$	-1	

However, this symmetrical condition ceases when the slack column is taken into consideration. Bishop's rule for a cost matrix requires that as large an assignment of the final inventory, I_f, as possible, be put into the *highest cost*, Final Inventory row. Then as much of the remainder as possible should be put into the next highest I_f cost row. As this procedure is continued an

---

[12] The Northwest Corner Method allocation has been used, resulting in a doubly degenerate pattern. The two epsilons have been entered to provide network points for the stepping stone method of transportation analysis.

[13] George T. Bishop, "On a Problem of Production Scheduling," *Operations Research*, 5: 1 (February, 1957), 97–103.

optimal solution will be found directly. Bishop's rule is much easier to use than the straight transportation algorithm.

Consider the previous example. We would have a final optimal solution if the 150 fifty units in the cell O_2, slack could be moved to the cell O_1, slack. This is directly accomplished.

	2	I_f	Slack
	⋮	⋮	⋮
O_1	200 −150	⋯	$\overset{.}{+}$ 150
R_2	⋯	⋯	⋯
O_2	+ 150	⋯	150 −150
	⋮	⋮	⋮

The epsilon entry, being strictly a device for treating degeneracy in the matrix, can be ignored.

Back Orders Permitted

When back orders are allowed, the Bishop rule can no longer be used. Our matrix appears as below.

Sales Period

	1	2	3	I_f	Slack	Supply
I_0	0	c	$2c$	$3c$	0	I_0
R_1	r	$r+c$	$r+2c$	$r+3c$	0	R_1
O_1	v	$v+c$	$v+2c$	$v+3c$	0	O_1
R_2	$r+b$	r	$r+c$	$r+2c$	0	R_2
O_2	$v+b$	v	$v+c$	$v+2c$	0	O_2
R_3	$r+2b$	$r+b$	r	$r+c$	0	R_3
O_3	$v+2b$	$v+b$	v	$v+c$	0	O_3
Demand	D_1	D_2	D_3	I_f	S	Grand total

It has the additional new cost, b, which is the back order cost per unit. This problem must be solved by conventional transportation techniques.

Is forecasting a mysterious art, prediction a conjecture no better than those obtained from crystal balls? The cost of clear crystal balls has actually soared over the past fifty years. No history of prediction can ignore the role of the oracle at Delphi. To whom does this role of professional foretelling of the future now belong? Has it been eradicated?

In terms of the physics and chemistry of systems—because of the nature of dynamics and inertia and since meaningful classification of information about what has been, and memory of what became of what has been is possible—*conjecture is reasonable*. To not be able to foretell the future in any way is a more mysterious thought by far than to propose that it can be done to some degree. Certainly, to not try to foretell some futures is unfortunate: for example, that pollution is bad and will get worse unless something is done about it. To not try to change the future in accord with a good plan is absurd. And, in this respect, it is widely believed by top executives that their expectations strongly influence event probabilities.

Inventory planning and *aggregate scheduling* are two "operations" areas that are highly sensitive to forecast and prediction abilities. That is why we intend to dwell at some length on the forecast and prediction area at this point. If a believable time series, $\{S_t\}$, cannot be derived so that the time series would have little error when compared to actuality, then all methods for aggregate scheduling, exemplified by those we have been describing, have no merit.

Although the distinction between forecasting and prediction has already been made, let us reiterate. Prediction is the choice of one particular state. It is chosen as the state that is most likely to happen from among a number of different states that appear to have some likelihood of occurring— e.g., betting on one horse in a race (to win, show, or place). The odds on the board are like the forecast. Turning to another analogy using meteorology, tomorrow's weather is *predicted* to be fair, based on the *forecast* that there is a 30 per cent probability of precipitation.[14] Aggregate scheduling uses *predictions*, which are frequently derived from forecasts. It is important to note that predictions of the behavior of aggregations tend to be more accurate than predictions of the behaviors of the individual components that make up the aggregate. For example, it is easier to predict next year's (total) aggregate sales level for a department store than next month's aggregate sales level, because the longer period has less erratic behavior than the small, short

---

[14] While this is not a universal distinction, R. G. Brown states, "I use *predict* to refer to . . . subjective estimates, and *forecast* to denote an objective computation." Brown's further explanation is entirely compatible with the definition suggested in the text. See R. G. Brown, *Smoothing, Forecasting and Prediction* (Englewood Cliffs, N.J.: Prentice-Hall, Inc., 1962), pp. 2–3.

interval sample; and it is easier to predict aggregate sales for all floors of the department store than for any one floor, because fluctuations in individual departments tend to cancel each other out. As shown in Figure 9.6, trajectories of big systems tend to be smooth; of little systems, erratic and unpredictable.

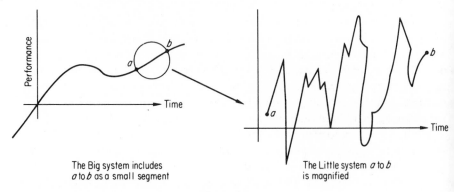

The Big system includes
a to *b* as a small segment

The Little system *a* to *b*
is magnified

Figure 9.6

As a result, it is not unusual to study the big system to explain the small system's behavior. Thus, the trend from *a* to *b* is quite clear in the big system and not readily apparent in the small system's chart. Similarly, the department store manager may estimate quarterly sales in aggregate terms and later proportionately divide this gross prediction into particular product-line sales.

It is usually easier to interpolate or extrapolate on aggregates and later convert to component predictions through proportioning. *Interpolation* is the process of trying to reconstruct history. For example, we know that (Figure 9.7, A) at t_0 the system was at *a* and at t_1 it was at *b*. Question: What happened in between? Answer. We can't say exactly; a likely guess is point *c* on the straight line; and anything greater than point *d* or less than point *e* is unlikely. Proceeding in this fashion, we try to find some reasonable rules for interpolating between *a* and *b*. The size of the intervals $t_1 - t - t_0$ plus the characteristic dynamics of the system are determinants of what is reasonable.

Extrapolation is the process of moving from observed data (past and present) to the unknown values of future points, Figure 9.7, B.
Extrapolation is typical of a great many forecasting and predicting activities. The same kind of reasoning concerning interval sizes, dynamics of the system, and inertial effect applies as was the case with interpolation. Often, interpolation is used to build up a history for the system so that new forecasts can be obtained.

Given a forecast, the mean, mode, or median of the forecast distribution might be the basis for a prediction of a particular event. Both forecasts and the predictions themselves can be based on: guesses; extrapolations of trends; belief that history repeats itself; the notion of leading index numbers; the belief that some ratio always holds; the mode of values based on expert opinions; and complex interactions of mathematical models, including the intersection of independent multiple forecast models. The list gives a pretty good sampling (later we shall explain details), but we still need some further distinctions.

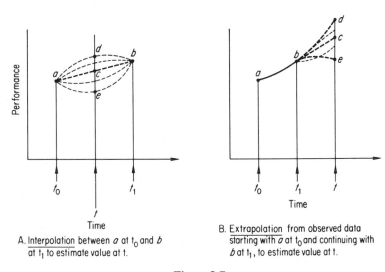

A. Interpolation between a at t_0 and b at t_1 to estimate value at t.

B. Extrapolation from observed data starting with a at t_0 and continuing with b at t_1, to estimate value at t.

Figure 9.7

Some forecasts (known as Bayesian forecasts) are based on *subjective* judgments, whereas *objective* forecasts are derived by *counting* the number of special events and dividing that number by the total number of all events— e.g., out of ten letters drawn at random, three are A's, so $p[A] = 3/10$.

Moving from past to present, we have a historical stream of data known as a time series. Contrast this with information that has lost its time tag. Such information that is bereft of specific time or even time sequence but is known to belong to a given interval of time is called cross-sectional data. The analysis of time series separates out any basic trends in the data that might exist; as well, the analysis isolates any cyclical variation (perhaps seasonal). And it identifies and removes a class of information associated with random variation, often called *noise*. Many methods exist for filtering out noninforming noise so that "pure" trends and "real" cycles can be spotted. Difficulty arises because noise often *hides* fundamental patterns. All control theory is concerned with this removal of noise, and Figure 9.8 represents the notion of filtering a time series (or cross-sectional data) to discern basic patterns.

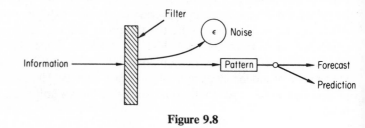

Figure 9.8

Predictive Error

The history of any system of predictions can be recorded as a difference between what was expected to happen and what actually happened—predicted − actual = the forecast error. For *systems of attributes,* where predictions take the form of "yes" or "no" (such as. it is or it is not oilbearing land), we can tally each individual's record to observe who was right *most* of the time. When choosing predictors, preference can only be given to good predictors if you know who they are. There appear to be strong psychological blocks against accurate evaluation by memory alone. Records help. For *systems of variables* (such as estimating next month's sales demand), forecasts of predictive error distributions, such as shown in Figure 9.9, could be obtained for each individual.

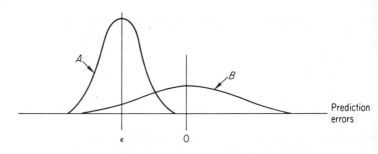

Figure 9.9

Although *B*'s prediction errors average out to zero (because he over- and underestimates equally), *A* is a better predictor. Somehow we should be able to correct *A*'s bias of ϵ, and *A*'s variance is less than *B*'s.

Predictive Tests

If a predictive test can be found and applied to determine what will happen, and if it is a perfect test, then a matrix of conditional probabilities with all unit diagonal entries would occur.

Matrix of Probabilities that a Specific Test Result Will Occur Given that the True State of Affairs Is Known

		If the "true" future state of the system will be:				
		A	B	C	$\ldots$	Z
The test T_1 is perfect. It indicates	A'	1				
that the future state of the	B'		1			
system will be:	C'			1		
	$\vdots$					
Prime indicates a test result.	Z'					1

But, if the only test available (call it T_2) is imperfect, we might get, for example

	A	B	C	$\ldots$	Z
A'	$\frac{1}{3}$	$\frac{1}{8}$	$\frac{1}{8}$		0
B'	$\frac{1}{3}$	$\frac{7}{8}$	$\frac{2}{8}$		0
C'	$\frac{1}{3}$	0	$\frac{5}{8}$		0
$\vdots$					$\frac{1}{5}$
Z'	0	0	0	$\ldots$	$\frac{4}{5}$

Should a predictive test such as T_2 be used? For that matter, if the test T_1 costs more than could possibly be gained by making a perfect prediction, no one will use it. Everything depends on how much it costs to use a specific test and what benefits it can provide.

To illustrate, consider the following decision situation where the matrix entries are profits:

Forecast (p_i)	$\frac{1}{4}$	$\frac{1}{4}$	$\frac{1}{2}$	
	A	B	C	Expected Profit
Strategy $S1$	1	0	0	$\frac{1}{4}$
Strategy $S2$	0	1	0	$\frac{1}{4}$

Should the manager use $S1$ or $S2$ or wait and use the predictive test first? Let the forecast (often called the a priori probabilities and frequently obtained subjectively) be $p_A = \frac{1}{4}$, $p_B = \frac{1}{4}$, and $p_C = \frac{1}{2}$. Then the expected values of strategies $S1$ and $S2$ are the same.

If the test matrix is:[15]

	A	B	C
A'	$\frac{1}{3}$	$\frac{1}{8}$	$\frac{1}{8}$
B'	$\frac{1}{3}$	$\frac{7}{8}$	$\frac{2}{8}$
C'	$\frac{1}{3}$	0	$\frac{5}{8}$

then multiply each column (j) by its respective p_j, and sum each row, yielding:[16]

p_j	$\frac{1}{4}$	$\frac{1}{4}$	$\frac{1}{2}$	
	A	B	C	Row Sum
A'	1/12	1/32	1/16	$(8 + 3 + 6)/96$ = 17/96
B'	1/12	7/32	2/16	$(8 + 21 + 12)/96$ = 41/96
C'	1/12	0	5/16	$(8 + 0 + 30)/96$ = 38/96

The sum of each matrix row is then divided *into* each of its own row entries. This produces:[17]

Table of Probabilities that a Specific State of Nature Will Exist Given that a Specific Test Result Has Occurred

	A	B	C
A'	8/17	3/17	6/17
B'	8/41	21/41	12/41
C'	8/38	0	30/38

These are the new forecast probabilities (called a posteriori). The a posteriori probabilistic results are often presented in tree form (see Figure 9.10). These values are interpreted as follows:

If the test is used and A' results (which occurs 17/96 of the time)

	8/17	3/17	6/17	
	A	B	C	*Expected Profit*
Strategy 1	1	0	0	8/17[18]
Strategy 2	0	1	0	3/17

[15] The entries of the test matrix are: $P[j'|j]$ where $j' = A', B', C'$ and $j = A, B, C$

[16] The entries of the second matrix are: $P(j)P[j'|j]$ for all j' and j; and the Row Sums are $\sum_j P(j)P[j'|j] = P(j')$ for each row i.

[17] $P(j)P[j'|j]/P(j') = P[j|j']$, which is Bayes' Theorem.

[18] Maximum profit for the specific conditions: $P[j|A']$, $j = A, B, C$.

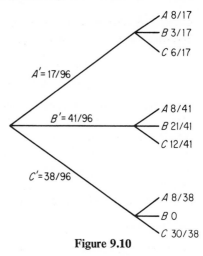

Figure 9.10

If the test is used and B' results (which occurs 41/96 of the time)

	8/41	21/41	12/41	
	A	B	C	Expected Profit
Strategy 1	1	0	0	8/41
Strategy 2	0	1	0	21/41[19]

If the test is used and C' results (which occurs 38/96 of the time)

	8/38	0	30/38	
	A	B	C	Expected Profit
Strategy 1	1	0	0	8/38[20]
Strategy 2	0	1	0	0

This gives us an expected profit with the test of:

Expected profit $= 17/96(8/17) + 41/96(21/41) + 38/96(8/38) = 37/96$

The expected profit *without the test* was equal to 1/4 for both strategies or 24/96. Therefore, $37/96 - 24/96 = 13/96$ measures the *savings* derived from the predictive test. The test *cannot* cost more than that amount if it is to be used.

Data-Based Predictions

A variety of methods for predictive extrapolation exists. For example, *moving averages* provide a simple means of obtaining future values. Thus, a

[19] Maximum profit for the specific conditions $P[j|B']$ $j = A, B, C$.
[20] Maximum profit for the specific conditions $P[j|C']$, $j = A, B, C$.

series of N observations is regularly updated to maintain recent information. We will use $\hat{x}_t$ to represent the predicted value of x in period t.

$$\hat{x}_{t+1} = (x_t + x_{t-1} + \ldots + x_{t-N+1})/N$$
$$\hat{x}_{t+2} = \hat{x}_{t+1} + (x_{t+1} - x_{t-N+1})/N$$

It will be noted that, say, each month's prediction is updated by dropping the oldest month of the series and adding the latest observation. In this way, new trends are taken into account, and old information is removed from the system. Here is an example, assuming a four-period moving average. The most recent observation was five; the prediction for the next period is four, i.e., $\hat{x}_{t+1} = 4 = (5 + 4 + 4 + 3)/4$. Let's say that instead of the prediction of four being validated, the actual result is six. Then, the following period prediction is 4.75, i.e., $\hat{x}_{t+2} = 4.75 = 4 + \left(\dfrac{6-3}{4}\right) = \dfrac{6+5+4+4}{4}$. The moving average is slowly increasing with the apparent trend. Such slowness of response will be appreciated only if there really is no trend.

We can influence this situation by using *weighted averages*. Let the sum of the weights w_t be one, thus, $\sum\limits_{t} w_t = 1$. Our system of predictive equations becomes:

$$\hat{x}_{t+1} = w_t x_t + w_{t-1} x_{t-1} + \ldots + w_{t-N+1} x_{t-N+1} \text{ or specifically,}$$
$$\hat{x}_{t+1} = .4x_t + .3x_{t-1} + .2x_{t-2} + .1x_{t-3}, \text{ for the given weights, .4, .3, .2, .1.}$$

With the previous moving averages, all the w_t were treated as being equal, viz.,

$$\hat{x}_{t+1} = \tfrac{1}{4}(5) + \tfrac{1}{4}(4) + \tfrac{1}{4}(4) + \tfrac{1}{4}(3) = 4$$

Using the weights (.4, .3, .2, .1) we obtain:

$$\hat{x}_{t+1} = .4(5) + .3(4) + .2(4) + .1(3) = 2 + 1.2 + 0.8 + 0.3 = 4.3$$

This system is responding more rapidly to the (possible) trend.

Introducing the new value of six (as we did before), we again observe an increase in reaction rate.

$$\hat{x}_{t+2} = .4(6) + .3(5) + .2(4) + .1(4) = 2.4 + 1.5 + 0.8 + 0.4 = 5.1$$

Prediction Through Exponential Smoothing

There is a lot of calculation involved in using moving and weighted averages, and often these methods are less effective than exponential smoothing, which requires less calculation. Many control systems utilize exponential smoothing. It has proven effective for such diverse applications as tracking aircraft and predicting demand levels for inventory systems. This method of exponential smoothing carries the last *average value* in memory and combines it with the most recent *observed value*. Thus, $\hat{x}_{t-1}$ is the last prediction made; x_{t-1} is the actual result observed for the period $t - 1$; and $\hat{x}_t$ is the new prediction to be made for period t.

$$\hat{x}_t = \alpha x_{t-1} + (1 - \alpha)\hat{x}_{t-1}$$

According to the weight α that is used, the response rate of the system can be changed markedly. Thus, using the same data as in our prior illustrations:

$$
\begin{aligned}
\hat{x}_t &= .1(6) + .9(4) = 4.2 && \alpha = .1 \\
&= .2(6) + .8(4) = 4.4 && \alpha = .2 \\
&= .3(6) + .7(4) = 4.6 && \alpha = .3 \\
& \qquad\qquad\qquad\quad 4.75 && \alpha = .375 \quad \leftarrow \text{Moving average result} \\
&= .4(6) + .6(4) = 4.8 && \alpha = .4 \\
&= .5(6) + .5(4) = 5.0 && \alpha = .5 \\
& \qquad\qquad\qquad\quad 5.1 && \alpha = .550 \quad \leftarrow \text{Weighted average result} \\
&= .6(6) + .4(4) = 5.2 && \alpha = .6 \\
& \qquad\qquad\qquad\quad\ \ . && \ \ . \\
& \qquad\qquad\qquad\quad\ \ . && \ \ . \\
& \qquad\qquad\qquad\quad\ \ . && \ \ . \\
&= 1.0(6) + 0(4) = 6.0 && \alpha = 1.0
\end{aligned}
$$

This simple, updating system requires only one operation. Small values of α are used for noisy, randomly fluctuating systems that have a basic stability, and larger values of α are used for emerging and evolving systems, where a goodly amount of weight can only be placed on the last observation. For many aggregate scheduling and inventory systems, α is kept quite small, in the neighborhood of 0.05 to 0.15, to decrease the system's response to random fluctuations.

The Properties of Prediction Systems

Note that in all the above methods, the assumption is implicit that successive values of x_t are independent of each other. In many systems, this is a false assumption. At the core of the forecast and prediction problem is the ability to discern the type of system that exists. The first step is to classify the situation as being one of risk, certainty, or uncertainty. If the problem requires risk analysis, then it is necessary to determine.

1. Whether the system's behavior is stable or unstable;
2. If it is stable, in what sense is it stable;
3. Whether it will continue to be stable; but
4. If it is not stable, whether it can be made so.

This approach presents an aspect of forecasting and prediction that is rarely recognized, but it is vital. Meaningful forecasts cannot be made until the initial conditions and structural properties of the event system have been established. Let us classify the various kinds of systems that might be encountered in business, government, or institutional operations.

A. *No Distribution Exists.* There is only one environment, therefore we have decision making under certainty; the forecast is the prediction.

B. *A Stationary Distribution Exists.* The probabilities associated with the environments are unchanging, ergo, decision making under risk; the same forecast prevails over time even though for managerial reasons the prediction may change.

C. *There Is Shewhart-type Stability.*[21] In this case, the probabilities or forecast associated with the environments can change in some *regular* fashion; however, aside from that regularity, environmental predictions are independent of the history of prior environments.

D. *There Is Markovian-type Stability.* In this case, the probabilities or forecast associated with the environments must change in some *regular* fashion; but environmental prediction is *dependent* on the *one preceding* environment that existed;

E. *There Is Non-Markovian Prior State Stability.* Here, the probabilities or forecast associated with the environments must change in some *regular* fashion; but environmental prediction is *dependent* on some *set* of preceding environments that existed;

F. *There Is Instability.* No knowledge exists or can be developed with respect to the probabilities or forecast of the environments, so there is decision making under uncertainty;

G. *There Is No Knowledge with Respect to Environments.* That is, we cannot describe or enumerate the relevant environments.

Markovian Predictive Systems

If an experiment is conducted at an early state, such as a test market, and there is reason to believe that the system is stable and of the Markovian-type, then a prediction model of the following type might be used. Assume that the universe is divided into two parts, for example, noncustomers at time t (called NC_t) and customers at time t (called C_t). Over a specified interval we observe that forty noncustomers become customers; sixty noncustomers remain noncustomers; seventy customers remain customers; and thirty customers become noncustomers. This information based on a sample, say, of two hundred people is assembled in matrix form. The matrix will be used to make a prediction concerning eventual market shares in a marketplace of 100,000 people. Since, we are dealing with a new product, all 100,000 people will initially be assumed noncustomers.

---

[21] Walter A. Shewhart, *Statistical Method from the Viewpoint of Quality Control* (Washington, D.C.: The Department of Agriculture, 1939).

| | | Time 2 | |
| | | NC_2 | C_2 |
→			
Time 1	NC_1	60	40
	C_1	30	70

We convert these numbers into transition probabilities such that each row sums to unity. Then:

| | | Time 2 | |
	→	NC_2	C_2
Time 1	NC_1	0.6	0.4
	C_1	0.3	0.7

We start at time 1 in a large market with 100,000 potential customers. To begin, all are noncustomers. How many customers will we have at time 2? This prediction is readily derived if the assumptions that we have made actually hold. Thus, at time 2, we have obtained forty per cent of the market:

$$NC_2 = 0.6(100,000) + 0.3(0) = 60,000$$
$$C_2 = 0.4(100,000) + 0.7(0) = \underline{40,000}$$
$$ 100,000$$

To determine the number of customers at times 3, 4, 5, and so on, we use the same relationship, viz.,

$$NC_t = 0.6NC_{t-1} + 0.3C_{t-1}$$
$$C_t = 0.4NC_{t-1} + 0.7C_{t-1}$$

Thus, for $t = 3$, we obtain:

$$NC_3 = 0.6(60,000) + 0.3(40,000) = 48,000$$
$$C_3 = 0.4(60,000) + 0.7(40,000) = \underline{52,000}$$
$$ 100,000$$

And for $t = 4$:

$$NC_4 = 0.6(48,000) + 0.3(52,000) = 44,400$$
$$C_4 = 0.4(48,000) + 0.7(52,000) = \underline{55,600}$$
$$ 100,000$$

We can continue this process until the results stabilize and there is only a very minor difference between NC_t and NC_{t-1}; similarly, almost no change between C_t and C_{t-1}. This is called the *steady state* of the system. Figure 9.11 shows the trajectory of the customer predictions over time. The steady state result is 57,143 customers.

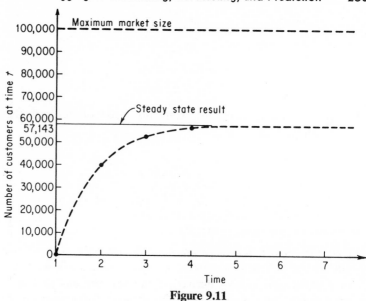

Figure 9.11

Predictions imply dynamic trajectories as well as steady states.

Temporal Regularities

When historical information is available, it is often found that the calendar has a big influence on what happens; sometimes we refer to this as a seasonal pattern. The so-called *historical forecast*[22] is based on the assumption that what happened last year will happen again. Thus, for example, if the demand in the previous January was x, then in the coming January it will also be x. Of course, this method is effective only if a *very stable* calendar pattern exists.

If the forecast means appear to be changing over time but the seasonal pattern remains fixed, then a *base series modification* can be used. For example, assume that in the preceding year the quarterly demands were successively 40, 20, 30, 10. This gives a yearly demand of 100 units. Now, let us assume that in the current year the yearly (aggregate) demand is expected to be 120 units. Then the quarterly forecasts would be $(40/100)120 = 48$; $(20/100)120 = 24$; $(30/100)120 = 36$; $(10/100)120 = 12$. These quarterly demands total to 120 units.

Regression Analysis for Prediction

When environmental occurrences appear related to other factors that *lead* or precede their occurrence, then, it is often possible to predict what will

[22] In our terms, historical prediction.

happen on the basis of observations of the other factors. For example, assume
the following data:

i	x_i = number of children born in year i (in millions)	$i + 5$	y_{i+5} = kindergarten attendance in year $i + 5$ (in millions)
1	3	6	2
2	4	7	3
3	6	8	5
4	4	9	5
5	8	10	6

Assuming that the number of children born in a given year leads kinder-
garten attendance by five years, we have paired the x_i's with the y_{i+5}'s that
occurred five years later. Let us fit a least-squares line to these data. We use
the normal equations (based on the assumption of a *linear* relationship
between x_i and y_{i+5}).

$$\sum_{i=1}^{i=N} y_{i+5} = aN + b \sum_{i=1}^{i=N} x_i$$

$$\sum_{i=1}^{i=N} x_i y_{i+5} = a \sum_{i=1}^{i=N} x_i + b \sum_{i=1}^{i=N} x_i^2$$

$N = 5$, which is the total number of pairs of x_i and y_{i+5}, for which we have
data available. Then:

i	x_i	y_{i+5}	$x_i y_{i+5}$	x_i^2
1	3	2	6	9
2	4	3	12	16
3	6	5	30	36
4	4	5	20	16
5	8	6	48	64
Σ	25	21	116	141

Therefore:

$$21 = a(5) + b(25)$$
$$116 = a(25) + b(141)$$

Solving for a and b, we obtain: $a = +61/80; b = +11/16$.
These values are introduced in the least-squares line:

$$y_{i+5} = a + bx_i = +\frac{61}{80} + \frac{11}{16} x_i$$

The appropriate line and the actual scatter of values are shown in Figure 9.12.
To use this line, suppose that when $i = 6$, $x_i = 10$. We see that y_{i+5} would
be predicted to be 7.6375 million. We would use this prediction only if the
data upon which the regression line is constructed appear to fit it well,
especially in recent years.

Different forecasts for the same phenomena frequently exist within a single organization. Sometimes, the production manager derives one forecast; the sales manager derives another; branch managers derive still others. Often a variety of different data bases coexist. Methods for pooling information to provide a stronger prediction should not be ignored. Also, it is of critical importance that all parties share the same forecasts, and usually, much stronger forecasts can be obtained if both data *and experience* are pooled.

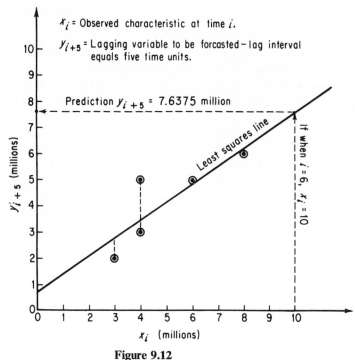

Figure 9.12

Least-squares linear relationship between a leading indicator and the variable to be predicted.

Autocorrelation and Predictions

To determine what interval best describes the temporal regularity of a time series or the most appropriate lag relationship between two different time series, the use of an autocorrelation function is warranted. Such a function can be represented in continuous form by:

$$R(\tau) = 1/T \int_0^T x(t)x(t - \tau)\, dt$$

where: $T =$ number of observations made or the time period.

$x(t)$ = the specific value of x observed at time t.

$x(t - \tau)$ = value observed at time $t - \tau$.

When the integral is divided by T, the variance of $f(x)$[23] results. We are really interested in the *auto correlation coefficient*, called ACC, which is:

$$\text{ACC} = \frac{R(\tau)}{\sigma^2}$$

In the discrete case, $R(\tau)$ is the variance of x_i with $x_{i+\tau}$, thus:

$$R(\tau) = ([\sum_i x_i \cdot x_{i+\tau}]/n) - \bar{x}^2$$

and

$$\sigma^2 = \sum_i (x_i - \bar{x})^2/n = \sum_i (x_i^2 - 2x_i\bar{x} + \bar{x}^2)/n$$

$$= \frac{\sum x_i^2}{n} - \frac{2\bar{x} \sum_i x_i}{n} + \frac{n\bar{x}^2}{n}$$

$$= \frac{\sum_i x_i^2}{n} - 2\bar{x}^2 + \bar{x}^2 = (\sum_i x_i^2/n) - \bar{x}^2.$$

Thus, σ^2 is the variance of $(x_i)^2$ or $R(0)$.

Certain observations can be made about the AC function and the ACC. The function produces a series of different values as τ is varied. Specifically, when $\tau = 0$, we are squaring the observations of the time series $[x(t) - \bar{x}]^2$.

The definition of a historical forecast is that $\tau = 0 \equiv \tau = 12$. If the historical forecast is valid, then the ACC should be close to 1.00. But for predictive purposes, an ACC of minus one is quite as useful. In fact, it might give the strongest lag-lead results where one series is x_i and the other $y_{i+\tau}$. A brief example may help to illustrate the use of autocorrelation. Let $\tau = 2$.

i	x_i	$x_{i+\tau}$	x_i^2	$x_i \cdot x_{i+\tau}$
1	1	3	1	3
2	2	4	4	8
3	3	5	9	15
4	4	4	16	16
5	5	3	25	15
6	4	2	16	8
7	3	1	9	3
8	2	2	4	4
9	1	3	1	3
10	2	4	4	8
11	3	5	9	15
$R(2) = \frac{98}{11} - (\bar{x})^2$			98	98

$$\frac{R(2)}{\sigma^2} = 1 = \text{ACC} \,(\tau = 2)$$

$$\sigma^2 = \frac{98}{11} - (\bar{x})^2$$

---

[23] The integral function.

A computer program can rapidly produce calculations of this sort. Figure 9.13 outlines a flow diagram that, if followed, will calculate the autocorrelation coefficient for any specified number of lag intervals.

Forecasting and prediction are hardly exhausted by our brief discussion in this chapter. However, at least a sufficient base is established to appreciate why aggregate scheduling techniques do not assist the manager who lacks the ability to achieve a synthesis with predictive techniques.

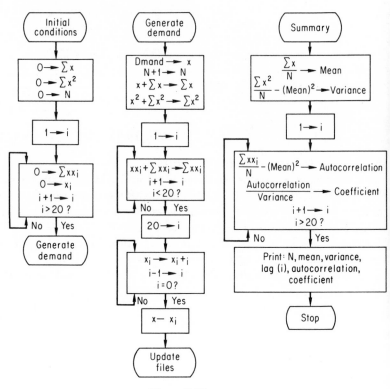

Figure 9.13

Approximate computations for autocorrelation. [From: *Statistical Forecasting for Inventory Control*, by Robert G. Brown (New York: McGraw-Hill Book Company, 1959) p. 183. Used with permission of McGraw-Hill Book Company.]

PROBLEMS

1. Actual monthly demands for the past year are available for item, Z54, a microswitch.

Month	Demand	Month	Demand
1	621	7	708
2	415	8	615
3	380	9	422
4	763	10	669
5	845	11	810
6	550	12	396

Can you find any useful patterns that will enable you to proceed with an aggregate scheduling problem?

2. Use the HMMS model with the above data divided into quarterly demands. Assume simple values for all the costs based on reasonable patterns for the curves in Figure 9.4, p. 235. Determine the optimum values for each of the four quarters of the coming year.

3. Set up the LP equivalent of the problem described in two above. Use the same costs and predictions for future quarterly demands. Compare the LP approach with that of numerical optimization.

4. Use Bishop's rule to resolve the aggregate scheduling problem below:

	1	2	3	Closing Inventory	Dummy	Supply
I_0				⌐10		100
R_1				⌐9		49
0_1				⌐8		80
R_2				⌐7		70
0_2				⌐6		100
R_3				⌐5		50
0_3				⌐4		51
Demand	80	120	100	100	100	500

5. It is believed that demand will follow a Markovian pattern for the next three months based on a present share of 30 per cent for our brand, A. Obtain the predicted demand for the next three months given a fixed total monthly sales volume of 100,000 units.

		Time 2			
	Share	$\rightarrow$	A_2	B_2	C_2
	.30	A_1	.6	.3	.1
Time 1	.40	B_1	.3	.6	.1
	.30	C_1	.2	.2	.6

6. Use transportation analysis for aggregate scheduling where regular production represents eight thousand units per month at a cost of fifty cents per unit and overtime can produce five thousand units per month at a cost of seventy-five cents per unit. The initial inventory is one thousand units, and the final inventory is to be no greater. The carrying cost rate is stated to be 2 per cent per month. This schedule is to cover the first quarter; the monthly demands are 9,000 to 12,000, and 16,000 respectively.

Chapter 10 concerns the shop loading or machine loading function. It is a task that is highly repetitive in most job shops. The requirement is to determine which facility or machine centers will be assigned specific jobs and how much of a load such centers shall carry. Clearly, this differs from aggregate scheduling in that the spotlight is thrown upon different facilities. A variety of approaches to this problem are available that tend to emphasize ease of computation.

Shop Loading 10

Following aggregate scheduling, the production plans, P_{t_i}, for individual items, i, are developed. Facilities and work force levels have also been scheduled, but the facilities have not been reserved for items nor have the items been assigned to facilities. In other words, $W_t = \Sigma_i W_{t_i}$ for $i = 1, 2, \ldots,$ and only the left-hand side of the equation is known. Shop loading is intended to accomplish this assignment of actual jobs to facilities.

Linear programming (or an equivalent network algorithm) can be used effectively for scheduling a variety of jobs through departments having many machines. We know that LP is a deterministic technique. So, those risk factors that exist, including machine breakdowns and man-machine interactions, that produce variability and other disturbances must be reserved for later interpretation and action by the manager.

This is no different from the Gantt approach to shop loading.

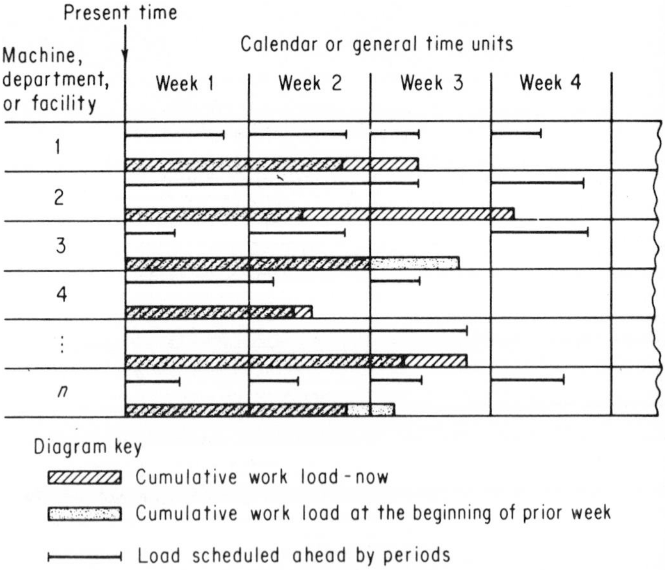

Figure 10.1

The Gantt load chart.

Gantt loading has been used for years (with the assumption of no unexpected events) to accomplish "general" work loading of departments and machine or facility centers. The reason that certainty is assumed, no matter what technique is used, is that the kinds of variations that occur are not usually fundamental determinants of process behavior, and process effectiveness is not particularly sensitive to them. When the process is really sensitive and responsive to one or more risk factors, then linear programming is not the right conceptual approach to accomplish the loading or assignment job, but then, neither is the Gantt approach. In most facility and job loading situations, it is vital to define the objectives that are to be accomplished. The reason is simple: One does not usually obtain the same job-machine assignment when the objective is to minimize time through the system as one obtains when the objective calls for minimization of cost. Similarly, profit maximization is quite likely to provide a third solution.

The Assignment Algorithm for Relatively Continuous Loading of Production Facilities

First, let us study the problem of assigning jobs on a relatively permanent basis, for example, jobs involving the use of heavy capital equipment requiring expensive set-up costs. This would epitomize situations where the facilities tend to be continuously employed on particular jobs—intermittent flow shops. We shall assume that four different jobs can be done by four different facilities. We shall postulate that economic lot size requirements call for almost continuous operation of the facilities. Furthermore, the set-up and take-down costs are prohibitively high for changeovers.

The assignment matrix must be square, i.e., same number of jobs as machines. No splitting of job assignments is allowed. In general, the assignment would be relatively stable because there is a corresponding psychological assumption (that may or may not match reality) that the relevant system is really stable. If this assumption is faulty, and a sequence of assignments are made over time, then there is no protection against the fact that such a sequence may not produce optimal solutions; in fact, it may produce quite poor ones. The type of relation that holds has much relevance to our ideas about synthesis, namely, with respect to the total time (or cost) to accomplish k jobs:

$$\text{Optimal } (t_1 + t_2 + \ldots t_k) \leq \text{Optimal } t_1 + \text{Optimal } t_2 + \ldots + \text{Optimal } t_k$$

With this criterion in mind, let us now turn to an assignment problem. We develop a matrix to indicate the operating *costs* per part for each job on each machine. Our objective will be to minimize the total cost of all assignments. Some hypothetical data are introduced in the matrix below, where the facilities are A, B, C, and D, and the jobs are 1, 2, 3, and 4.

	M_A	M_B	M_C	M_D
J_1	3	5	7	4
J_2	6	4	7	2
J_3	2	5	3	5
J_4	8	2	6	1

For job 1, machine A is preferred because it has the lowest cost of $3.00. However, job 3 is also best suited for machine A. We have defined *best suited* to mean that the cost per part is lowest. Thus, *a conflict exists with respect to machine A for jobs 1 and 3*. Now let us compare the relative advantages of different machines for a specific job, for example, job 4. We find that the best machine B assignment is job 4 and the best machine D assignment is also job 4. There is a *conflict with respect to the fourth job*. Machines B and D are both best when employed on job 4.

To resolve this problem we shall derive a set of *opportunity costs*. First, we can subtract the lowest cost in each column from all the costs in that column—doing this for every column in the matrix. For machine A, $2.00 is the best possible cost. Therefore, if we assign machine A to job 3, we would have a zero opportunity cost. On the other hand, if we assign job 1 to machine A, there is a penalty of $1.00 to be paid (that is, $3.00—$2.00). Similarly, with respect to M_A, job 2 incurs an opportunity cost of $4.00, and job 4 has an opportunity cost of $6.00. Turning to machine B, we proceed to do the same thing. When machine B is assigned to job 4 the *best* possible result occurs, that is, a *zero* opportunity cost. The matrix shown below is the *opportunity cost matrix* with respect to jobs for each given machine.

	M_A	M_B	M_C	M_D
J_1	1	3	4	3
J_2	4	2	4	1
J_3	0	3	0	4
J_4	6	0	3	0

If each zero appeared in such a way that the four jobs could be assigned to four different machines—assignments being made to zero cells—the problem would be solved. The result would be a minimum cost assignment. Sometimes alternative assignment patterns exist, all of which have the *same* minimum cost. In the present case, we see that conflicts exist. Zero opportunity cost assignments for job 3 can be obtained in two ways, that is, machines A and C; job 4 could be placed on machines B and D; and no assignment has been indicated for jobs 1 and 2.

Our next step is to subtract within rows. In this way we obtain *job opportunity costs* with respect to machines. Thus, the assignment of job 1 to machine A produces zero opportunity cost. The assignment of job 2 to machine *D* produces a zero opportunity cost. We develop a matrix of two-way opportunity costs—first, using column, then row subtraction[1]—which must, therefore, have a zero in every row and every column. This matrix is shown below.

	M_A	M_B	M_C	M_D
J_1	0	2	3	2
J_2	3	1	3	0
J_3	0	3	0	4
J_4	6	0	3	0

(Because the third and fourth rows obtained their zeros in the previous step of column subtraction, row subtraction produces no further modification.)

We must find out if we have a unique assignment that meets our *requirement of a different job on each machine*. Let us begin by circling all zeros that are *unique* in either their rows or their columns. Thus, select the zero representing the assignment of job 3 to machine *C*. It is the only zero in column 3. Similarly, circle J_1M_A—unique in its row; circle J_2M_D—unique in its row; circle J_4M_B—unique in its column. Because a different machine is unambiguously assigned to each job, the schedule is completed. The assignments should be made as follows:

Assignment		
Job	Machine	Unit Cost in Dollars
1	A	3.00
2	D	2.00
3	C	3.00
4	B	2.00

This is the minimum cost schedule. There are no alternatives.

It is interesting to note that initially the number of possible assignments that can be made is *n*! In this case, *n* is four, and, therefore, twenty-four different assignments are possible. Allowing one minute to evaluate each assignment, the job of determining the optimal schedule would take almost a half hour. By using the assignment algorithm we obtain the optimal solution in one or two minutes. The comparison of computing times—with and without the algorithm—becomes impressive, indeed, as the number of job-machine assignments to be made increases. With ten machines and ten jobs there are over three and a half million possible assignments; with $n = 15$, over a trillion unique assignments exist.

Now, let us consider the situation that arises when row and column

---

[1] The order can be reversed at will.

subtractions do not yield a solution directly. As footnoted before, the final solution will always be invariant to whether row subtraction or column subtraction is used first. At most, an extra calculation may be required because one is used instead of the other.

We construct the following matrix, using machines P, Q, R, and S with jobs, 1, 2, 3, and 4:

	M_P	M_Q	M_R	M_S
J_1	3	5	9	4
J_2	6	3	7	4
J_3	2	5	8	5
J_4	8	2	6	1

This time, use row subtraction first. The matrix derived is:

	M_P	M_Q	M_R	M_S
J_1	0	2	6	1
J_2	3	0	4	1
J_3	0	3	6	3
J_4	7	1	5	0

We see that no solution is arrived at in this manner. Let us, therefore, proceed to the next step—the use of column subtraction. We obtain:

	M_P	M_Q	M_R	M_S
J_1	0	2	2	1
J_2	3	0	0	1
J_3	0	3	2	3
J_4	7	1	1	0

which does not constitute a solution. To reduce this matrix further we can apply the following steps.

Assignment Rules After Row and Column Subtraction

1. Cover all the zeros in the matrix with the *minimum number* of lines possible.[2] We see that three lines will achieve our objective. They can be

---

[2] When the problem is large, an algorithm for finding the minimum number of lines is desirable. See, for example, M. Sasieni, A. Yaspan, and L. Friedman, *Operations Research: Methods and Problems* (New York: John Wiley & Sons, Inc., 1959), pp. 189–90.

drawn in several different ways. It is possible to cover with four lines, but this is not the minimum number of lines which we have specified. The matrix below shows one way of covering all zeros with three lines.

	M_P	M_Q	M_R	M_S
J_1	0	2	2	1
J_2	3	0	0	1
J_3	0	3	2	3
J_4	7	1	1	0

2. Choose the *smallest uncovered number*, which in this case is 1 at J_1M_S.

3. Subtract this number, that is, 1, from every uncovered number in the matrix, including itself. Then *add* this number to all values that appear at line intersections. This procedure yields:

	M_P	M_Q	M_R	M_S
J_1	0	1	1	0
J_2	4	0	0	1
J_3	0	2	1	2
J_4	8	1	1	0

4. We now test to see whether this result is a solution. In the present case it is not.

5. Therefore, cover all zeros with the minimum number of lines, which is three, as before. This is shown below.

	M_P	M_Q	M_R	M_S
J_1	0	1	1	0
J_2	4	0	0	1
J_3	0	2	1	2
J_4	8	1	1	0

6. We repeat steps two, three, and four described above as many times as required until the final solution is determined.

For this example, at the end of the next cycle of matrix operations we obtain the final solution, viz.:

	M_P	M_Q	M_R	M_S
J_1	0	0	0	0
J_2	5	0	0	2
J_3	0	1	0	2
J_4	8	0	0	0

We observe that there are five equally desirable alternative schedules indicated by the final matrix. Each of these produces a total cost for one unit of
each part of $15.00. Figure 10.2 illustrates the alternate assignments that pro-
vide a final solution. The manager is now in a position to consider the intangible advantages of the various alternatives, which in strictly quantitative
terms are equivalent.

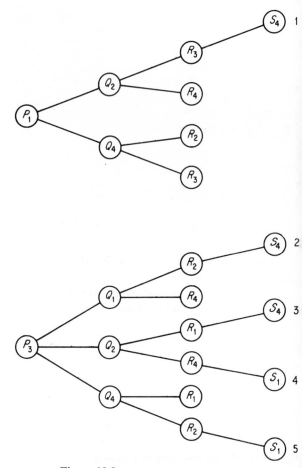

Figure 10.2

Five feasible optimal alternatives for machine assignments. (Jobs 1 and 3 can be assigned to
Machine P, that is, P_1 and P_3. The same reasoning applies to Q, R, and S.

The use of a dummy job, J_*, illustrates some additional strengths of this
assignment approach. It permits alternative facilities to compete for investment funds. Assume that the company can afford to buy only four different
machines, but five different choices are available. How should the choice be

made? We will call the new machine option, M_T, and assume that the matrix below applies:

	M_P	M_Q	M_R	M_S	M_T
J_1	3	5	9	4	5
J_2	6	3	7	4	3
J_3	2	5	8	5	1
J_4	8	2	6	1	2
J_*	0	0	0	0	0

Note that when a fifth machine is considered, there being only four jobs to be assigned and only four machines to be used, a dummy job called J_* was created. Because this job does not really exist, we utilize all zero costs for its row in the matrix. Thus, we express the fact that we are indifferent as to which machine this dummy job, J_*, will be assigned. In this way, the relative qualities of other jobs with respect to machines will force their assignments *before* the dummy assignment is made. Whichever machine the dummy job is assigned to will be dropped from the list of equipment to be selected. Clearly, the machine that is given the dummy job assignment will be the least desirable machine from the point of view of minimizing operating costs. It is the expendable machine.

Going through the steps required by the assignment algorithm, we find the following solution:

	M_P	M_Q	M_R	M_S	M_T
J_1	⓪	2	6	1	2
J_2	3	⓪	4	1	0
J_3	1	4	7	4	⓪
J_4	7	1	5	⓪	1
J_*	0	0	⓪	0	0

The dummy job is assigned to machine R. Machine T, the alternative that was being considered, *should be obtained* to replace machine R. The same kind of comparisons can be made for other machines options that might be specified, such as M_U, M_V, M_W, and so on.

If the problem is couched in terms of profit maximization instead of cost minimization, a simple transformation is required. We subtract all the numbers that appear in the profit matrix from the *largest number* in the matrix. In effect, this converts the profit matrix into a cost matrix. We then follow the same rules as before. If a given job cannot be assigned to a certain machine for technological reasons—or because a job is already in process on the machine—then we block the assignment by entering a very large cost in the appropriate cell. This will prevent impossible, unwanted, and undesirable assignments from being made. From a systems point of view, the loading problem interacts with facility selection. The *effective* solution cannot be indifferent to this point of view although, historically, the assignment effort has been limited to finding *cost efficient* solutions

Network Version of the Assignment Method

The Ford-Fulkerson methods for determining maximum flow in a network of fixed capacities can be explained, in an interesting way, by means of a *string model*. This is a network analog that permits minimum distance, minimum time, or maximum capacity paths to be discovered through a complex maze. The knots, when the pieces of string are joined together, are the nodes of the network. For example, they can represent machines or stations at which specific operations are to be performed. The length of string between the nodes (the network arc) can be made proportional to the distance between machines that a given layout calls for (see Figure 1.19, p. 22). The length could also be made proportional to traverse time between stations, to the cost of transporting an item between stations, or to the capacity of each network arc.[3] When the string is stretched taut between any two nodes, we immediately obtain the minimum path between these nodes. Thus, for different input (receiving) and output (shipping) portals, a given layout can be rather quickly compared with alternative designs. The ease with which this model can be applied to small systems is its only practical recommendation; however, as a conceptual device for understanding network behaviors it is excellent.

The assignment problem is another form of network algorithm. Given that each job must be assigned to a unique machine—that is, no duplicate machine assignments can be made—a string analog can be devised. Let us take the simplest example of a 2 × 2 system. This is shown both in matrix and network form in Figure 10.3.

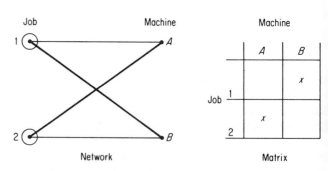

Figure 10.3

The assignment *A*2, *B*1 is represented by heavier lines and the *x*'s in the matrix.

[3] See Chapter 14, pp. 431–436.

There are only four possible patterns of assignments:

	1		2		3		4	
1	0	0	1	1	0	0	1
1	0	1	0	0	1	0	1
	No		Yes		Yes		No	Feasibility

Only two of these are feasible. In general, for an $n \times n$ system, there are $n!$ *feasible* assignments; the first job can be assigned in n ways, the second job in $n - 1$ ways, . . . the last job in only one way.

Now, let us visualize how network algorithms operate by the admittedly tedious analysis of how a string network can be manipulated to provide a solution. We will use the network algorithm, say, for minimum cost:

1. Cut shortest line among $1A$, $2A$, . . . etc., in Figure 10.4; this is equivalent to finding the zero opportunity cost in the first column of the job-machine matrix.

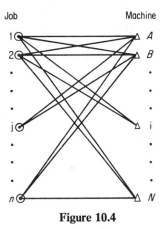

Figure 10.4

2. Shorten all other jA lines by the amount of the cut string; i.e., all column A's opportunity costs are derived.
3. Repeat for jB's, jC's, etc.; opportunity costs for each column of the entire matrix are obtained.
4. How can you tell if you have a solution? Answer: if each ⊙ (or j) is connected to a different △ (or i).
5. If this is not the case, then cut shortest line among $A1$, $B1$, . . . etc. This is equivalent to finding the zero opportunity cost in the first row. Note that one or more of these lines may have been cut previously, i.e., a zero already exists in the first row.
6. Shorten all other $1i$ lines by the amount of the cut string.
7. Repeat for $2i$'s, $3i$'s, etc.

8. Apply the same test as in four above.
9. If no solution is obtained, this string explanation of the network algorithm can be extended to include the matrix zeros line covering steps that are a conventional part of the assignment method. We are not doing this because our purpose in this explanation being conceptual is not aided by further complexity.

Machine Loading with the Transportation Algorithm

Having discussed assignment problems for which relatively permanent selections can be made, we shall proceed to the situation in which more frequent rearranging of the load is expected. In the case of the relatively permanent assignment, a best facility selected from among a set of alternative facilities could be found for a given job. Because all the jobs were expected to continue for some time, it would have been pointless to break up or *split* jobs, assigning portions to different facilities. For the situations we are about to describe, this condition will no longer apply. Consequently, whatever technique we utilize should enable us to place part of a job on one facility and the remainder of it on another. Sometimes it will be reasonable to break the jobs 50-50; at other times, 10 per cent might be assigned to each of six facilities, the remaining forty per cent to a single facility.

The model that we will employ is based upon the transportation algorithm previously discussed on pp. 240–246. We must now reexamine this transportation matrix in a different light. We should note that in the usual transportation model both the column and the row restrictions have identical dimensions. In other words, factory A can ship *x units of goods* to warehouse B that, in turn, requires *x units of goods*. The dimension, units of goods, is the same for all rows and columns. This is not true for the machine loading problem. Here the resources of the facilities are measured by the number of productive hours available per week, and the demand is measured in units of goods. Then, the only way to proceed is to find some means of converting all information to a standard data form. Perhaps this is more easily understood if the LP form of the transportation network is presented first. This would be:

$$\sum_j x_{ij} \geq b_i \quad i = 1, 2, \ldots n, \quad x_{ij} \geq 0$$

$$\sum_i x_{ij} \leq r_j \quad j = 1, 2, \ldots m$$

$$\sum_i b_i = \sum_j r_j$$

Minimize $(\sum_i \sum_j c_{ij}x_{ij})$

Or, in matrix form:

	M_A	M_B	...	M_N	Demand (number of pieces)
J_1	C_{1A} x_{1A}	C_{1B} x_{1B}	...	C_{1N} x_{1N}	b_1
J_2	C_{2A} x_{2A}	C_{2B} x_{2B}	...	C_{2N} x_{2N}	b_2
$\vdots$					$\vdots$
J_n	C_{nA} x_{nA}	C_{nB} x_{nB}	...	C_{nN} x_{nN}	b_n
Machine Time Available	r_1	r_2	...	r_N	

Note: The c_{ij} can be times, costs, or profits—but whichever, they must be dimensioned per standard machine hour. The x_{ij} will have to produce assignments in terms of standard machine hours. To accomplish this, the b_i that are job demands and the r_j that are machine hours available must be converted to standard machine hour terms.

A productivity matrix, such as the one below is essential for the standard hour transformation.

	M_A	M_B	M_C	M_D	Demand (number of pieces)
J_1	3	6	4.8	3.6	300
J_2	3.5	7	5.6	4.2	210
J_3	3	6	4.8	3.6	240
J_4	15	30	24	18	1800
J_5	12.5	25	20	15	400
Index	0.5	1.0	0.8	0.6	
Available Hours	40	60	80	$41\frac{2}{3}$	

Matrix of Production Rates (All matrix entries in pieces per hour)

We require a *standard machine* against which the other machines can be compared. Machine B has been arbitrarily chosen as the standard machine. Once we obtain a standard unit we can transform all the elements of the transportation matrix into comparable dimensional terms. Observe the productivity rates of the various machines. The numbers in the matrix represent the production rates that characterize each job and each machine. Productivity is given in terms of pieces per hour. Thus, machine A produces three pieces of job 1 per hour. These matrix entries are comparable to the shipping costs ordinarily utilized for distribution problems. Machine B is capable of the greatest production rates for all jobs. Machine A has only one-half of machine B's productivity. Machine C has 0.8 of machine B's productive capacity, and machine D has 0.6 of machine B's productive capacity. Consequently, we can use index numbers to rate the relative productivities of each machine. The index ratings have been shown in the matrix. We call machine B the *standard machine*, and we have assigned it an index of 1.

The key to the concept of the standard machine is that the *relative productivities of the facilities are proportional to each other* for all jobs. When this is not exactly true, we try to approximate it. Usually, some acceptable approximation is possible. *It doesn't matter which machine we call the standard machine.* We have arbitrarily chosen the machine that has the greatest productivity rate for the assignment of an index of 1.

Now, turning to the column constraints, the first machine has 40 hours available per week; the second, 60 hours available per week; the third, 80 hours available per week; and the fourth, $41\frac{2}{3}$ hours available per week. Why is there this difference between machines? First, there may be two machines of the M_C type that together give a total of 80 hours in a normal work week. On the other hand, extra shifts may be utilized for M_C. How about M_B? There may be two of these machines, but part of the week is blocked by a previous assignment for one of the two machines. Furthermore, some of the machines may be scheduled for maintenance work and, therefore, would not be available on the production load chart.

We must convert the machine hours available per week into standard machine hours available per week. We do this in the following table.

Machine	Hours Per Week Available	Per Cent Utilization	Effective Hours Available Per Week	Index	Standard Machine Hours Available Per Week
A	40	0.9	36	0.5	18
B	60	0.9	54	1.0	54
C	80	1.0	80	0.8	64
D	$41\frac{2}{3}$	0.8	$33\frac{1}{3}$	0.6	20
			$203\frac{1}{3}$		156

To begin, we list the number of available hours per week for each machine. Then, for realism, a per cent utilization column is also given. This per cent utilization, which is derived from operating records, is intended to account for breakdowns, adjustments, and other factors that subtract *real* time from productive time. By multiplying available hours per week by per cent utilization, we determine effective hours available per week. Next, we multiply the effective hours by the appropriate index rating for each machine. For example, the index of M_A is 0.5; the effective hours are 36; the product is 18 *standard hours* available per week. Effective hours and standard hours are equal for machine B because the index of M_B is 1. The total standard machine hours available per week is 156 hours.

The row constraints must be transformed into standard units. There are five jobs to be scheduled for the week. Allowance has been made for those jobs that are already on machines and have been assigned blocked time. In some cases, it is desirable to reschedule the total set of jobs on hand, including those with prior assignments. This is particulary apt when set-up costs are low. In fact, throughout our present discussion we shall assume that set-up costs are not significant. If they were large, we would have to take them into account. Frequently, this would prohibit splitting jobs between facilities. The five jobs have specified demands of 300, 210, 240, 1800, and 400 pieces. Job 1 has a requirement of 300 pieces per week. If we divide these numbers by the productivity rate of the standard machine, we will transform the dimension of requirements into standard hours per week. For example:

$$(300) \frac{\text{Pieces}}{\text{Week}} \div (6) \frac{\text{Pieces}}{\text{Standard Machine Hour}} = (50) \frac{\text{Standard Machine Hours}}{\text{Week}}$$

Following through this operation for all jobs, we obtain the following:

Job	Standard Row Restrictions
1	300/6 = 50
2	210/7 = 30
3	240/6 = 40
4	1800/30 = 60
5	400/25 = 16
	196 Standard Hours

Now we discover that 196 standard hours are required to do all the jobs, but we have only 156 standard hours available from our machines. Accordingly, we can appoint a *dummy machine* to absorb the overrequirement of 40 standard hours. One of the jobs will not be completed in the period.

We shall assume that our objective is to maximize profit.[4] Let us determine the profit rate for each job-machine combination in terms of standard machine hours. First, we observe that each machine requires a different level of operator skill and that each labor skill level has a different wage rate per hour.

Machine	Labor Skill	Wage Rate (dollars per hour)
A	a	6.00
B	c	4.20
C	b	4.80
D	d	3.60

[4] We reiterate that profit maximization solutions are not necessarily the same as those of cost minimization. Both might be different from the solution for delivery time minimization. The profit objective is *global*, and, consequently, we utilize it for this problem.

Next, we determine a *labor-cost matrix* in dollars per piece. Job 1 on machine *A* has a production rate of three pieces per hour. If we divide the labor cost per hour by the production rate, we discover that the labor cost is $2.00 per piece for job 1 on machine *A*.[5] Similarly, consider job 4 on machine *C*. This is skill level *b*—rated at $4.80 per piece. The productivity rate is twenty-four pieces per hour. We divide twenty-four into 4.8 and obtain a labor cost of $0.20 per piece. In this way we derive the labor-cost matrix shown below.

Labor-Cost Matrix—Dollars Per Piece

Job	M_A	M_B	M_C	M_D
1	2.00	0.70	1.00	1.00
2	1.71	0.60	0.86	0.86
3	2.00	0.70	1.00	1.00
4	0.40	0.14	0.20	0.20
5	0.48	0.17	0.24	0.24

Next, consider the material cost for each job. The relevant data might be:

Job	Material Cost (dollars per piece)
1	0.50
2	0.60
3	0.80
4	1.00
5	1.20

Materials for job 1 cost $0.50 per piece. Materials for job 5 cost $1.20 per piece. We can now develop a labor + materials-cost matrix in dollars per piece by adding the appropriate materials cost to each row of the labor-cost matrix. The result is:

Labor + Materials Cost Matrix—Dollars Per Piece

Job	M_A	M_B	M_C	M_D
1	2.50	1.20	1.50	1.50
2	2.31	1.20	1.46	1.46
3	2.80	1.50	1.80	1.80
4	1.40	1.14	1.20	1.20
5	1.68	1.37	1.44	1.44

[5] Thus: $(6) \dfrac{\$}{\text{hr.}} \div (3) \dfrac{\text{pieces}}{\text{hr.}} = (2) \dfrac{\$}{\text{piece}}.$

The next set of computations will produce the *profit-per-piece matrix*. To obtain this we must know the selling price per piece for each job. Thus:

Job	Selling Price (dollars per piece)
1	4.00
2	4.00
3	5.00
4	3.00
5	3.00

For each row of the cost matrix, only one selling price applies. From this selling price, row by row, the appropriate labor plus material costs are to be subtracted. For example, job 2 sells at $4.00 per piece. Each job 2 row entry is subtracted from four; thus, $4.00 − $2.31 = $1.69, $4.00 − $1.20 = $2.80, $4.00 − $1.46 = $2.54, and so forth. By utilizing this approach we have derived the profit-per-piece matrix.

Profit-Per-Piece Matrix in Dollars

Job	M_A	M_B	M_C	M_D
1	$1.50	$2.80	$2.50	$2.50
2	1.69	2.80	2.54	2.54
3	2.20	3.50	3.20	3.20
4	1.60	1.86	1.80	1.80
5	1.32	1.63	1.56	1.56

We now convert the profit-per-piece matrix into a *profit-per-standard-machine-hour matrix*. To achieve this conversion we utilize the *productivity rates of the standard machine* (see p. 279). Thus, for example, all elements in the first row of the profit-per-piece matrix are multiplied by six—the job 2 productivity of the standard machine. All elements in the second row of the profit-per-piece matrix are multiplied by seven—the job 2 productivity of the standard machine. All elements in the fourth row of the profit-per-piece matrix are multiplied by thirty, and so forth. The reason that this succeeds in producing a new matrix transformed into terms of profit per standard machine hour is shown by the following relationship.

$$\frac{\text{Profit}[6]}{\text{Piece}} \times \frac{\text{Pieces}}{\text{Standard Hour}} = \frac{\text{Profit}}{\text{Standard Hour}}$$

[6] Or cost (per piece yielding cost) per standard hour.

The profit-per-standard-machine-hour matrix is given herewith:

Profit Per Standard Machine Hour in Dollars

Job	M_A	M_B	M_C	M_D
1	$ 9.00	$16.80	$15.00	$15.00
2	11.80	19.60	17.80	17.80
3	13.20	21.00	19.20	19.20
4	48.00	55.80	54.00	54.00
5	33.00	40.80	39.00	39.00

The complete matrix, entirely in terms of standard machine hours will be:

Matrix of Profit Per Standard Machine Hour

	M_A	M_B	M_C	M_D	Δ	Demand (standard machine hrs.)
J_1	$ 9.00	$16.80	$15.00	$15.00	$0	50
J_2	11.80	19.60	17.80	17.80	0	30
J_3	13.20	21.00	19.20	19.20	0	40
J_4	48.00	55.80	54.00	54.00	0	60
J_5	33.00	40.80	39.00	39.00	0	16
Available Standard Hours	18	54	64	20	40	196

The profits per standard hour assigned to the dummy (called Δ) are all set at zero so that no preference exists with respect to which job will be assigned to the dummy machine. Whichever job is eventually assigned, it will not be done in this week.

To summarize, the transformations to dimensions of standard hours (*) are dependent upon the use of a column vector $[P_{is}]$ of productivity measures for the ith job on the standard machine, S. Then,

1. $[c_{ij}] \times [P_{is}] = [c_{ij}^*]$
2. $[Demand] \div [P_{is}] = [Demand^*]$
3. $[Effective\ Hours] \times [Index] = [Machine\ Hours^*]$

The transportation algorithm can now be used. The objective, in this case, is to maximize profit. Logically, therefore, all changes in assignments should be made to cells that improve the total profit. The initial assignments can be set down as a Northwest Corner allocation. It has a profit π of $3985.20.

Northwest Corner Allocation of Standard Machine Hours

	M_A	M_B	M_C	M_D	Δ	*Demand*
J_1	18	32				50
J_2		22	8			30
J_3			40			40
J_4			16	20	24	60
J_5					16	16
Available Hours	18	54	64	20	40	196

We continue to rearrange these assignments until there is no longer any possibility of improving the profit. The matrix of the fifth and final solution is shown below as well as the profit levels associated with the first and last iterations.

Profit Levels

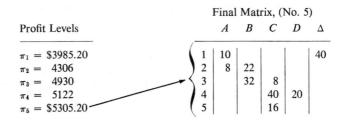

Final Matrix, (No. 5)

	A	*B*	*C*	*D*	Δ
1	10				40
2	8	22			
3		32	8		
4			40	20	
5			16		

$\pi_1 = \$3985.20$
$\pi_2 = 4306$
$\pi_3 = 4930$
$\pi_4 = 5122$
$\pi_5 = \$5305.20$

Also, the cost analysis indicates that there are many alternative assignments. Job 1 has been assigned to both M_A and to the dummy. Job 2 has been assigned to M_A and M_B and so on. The transportation matrix of standard hours for each assignment can be written.

Final Solution in Standard Hour Assignments

	M_A	M_B	M_C	M_D	Δ	*Demand*
J_1	10				40	50
J_2	8	22				30
J_3		32	8			40
J_4			40	20		60
J_5			16			16
Available Hours	18	54	64	20	40	

Now we reconvert from the standard machine hour system to actual machine hours. We divide each standard hour job assignment by its appropriate index number. Thus, all M_A assignments are divided by 0.5; all M_B assignments are divided by 1; all M_C assignments are divided by 0.8, and so on. We ignore the dummy, because the assignment of job 1 to the dummy is not real. This gives us:

Actual Machine Hour Assignments

	M_A	M_B	M_C	M_D
J_1	20			
J_2	16	22		
J_3		32	10	
J_4			50	$33\frac{1}{3}$
J_5			20	
Actual Machine Hours Available	36	54	80	$33\frac{1}{3}$

To determine the number of pieces that will be obtained for each job, we multiply actual assignment hours by the appropriate, real productivity rates of each machine. Thus, for example, for job 4 assigned to M_D, the productivity rate is eighteen pieces per hour. We multiply $33\frac{1}{3}$ hours by eighteen pieces per hour, which yields six hundred pieces. The matrix of total pieces is shown below.

Matrix of Actual Pieces Produced by Each Assignment

	M_A	M_B	M_C	M_D	Total Units	Requirements
J_1	60				60	300
J_2	56	154			210	210
J_3		192	48		240	240
J_4			1200	600	1800	1800
J_5			400		400	400

Job 1 is the only demand that is not fully supplied. It is short 240 units. This fact does not surprise us because demand exceeded productive capacity. The manager may decide that job 1 is not the one to be held over to the following week in spite of this result, because job 1 may be for a valued customer. Some other job, then, would not be finished. Any formal solution is always subject to reinterpretation and the use of good judgment on the part of the manager. At least, however, this loading algorithm provides him with a *reasonable base schedule*.

Many hours of clerical work can be saved by using this transportation approach. It is possible to speed up the time to solution even further by using a modified Northwest Corner rule. Namely, arrange machines from left to right in order of descending productivity—1, $\frac{4}{5}$, $\frac{3}{5}$, $\frac{1}{2}$. Then, arrange jobs from top to bottom in order of profit per standard machine hour. This will be found to be: 4 (top), 5, 3, 2, 1 (bottom). The matrix, so arranged, yields an optimum solution directly when the Northwest Corner assignment procedure is used. It will be noted that it is an alternative solution. The load matrix in standard hours is:

	M_B	M_C	M_D	M_A	Δ	Standard Machine Hours Required
4	54	6				60
5		16				16
3		40				40
2		2	20	8		30
1				10	40	50
Standard machine hours available	54	64	20	18	40	196

The model we have just discussed is exceedingly useful when it is possible to approximate the conditions of a standard machine. With ingenuity and good judgment, extraneous factors such as set-up costs, variability in production rates, job priorities, and other occurrences that are likely to be encountered in a real production system can be taken into account. Also, it is not unreasonable to compare schedules obtained for maximum profit with those derived for minimizing production time.

Shop Loading with the Index Method[7]

It is not surprising that a heuristic method for shop loading exists. The activity of shop loading is repeated so often that a relatively fast heuristic that allows assignment splitting, if desired, and that is designed strictly for hand computation becomes highly desirable.

A row of index numbers is computed for each job i with respect to its performance at the machine centers j. When the performance criterion is of the cost per part type, the ith row of index numbers will be $(c_{j_i} - c^*_{j_i})/c^*_{j_i}$ and when the performance criterion is for profit per part, we have $(p^*_{j_i} - p_{j_i})/p^*_{j_i}$. (In both cases, the asterisk represents the ideal machine assignment—lowest cost or highest profit per part.) These index numbers show the relative *penalties* of assigning each of the given jobs to the different machine centers.

In many companies, for every part, a schedule card is maintained that presents relevant information concerning processing times and costs on different machines. For example:

Part Name—4x		Order Quantity—100	
Machine:	A	B	C
Time per Part:	$\frac{2}{5}$	1	$\frac{4}{5}$
Total Time (Hrs.):	40	100	80
Cost per Hour:	$4	$2	$3
Total Cost:	$160	$200	$240
Time Index:	0	1.5	1
Cost Index:	0	0.25	0.50

[7] See R. O. Ferguson and L. F. Sargent, *Linear Programming* (New York: McGraw-Hill Book Co., Inc., 1958), pp. 149–59.

Consider the following matrix of total times where parts are identified with jobs:

		Machines		
Job	A	B	C	
1X	⌐1/4⌐ 50	⌐0⌐ 40	⌐7/8⌐ 75	
2X	⌐0⌐ 25	⌐3/5⌐ 40	⌐1⌐ 50	
3X	⌐0⌐ 27	⌐1/9⌐ 30	⌐1⌐ 54	
4X	⌐0⌐ 40	⌐1.5⌐ 100	⌐1⌐ 80	
5X	⌐0⌐ 20	⌐4⌐ 100	⌐1.5⌐ 50	
Available Time	75	75	75	

The index numbers have been determined and entered into the little boxes in each cell of the matrix. Available time is a capacity constraint at each center based on double shifts less cleanup and maintenance times. An investment in another type-A machine would be required to increase the total available time at center A.

First assignments are always made to zero index measures. Then, to satisfy capacity constraints if some machines are overloaded, jobs are shifted to other machines that have the lowest possible set of alternative index numbers. The reassignments are done in the order of increasing index values.

Returning to our example, the assignments based on zero index would be:

	Machines		
Jobs	A	B	C
1X		40	
2X	25		
3X	27		
4X	40		
5X	20		
Available Time	75	75	75
Assigned Time	112	40	0
Excess	+37	−35	75

Machine A is overloaded with an excess of 37 hours. Machines B and C are underutilized. So, we shall shift job 3X because in its row the smallest alternative index appears, $\frac{1}{9}$ at $3X$, B. When we shift $3X$ from A to B, it takes 30 hours to do the job instead of 27.

		Machines	
Jobs	A	B	C
$1X$		40	
$2X$	25		
$3X$		30	
$4X$	40		
$5X$	20		
Excess	+10	−5	−75

The heuristic rule can be applied in several ways at this point. For example, since $\frac{1}{4}$ is now the next best index, at $1X$, A, this would mean that $1X$, B should be shifted to $1X$, A. Generally, however, we refuse to further overload a machine center, and instead, we try to move jobs from it to the best possible alternative positions. Here, for machine A either $2X$, $4X$, or $5X$ could be shifted from A to C. Since $5X$'s index for C is larger than the others, we eliminate it as a choice. And $4X$, when moved, will cause an overload at center C, so move $2X$. The result is:

		Machines	
Jobs	A	B	C
$1X$		40	
$2X$		5	43.75[see footnote 8]
$3X$		30	
$4X$	40		
$5X$	20		
Excess	−15	0	−31.25

Total Time = 60 + 75 + 43.75 = 178.75 hours

Still further improvement is available to allow splitting because machine A, which is fast for every job except $1X$, is underutilized. So, we return 15 hours of job $2X$ to A.

		Machines	
Jobs	A	B	C
$1X$		40	
$2X$	15	5	13.75[see footnote 9]
$3X$		30	
$4X$	40		
$5X$	20		
Excess	0	0	−61.25

Total Time = 75 + 75 + 13.75 = 163.75 hours

[8] ($5/40 = 1/8$ of job $2X$ is completed at B, thus $7/8 \times 50 = 43.75$ hours remain to be done at C.)

[9] ($1/8$ of job $2X$ is completed at B, $15/25 = 3/5$ of job $2X$ is completed at A; this leaves ($1 - 1/8 - 3/5 = 11/40$) to be done at C and ($11/40) \times 50 = 13/75$ hours.)

While promising only "approximately optimal" solutions, the simplicity of this index method proves attractive in many circumstances. Also, it can be used even when the standard machine concept is invalid.

Trim Problem

A particular kind of loading problem involves the question of how to minimize waste. This problem is quite characteristic of the paper industry. We shall give a brief description of a clever LP solution of this so-called "trim problem."[10] We will use Vajda's numbers; assume, therefore, that a roll of paper is 215 inches wide and that orders for 90 feet of 35-inch, 90 feet of 60-inch, and 180 feet of 64-inch cuts are on hand. Further, we will allow that cuts of each width can be joined together to form a continuous length of that width. That is, a feasible solution would be the combinations of the two cuts shown in Figure 10.5.

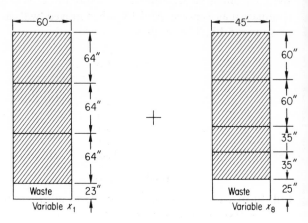

Figure 10.5

This solution meets the feasibility requirements, as would many other arrangements, but the waste is not minimized. In this case, the waste is: $(60' \times 23'') + (45' \times 25'')$. Since our purpose is to minimize waste, we can use LP as follows:

Let x_j = different combinations of cuts; for example, the cut of three 64-inch widths plus 23 inches of waste is called x_1; the cut of two 60-inch widths plus two 35-inch widths plus a 25-inch width of waste is called x_8. The tableau is set up:

[10] See S. Vajda, *Readings in Linear Programming* (New York: John Wiley & Sons, Inc., 1958), pp. 78–84.

	Waste	23"	27"	17"	31"	21"	11"	0"	25"	15"	5"	
Dual Variable	Order	x_1	x_2	x_3	x_4	x_5	x_6	x_7	x_8	x_9	x_{10}	b_i
y_A	64"	3	2	2	1	1	1	0	0	0	0	180
y_B	60"	0	1	0	2	1	0	3	2	1	0	90
y_C	35"	0	0	2	0	2	4	1	2	4	6	90

Objective: Minimize $[z = 23x_1 + 27x_2 + 17x_3 + \ldots + 5x_{10}]$ subject to the set of constraints:

$$3x_1 + 2x_2 + 2x_3 + x_4 + x_5 + x_6 \geq 180$$
$$x_2 + 2x_4 + x_5 + 3x_7 + 2x_8 + x_9 \geq 90$$
$$2x_3 + 2x_5 + 4x_6 + x_7 + 2x_8 + 4x_9 + 6x_{10} \geq 90$$

But, a clever transformation of the objective function is available. We can minimize waste by minimizing the total area cut, minus the area of the orders. This is:

Objective: Minimize $z = 215 \Sigma_j x_j - (180 \times 64) - (90 \times 60) - (90 \times 35)$ which is equivalent to Minimize $\Sigma_j x_j$ since all other terms are constants. That is, the objective function becomes simply:

$$\text{Minimize } [z = (1)x_1 + (1)x_2 + \ldots + (1)x_{10}]$$

Further, computing time may be saved by transforming to the dual:[11]

$$
\begin{aligned}
3y_A &\leq 1 & y_A + 4y_C &\leq 1 \\
2y_A + y_B &\leq 1 & 3y_B + y_C &\leq 1 \\
2y_A + 2y_C &\leq 1 & 2y_B + 2y_C &\leq 1 \\
y_A + 2y_B &\leq 1 & y_B + 4y_C &\leq 1 \\
y_A + y_B + 2y_C &\leq 1 & 6y_C &\leq 1
\end{aligned}
$$

Objective: Maximize $[z = 180y_A + 90y_B + 90y_C]$

The solution after converting from dual to primal is $x_1 = 60$, $x_7 = 30$, $x_{10} = 10$. The $\Sigma_j x_j = 100$, which is the minimum, so $215(100) - (180 \times 64) - (90 \times 60) - (90 \times 35) = 1430$. In other words:

	64"	60"	35"	Waste
x_1	3 × 60'			23" × 60
x_7		3 × 30'	1 × 30'	0 × 30
x_{10}			6 × 10'	5" × 10
	180'	90'	90'	1430"

[11] See pp. 137–138.

PROBLEMS

1. Use the assignment method to achieve a satisfactory shop loading arrangement for an intermittent flow shop where the per unit profits are given in the matrix below and relatively continuous production (in the quarter) can be expected for each assignment.

			Machines		
Jobs	A	B	C	D	E
1	19	17	15	15	13
2	12	30	18	18	15
3	13	21	29	19	21
4	49	56	53	55	43
5	33	41	39	39	30

2. For the data in problem 1, a new machine F has become available that can only work on jobs 1, 2, or 3, with unit profits of 14, 11, and 12. Would it be worthwhile to replace one of the present machines with F? After analysis, what information is still lacking?

3. Use the data below to develop a shop loading analysis where splitting of assignments is permitted and assumed to have negligible costs. Assume that the objective is to minimize total job times.

	Parts per Hour				
	Machines				
Jobs	A	B	C	D	Demand/Week
1	7.5	15	10	20	400
2	4.5	9	6	12	300
3	3	6	4	8	200
Available Hours per Week	40	40	40	40	

4. Work with the same data to develop an index loading model and find a solution in this way. Compare your results.

5. Convert the load matrix given in standard hours on p. 287 into the appropriate nonstandard hour matrix.

6. Let the roll in the trim problem be 150 inches wide. Assume that we require 100 feet of 30-inch width, 80 feet of 50-inch width and 70 feet of 90-inch width. What is the waste minimizing solution?

7. Reconsider problem 7 in Chapter 1, p. 22. Would you answer the question in the same way now?

Loading, discussed in Chapter 10, is accomplished without regard to the **order** or **precedence** in which operations will be done at a particular machine center. Sequencing establishes the **priorities** for jobs (operations) in the machine center's queue. When there are many jobs and machines, this repetitive task can have considerable economic importance. Recently, the general problem of ordering various operations through a specific facility has received a great deal of attention. As Conway, Maxwell, and Miller point out, "An inherent sense of fair play has elevated the 'first-come, first-served' solution of sequencing problems to an eminence out of all proportion to its basic virtue." [1] In fact, as we shall see, the shortest processing time (SPT) should be the important criterion. It "plays fair" only with the system.

[1] R. W. Conway, W. L. Maxwell, and L. W. Miller, **Theory of Scheduling** (Reading, Mass.: Addison-Wesley Publishing Co., 1967), p. 1.

Sequencing 11
Operations

The sequencing problem is: to establish the exact ordering, priorities, of jobs that have already been assigned to machine centers—using loading algorithms as previously described. The Gantt Layout Chart in Figure 11.1 *sequences* jobs through facilities. It should be contrasted with the Gantt Load Chart in Chapter 10, p. 268, which assigns work levels unspecified by jobs.

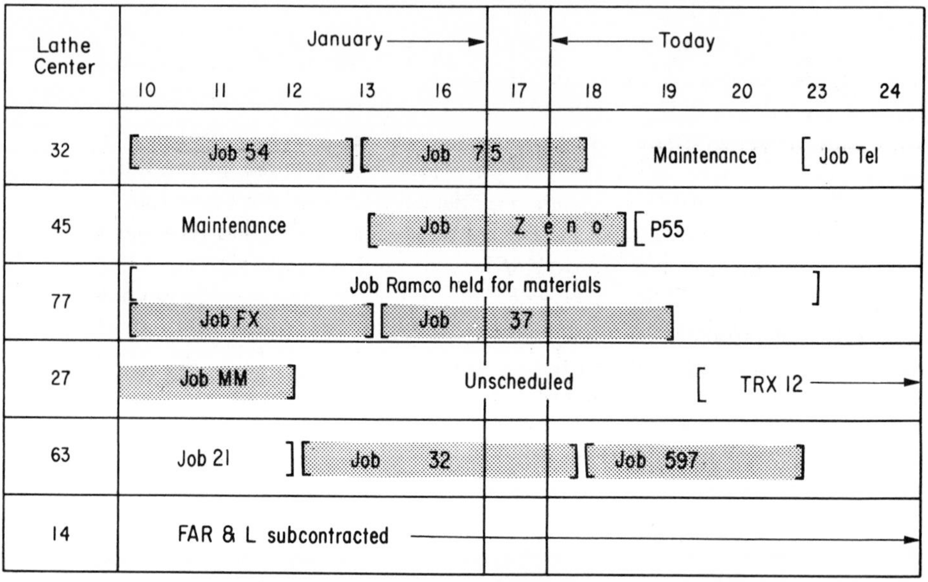

Lathe Center	January ———————▶		◀——— Today	
	10 11 12 13 16	17	18 19 20 23 24	
32	[Job 54][Job 7 5	]	Maintenance	[Job Tel
45	Maintenance [Job Z e n o][	P55		
77	[Job Ramco held for materials]			
	[Job FX][Job 37]			
27	[Job MM] Unscheduled		[TRX 12 ———————▶	
63	Job 21][Job 32][Job 597]			
14	FAR & L subcontracted ——————————————————————————▶			

Figure 11.1

The Gantt layout chart (a reserved time planning system). Status: (1) job P-284 is ahead 1.5 days; (2) job J20 is ahead 3.0 days; (3) job O22 is ahead 5.5 days; (4) job M21 is ahead 1.0 days; (5) job R65 is 2 days short of completion—and 3 days late (M); (6) job P-285 is 1.5 days short and 1.5 days late (set-up time; will catch up); (7) job T10-X is 1.5 days short and about 4 days late (M) (E).

Classification of Sequencing Problems

There are at least four factors that are essential for classifying sequencing problems.[2] The *first* describes job-arrival patterns, where the jobs come for service at the machines. The symbol, n, refers to the number of jobs that are *waiting* to be sequenced through the facility. Typically, in the job shop, n is a number that varies a good deal. *Second*, it is necessary to specify the number of machines, m, in a machine group through which the jobs must pass. *Third*, the flow pattern in the shop must be identified. When a set of jobs follows a fixed machine ordering, the conditions exist for an intermittent flow shop, see pp. 24–25. On the other hand, when many technological orderings are required, job shop sequencing prevails. The sizes of the orders, the length of production runs, the importance of set-ups—changing jigs and fixtures between jobs, etc.—are, however, the ultimate determinants of what type of shop exists. *Fourth*, a variety of criteria exists for evaluating the performance of the schedule.

Evaluatory Criteria

In our discussion, we will emphasize the evaluation measure of flow time and mean flow time as defined in the following way.

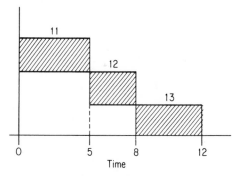

Figure 11.2

Three jobs (11, 12, and 13) in Figure 11.2 are sequenced through a facility in that order. Job 11, which goes first, is completed after five minutes; meanwhile, jobs 12 and 13 have waited five minutes. Job 13 then must wait an additional three minutes before it can begin its own processing. We define for job i, a waiting time, W_i, and a processing time, t_i. Assuming job 11 begins

[2] Conway *et al.*, *op. cit.*, pp. 6–8.

at time zero[3] then the completion time is $C_i = W_i + t_i$. For our three jobs this yields the following table:

Job i	W_i	t_1	C_i
11	0	5	5
12	5	3	8
13	8	4	12
Sum	$13 + 12 = 25$		

The $\Sigma_i C_i$ is the *flow time*, in this case twenty-five, and *mean flow time* would be $\left(\overset{n}{\underset{i}{\Sigma}} C_i\right)/n = 25/3$.

There are other measures often used in evaluating operation sequences. For example, define d_i as the due date of a job. Then $L_i = C_i - d_i$ is a measure of the lateness of job i. There are also degrees of facility idleness that may play a critical role in sequence determination. The fact is, however, that sequencing models to simultaneously optimize many of these terms are not readily available. There are no overall, general solution models. Linear programming provides minimum help in this area, and network theory is awkward in application. As a result, many heuristics have been developed to try to cope with the level of detail involved in making the highly repetitive sequencing decisions required by many firms.

n Jobs—1 Machine

A common objective of facility sequencing is to minimize mean flow time. For reasons apparent from our previous discussion, in many problems this is equivalent to minimizing average job waiting times, i.e.,

$$\min \frac{\overset{n}{\underset{i}{\Sigma}} C_i}{n} = \min \frac{\overset{n}{\underset{i}{\Sigma}} (W_i + t_i)}{n}$$

And it also turns out that facility idleness is often minimized. A simple rule applies. Namely, it can be shown that if a set of n jobs in one machine's queue are ordered so that the operations having the shortest processing times t_i are done first, that the mean flow time, mean completion time, and mean waiting time will all be minimized. Ordering jobs according to shortest processing times is called the SPT rule. Using this rule, jobs are rank ordered by least t_i as in Figure 11.3. Note that the area under the curve is minimized. In Figure

---

[3] That is, the release time, often called r_i equals zero (say at the start of the day).

11.4, the jobs are randomly ordered without regard to SPT, and the area under the curve is not minimized nor is mean flow time.

An example of SPT, shortest processings time rule, where $t_4 < t_5 < t_2 < t_6 < t_3 < t_{10}$
There are $n=6$ jobs and $m=1$ machine.

Job i	W_i	t_i	C_i
4	0	5	5
5	5	7	12
2	12	8	20
6	20	10	30
3	30	12	42
1	42	14	56
	109 +	56 =	165

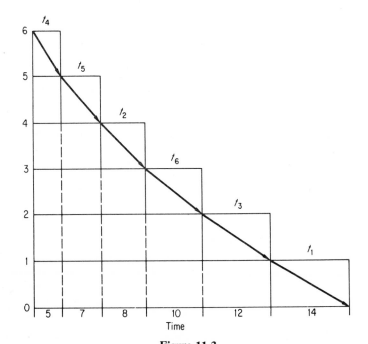

Figure 11.3

Jobs ordered by ranked access times.

In practice, sequencing according to due date, d_i, is not unusual, the purpose being to maximize the fulfillment of delivery promises. It is, therefore, to be

An n x 1 problem where SPT is not used.

Job i	W_i	t_i	C_i
1	0	14	14
2	14	8	22
3	22	12	34
4	34	5	39
5	39	7	46
6	46	10	56
	155	+56	=211

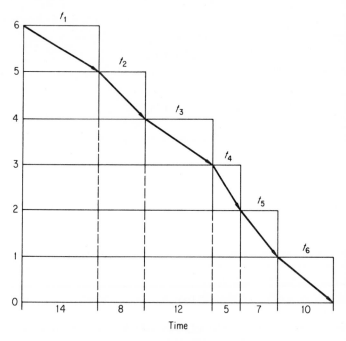

Figure 11.4

noted that ordering jobs by the SPT rule also succeeds in minimizing average delivery lateness, L_i. As an additional strength, the SPT rule can be modified to take into account the fact that some jobs are more important than others. For example, in Figure 11.5, the importance weight w_3 is larger than any

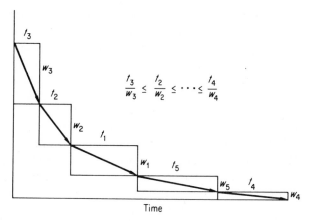

Figure 11.5

Jobs ordered by smallest ratios of weighted processing time.

other job weight. It happens that t_3 is the shortest processing time; in any case, the ratio t_i/w_i is smallest for job 3, and so it is placed first in the sequence. It is clear that this ratio rule assures a smooth convex function that will minimize the area under the curve.

n Jobs—2 Machines

Essentially, the same kind of reasoning applies when jobs must pass through *two* machine centers in a given (flow shop) technological order, e.g., $M1$ followed by $M2$ or cast followed by trim. For example,

Job	Machine 1	Machine 2
a	6	3
b	8	2
c	7	5
d	3	9
e	5	4

S. M. Johnson's algorithm[4] solves this problem for all "no passing" cases in terms of minimum completion time. ("No passing" means that the *order* of processing jobs by the first facility *must be preserved* for all subsequent facilities).

To use the algorithm for the above table, where $M1$ must be first, select the job with the shortest processing time on either $M1$ or $M2$. If this minimum value is in the $M2$ column, place the job *last* in sequence (here in fifth place); if it is in the $M1$ column, award that job *first* place. For our example, job b with 2 in the $M2$ column will be done last. Remove job b from further consideration, then continue in the same way. Select the smallest number remaining in the matrix. If it is in the $M2$ column, assign that job to the last place if available or the next to last place if not; should the number be in the first column, that job gets first or next to first place. (Ties are resolved by randomly selecting either position for assignment.) For the example above, job b goes last; job d goes first in sequence; job a, next to last; job e precedes job a; job c fills the remaining slot. The minimum total completion time is 31, shown in the Gantt chart of Figure 11.6.

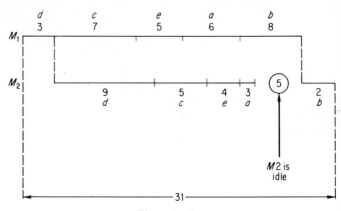

Figure 11.6

Although we will not directly show a proof of Johnson's algorithm, we can develop an intuitive notion as to why it works. Referring to Figure 11.6, we observe that the last job (call it n) cannot ever begin processing on machine 2 until all jobs have completed processing on machine 1. Therefore, we can establish one possible lower limit (L_1) for total processing time (TPT), meaning that TPT may have to be longer than this amount but it can't be less.

$$L_1 = \sum_{i=\alpha}^{i=n} t_{i,M1} + t_{n,M2}$$

[4] S. M. Johnson, "Optimal Two- and Three-Stage Production Schedules with Set-up Times Included," *Naval Research Logistics Quarterly*, 1: 1 (March, 1954), 61–68.

Here, $t_{n,M2}$ = processing time for nth and last job in sequence on machine 2; also $t_{i,Mj}$ = processing time for the ith job on the jth machine. The first job in sequence is denoted by α. We should note that $L_1 = 31$ in Figure 11.6.

Another potential limit exists. We see that none of the jobs can begin processing on machine 2 until the first job in the sequence (α) has completed processing on machine 1. This gives another lower limit, $L_2 = t_{\alpha,M1} + \sum_{i=\alpha}^{i=n} t_{i,M2}$. For our example, $L_2 = 26$. So L_1 dominates L_2. In all cases, the higher of these two lower limits is controlling, and we can state that the *lower bound* for minimum total processing time is the largest of the two, that is: lower bound $= \max(L_1, L_2)$.

We observe that the summations in each expression are constants for any given problem, the only factors affecting the minimum total processing time are the processing times for the first job on machine 1 and the last job on machine 2. Therefore, for an $n \times 2$ sequence problem, we choose the lowest of all the t_{ij}'s and place the job i first if $j = M1$ or last if $j = M2$. By similar reasoning, we select a second job to be assigned from the remaining $n - 1$ jobs. Its position should be determined in the same way, and parenthetically, we note that the rules we have just derived are those developed by Johnson.

n Jobs—3 Machines

Johnson proposed a variant of his two-machine algorithm that will find the optimal sequence for three machines—if certain conditions are met. Suppose we have three machines with the technological ordering $M1$, $M2$, $M3$. As before, no passing is allowed, and we define t_{ij} = processing time of the ith job on machine j.[5] Then if at least one of the following restrictions holds, we can apply Johnson's method:

$$\min t_{i1} \geq \max t_{i2}$$

or

$$\min t_{i3} \geq \max t_{i2}$$

In words, the middle machine may not have any operation times that are greater than the minimum operation times of *both* the other machines. For example, the method can be applied to the matrix of processing times below.

			Job			
Machine	a	b	c	d	e	
1	4	7	5	3	3	Min $t_{i1} = 3$
2	2	1	2	0	2	Max $t_{i2} = 2$
3	1	1	3	9	2	Min $t_{i3} = 1$

[5] There is no solution that allows passing which can produce a shorter completion time than the no-passing solution for up to $n = 3$. See Conway, et al., pp. 80–83.

If there had been a four in the *M2* row, the method we are about to describe could not be used.

We reformulate the problem as a two-machine system. Then we apply the two-machine algorithm. That is, let $p_i = t_{i1} + t_{i2}$ and $q_i = t_{i2} + t_{i3}$. Then, we proceed as we did before: Job i should precede job k in the optimal sequence if

$$\min (p_i, q_k) < \min (p_k, q_i)$$

For the numbers in the matrix:

	Job				
	a	*b*	*c*	*d*	*e*
$(M1 + M2)\, p$	6	8	7	3	5
$(M2 + M3)\, q$	3	2	5	9	4

So the optimal sequence is unchanged from the one previously developed for the $n \times 2$ case. Giglio and Wagner[6] applied this method to a series of problems where the restrictive condition did not hold and found that fairly good results were achieved. Of the twenty problems solved, the optimal sequence was achieved in nine cases, and in eight others it would have been reached if two adjacent jobs in the sequence exchanged positions. More importantly, the average error—measured from the true optimum that was found by enumeration—was under 3 per cent for the twenty problems tested. Therefore, by relaxing the restrictive conditions and applying Johnson's algorithm, we have what amounts to a heuristic method for finding a pseudo-optimum sequence.

Branch and Bound Algorithm

Ignall and Schrage[7] developed a *branch and bound* algorithm for *any* three-machine problem. It uses reasoning similar to that followed by Johnson's two-machine algorithm. If we were to examine all possible sequences of n jobs we would be considering $n!$ branches of a tree in which each node represents a partial solution. See Figure 11.7. For a four-job problem we would only have to look at twenty-four (4!) possible sequences to determine the optimum sequence. However, for larger problems the computation required to examine all branches becomes horrendous with twelve jobs we have $12! = 4.7900 \times 10^8$).

[6] R. J. Giglio and H. M. Wagner, "Approximate Solutions to the Three-Machine Scheduling Problem," *Operations Research*, 12: 2 (March–April, 1964), 305–324.

[7] E. Ignall and L. Schrage, "Application of the Branch and Bound Technique to Some Flow Shop Scheduling Problems," *Operations Research*, 13: 3 (May–June, 1965), 400–412.

The branch and bound process allows us to prune away many of these branches and only examine those that offer promising solutions. To determine which branches to investigate we need to establish lower bounds for

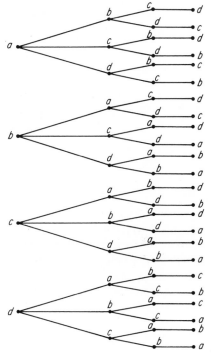

Figure 11.7

partial sequences and then follow the branch that has the smallest lower bound until we find another branch that has a smaller lower bound. How can we determine the lower bound for a specified node or partial sequence? In the two-machine case we found (see p. 301) that the lower bound for our problem was given by max (L_1, L_2).

We can follow similar reasoning for the three-machine problem. Note in Figure 11.8 that

1. The last job c cannot begin processing on machine 3 until it has completed processing on machine 2, and it cannot begin processing on machine 2 until all jobs have completed processing on machine 1.
2. The last job cannot start processing on machine 3 until all jobs have finished on machine 2, and none of the jobs can begin processing on machine 2 until the first job is through machine 1.
3. None of the jobs can begin processing on machine 3 until the first job has finished processing on machines 1 and 2.

These three statements yield the following lower limits where $\alpha = $ first in sequence:

$$L_1 = \sum_{i=\alpha}^{n} t_{1,M1} + t_{n,M2} + t_{n,M3}$$

$$L_2 = t_{\alpha,M1} + \sum_{i=\alpha}^{n} t_{i,M2} + t_{n,M3}$$

$$L_3 = t_{\alpha,M1} + t_{\alpha,M2} + \sum_{i=\alpha}^{n} t_{i,M3}$$

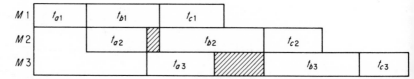

Figure 11.8

Our lower bounds will be computed for partial sequences such as d, bc, adc, etc. Therefore, we need to redefine the lower bounds so as to distinguish between the assigned and the unassigned portions of the sequencing network. Let T_j be the time at which all jobs of the assigned portion of the sequence will be completed on machine j; and U_j be the total time of the unassigned portion of the sequence on machine j. Then, new lower bounds can be written:

$$L_1 = T_1 + U_1 + \min* (t_{i,M2} + t_{i,M3})$$
$$L_2 = T_2 + U_2 + \min* (t_{i,M3})$$
$$L_3 = T_3 + U_3$$

where * signifies that only the t_{ij}'s of unassigned jobs qualify. Then, our lower bound for a specified sequence or partial sequence $S*$ is:

$$\text{LB}(S*) = \max (L_1, L_2, L_3)$$

Let us illustrate the method with an example that could not be resolved with the S. M. Johnson modified sequencing algorithm for the $n \times 3$ problem.

Job	Machine 1	2	3
a	13	3	12
b	7	12	16
c	26	9	7
d	2	6	1

We will start our examination with calculations for node a, meaning that job a would be assigned to first position in the sequence; b, c, and d are unassigned.

$L_1 = (13)$ $+ (7 + 26 + 2) + \min (12 + 16, 9 + 7, 6 + 1) = 55$
$L_2 = (13 + 3)$ $+ (12 + 9 + 6) + \min (16, 7, 1)$ $= 44$
$L_3 = (13 + 3 + 12) + (16 + 7 + 1)$ $= 52$

Then $LB(a) = 55$. Similar calculations must be made for $LB(b)$, $LB(c)$, and $LB(d)$. The initial list would be:

First List

Node	LB(node)
a	55
b	55
d	63
c	71

The branch and bound algorithm begins with just such a list that contains all reasonable starting points. Later lists contain all partial sequences and their lower bounds, arranged so that the smallest lower bound is first.

We shall now examine the method by which certain nodes are deleted from the list. Thus, select the first, lowest bound node from the list. Write down all nodes that immediately follow the selected node, compute their lower bounds, and insert these nodes in their proper positions in the list. Then delete from the list the node that you have just branched from. Continue selecting from the top of the list until a complete sequence is specified that has a lower bound less than that for any other node sequence on the list. Since nodes a and b tie for the *lowest*, lower bound, we could select either one from which to branch—but not any of the others. Arbitrarily, let us branch from node a first. Here is the calculation for the partial sequence, ab.

$L_1(ab) = (13 + 7)$ $+ (26 + 2) + \min (9 + 7, 6 + 1) = 55$
$L_2(ab) = (13 + 7 + 12)$ $+ (9 + 6) \ + \min (7, 1)$ $= 48$
$L_3(ab) = (13 + 7 + 12 + 16) + (7 + 1)$ $= 56$

Then $LB(ab) = 56$

Continuing in this way, our list changes as follows:[8]

Second List

Node	LB(node)
b	55
ab	56
d	63
ad	64
c	71
ac	72

[8] David Dannenbring's program of the branch and bound algorithm produced the results that follow.

The node *b* retains the lowest, lower bound value, which is why it continues to head the list. Also, the next set of branchings begin with *b*.

We derive a new list:

Third List	
Node	*LB(node)*
ba	55
ab	56
bc	62
bd	63
d	63
ad	64
c	71
ac	72

Since node *ba* has the lowest lower bound, we branch from it to *bac* and *bad*, the only possible branches. The partial sequence *ab* moves to the head of the list.

Fourth List	
Node	*LB(node)*
ab	56
bc	62
bac	63
bd	63
d	63
bad	64
ad	64
c	71
ac	72

We next branch from node *ab* to *abc* and *abd* and revise our list to:

Fifth List	
Node	*LB(node)*
bc	62
abc	63
bac	63
bd	63
d	63
abd	64
bad	64
ad	64
c	71
ac	72

From node *bc* we branch to nodes *bca* and *bcd* and change our list to read:

Final List

Node	LB(node)
bca	62
bcd	63
abc	63
bac	63
bd	63
d	63
abd	64
bad	64
ad	64
c	71
ac	72

At this point, the solution is complete. Node *bca* tops the list and represents a complete sequence (*b, c, a, d*). The lower bound for this sequence, 62, represents the *minimum total processing time* for this $n \times 3$ problem. (*Note:* It would be impossible for any sequence beginning with job *d* to have a lower time than the sequence *bcad* because the lower bound for node *d* is 63, which is greater than the time 62 for *bcad*. This relation holds true for all the other nodes on the list, so we do not need to explore further.) If we had used the S. M. Johnson algorithm, we would have obtained the same sequence that adds an impressive confirmation to the Giglio-Wagner finding that was previously reported, p. 302.

One important, additional aspect of branch and bound remains to be discussed here. That is, an *upper bound* that can substantially reduce the size of the problem. Say that arbitrarily we chose the sequence *abcd*. (If any intuition is available that prompted this choice or a better one, so much the better.) The Gantt chart in Figure 11.9 shows that the sequence *abcd* has a completion time of 63.

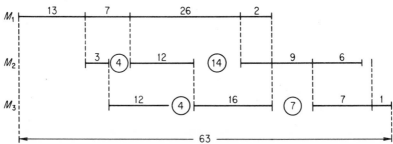

Figure 11.9

We can confirm this calculation by noting that in the final list, the sequence *abc*(*d*) was third down with a lower bound of 63. But, we would not have had this final list available at the beginning of the problem. No sequence having a value greater than the (arbitrary) upper bound need ever be considered. This knowledge would have reduced the size of our lists. For example, in the first list, the node c would have been deleted. In the second and third lists, delete nodes ad, c, and ac. In the fourth list, delete bad, ad, c, and ac. In the fifth and final lists, delete abd, bad, ad, c, and ac. This choice of an upper bound of 63 would not have helped much, but it is clear that a well-chosen, upper bound could substantially reduce the size of the problem.

n Jobs—m Machines

There is no *general* solution for any problem where $m > 2$. But there are *heuristic* approximations of the optimal solution. Campbell, Dudek, and Smith report on the successful performance of a heuristic algorithm that generates a series of sums for each job similar to the two new sets of sums generated in the prior discussion of $n \times 3$ systems.[9] Thus, with m machines, we can develop $m - 1$ two column sets of job times that can then be treated by the S. M. Johnson $n \times 2$ algorithm, assuming the technological ordering $1 \to 2 \to \ldots \to m$ and no passing. For example, consider the following six-job, four-machine problem.

	Processing Time on Machine			
Job	*1*	*2*	*3*	*4*
a	50	43	15	4
b	89	99	95	77
c	7	47	20	98
d	8	64	12	94
e	61	19	65	14
f	1	80	66	78

We would calculate:

Set	*Column 1*	*Column 2*
1[10]	t_{M1}	t_{Mm}
2[11]	$t_{M1} + t_{M2}$	$t_{Mm} + t_{M(m-1)}$
.		
.		
.		
k[12]	$t_{M1} + t_{M2} + \ldots + t_{Mk}$	$t_{Mm} + t_{M(m-1)} + \ldots + t_{M(m+1-k)}$
.		
.		
$m - 1$	$t_{M1} + t_{M2} + \ldots + t_{M(m-1)}$	$t_{Mm} + t_{M(m-1)} + \ldots + t_{M2}$

[9] H. G. Campbell, R. A. Dudek, and M. L. Smith, "A Heuristic Algorithm for the n Job, m Machine Sequencing Problem," *Management Science*, 16: 10 (June, 1970), B630–B637.

[10] When $m = 2$, this is the standard S. M. Johnson algorithm.

[11] When $m = 3$, this is the *special* $n \times 3$ case, see pp. 301–302.

[12] We can represent these sums for the jth job as $\sum_{i=1}^{k} t_{ji}$ for column 1 and $\sum_{i=m+1-k}^{m} t_{ji}$ for column 2.

The completion time for the sequence generated by each set is calculated, and that sequence is chosen which produces the minimum completion time.

$k = 1$

For our first two-machine problem, we need to reformulate the above table so that we are considering the times for machines 1 and 4 only. Our new table is:

Job	Machine 1	Machine 4
a	50	4
b	89	77
c	7	98
d	8	94
e	61	14
f	1	78

Applying the two-machine algorithm we get (*fcdbea*) as the solution to our first subproblem.

$k = 2$

For $k = 2$, processing times for machine $(1 + 2)$ are equal to the sum of the times for machines 1 and 2 and those for $(3 + 4)$ are equal to the sum of the times for machines 3 and 4.

Job	Machine $(1 + 2)$	Machine $(3 + 4)$
a	$50 + 43 = 93$	$15 + 4 = 19$
b	$89 + 99 = 188$	$95 + 77 = 172$
c	$7 + 47 = 54$	$20 + 98 = 118$
d	$8 + 64 = 72$	$12 + 94 = 106$
e	$61 + 19 = 80$	$65 + 14 = 79$
f	$1 + 80 = 81$	$66 + 78 = 144$

Solving this subproblem we find the solution to be the sequence (*cdfbea*).

$k = 3$

The last subproblem to be solved, in this case, consists of machine $(1 + 2 + 3)$ that is the sum of the times on machines 1, 2, and 3 and machine $(2 + 3 + 4)$ that is the sum of the times on machines 2, 3, and 4.

Job	Machine $(1 + 2 + 3)$	Machine $(2 + 3 + 4)$
a	$50 + 43 + 15 = 108$	$43 + 15 + 4 = 62$
b	$89 + 99 + 95 = 283$	$99 + 95 + 77 = 271$
c	$7 + 47 + 20 = 74$	$47 + 20 + 98 = 165$
d	$8 + 64 + 12 = 84$	$64 + 12 + 94 = 170$
e	$61 + 19 + 65 = 145$	$19 + 65 + 14 = 98$
f	$1 + 80 + 66 = 147$	$80 + 66 + 78 = 224$

The solution sequence for this subproblem is the same as for subproblem two, (*cdfbea*). Each of the sequences is evaluated in terms of total processing time. The results are shown below:

Sequence	Total Processing Time
(*fcdbea*)	512
(*cdfbea*)	487

Based on these figures, we would choose the sequence (*cdfbea*) as our quasi-optimal sequence for this problem. Actually, our chosen sequence did not fare badly at all with the true optimum for the problem. By enumeration we would find that the sequences (*cdbfae*) and (*cdbfea*) are optimal with a total processing time of 485. Thus, we could calculate the degree of error as:

$$\frac{487 - 485}{485} \times 100 = 0.41 \text{ per cent error}$$

2 Jobs—m Machines

Akers has shown that where two jobs pass through *m* machines (each job with its own specific technological ordering) that graphical analysis can *help* to determine the optimal sequencing of operations for minimum completion time.[13] The graphical approach has also been treated more formally.[14] Except in special cases, these algorithms remove infeasible solutions but do not identify the optimal solution.

In this case, different technological sequences exist *for each job*. The intermittent flow shop is replaced by the job shop. We must limit ourselves to two jobs, J_I and J_{II}. However, the number of facilities through which these

[13] S. B. Akers, Jr., "A Graphical Approach to Production Scheduling Problems," *Operations Research*, 4: 2 (April, 1956), 244–45.

[14] Wlodzimierz Szwarc, "Solution of the Akers-Friedman Scheduling Problem," *Operations Research*, 8: 6 (November–December, 1960), 782–88. See also, W. W. Hardgrave and G. Nemhauser, "A Geometric Model and Graphical Algorithm for a Sequencing Problem," *Operations Research*, 11: 6 (November, 1963), 889–900.

two jobs can be scheduled may be as large as required. Let the facilities be called $A, B, \ldots, M$. The objective is to complete both jobs in the shortest possible time. An additional piece of information is needed. How much time is required for each job at each facility? We shall let these times be denoted by a subscript, for example, A_5 represents five hours spent at facility A.

Now, let us turn to a specific example.

Job	Technological Sequence and Times (in hours) at Each Facility
J_I	Begin $\;\;A_5 \to B_2 \to C_3 \to E_5 \to D_4\;\;$ End
J_{II}	Begin $\;\;C_3 \to D_3 \to B_3 \to E_2 \to A_{10}\;\;$ End

Figure 11.10 represents the technological sequences of two jobs in terms of Cartesian coordinates. (We can see why only two jobs can be handled by this approach.) Along the abscissa we have laid out the technological sequence

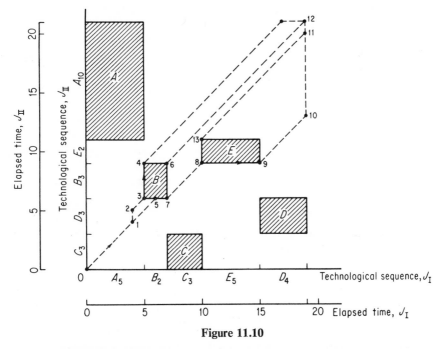

Figure 11.10

Graphical sequencing model with several feasible production plans traced out.

specified for J_1. The same thing has been done for J_{II} along the ordinate. We then block off the area that is common to each of the facilities, A, B, C, D, and E. The intersection space of each facility has an area equal to the product of the time requirements of each job at the facility.

Examination of this diagram reveals that it is impossible to utilize any of the blocked intersection space that has been cross-hatched. To do so would require either the *simultaneous* use of one facility for both jobs or replacing an unfinished job with an unstarted job. On the other hand, a point such as 2 represents work being done for J_I at facility A and for J_{II} at facility D. Point 2 also signifies that four hours of work have been completed on J_I and five hours of work have been completed on J_{II}. Further, J_{II} has completed its stay at facility C and has only one more hour to go at facility D. Any point in the space can be interpreted in this manner. Point 12 signifies that both J_I and J_{II} are completed.

Any path for completing these jobs must avoid the shaded blocked areas. We start at the origin, point 0, and begin to move upward and to the right, following a diagonal. The diagonal is the most efficient policy because it indicates that we are *simultaneously* working on both jobs, each at different facilities. As long as we remain on the diagonal we are obtaining full utilization of our productive capacity; however, we cannot always do so. When we reach point 5, we have no alternative but to change direction to the horizontal, because we cannot enter blocked space. A number of different paths have been illustrated in the figure, and all *must* reach point 12, which represents the completion time of both J_I and J_{II}. It requires nineteen hours on the x-axis and twenty-one hours on the y-axis.

There are only three kinds of movements that can be made through this chart. These are: (1) the diagonal movements, representing simultaneous operations; (2) vertical movements, indicating that J_I is not being worked on; and (3) horizontal movements that indicate J_{II} is idle. Obviously, we would like to be able to trace a path directly along the diagonal from point 0 to point 12.[15] This cannot be done if blocked intersection space interferes. In our example, facility B stops the diagonal movement. Every situation produces its own unique configuration, and we are stuck with ours. There is a variety of alternate routes that can be taken to avoid going through the space blocked by facility B. We have illustrated some of these. For the purpose of this discussion, we shall only consider four of them:

> Path *a*—0, 1, 2, 3, 4, 12
> Path *b*—0, 1, 5, 7, 8, 9, 10, 11, 12
> Path *c*—0, 1, 5, 7, 6, 12
> Path *d*—0, 1, 5, 7, 8, 13, 11, 12

None of the paths is necessarily optimal. The method we are explaining cannot locate the one path that is optimal for sequencing these jobs through the facilities. Our objective is to discover the path of minimum total elapsed time,

---

[15] Since the sum of J_I's process times is 19 and the sum of J_{II}'s process times is 21, the diagonal could only be followed to (19, 19) and then the line would go vertically to (19, 21).

but we can only generate a number of alternative paths that are likely to include the optimal sequence. Let us consider, therefore, the four sequencing paths previously described and determine which one of these provides the best result.

It is simple enough to compute elapsed time. To the total time for J_I operations—this is $(5 + 2 + 3 + 5 + 4) = 19$ hours—add any J_I idle time. The idle time for J_I is represented by the sum of all vertical segments along any given path. Consider the path 0, 1, 5, 7, 8, 9, 10, 11, 12. The vertical segments total eight. Therefore, total elapsed time for both jobs will be $19 + 8 = 27$ hours. To check this result, J_{II} operations require twenty-one hours. Along the path that we have just followed, the horizontal segments (J_{II}'s idle time) total six. Then, $21 + 6 = 27$ hours, which is identical to our previous result. Proceeding in the same way, we can obtain the following table for paths a, b, c, and d.

Path	Total Elapsed Time	Job I Idle Time	Job II Idle Time
a	23	4	2
b	27	8	6
c	22	3	1
d	22	3	1

We observe that paths c and d provide equal and minimum times. There may be a better sequence than this, but we have not found it.

The graphical sequencing model is certainly useful. It clearly illustrates that many schedule control difficulties are problems of coping with enormous diversity. When we add more realism through the inclusion of full-scale problems and recognition of risk, analytic, mathematical models are simply overwhelmed. Consequently, for complex sequencing problems, we frequently require the use of simulation techniques for determining near-optimal paths through the system. In the last analysis, we will be satisfied, as we almost always have been, with doing a good, even if not a *perfect*, job.

Sequencing to Minimize Setup Costs

Another aspect of sequencing arises when each new job assigned to a specific machine has a significant set-up cost. The objective of minimizing set-up costs might override the other objectives that we have previously considered. To get a real sense of this kind of problem, assume that a matrix of set-up costs such as the one shown below is available.[16]

[16] Conway *et al.*, *op. cit.*, p. 58.

		Successor Job				
$\rightarrow$		*a*	*b*	*c*	*d*	*e*	*f*

		a	*b*	*c*	*d*	*e*	*f*
	a	—	1	7	3	14	2
	b	3	—	6	9	1	24
Predecessor	*c*	6	14	—	3	7	3
Job	*d*	2	3	5	—	9	11
	e	15	7	11	2	—	4
	f	20	5	13	4	18	—

The character of this particular matrix configuration is analogous to the well-known *traveling salesman problem*. The salesman's requirement is to complete a minimum time (or cost) circuit of all cities on his itinerary of cities without any doubling back. A square assignment matrix can be used, representing preceding jobs as rows (i) and succeeding jobs as columns (j). Thus, an ordering must be found for a set of jobs, where $t_{ij} > 0$ ($i \neq j$) is the set-up time needed to change facilities from the ith to the jth job, and it is not required that $t_{ij} = t_{ji}$. An initial job is chosen, and the problem is to find a sequence with no internal cycles that minimizes the *total* set-up time. Similar statements can be made for facility downtime. The assignment method, as it is ordinarily used, can produce internal cycles (such as $ABCBC . . .$), and so, in general, another solution method is required. An exact solution can be found by the previously described iterative process of branch and bounding. We shall also describe several heuristic approaches that have great appeal for their simplicity.

Little, Murty, Sweeney, and Karel developed the "branch and bound" algorithm to provide solutions of optimum tours.[17] The method, as with all branch and bounding, is based on *opportunity cost analysis* in conjunction with rules of logic that delete nonoptimal solutions. Opportunity costs are derived by row and column subtraction of the assignment method (see pp. 270–272). The total amount subtracted is the initial lower bound. Using the matrix above, we obtain with row and then column subtraction the following values:

		Successor Job						
$\rightarrow$		*a*	*b*	*c*	*d*	*e*	*f*	*Subtract*

		a	*b*	*c*	*d*	*e*	*f*	*Subtract*
	a	—	0	3	2	13	1	1
	b	2	—	2	8	0	23	1
Predecessor	*c*	3	11	—	0	4	0	3
Job	*d*	0	1	0	—	7	1	2
	e	13	5	6	0	—	2	2
	f	16	1	6	0	14	—	4
Subtract		0	0	3	0	0	0	$3 + 13 = 16$

Sixteen, the initial lower bound, would also be the *optimal* cost if these first

[17] J. D. C. Little, K. G. Murty, D. W. Sweeney, and C. Karel, "An Algorithm for the Traveling Salesman Problem," *Operations Research*, 11: 6 (November, 1963), 972–989.

subtractions produced a final solution. Since they do not, further opportunity costs must be incurred. The matrix solution, in this particular case, provides an incomplete tour, *abedcfd*, which is not a final resolution of the problem. Therefore additional calculations can be made by identifying each zero in the matrix with the sum of its minimum row and minimum column values, which is an opportunity cost measure of not making that particular zero assignment.

		Successor Job					
	$\rightarrow$	a	b	c	d	e	f
	a	—	0^2				
	b		—			0^6	
Predecessor	c			—	$0°$		0^1
Job	d	0^3		0^2	—		
	e				0^2	—	
	f				0^1		—

Branching is performed on the highest opportunity cost zero, that is $b \rightarrow e$. A logical partitioning of sequencing possibilities is now made into those sequences that have the assignment $(b \rightarrow e)$ and those sequences that do not. The opportunity costs of each possibility increase and become two new lower bounds from which the tree of possibilities will continue to grow as the next zero in the matrix is analyzed and used for further partitioning. The process stops when closure is obtained with a specific lower bound value. If other possibilities that have lesser lower bound values still remain in the tree, they must be followed out until they equal or exceed the completed tour's lower bound value—or beat it. This approach is clearly explained in the material from Conway, Miller, and Maxwell that follows:[18]

Say that a problem S, fully reduced, is being considered for solution by the partitioning routine. One is concerned with the selection of a particular path, say from i to j, that will be the basis for creating two new problems:

1. S_{ij}, the problem of finding the best solution from among all the solutions to S that include the step (i, j).
2. $S_{n(ij)}$, the problem of selecting the best from among all the solutions to S that do not include the step (i, j).

Since in problem S_{ij} it has been decided to go from i to j, one can prohibit going from i to any other city and prohibit arriving at j from any other city, by making all the entries in the ith row and the jth column, except s_{ij}, equal to infinity. One must also prohibit the future selection of the element s_{ji}, by making it infinite also, since a tour cannot include s_{ij} and s_{ji} and still visit all n cities before returning to the starting point. Since these prohibitions may have eliminated some of the zeros of S, one can possibly further reduce S_{ij} and thus establish a new and greater lower bound on solutions of S obtained by solving S_{ij}.

In problem $S_{n(ij)}$ one prohibits travel from i to j by making $s_{ij} = \infty$. Again, a

[18] Conway, Maxwell, Milles, *Theory of Scheduling* (Reading, Mass.: Addison-Wesley Publishing Co., 1967), pp. 58–60.

further reduction of this modified matrix may be possible that will give an increased lower bound on solutions obtained through problem $S_{n(ij)}$. Now the objective of the selection of (i, j) is to make the lower bound on $S_{n(ij)}$ as great as possible in hopes that it can be discarded from the list of unsolved problems by the elimination routine without further partition. To accomplish this, one looks ahead at the reduction that will be possible in $S_{n(ij)}$ for each possible (i, j) and makes the selection such that the sum of the two subsequent reducing constants will be a maximum. It should be obvious that it is necessary to consider only the zero elements of S as candidates, since if a nonzero element is selected no further reduction of $S_{n(ij)}$ will be possible. At stage (1) of the procedure, the list consists of problem S-(16), the (16) indicating that any solution to the original problem obtained through S-(16) will have a value of at least 16. A solution 1–2–3–4–5–6 is, of course, known so that at this point $Z = 43$. The superscripts to each of the zeros of S-(16) indicate the reduction that would be possible if the zero were prohibited. The greatest of these is 6, for element s_{25}, so the partition is based on this element, yielding the problems shown below:

List, stage (2) ($Z = 43$)

S₂₅-(16)
S_{n(25)}-(22)

S_{25}-(16)

—	0^2	3	2	—	1
—	—	—	—	0	—
3	11	—	0^0	—	0^1
0^3	1	0^3	—	—	9
13	—	6	0^2	—	2
16	1	6	0^1	—	—

$S_{n(25)}$-(22)

—	0	3	2	9	1
0	—	0	6	—	21
3	11	—	0	0	0
0	1	0	—	3	9
13	5	6	0	—	2
16	1	6	0	10	—

At stage (2) the list consists of problems S_{25}-(16) and $S_{n(25)}$-(22). Note that $S_{n(25)}$ has been further reduced by 6 (4 in the 5th column and 2 in the 2nd row), giving a bound of 22. In problem S_{25} the element s_{25} has been underlined, indicating that this is *required* in the solution, and the other elements in that row and column have been prohibited. Note also that element s_{52} has been prohibited. Since solutions to this problem are known to contain s_{25}, it is clear that they cannot contain s_{52}, which would cause a cyclic subtour of fewer than n cities. Since both problems on the list have bounds of less than Z and more than two cities to specify, they cannot yet be either *solved* or *eliminated*, and one of them must be attacked with the *partitioning* routine. With more cities specified, and a lower value of Y, S_{25} is probably the more promising of the two problems. Again, the value of each zero as a basis for partition is given as a superscript. Selecting element s_{41} produces problems $S_{25,41}$-(19) and $S_{25,n(41)}$-(19); $S_{n(25)}$-(22) remains on the list from stage (2).

List, stage (3) ($Z = 43$)

S_{n(25)}-(22)
S₂₅,₄₁-(19)
S_{25,n(41)}-(19)

$S_{25,41}$-(19)

—	0^1	0^3	—	—	1
—	—	—	—	0	—
—	11	—	0^0	—	0^1
0	—	—	—	—	—
—	—	3	0^2	—	2
—	1	3	0^1	—	—

$S_{25,n(41)}$-(19)

—	0^2	3	2	—	1
—	—	—	—	0	—
0^{10}	11	—	0^0	—	0^1
—	1	0^4	—	—	9
10	—	6	0^2	—	2
13	1	6	0^1	—	—

List, stage (4) (Z = 43) $S_{25,41,13}$-(20) $S_{25,41,n(13)}$-(22)

$S_{n(25)}$-(22)	—	—	0	—	—	—	—	0	—	—	—	1
$S_{25,n(41)}$-(19)	—	—	—	—	0	—	—	—	—	—	0	—
$S_{25,41,13}$-(20)	—	10	—	—	—	0^{12}	—	11	—	0	—	0
$S_{25,41,n(13)}$-(22)	0	—	—	—	—	—	0	—	—	—	—	—
	—	—	—	0^2	—	2	—	—	0	0	—	2
	—	0^{10}	—	0^0	—	—	—	1	0	0	—	—

List, stage (5) (Z = 43) $S_{25,41,13,36}$-(20) $S_{25,41,13,n(36)}$-(32)

$S_{n(25)}$-(22)	—	—	0	—	—	—	—	—	0	—	—	—
$S_{25,n(41)}$-(19)	—	—	—	—	0	—	—	—	—	—	0	—
$S_{25,41,n(13)}$-(22)	—	—	—	—	—	0	—	0	—	—	—	—
$S_{25,41,13,36}$-(20)	0	—	—	—	—	—	0	—	—	—	—	—
$S_{25,41,13,n(36)}$-(32)	—	—	—	0	—	—	—	—	—	0	—	0
	—	0	—	0	—	—	—	0	—	0	—	—

Note that at stage (4) when $S_{25,41}$ is partitioned on the basis of element 13, the blocking of elements of $S_{25,41,13}$ which cannot be used includes the usual symmetric element 31 and also element 34. Since both 41 and 13 are required steps in the path, element 34 would close a three-city subtour 4–1–3–4.

Partitioning is continued until at stage (5) there is a solvable problem on the list—$S_{25,41,13,36}$-(20) has only two steps remaining to be specified. Four specified steps must involve a minimum of five cities; there is at most one city remaining, and only one way that it can be fitted in to give a valid tour. In this case the four steps happen to involve all six cities in two disconnected trips: 2–5 and 4–1–3–6. The solution routine connects these trips, specifying s_{54} and s_{62} (there is no choice) to produce a solution 6–2–5–4–1–3 with a value of 20.

This new value, $Z = 20$, allows the *elimination* routine to discard three problems from the list, so that all that remains is problem $S_{25,n(41)}$,-(19). It is still possible that this problem could yield a solution with a value less than 20. This problem is partitioned on s_{31} to produce $S_{25,n(41),31}$-(20) and $S_{25,n(41),n(31)}$-(29). Both these problems can be discarded by the elimination routine so that the list becomes empty and the problem is solved.

List, stage (7) (Z = 20) $S_{25,n(41),31}$-(20) $S_{25,n(41),n(31)}$-(29)

$S_{25,n(41),31}$-(20)	—	0	—	2	—	0	—	0	3	2	—	1
$S_{25,n(41),n(31)}$-(29)	—	—	—	—	0	—	—	—	—	—	0	—
	0	—	—	—	—	—	—	11	—	0	—	0
	—	1	0	—	—	8	—	1	0	—	—	9
	—	—	6	0	—	1	0	—	6	0	—	2
	—	1	6	0	—	—	3	1	6	0	—	—

One can conveniently show the partitioning of the various problems by means of a tree. Each node in Figure 11.11 corresponds to a problem on the list.[19]

[19] Conway, *et al.*, *op. cit.*, pp. 58–61.

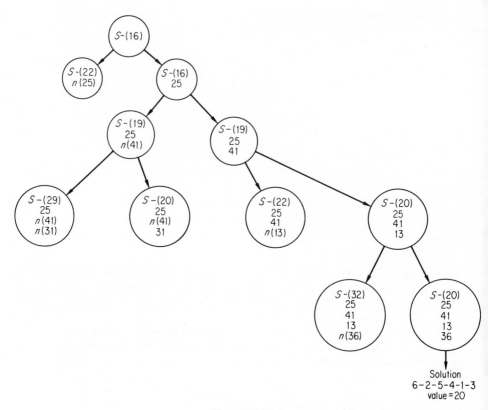

Figure 11.11

Partitioning tree for the traveling-salesman problem.

Another Approach to Branch and Bounding

In as yet unpublished material, Dannenbring has programmed a branch and bound algorithm that offers an alternative explanation of the branch and bound process applied to the traveling salesman model of the set-up sequencing problem. Although differing procedurally from the algorithm proposed by Little *et al.*, it has much in common with it.

The process involves creating a list of unsolved partial problems each of which has a lower bound, below which that partial sequence is guaranteed not to produce a solution. A dynamic upper bound is also used to eliminate potential solutions whose lower bounds are not less than the upper bound for the problem. The smallest lower bound of all partial solutions is considered the lower bound for the problem. As branchings occur, the lower bound increases and the upper bound decreases until such time as they *converge* to a solution.

The process is: Select an initial node. Branch from that node to all immediately following nodes. Calculate lower bounds for each branched-to node. Discard the branched-from node and any nodes whose lower bounds are not less than the upper bound. Arrange the remaining nodes so that the node with the smallest lower bound is first, the node with next smallest lower bound is second, etc. Then select the first node from the list, and branch from it to all possible immediately succeeding nodes. Add these nodes to the list in their proper positions. Discard the branched-from node and any nodes with lower bounds greater than or equal to the problem's upper bound. The branching process continues until the problem's lower bound and upper bound converge. The upper bound value (say, 43) changes (to say, 25) when a branch has been followed to form a complete cycle and the solution value of say, 25) is less than the present upper bound for the problem.

The lower bound for any given node can be calculated according to the following steps. Each node is designated by a number, such as 1246, which represents a partial solution. The node 1246 specifies a partial tour from city 1 to city 2 to city 4 to city 6. Its lower bound would be calculated by:

$$LB(1246) = C_{12} + C_{24} + C_{46} + \sum_{\substack{i \neq \\ 1,2,4}} \min C_{ij}, j \neq 2,4,6$$

or in general

$$LB(abc \ldots n) = C_{ab} + C_{bc} + \ldots + C_{mn}$$
$$+ \sum_{\substack{i \neq \\ a,b,\cdots,m}} \min C_{ij}, j \neq b, c, \ldots, n$$

where C_{ab} = cost (distance) associated with city b following city a in the tour.

This lower bound computation is followed in the example below. The initial cost matrix we will use is:[20]

$\rightarrow$	1	2	3	4	5	6
1	—	1	7	3	14	2
2	3	—	6	9	1	24
3	6	14	—	3	7	3
4	2	3	5	—	9	11
5	15	7	11	2	—	4
6	20	5	13	4	18	—

Before we begin with lower bound calculations, let us arbitrarily choose the tour 123456 to provide an upper bound of 43, i.e., $1 + 6 + 3 + 9 + 4 + 20$.

[20] Using this matrix, note that

$$LB(1246) = 1 + 9 + 11 + \min[6, 7] + \min[15, 11] + \min[20, 13, 18]$$
$$= 21 + 6 + 11 + 13 = 51$$

First List.

Select an initial node to branch from. At random we will choose node 1. (The initial node selected will only affect the speed with which an optimal solution will be reached.) Determine all possible branches from the initial node. See Figure 11.12.

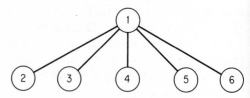

Figure 11.12

For each possible branch, calculate its lower bound. Record the partial sequence and lower bound on the list of potential solutions, which is arranged with the smallest lower bound first. The lower bound for nodes 12 and 13 are calculated:[21]

$$LB(12) = C_{12} + \sum_{i \neq 1} \min C_{ij}, j \neq 2$$

$$LB(12) = 1 + 1 + 3 + 2 + 2 + 4 = 13$$

Similarly

$$LB(13) = C_{13} + \sum_{i \neq 1} \min C_{ij}, j \neq 3$$

$$LB(13) = 7 + 1 + 3 + 2 + 2 + 4 = 19$$

The first list would be:

Node:	12, 16, 14, 13, 15
Lower Bound Value:	13, 14, 18, 19, 28

Second List.

Since node 12 has the smallest lower bound, we branch from that node to all possible partial sequences (see Figure 11.13).

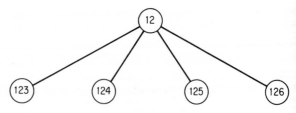

Figure 11.13

[21] We note the similarity of these calculations with the determination of the zero opportunity costs, previously described on pp. 314–317.

We will compute the lower bound for the partial sequence 123.

$$LB(123) = C_{12} + C_{23} + \sum_{i \neq 1,2} \min C_{ij}, j \neq 2, 3$$

$$LB(123) = 1 + 6 + 3 + 2 + 2 + 4 = 18$$

After all calculations are completed, the second list contains:

Node:	125, 16, 123, 14, 13, 15, 124, 126
Lower Bound Value:	13, 14, 18, 18, 19, 28, 32, 36

Note that node 12, the originally branched-from node, has been dropped from the list. In case of ties for position on the list (nodes 123 and 14), the node with the most complete sequence (123) is placed first. This facilitates finding upper bounds so that we can eliminate nodes from the bottom of the list (keeping the list shorter and easier to manage).

Third List.

Again we branch from the node at the top of the list—node 125. Lower bounds are calculated, and the third list is:

Node:	16, 1256, 123, 14, 13, 1253, 1254, 15, 124, 126
Lower Bound Value:	14, 15, 18, 18, 19, 22, 22, 28, 32, 36

Fourth List.

This time we branch from node 16, and our fourth list is:

Node:	1256, 162, 123, 14, 13, 1253, 1254, 163, 164, 15, 165, 124, 126
Lower Bound Value:	15, 15, 18, 18, 19, 22, 22, 23, 25, 28, 30, 32, 36

Fifth List.

Node 1256 is branched-from, and the two resulting nodes, 12563 and 12564, completely specify solutions—1256341 and 1256431—which can be evaluated and used as new upper bounds to prune the list.[22] Of course, if one of these had a lower bound value less than any unbranched-from node, we would have the optimal sequence and computation would terminate. That was not the case here, and our fifth list appears as follows:

Node:	162, 123, 14, 13, 1256431[23]
Lower Bound Value:	15, 18, 18, 19, upper bound: 21

[22] Our previous upper bound has been of no assistance because it was always larger than any of the lower bound values that appeared in the lists.

[23] This upper bound gets rid of all branchings having values greater than 21 and also the former upper bound of 43.

Sixth List.

Continuing with a branch from node 162, we arrive at:

Node:	1625, 123, 14, 13, 1623,	1256431
Lower Bound Value:	15, 18, 18, 19, 19, upper bound:	21

Seventh List.

Branching from 1625, we find that neither branch can better the upper bound, and we reach:

Node:	123, 14, 13, 1623,	1256431
Lower Bound Value:	18, 18, 19, 19, upper bound:	21

Eighth List.

Node:	1236, 14, 13, 1623,	1256431
Lower Bound Value:	18, 18, 19, 20, upper bound:	21

Ninth List.

Node:	14, 13, 1623,	1256431
Lower Bound Value:	18, 19, 20, upper bound:	21

Tenth List.

Node:	13, 1623,	1256431
Lower Bound Value:	19, 20, upper bound:	21

Eleventh List.

Node:	136, 1623,	1256431
Lower Bound Value:	19, 20, upper bound:	21

Twelfth List.

Node:	1362, 1623,	1256431
Lower Bound Value:	20, 20, upper bound:	21

Thirteenth List.

Node:	1362541
Lower Bound Value: upper bound:	20

At this point the algorithm has converged to the optimum solution, which has a value of 20.

Note that the list could have been kept shorter in the earlier solution steps by picking an appropriate upper bound before the solution begins. As Little *et al.* suggested, we did select the naïve tour sequence of {1, 2, 3, 4, 5, 6, 1}. However, in this problem the value obtained was of no use since it was higher than any lower bound computed. A better approach might be to use Gavett's "closest-unvisited-city" heuristic to determine an initial upper bound.[24] We shall explain this now.

Sequencing Heuristics

Gavett has shown that heuristic approaches can be both simple and satisfactory.[25] He first proposes using the "next best" (NB) rule. Given a specific starting job, this NB rule selects as next the job that has the least set-up time in relation to the job just finished. A second heuristic (called NB′) tests the initial job followed by all $n - 1$ other jobs. The (NB) rule is then applied to each of the $n - 1$ sequences. (Note that the one sequence derived by the NB heuristic must be included in the $n - 1$ sequences of the second rule.) The sequencing strategy among $n - 1$ choices that produced the best result is chosen. Gavett's third heuristic (NB″) uses column subtraction first (to obtain opportunity costs with respect to each job as a successor) and then applies the (NB) rule. Each of these approaches entails less work than the "branch and bound" calculations yet provides improved performance as compared to random assignments.

There are real advantages to be gained by using Gavett's heuristic approaches to obtain a "good" upper bound solution for the branch and bound solution of the traveling salesman-type of sequencing problem. Also of importance, in that case, is whether one origin, arbitrarily chosen as the starting point, is used or whether instead all possible origins are tested.

---

[24] By using the NB rule described in the next section in conjunction with all origins being tested, an upper bound of 22 was found for the problem we have been discussing. This knowledge would have kept the list substantially smaller.

[25] J. William Gavett, "Three Heuristic Rules for Sequencing Jobs to a Single Production Facility," *Management Science*, 11: 8 (June, 1965), B166–B176.

PROBLEMS

1. Examine several alternative sequences for the following $n \times 1$ system, with six jobs and processing times, t_i.

i	t_i	i	t_i
a	5	d	9
b	4	e	12
c	6	f	8

Especially study the SPT and also the effect of LPT (longest processing time).

2. What effect does the information that jobs a, b, and c are half as important as jobs d, e, and f have on the sequence solution?

3. Sequence the jobs whose processing times are given below through their two machine centers. All jobs have the same technological sequence $MC_1 \rightarrow MC_2$. No passing is allowed.

				Job				
	a	b	c	d	e	f	g	h
MC_1	8	10	4	6	5	12	20	11
MC_2	16	16	16	3	5	8	12	7

4. Our company has four orders on hand, and each must be processed in the sequential order:

Department A—press shop

Department B—plating and finishing

The table below lists the number of days required by each job in each department. For example, Job IV requires one day in the press shop and one day in the finishing department.

	Job I	Job II	Job III	Job IV
Department A	8	6	5	1
Department B	8	3	4	1

(a) Assume that no other work is being done by the departments. Use a Gantt layout chart technique to try to find the best work schedule. By best work schedule, we mean minimum time to finish all four jobs.

(b) Determine the total time to complete all four jobs when the optimal schedule is used.

(c) Compare the results obtained in (a) and (b), and comment on the complexity of such problems when many departments and many jobs are involved.

(d) What is the effect of working Department A on a double shift? How about the effect of working both departments on half time?

5. (a) Sequence the jobs whose processing times are given below through the three machine centers. All jobs are constrained by the same technological sequence, (1, 2, 3,) and no passing is permitted.

| | Job | | | | |
	a	b	c	d	e
MC_1	13	14	15	18	12
MC_2	6	12	8	10	5
MC_3	20	8	4	16	24

(b) Use the branch and bound approach to solve this same problem.

6. Why will a string model not work for finding the minimum distance tour in the traveling salesman-type of sequencing problem?

7. Using the same data as the sequencing matrix in the text (pp. 319) use branch and bound methodology starting with node 3 to solve the problem. (It will be found that the list converges to a solution more rapidly than was the case for node 1.)

8. Apply various heuristic rules such as discussed on pp. 323 to the traveling salesman-type sequencing matrix below.

| | | Successor Job | | | | |
	→	a	b	c	d	e
	a	—	16	8	9	5
Predecessor	b	4	—	12	20	6
Job	c	12	9	—	4	10
	d	18	15	1	—	11
	e	8	7	13	3	—

9. Use the graphical sequencing method for the following problem:

$$J_I \quad A_8 \quad B_6 \quad C_5 \quad D_1$$
$$J_{II} \quad C_8 \quad D_4 \quad A_3 \quad B_1$$
$$\text{technological} \quad \rightarrow \quad \text{sequence}$$

A, B, C, and D are the facilities, and the notation is equivalent to that used on pp. 310–313.

Inventoried materials with regulated flows are one of the major classes of inputs to the transformation system. In general, the stock levels are simple to control. For the most part, orders for raw materials, purchased parts, in-process inventories, finished goods inventories, and maintenance supplies are representative of repetitive decision problems. Therefore, a single decision that deviates from the optimal cannot do much harm. Only the **cumulative** effects of repeated divergencies from optimal results can impose severe penalties over time. Materials are involved with direct costs. When all material costs are added together, they constitute a major share of operating costs. Even in labor-intensive industries material costs often account for a surprisingly large per cent of all direct costs. Many service systems also require a great deal of purchasing, and inventory turns out to play a critical role for them. Inventories are mainly associated with the variable-cost line of the break-even chart. This area of cost control is most familiar to operations managers.

Inventory

Management 12

Companies have been moving toward an organizational integration of materials control functions.[1] In many firms these activities were fragmented, attended by individuals who seldom communicated with each other. Eventually, in the search for greater control, a *single, central materials control department* appeared in numerous organizations.

Materials Management

Today, many organizations have a vice president in charge of materials control. The responsibilities vested in a materials control department include at least three subfunctions: namely, *purchasing, inventory control,* and *receiving* (the last includes inspection, acceptance sampling, and storage).[2] We will treat each of these topics but concentrate our attention on inventory control (and acceptance sampling).

Figure 12.1 is a flow diagram depicting the various communications that unite the materials control area. We observe that many forms of communication flow between the organizational units to achieve an integrated materials control department. In addition, the materials control department communicates with other operating divisions of the company and with the external world.

Purchasing

The purchasing division occupies a unique organizational position. Through its purchasing function, the organization operates as a *customer.*

[1] See, for example, AMA Management Report Number 35, *Managing the Materials Function* (New York: Manufacturing Division, American Management Association, Inc., 1959).

[2] Attention has also been paid to the specification of appropriate materials for the job—a subject sometimes called value analysis. See, for example, Lawrence B. Miles, *Techniques of Value Analysis* (New York: McGraw-Hill Book Co., Inc., 1961).

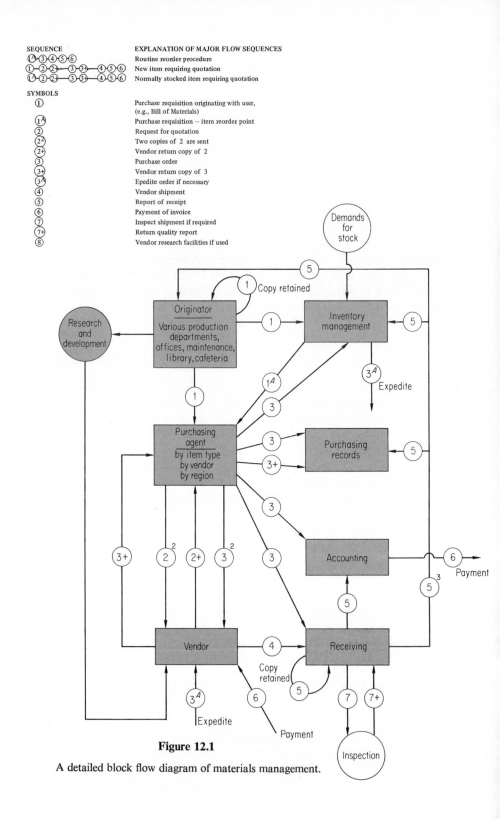

Figure 12.1

A detailed block flow diagram of materials management.

Accordingly, it is susceptible to the marketing strategies of the vendors from whom it obtains the materials that are required for its operations. Depending upon the extent to which the company requires outside suppliers—and is not self-sufficient—the importance of the buying function increases. For example, a mail order company produces a small fraction of the total items that it offers for sale. Buyers in such enterprises are responsible, in large measure, for the success of their companies. Commensurate with this responsibility is the remuneration that such buyers receive. At the same time, they must accept the risk of making errors in carrying out their functions. The penalties of errors can be high.

The purchasing function is deeply involved with human behavior. Relations with vendors cannot be pinned down to a formula. They can affect "deals" that are made, favors that are rendered, and the continuity of suppliers. Purchasing operations are immersed in a maelstrom of human relations. There are many mechanical aspects to the achievement of a successful purchasing function, but the human factors cannot be overlooked. Buyers can succeed in achieving special arrangements because of friendly relationships that exist. These are not dishonorable relationships because they include the evaluation of both buyer and vendor of the long-term stability and goodwill of their relationship. Thus, in the business environment of North America, personal friendships are not considered to be a reasonable basis for enterprise decisions. In other business environments, for example, Latin America and the Middle East, personal friendships are considered to be business assets that reduce risk and have monetary value. Part of this cultural difference can be traced to the importance placed upon legal contracts in North America that does not exist elsewhere. Because of the enormous growth of international operations, these factors can play a significant role in determining the success of management in handling the affairs of subsidiaries outside the U.S.A.[3]

Purchasing records provide a history of what has been done in the past, what costs were involved, who the major suppliers were as well as the costs, discounts, quality levels, and delivery periods for specific items. But purchasing is a function that is not even roughly similar in many different companies. Differentiated skills exist that emphasize types of materials and vendor purchasing *traditions*. It would be impossible to discuss all the intricate relationships that have been developed by buyers and vendors in order to achieve maximum satisfaction for both parties. One important procedure, however, should be mentioned. It is called *vendor releasing*. In this case, a buyer contracts for a substantial number of units and, thereby, obtains discount prices. The vendor agrees to ship fixed or varying amounts of the purchased material at stated intervals. Often, only the approximate shipping quantities for each time period are agreed upon. Generally, the buyer is in a position to

---

[3] For a useful discussion of these points, see: Edward T. Hall, "The Silent Language in Overseas Business," *Harvard Business Review*, 38: 3 (May–June, 1960), 87–96.

change the quantities, from time to time, if he does so with sufficient notice. We can observe how an arrangement, such as vendor releasing, is dependent upon a reasonable forecast of demand and a reasonably accurate specification of the vendor's lead time.[4] It requires a fairly long-term commitment to obtain the benefits of quantity discounts. We will be discussing many of these factors as we proceed.

Commodity Purchasing

To examine how vendor relations depend on the nature of a company's operations, let us divide purchased inventory into two major groups: (1) materials required for production; and (2) materials required for maintenance of plant and equipment. With respect to the first class, some companies purchase manufactured and assembled items; other companies deal primarily with basic raw materials and commodity markets. There is a real difference in the purchasing agent's approach to each of these situations.

Let us consider, as an example, the green coffee commodity market from the point of view of a coffee producer. A larger than normal inventory may have to be built up, at a particular time, as a result of favorable coffee prices. The cost of holding this inventory must be balanced against the advantage to be gained by overbuying. If the problem is one of underbuying while waiting for a more favorable market, then the cost of running out of stock must be taken into account. Under certain circumstances, specialized buying techniques may be involved. These include hedging[5] and speculative purchases, both of which require forward buying.

Hedging involves the buying and selling of commodity futures. Thus, a company fearing that commodity prices will rise buys a given amount of the material for delivery in a *future month*. The market price is paid plus carrying charges. When the material is actually required for production—before the *future month*—a spot purchase is made for cash and immediate delivery. Simultaneously, a sale is made for delivery in the *future month*. If the price of the commodity has risen, then the selling price of the future contract reflects this as compared to the buying price of the futures. This profit, when applied to the purchase price of the spot transaction, smooths out the rise in price that has occurred. Thus:

1. Our company counts on a raw material cost of $1.00 per pound.
2. Fearing a price rise in this raw material but having sufficient supply on hand, the purchasing agent buys one thousand pounds for delivery to his

---

[4] Lead time, or lag time, is the interval that elapses between the placement of an order with the vendor and the receipt of the ordered goods.

[5] Hedging can only be carried on if an organized commodity exchange exists.

company *at some specific future date*—at $1.03 per pound. ($1.00 is the present price, the $0.03 reflects carrying costs.)

3. After a period of time, prices have risen. The cost per pound is now $1.50. The company requires and buys one thousand pounds at this price, expecting rapid delivery.
4. But on the same date, the company agrees to sell one thousand pounds for delivery at the *same* future date (as in two above) at $1.53 per pound.
5. In this way, the company sells the commodity for future delivery and receives income, on a per pound basis, of $1.53. It has previously purchased material to cover this sale at $1.03. This yields a profit per pound of $0.50.
6. But the company had to pay $1.50 instead of $1.00 per pound to take care of its production requirements—or an increase per pound of $0.50.
7. This results in a *net* change for our company in the price per pound of $0.00. If the price had fallen, similar reasoning would apply. The company doesn't benefit from the drop in price but ends up with zero net change.

The purchase of coffee is only one example of this type of situation. We could, as well, have cited the grain commodity market, which affects distilleries and flour mills, or the cattle commodity market for both meat and skins. Soft drink manufacturers must adapt their activities to the sugar market. Textile manufacturers deal with cotton commodities. The confectionery industry buys cocoa. Other commodities include rubber, potatoes, zinc, and cottonseed oil.

Although it is exceedingly complicated, commodity buying can be analyzed in terms of a formal model.[6] We shall present a simple example of such a model with the intention of indicating the conceptual basis upon which the problem can be approached and to highlight the kind of information that is required. The objective is to minimize the cost of a primary raw material input that is characteristically subject to fluctuating prices.

A Dynamic Programming Buying Model

Step 1. Obtain probability estimates that describe the relative likelihood for different commodity prices in each quarter of the year. Such estimates could be obtained by consulting historical records of the particular commodity market. For simplicity, class the price by whole dollars and use time breaks of three months. In practice, these divisions can be made as fine as appears to be warranted.

[6] William T. Morris, "Some Analyses of Purchasing Policy," *Management Science*, V: 4 (July 1959), 443–52. With respect to the method used, see also Richard E. Bellman, *Dynamic Programming* (Princeton, N.J.: Princeton University Press, 1957).

| | | *Quarter* | | |
Price	1	2	3	4
$4.00	.40	.30	.40	.10
5.00	.40	.30	.30	.40
6.00	.20	.40	.30	.50
Expected Price	$4.80	$5.10	$4.90	$5.40

Step 2. Assume that we have to make one purchase in the year. If we defer buying until the fourth quarter, the expected price will be $5.40. Can we do better than this? We note that if we buy in the third quarter there is a 70 per cent chance of doing better, viz., a 30 per cent chance of buying at $5.00 and a 40 per cent chance of buying at $4.00.[7] Then, Decision Rule A follows:

1. Buy in the fourth quarter if the price in the third quarter is $6.00.
2. Buy in the third quarter if the price in the third quarter is $5.00 or less.

The probability that two will occur is 0.70. Consequently, the probability that one will occur is $1.00 - 0.70 = 0.30$. From this we derive the expected value of Decision Rule A.

Expected price (Decision Rule A) = 0.40($4.00) + 0.30($5.00)
$$+ \, 0.30(\$5.40) = \$4.72.$$

Step 3. If the price in the second quarter is $4.00, we can do better than this expected price of $4.72. Decision Rule B is then:

1. Use Decision Rule A if the price in the second quarter is $5.00 or greater.
2. Buy in the second quarter if the price in the second quarter is $4.00.

The probability that two will occur is 0.30. Hence:

Expected price (Decision Rule B) = 0.30($4.00) + 0.70($4.72) = $4.504.

Step 4. If the price in the first quarter is $4.00, we can do better than this expected price of $4.504. Decision Rule C follows:

1. Use Decision Rule B if the price in the first quarter is $5.00 or greater.
2. Buy in the first quarter if the price in the first quarter is $4.00.

The probability that two will occur is 0.40. Thus:

Expected price (Decision Rule C) = 0.40($4.00) + 0.60($4.504) = $4.3024.

We have derived an optimal policy that has an expected price of $4.3024. The decision tree in Figure 12.2 recapitulates this policy.

---

[7] Because of the crude categorization for dollars, we are forced to treat this problem as: ($4.00 and $5.00) < $5.40 < $6.00. With finer price breaks this could be avoided.

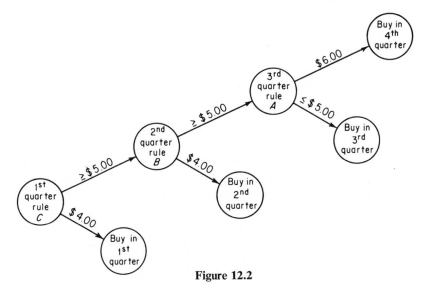

Figure 12.2

A decision tree for commodity buying policy.

The importance of commodity buying has induced us to present a commodity buying model. Inventory control and production scheduling and control are strongly affected by such considerations.

Usually, the purchase of fabricated units and components tends to involve more *stable* price structures than apply to commodities. An organization will contract with a producer to supply a given number of units of some specific quality. Under some circumstances, the contract may be given on the basis of bids that are offered by potential vendors. The bid system is commonly associated with governmental acquisition of materials. It is also familiar in situations where industrial organizations have no prior vendor arrangements and in which substantial acquisitions are to be made. It is only useful when true competition exists for the items to be supplied.

A company does not, of necessity, choose to make its purchases from the organization presenting the lowest bid. Price is not the only factor that should be taken into consideration when awarding a contract. Among other things, it is necessary to consider the guarantees of quality, the experience of the vendor, the certainties of delivery, and the kind of long-term supplier-producer relationship that is likely to develop. Transportation costs further complicate the picture. A high bid received from a vendor that is two miles away may be less costly—after transportation—than a lower bid from a potential supplier located three thousand miles away. Thus, it is not enough to compare bids on an FOB point of origin basis.[8]

[8] FOB Detroit. This familiar expression is read "freight on board," Detroit. It means that the price is quoted *without* shipping charges from Detroit to whatever point of destination is involved.

Maintenance Inventories

Previously, we mentioned inventories that are primarily maintenance inventories. Consider, for example, an oil refinery: For lack of a few critical parts, an entire refinery can be shut down. The cost of lost production may well run into millions of dollars. Should all parts be kept in stock? If so, how many of each kind? How likely is it that a spare part kept in stock for an emergency is, in fact, a reject—a faulty part—that will fail immediately upon use? There are many different kinds of problems that are faced by purchasing agents for maintenance parts. Often, severe *technical* problems are involved in purchasing for the maintenance function of complex technological systems.

Maintenance parts buyers, in particular, must be familiar with production equipment and its requirements. They must also be able to evaluate the quality of the merchandise they acquire. A rational plan should be developed for purchasing and stocking such items. Maintenance inventory policies are a function of the type of maintenance that is used, that is, *preventive* or *remedial* maintenance or a combination of the two. In many systems, the technical basis used for purchasing decisions can be exceedingly critical. When reliability and failure are of major importance, the purchasing function is frequently assigned to a scientifically trained individual. This is particularly necessary when critical specifications are couched in engineering terminology.

A Model for Maintenance Inventories

An important class of maintenance inventories is identified with the fact that at the time a major facility is purchased, spare parts can be obtained inexpensively. Later on, however, if it turns out that an insufficient supply of spare parts was acquired, the cost of obtaining additional spares is much higher.

To illustrate, assume that a large punch press has a part that engineering data indicate has a probability of i failures, $\{p_i\}$ over the lifetime of the machine. There is a cost, c, for each spare part purchased at the time that the press is acquired. When a spare part must be purchased at a later time, because not enough were originally purchased, the cost is estimated to be C_u (which includes downtime costs on the press and the larger cost per part charged by the vendor who must treat the spare part request as a special order).

For a simple example of this model,[9] let $i = 1, 2, 3$ and $p_1 = p_2 = p_3 = \frac{1}{3}$.

---

[9] We could complicate the problem considerably by adding a charge for carrying a part in stock, by treating the intervals between failures, by questioning how many spares should be *reordered* at one time, etc. All such issues, and others as well, could be treated in a realistic model.

Also, assume that $c = \$5$ and $C_u = \$40$. The question we wish to answer is: How many spare parts, k, should be ordered at the time of the original purchase? A decision matrix can be constructed to represent this problem. Thus:

		Number of Failures i			
		1	2	3	Expected Cost
	p_i	$\frac{1}{3}$	$\frac{1}{3}$	$\frac{1}{3}$	
Original order	1	5	$5 + 40$	$5 + 80$	45
size, k	2	10	10	$10 + 40$	$23\frac{1}{3}$
	3	15	15	15	15 Min. cost

The outcome entries in the matrix are computed by the equation:

$$TC_{ki} = kc \qquad\qquad i \leq k$$
$$TC_{ki} = kc + (i - k)C_u \qquad i > k$$

where TC_{ki} is the total cost of ordering k spare parts when it turns out that i are required.

The expected cost for each strategy of ordering k spare parts is computed:

$$EC_k = \sum_{i=0}^{k} kcp_i + \sum_{i=k+1}^{N} [kc + (i - k)C_u]p_i$$

In our example, the optimal strategy is to order three spare parts with the press. Clearly, the decision matrix lends itself nicely to representing this static[10] form of inventory problem.

Before moving on to an expanded view of inventory control, let us examine the opportunity cost transformation of the total cost decision matrix that is obtained by column subtraction.

Total Cost Matrix			Opportunity Cost Matrix		
5	45	85	0	35	70
10	10	50	5	0	35
15	15	15	10	5	0

We observe zeroes on the diagonal of the opportunity cost matrix. This is expected, because when $k = i$, there is no overstock cost, no understock cost, and no regret. When $(k > i)$, there is an overstock cost of $5 (per unit over), and when $(k < i)$, there is an understock cost of $35 (per unit under). The cost of $35 is derived by recognizing that you would have had to pay $c = \$5$ in any case, so $C_u - c = \$40 - \$5 = \$35$. This opportunity cost analysis sheds important insight on the nature of inventory costs.

---

[10] "Static" is defined in the next section.

Classification of Inventory Systems

There are many significant distinctions between types of inventory items that need to be made. First, let us note, there are items that are functionally critical to operations, no matter how much or how little they cost. For example, the lack of some small spare engine part could ground a 747 aircraft. The need for a cheap pump part might severely slow down a refinery.

Second, there are items that are important because their transactional dollar volume is high. Previously, we discussed a lognormal type of distribution (see p. 26). Let us do so again, this time in the context of the many items in the system's total inventory. Figure 12.3 portrays the not unusual case where 25 per cent of all items accounts for between 60 and 75 per cent of the company's total dollar volume. This is the A class of inventory items.

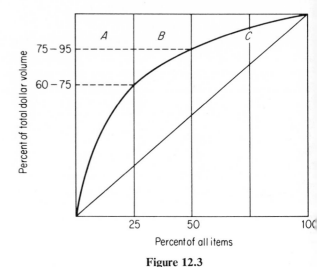

Figure 12.3

The ABC or lognormal type of distribution

Since dollar volume relates directly to inventory costs, *potential savings* available as a result of better inventory policies will be far greater in this class than any other. This is particularly apparent when it is pointed out that the cost of inventory policy studies tends to be proportional to the number of items under consideration. The B class (another 25 per cent of all items) may account for 15 or 20 per cent of dollar volume. The C class often deals with no more than 5 to 10 per cent of the company's total dollar volume although 50 per cent of all items inventoried belong in that group. There is no commitment to breaks occurring at 25 and 50 per cent nor a need to abide by three classes. It is essential, however, that the operations manager recognize the unequal contributions of different items in his inventory and the fact that equivalent effort should not be spent on improving the inventory policies of all items.

Another important classification is based on the difference between *static* and *dynamic* situations. In the *static* case, only one inventory decision can be made. The spare parts model is a static case. A well-known problem that is often cited to explain the static situation is the "Christmas tree problem." The man selling Christmas trees can only place a single order for trees. Then, on Christmas day, he finds out whether he estimated exactly right or guessed over or under. In the case of overestimated demand, salvage value is sometimes available. For example, a department store that overbuys on toys, shipped from abroad in time for the holiday season, can often sell those toys at a discount after the selling season is finished. *Dynamic* situations do not require these same considerations because the demand for such items is continuous. The problem becomes one of adjusting inventory levels so as to balance the various costs that apply.[11]

Inventory Costs

The inventory control area is even more susceptible to formalism and rationality than production control. This is not to say that uncertainties arising from human nature and natural phenomena do not enter into the inventory problem. But the uncertainties are within the bounds that can normally be included in an analytic system. Also, the payoffs that can be derived from the rational approach are usually of significant magnitude. As a matter of fact, a company that has been employing traditional, intuitive methods exclusively would be best advised to begin to introduce analytic procedures, *starting* with the inventory area. This statement is particularly applicable to companies requiring large inventories for both production requirements and maintenance items.

The heart of inventory analysis resides in the identification of relevant costs. There are many kinds of costs that apply to the inventory situation. We shall now itemize some of those that are most frequently encountered.

1. *Cost of Ordering.* Each time a purchase requisition is drawn up, both fixed and variable costs are incurred. The fixed costs of ordering are associated with the salaries of the permanent staff of the order department. We also include investments in equipment and properly assigned overhead charges. Fixed costs are not affected by the inventory policies that are followed. The variable cost component consists of the purchase requisition

[11] We shall deal with other significant differences as we proceed. For example, certain demand (say, by contract) v. probabilistic demand. Inventory decisions also differ according to "make v. buy."

form, the cost of sending this purchase requisition to the vendor, in fact, any costs that increase as the number of purchase requisitions increase. Not to be overlooked are opportunity costs associated with alternative uses of both time and equipment. Thus, the ordering cost for a self-employed shopkeeper must take into account the fact that he could be redecorating his windows, talking longer with a customer, or using his time in some other fruitful manner. Then, by definition, as the number of orders increases, the fixed costs remain constant; the variable costs increase. For example, a company may be able to process 100 orders per week. If a new inventory policy requires that 150 purchase requisitions—on the average—be processed in a week, then the ordering department must be enlarged. The increase in labor costs and equipment and overhead is considered to be additional variable cost. In this way the ordering cost is determined on top of a base ordering system.

2. *The Cost of Carrying Inventory.*   It is well-known that manufacturers prefer to maintain minimum inventories. We frequently hear that in times of uncertainty companies begin to cut back on their inventory. Why is this so? The answer is that a company maintains an investment in the form of inventory. Their capital is tied up in materials and goods. If the capital were free, alternative uses might be found for it. For example, the company could put it in the savings bank, thereby earning interest on the money. On the other hand, somewhat more speculative investments could be made in stocks. The company could purchase additional equipment and expand capacity or even use this money to diversify. Thus, we see that an opportunity cost exists. By holding inventory the company foregoes investing their capital in alternative ways.

Inventory carrying costs must also include the expense of storing inventory. As was the case for the ordering department, costs should be measured from a fixed base. We must only consider the variable cost component associated with storage—the costs over which the production manager can exercise control in terms of the inventory policies. Thus, if a company has shelf space for one thousand units but can get a discount if they stock a maximum of two thousand units, then to get this discount they must expand their storage capacity or rent additional space. An appropriate inventory cost analysis must be made to determine whether or not the discount should be taken. The extra costs incurred are a variable cost component associated with holding inventory. It should be noted that interest charges are a variable cost that depend upon the number of units stocked, the price per unit, and the interest rate that is determined to be applicable.

Items that are carried in stock are subject to pilferage losses, obsolescence, and deterioration. These costs represent real losses in the value of inventory. Pilferage is particularly characteristic of certain items. Small items, for example, are more likely to disappear than large ones. Tool cribs are provided with attendants and frequently kept locked when the plant is shut down for the night and over the weekend. Tools have general appeal and almost universal utility. They are small enough to filch, ergo, the tool crib concept. Obsolescence can occur quite suddenly because of technological change. Or loss can be the kind that is associated with fashion goods, toys, and Christmas trees going out of style or being out of season. The problem of determining how much inventory to carry will be affected by the way in which units lose value over time. An additional component of the holding cost includes both taxes and insurance. If insurance rates and taxes are determined on a per unit basis, then the amount of inventory that is stocked will determine directly the insurance and tax components of the carrying costs.

As a guide, we can furnish the following table. Hypothetical figures have been entered similar to the carrying cost computations of many companies in the U.S.A. But each situation is different, and the manager must deal with those costs that apply to his situation.

A Sample Determination of Carrying Cost

Loss due to inability to invest funds in profit-making ventures, including loss of interest	14.00
Obsolescence	3.00
Deterioration	3.00
Transportation, handling, and distribution	2.00
Taxes	0.50
Storage cost	0.50
Insurance	0.50
General supplies	0.25
Pilferage	0.25
C_c = carrying cost *expressed as per cent per year* =	24.00

3. *Cost of Out of Stock.* If a company cannot fill an order, there is usually some penalty to be paid. Sometimes, the customer goes elsewhere, and the penalty is the value of the order that is lost. If this customer is annoyed because he had to do without or find a new supplier and he continues to hold a grudge against the company, then the loss of a sale plus the loss of goodwill must be translated into a cost. If the buyer is willing to wait to have his order filled, then the company treats this situation as a back order. Back orders cost money. They can annoy the customer even though he appears to be willing to wait. Many times, a company will attempt to fill the customer's order with a more expensive substitute. The cost factor is not difficult to determine in this case. Whatever the system: Fill or kill,[12] back ordering, material substitutions, and so on, some costs of being out of stock will occur. The lost goodwill cost is considered to be one of the most significant and one of the most difficult to evaluate.

---

[12] No back orders allowed; note the assumption on p. 246 in connection with the transportation algorithm for aggregate scheduling.

4. *Other Costs.*   The above named costs are the ones that usually are considered most relevant in the determination of inventory policy. Many other costs also play a part in specific cases. Thus, for example, there are systemic costs associated with running the inventory system, costs of delays in processing orders, costs of discounts not realized, set-up costs, costs of production interruptions, salvage costs, and expediting costs. In some instances, one or more of these costs will dominate the inventory policy evaluation.

The Economic Order Quantity Model

Now let us see how these costs operate in an inventory system and the way in which they can be balanced so that an optimal inventory procedure is followed. We will treat a *dynamic* system under certainty where no stock outages are allowed to occur. By dynamic we mean that inventory does not lose value after a given date, such as Christmas, and that a continuing, certain level of demand will exist over the long run. Figure 12.4 pictures the relation-

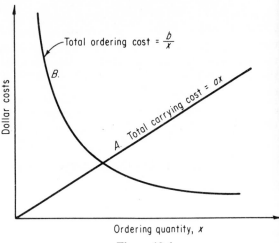

Figure 12.4

Total ordering costs and total carrying costs as a function of the order quantity, x.

ship of the order quantity x with *total ordering costs* and *total carrying costs*. Let x = the number of units purchased per order. We see that as the number of units that are purchased at one time increases, the carrying costs rise. This is line A. On the other hand, as the number of units per order increases, the number of orders that must be placed in a year will decrease. This declining ordering cost is line B. Thus, if the demand for a particular item amounts to 500 units per year, we could order all 500 units at one time. Only one order would have to be placed per year. The 500 units would gradually decrease from the beginning to the end of the year so that an average of approximately 250 units would be carried in stock for that year. Figure 12.5 portrays the withdrawal pattern. The carrying cost rate must be applied to the average dollar value of the 250 units. Only one order is to be made, so the ordering cost would be incurred only once.

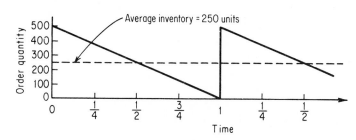

Figure 12.5

Continuous withdrawal pattern when $x = 500$ and only one order is placed per year.

Now let us consider the policy of ordering twice a year. There would be 250 units ordered with each of two purchase requisitions. These 250 units get used up gradually[13] until nothing is left. At that point the next order of 250 units arrives. The stock level shoots back up to a full bin of 250 units. Then the decline begins again until, at the end of the year, nothing is left and another new shipment will be immediately received. We now have *half* of the 250 units as the measure of the average number of units of inventory, viz., 125 units. The ordering cost is incurred twice, but the carrying cost is applied to

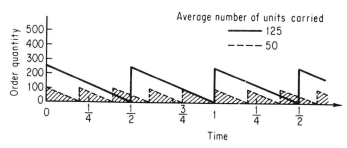

Figure 12.6

Continuous withdrawal pattern when $x = 250$ and two orders are placed each year; also when $x = 100$ and five orders are placed each year.

the smaller average inventory of only 125 units. Figure 12.6 illustrates this, and also shows what would happen with five orders per year. Each purchase

---

[13] Regularly, at the same rate; but, if this assumption is not exactly met, it is seldom a serious problem—as long as the total demand in the interval is fixed in size.

requisition consists of a request for 100 units. The average number of units on hand would now be 50, and the variable cost per order is incurred five times.

In each case, the total variable cost is the sum of the total variable ordering cost component and the total variable carrying cost component. Thus:

$$\text{Total Cost} = \text{Total Carrying Cost} + \text{Total Ordering Cost}$$

The basis of inventory theory is to write an appropriate cost equation including all relevant costs, such as obsolescence, pilferage, and so on. Then we minimize this total cost equation. It is clear that different costs result from different ordering policies. The smallest possible carrying charges would occur when we placed 500 orders for one unit apiece. On the other hand, a very small ordering cost could be achieved by ordering infrequently, say once every five years. Figure 12.7 shows the total-cost equation, the sum of the ordering cost B and carrying cost A.

The average number of units carried in stock is $x/2$, where x is the number of units purchased per order.

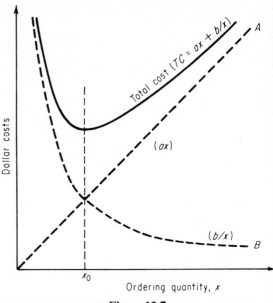

Figure 12.7

The total cost resulting from different ordering policies is the sum of the carrying costs, line *A*, and the ordering costs, line *B*.

The average dollar inventory carried is $cx/2$, where c is the per unit cost of the item.

The total carrying cost per year would be $(cx/2)C_c$, where C_c is the carrying cost rate per year (as previously described). This is the first term of the total-cost equation.

The number of orders placed per year is z/x, where z is the total demand per year, and x is as has been defined previously.

The total ordering cost per year will then be $(z/x)C_r$, where C_r is the variable cost per order. This is the second term of the total-cost equation.

The total cost (TC) is as follows:

$$TC = \left(\frac{cx}{2}\right) C_c + \left(\frac{z}{x}\right) C_r$$

We can minimize TC in a number of ways:

We can take the derivative of total cost with respect to x and set that quantity equal to zero (that is, $dTC/dx = 0$) in order to determine the point at which zero slope and minimum TC occurs. We call this optimal order quantity, x_o. The use of the derivative to determine either maximums or minimums is a general approach. It can be used for complex total cost equations that have many terms.

Here,

$$\frac{dTC}{dx} = \frac{cC_c}{2} - \frac{zC_r}{x^2} = 0$$

whence:

$$x_o = \sqrt{\frac{2zC_r}{cC_c}}$$

We can use a graphical method. This requires plotting each cost component and then adding them together, as in Figure 12.7.

We could use trial and error methods, by substituting different values of x into the total cost equation until the minimum total cost was obtained.

Still another approach can be employed. The minimum total cost will occur, for this equation, when the total carrying cost is equal to the total ordering cost. To illustrate this point, let us assume the following values: $C_c = 0.10$ per year, $c = \$200$ per unit, $z = 10$ units per year, $C_r = \$4$ per order, so $TC = 10x + 40/x$.

We list the values of TC as a function of x in the table below:

x	TC	$10x$	$40/x$
1	50	10	40
2	40	20	20
3	$43\frac{1}{3}$	30	$13\frac{1}{3}$
4	50	40	10

Minimum total cost occurs when $x = 2$. Also, for this value of x, the total carrying cost is equal to the total ordering cost, viz., twenty. The significant fact, however, is that the *rate of change* of these costs is equal at this point. With an additional increment of x, the carrying cost increases at a faster rate than the ordering cost decreases. When we subtract an increment of x, the ordering cost increases at a faster rate than the carrying cost decreases. Thus, at $x = 2$, the respective rates of change of the two kinds of cost are exactly balanced. This is what is meant by the statement that the marginal costs of the system are balanced. It is the underlying condition for our cost minimization.

Setting the total carrying cost equal to the total ordering cost, we obtain:

$$\left(\frac{cx}{2}\right)C_c = \left(\frac{z}{x}\right)C_r \quad \text{and} \quad x_0 = \sqrt{\frac{2zC_r}{cC_c}}$$

Using the same numbers that were previously employed for the example above, we get the same result.

$$x_o = \sqrt{\frac{2(10)4}{200(0.10)}} = 2$$

This inventory model provides the *economic order quantity, EOQ*. It has great utility. Even when probabilistic demand does exist in the system, the EOQ model can be employed, and then, as we shall show shortly, a *reserve stock level* would be added. Other modifications of this model permit stock outages to occur at some set level. Discounts can be examined to see whether it would benefit the company to take advantage of them. When the inventory is self-supplied by the production system, rather than purchased from an external vendor, the model can be converted to indicate the optimal run size. This variant is called the economic lot size model. For all these cases, and many others as well, the appropriate value of x_o that will produce a minimum cost can be readily determined.

Shortages Allowed

It is useful to extend the EOQ model by considering the cost of back-orders, C_b. Figure 12.7a helps us to define the symbols and terms that will be used.

The total cost equation now has three terms:

$TC = cC_c$ (Average inventory) $+ C_b$ (Average backorders) $+ C_r$ (Number of orders)

Average inventory is simple to derive: $\frac{S}{2}\left(\frac{t_1}{t}\right) + 0\left(\frac{t_2}{t}\right)$, and average back-order quantity is obtained in the same way. Whence,

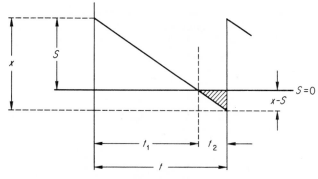

Figure 12.7a

The stock level is S, stock outages are measured by $x - S$, where x is the order quantity.

$$TC = cC_c\left(\frac{St_1}{2t}\right) + C_b\left(\frac{x - S}{2} \cdot \frac{t_2}{t}\right) + \frac{z}{x}Cr.$$

Using the geometric relations: $S/t_1 = x/t$ and $(x - S)/t_2 = x/t$ we remove t_1, t_2 and t from the total cost equation. Thus,

$$TC = \frac{cC_cS^2}{2x} + \frac{C_b(x - S)^2}{2x} + \frac{z}{x}Cr.$$

We obtain the partial derivatives $\partial TC/\partial S$ and $\partial TC/\partial x$, setting them both equal to zero.

$$\frac{\partial TC}{\partial S} = \frac{ScC_c}{x} - C_b + \frac{SC_b}{x} = 0$$

We solve for S_o, the optimal value of S: $S_o = \dfrac{xC_b}{cC_c + C_b}$ Further,

$$\frac{\partial TC}{\partial x} = -\frac{cC_c}{2}\left(\frac{S}{x}\right)^2 + \frac{C_b}{2} - \frac{C_b}{2}\left(\frac{S}{x}\right)^2 - \frac{z}{x^2}Cr = 0$$

We substitute S_o in this equation to obtain x_o, the optimal value for x when shortages are allowed. Thus,

$$x_o = \sqrt{\frac{2zCr}{cC_c}}\sqrt{\frac{cC_c + C_b}{C_b}}$$

It should be noted that when $C_b = \infty$, then the *EOQ* model, previously derived, will hold. Accordingly, for the *EOQ* model, infinite penalties are assumed for shortages.

The Economic Lot Size Model

Having investigated the relationship that describes the optimal order quantity when purchase orders are placed with an outside vendor, let us now consider the comparable problem—identical in all respects except that the company is its own supplier. We call this formulation the economic lot size model, ELS, because the production run quantity is called a "lot." Figure 12.8 shows the variations in stock level over time for the self-supplier situa-

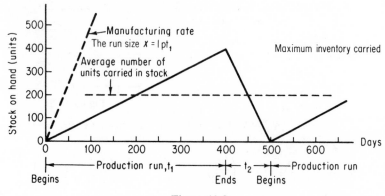

Figure 12.8

The economic lot size model, *ELS*, is used to determine the optimal production run.

tion. The sharp, *saw-tooth* form that applied to the EOQ case, where a total shipment of stock was received at one point in time, has been replaced by a gradual stock build-up. The rate of decline would be equivalent in both situations. In this case, x_o is the optimal *run size*. The cost of an order is no longer relevant. In its place we substitute C_s, which is the set-up cost and is usually larger than the order cost.[14] The set-up cost is composed of at least two parts. (1) the cost of labor required to prepare the facility for the new production run; and (2) the cost of lost production occasioned by the facility being down while being prepared for the new job. In addition, we need two other variables:

$p =$ production rate in units per day, and

$d =$ demand rate in units per day

Our total cost equation would be:

$$TC = \left(\frac{cx}{2}\right)\left(\frac{p-d}{p}\right)C_c + \left(\frac{z}{x}\right)C_s$$

where:

$\left(\frac{p-d}{p}\right)\frac{x}{2}$ is the average number of units carried in the inventory.

[14] All other things being equal, then, we would expect that the optimal run size would be larger than the optimal order size. This effect is further emphasized by the fact that the per unit cost of purchase is usually higher than that of self-supply.

Again, we can use the derivative approach:

Here,
$$\frac{dTC}{dx} = \frac{cC_c}{2}\left(\frac{p - d}{p}\right) - \frac{zC_s}{x^2} = 0$$

And, therefore:
$$x_o = \sqrt{\frac{2zC_s}{cC_c}\left(\frac{p}{p - d}\right)}$$

The graphical approach could be used or the equivalence of marginal opposing costs. We observe that if d is almost equal to p, then x_o becomes large, approaching infinity. This result makes sense. In effect it states: If the demand rate is as great as the production rate, then run the process continuously. On the other hand, if p is much greater than d, that is, $p > > > d$, then x_o equals EOQ. This result is also reasonable. The condition that is given approximates the state of being able to receive total replenishment upon request.

As an example of the ELS model, let us use the following numbers:

$z = 1000$ parts per year $= 4$ parts per day.
$C_s = \$200$ per setup.
$c = \$5$ per part.
$C_c = 0.10$ per dollar per year.
$p = 5$ parts per day $= 1250$ parts per year.
$d = 4$ parts per day $= 1000$ parts per year.

The optimal lot size, x_o, would be:

$$x_o = \sqrt{\frac{2(1000)(200)}{5(0.10)(0.20)}} = 2000 \text{ parts}$$

The result is a run of four hundred days, that is,

$$t_1 = \frac{x_o}{p} = \frac{2000}{5} = 400$$

The period between runs would be one hundred days, that is,

$$t_2 = \left(\frac{p - d}{pd}\right)x_o = \frac{1}{20}(2000) = 100$$

There would be one run every two years, that is,

$$t = t_1 + t_2 = \frac{x_o}{z} = \frac{2000}{1000} = 2$$

Lead Time

For both the EOQ and the ELS systems, the lead time required to supply items for inventory must be known. In Figure 12.9, the lead time or replenishment time is called LT.

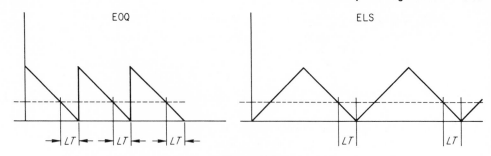

Figure 12.9

Consider the EOQ case. The obvious components of lead time include the period for recognition of the fact that it is time to reorder; the interval for doing whatever clerical work is needed (vendor releasing has advantages here, see p. 330), mail or telephone intervals for communicating with the vendor; then, recognition of the order by the vendor who will see whether the requested items are in stock or, if not, will set up to make them. Then the vendor ships the items, so there is delivery time. The items are delivered but must be processed by the receiving department, which may require inspection. Until the items are entered on the warehouse stock cards, the lead time continues. Similar descriptions could be given for the ELS case where the sometimes illusory advantages of dealing within your own firm, and thereby having greater control, appear.

Job Shop Self-Supply and Flow Shop Multi-Item Systems

It should be noted that when the job shop configuration exists the EOQ model can be applied to self-supply with batch production systems. Figure 12.10 helps to illustrate why this is so.

A multiple-item variant of these models should be mentioned. It is not unusual for a variety of *different* items to *follow one another* through the serial production system. This is an intermittent flow shop, all items operating on the same equipment, in the same sequence, but requiring some new setups as each different item begins production. Our previous discussion concerning the traveling salesman variant of the sequencing model might well be applied here. Given that a best sequence of items is known (or if the order of processing is not relevant to cost), then a simple formulation has been suggested concerning the amount of each item to run.[15] There are n different products that are all made on the same equipment, and each product is made only *once*

---

[15] See J. F. Magee and D. M. Boodman, *Production Planning and Inventory Control*, 2nd ed. (New York: McGraw-Hill Book Co., Inc., 1967), pp. 354–56.

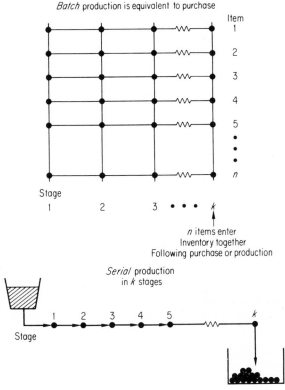

Figure 12.10

in the cycle. Using i to denote specific products, the optimal run sizes would be:

$$x_{0_i} = \sqrt{\frac{2z_i^2 \sum\limits_{i}^{n} C_{s_i}}{\sum\limits_{i}^{n} (cC_c)_i z_i \left(1 - \dfrac{d_i}{p_i}\right)}}$$

Quantity Discount Model

If a quantity discount is offered, should it be taken? When does the discount potential override the selection of x_o without the discount? By using sets of total cost equations, it is possible to analyze whether or not a quantity discount that is offered should cancel out the x_o value associated with undiscounted minimum total cost. Consulting Figure 12.11, we see that two total cost equations are drawn.

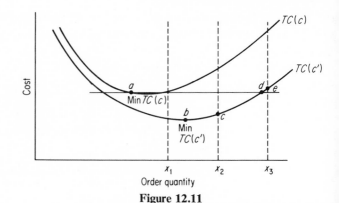

Figure 12.11

The top curve $TC(c)$ is based on an undiscounted cost, c. The bottom curve $TC(c')$ is applicable when a discount is available, *but it is only applicable at and above the quantity needed* to obtain the discount. Let x_j be the specified quantity required to obtain the discount. If x_j is x_1 in Figure 12.11, then the discount must be taken, and, in fact, the order quantity should be increased to intersect point b, which is the minimum total cost that can be obtained. Note, the top curve applies from $x = 0$ to $x < x_1$; the bottom curve applies for $x \geq x_1$. Figure 12.12 illustrates this discontinuity. Point b's cost is lower than that of point b'.

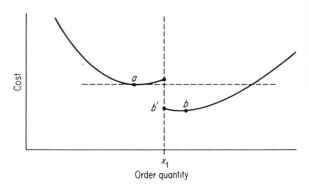

Figure 12.12

When x_j is specified at x_2, in Figure 12.11, then point c provides a lower cost than point a—the minimum total cost without the discount. Also, point c is the lowest total cost that is available in the discount region. So x_2 units should be purchased. If $x_j = x_3$, the intersected cost point is e, which is a greater cost than a; therefore, the order quantity corresponding to point a should be used.[16] The same reasoning can be extended to more than one price break

[16] If the price break were to the left of both minimums, then the discounted minimum cost quantity would be chosen.

for quantity discounts, and a purely mathematical approach can be used as well.[17] If the quantity specified for discount intersected point d (theoretically) the manager would be indifferent between buying the small amount at point a or buying the large amount at point d. In fact, the manager would consider a variety of intangibles such as: Is the item ordinarily hard to get; is there possibility of a strike; could we corner the supply to our competitive advantage? All these notions favor point d. On the other hand, does this item spoil easily; does it require a lot of storage space; does it experience a high pilferage rate? These last thoughts favor point a.

Sensitivity to Estimates

The sensitivity of these models can be explored in various ways. For example, let the "true" state of the numerator of the EOQ model be $2zC_r$, and the "estimate" of that numerator be $2zC_r\alpha$. Similarly, let the "true" denominator be cC_c, and the "estimate" of the denominator be $cC_c\beta$. Then the "true" optimal value of x will be $x_o = \sqrt{\dfrac{2zC_r}{cC_c}}$; the "estimated" optimal value of x will be $x'_o = \sqrt{\dfrac{2zC_r}{cC_c}\left(\dfrac{\alpha}{\beta}\right)}$.

When we introduce the values into their corresponding total cost equations, we obtain:

$$\text{``true'' optimal } TC(x_o) = \frac{cC_c}{2}\sqrt{\frac{2zC_r}{cC_c}} + zC_r\sqrt{\frac{cC_c}{2zC_r}}$$

$$= \sqrt{\frac{zcC_cC_r}{2}} + \sqrt{\frac{zcC_cC_r}{2}} = \sqrt{2zcC_cC_r}$$

$$\text{``estimated'' optimal } TC(x'_o) = \frac{cC_c}{2}\sqrt{\frac{\alpha}{\beta}}\sqrt{\frac{2zC_r}{cC_c}} + zC_r\sqrt{\frac{\beta}{\alpha}}\sqrt{\frac{cC_c}{2zC_r}}$$

$$= \left(\sqrt{\frac{\alpha}{\beta}} + \sqrt{\frac{\beta}{\alpha}}\right)\sqrt{\frac{zcC_cC_r}{2}}$$

The "estimated" optimal TC will be larger than the "true" optimal according to the ratio

$$\frac{TC(x'_o)}{TC(x_o)} = \frac{\left(\sqrt{\frac{\alpha}{\beta}} + \sqrt{\frac{\beta}{\alpha}}\right)\sqrt{\frac{zcC_cC_r}{2}}}{\sqrt{2zcC_cC_r}} = \frac{1}{2}\left(\sqrt{\frac{\alpha}{\beta}} + \sqrt{\frac{\beta}{\alpha}}\right)$$

[17] M. K. Starr and D. W. Miller, *Inventory Control: Theory and Practice* (Englewood Cliffs, N.J.: Prentice-Hall, Inc., 1962), pp. 84–86.

First, we observe that symmetry exists with respect to α- and β-types of errors. The α errors include incorrect estimates for demand and for the ordering cost. The β errors relate to cost and carrying cost rates. If these errors should not be considered in pairs, then a different set of sensitivity coefficients could be designed, following the same basic procedure that we have used, e.g., four coefficients could be studied.

Second, because α and β appear in ratio, it is clear that errors in the numerator and denominator of the same magnitude and direction will cancel each other out. On the other hand, errors of opposite direction are magnified. Thus, it would be advantageous to overestimate demand if carrying costs are more likely to be overestimated than underestimated. When α and β are equal, the total cost ratio equals one, as it should.

Third, let either α or $\beta = 1$. Then, we derive:

$$\frac{TC(x_0')}{TC(x_o)} = \frac{1}{2}\left(\frac{1+\beta}{\sqrt{\beta}}\right).$$

A brief examination of this relationship will reveal that the total cost ratio (with a minimum value of one) increases much faster with underestimates ($\beta < 1$) than with overestimates ($\beta > 1$). Thus, in general, overestimation is preferable to underestimation.

Aggregate Inventories

In the previous section, while examining the properties of the total cost curve, we observed that:

$$TC(x_o) = \frac{cC_c}{2}\sqrt{\frac{2zC_r}{cC_c}} + C_r z\sqrt{\frac{cC_c}{2zC_r}} = \sqrt{2zcC_cC_r}$$

For fixed costs C_c and C_r this is equal to $K\sqrt{zc}$, where K is a constant. In other words, total cost is a function of the square root of the dollar volume, cz. This reminds us of our previous statement concerning the lognormal distribution and the fact that dollar volume plays a major role in item classification. We can extend this formulation to encompass many items. Company inventories are seldom composed of only one A-type item. Usually, a number of different (important) items are carried in stock. Even for a single item, it is not unusual to have associated *stockkeeping units* (called SKU). For example, in the category "screws," a typical manufacturer's inventory will include various lengths, diameters, number of threads to the inch, wood screws, machine screws, Phillips-head screws, brass screws, steel screws, and so on. In the same way, a department store will carry many different sizes, colors, materials, and styles of socks, and the supermarket stocks a great variety of soups and soaps. We could, if we had enough information, obtain the optimal order quantity or lot size for each SKU. This would give us a theoretical value for the minimum *overall* total cost system. But, two factors intervene.

First, it costs money to study inventories and to develop policies for each item or SKU. From the point of view of the break-even chart, the cost of the inventory study increases fixed costs. The savings obtained from the study tend to decrease variable costs. The resultant must represent a sufficient return on investment (ROI) in the inventory study to make this particular investment preferable to alternative investments in bonds and stocks, machinery, or additional personnel. Because savings to be realized are a function of dollar volume, it is clear why the A class items would be singled out for attention.

Second, the company's resources are limited. It is frequently unreasonable to carry the total average dollar inventory that the individual item's optimal policies would require. The capacity of the ordering department may be overtaxed; storage facilities may be filled to capacity; the amount of capital invested in inventory may exceed the amount that the company has available. These limitations, if they exist, require a modification of inventory policy. That is, the theoretical system's optimal is not feasible because it violates other practical system's constraints.

Let us first relax the requirement with respect to unlimited capital resources. We will assume that company policy calls for no more than $2000 to be invested in inventory, on the average. But the sum of the optimal policies for each product requires a total average inventory investment of $2600. What then should be done? The cash limit prevents the use of the individual item optimal inventory policies. The figures for this example are given below, where $C_c = 0.24$ per year and $C_r = \$48.00$ per order.

Item No. j	c_j	z_j (per year)	x_o^j	$c_j x_o^j$	$c_j x_o^j/2 = a_j$
1	$3.50	1400	400	1400	700
2	$2.00	5000	1000	2000	1000
3	$1.00	2500	1000	1000	500
4	$2.00	800	400	800	400
			A = Total average dollar inventory		= $2600

Let A = Total average dollar inventory, and
   a_j = Average dollar inventory of the jth item.

Then, it can readily be shown that for a *rational* ordering policy:

$$\frac{\text{average dollar inventory of an item } j}{\text{total average dollar inventory of all items}} = \frac{\sqrt{c_j z_j}}{\sum\limits_j \sqrt{c_j z_j}} = \frac{a_j}{A}$$

The minimum total cost for each item is: $TC(x_j) = \sqrt{2C_c C_r} \sqrt{c_j z_j}$. The sum of the minimum costs is then:

$$\sum_j TC(x_j) = \sqrt{2C_c C_r} \sum_j \sqrt{c_j z_j}$$

The ratio of these two equations represents the ratio of optimal item policy to optimal total policy no matter what the constrained value of $\sum_j TC(x_j)$ might be set at, so:

$$\frac{TC(x_j)}{\sum_j TC(x_j)} = \frac{\sqrt{c_j z_j}}{\sum \sqrt{c_j z_j}}$$

We can explain the relationship given above for a_j/A in even more detail. The ratio of j's optimal dollar inventory to the optimal total dollar inventory is:[18]

$$\frac{a_j}{A} = \frac{\dfrac{c_j}{2}(x_o)_j}{\sum_j \dfrac{c_j}{2}(x_o)_j} = \frac{\dfrac{c_j}{2}\sqrt{\dfrac{2z_j C_r}{c_j C_c}}}{\sum_j \dfrac{c_j}{2}\sqrt{\dfrac{2z_j C_r}{c_j C_c}}} = \frac{\sqrt{\dfrac{C_r}{2C_c}}\sqrt{c_j z_j}}{\sqrt{\dfrac{C_r}{2C_c}}\sum_j \sqrt{c_j z_j}} = \frac{\sqrt{c_j z_j}}{\sum_j \sqrt{c_j z_j}}$$

Then, let us derive the values for our example, letting $A = \$2000$, as previously specified.

Item No. j	$c_j z_j$	$\sqrt{c_j z_j}$	$A\sqrt{c_j z_j}/\sum_j \sqrt{c_j z_j} = c_j x_j/2$
1	4,900	70	(2000)(70)/260 $ 538
2	10,000	100	(2000)(100)/260 = 769
3	2,500	50	(2000)(50)/260 = 385
4	1,600	40	(2000)(40)/260 = 308
		260	$= \sum_j \sqrt{c_j z_j}$ $A = \$2000$

We can recompute the rational order quantities directly.

Item No. j	$c_j x_j/2$	x_j
1	$538	2(538)/3.50 = 308
2	769	2(769)/2.00 = 769
3	385	2(385)/1.00 = 769
4	308	2(308)/2.00 = 308

This problem is resolved. We should order 308 units of item 1 instead of the optimal order quantity of 400. Similarly, order 769 units of item 2 instead of 1000 units; order 769 units of item 3 instead of 1000 units; and order 308 units of item 4 instead of 400 units.

The same kind of thinking can be applied to the number of orders that are placed assuming that no constraint exists for A. Thus,

$$\frac{n_j}{N} = \frac{\sqrt{c_j z_j}}{\sum_j \sqrt{c_j z_j}}$$

[18] The same result can be shown to hold for n_j/N, see ahead.

where n_j represents the number of orders to be placed for the jth item, and N stands for the total number of orders that can be made by the order department. This formulation is used when there is an upper limit to the capacity of the ordering department.

The reason that the multiple item inventory policies that we have just described are rational—as compared to other policies that would be irrational—is based on two points.

1. It is not irrational to find oneself unable to achieve the system's overall optimal state because resource limitations make it impossible to operate at this overall optimal level.

2. The existence of constraints of one kind or another, if they prohibit the use of the overall optimal policy, imply the fact that the costs, C_c and C_r, that have been used to determine the overall optimal policy, cannot both be correct measures of the situation. Therefore, a rational policy is one where an appropriate change in these costs would provide an optimal policy that would meet the constraints. This is what the above formulation succeeds in doing.

We note that $A \times N = \sum_j \dfrac{c_j}{2} (x_o)_j \left(\sum_j \dfrac{z_j}{(x_o)_j} \right)$

$$= \left(\sqrt{\frac{C_r}{2C_c}} \sum_j \sqrt{c_j z_j} \right) \left(\sqrt{\frac{C_c}{2C_r}} \sum_j \sqrt{c_j z_j} \right) = \frac{1}{2} \left(\sum_j \sqrt{c_j z_j} \right)^2$$

For any specific situation, this is equivalent to $A \times N = K$, where K is a constant. The rectangular hyperbola shown in Figure 12.13 represents the *rational* surface of all solutions that could be optimal under different cost constraints. For our data $A \times N = 1/2(260)^2 = 33,800$.

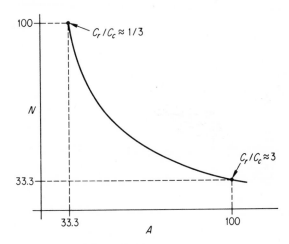

Figure 12.13

Thus, the ratio $A/N = C_r/C_c$ allows that every possible point on the curve in Figure 12.13 can be represented.

Lagrangian Formulation

The discussion we have just completed can be represented in more compact form by Lagrangian multipliers. Thus, for the aggregate total cost equation, we have:

$$\Sigma_j TC(x_j) = \Sigma_j \left(\frac{c_j x_j}{2}\right) C_c + \Sigma_j \left(\frac{z_j}{x_j}\right) C_r$$

If we wish to minimize $\Sigma_j TC(x_j)$ subject to a constraint on the total number of orders (N), we can minimize $\Sigma_j \left(\frac{c_j x_j}{2}\right)$ with respect to the constraint on $\Sigma_j \left(\frac{z_j}{x_j}\right)$. Since C_c and C_r are constants, they perform no useful service in these equations.

The Lagrangian would be: $L = \Sigma_j \left(\frac{c_j x_j}{2}\right) + \lambda \left(\Sigma_j \frac{z_j}{x_j} - N\right)$ where N is a limit on total order size. The conditions for minimum L are obtained by setting the partial derivatives $\partial L/\partial x_j$ and $\partial L/\partial \lambda$ equal to zero. Thus,

$$\frac{\partial L}{\partial x_j} = \frac{c_j}{2} - \lambda \left(\frac{z_j}{x_j}\right) = 0$$

$$\frac{\partial L}{\partial \lambda} = \Sigma_j \frac{z_j}{x_j} - N = 0$$

Solving these simultaneous equations we obtain: $x_{j_o} = \frac{1}{N} \sqrt{\frac{z_j}{c_j}} \Sigma_j \sqrt{c_j z_j}$.

When the constraint applies to average dollar inventory, then the Lagrangian would be: $L = \Sigma_j \left(\frac{z_j}{x_j}\right) + \lambda \left(\Sigma_j \frac{c_j x_j}{2} - A\right)$ where A is a limit on total average dollar inventory. In this case,

$$\frac{\partial L}{\partial x_j} = -\frac{z_j}{x_j} + \lambda \left(\frac{c_j}{2}\right) = 0$$

$$\frac{\partial L}{\partial \lambda} = \Sigma_j \frac{c_j x_j}{2} - A = 0$$

Solving the simultaneous equations yields,

$$x_{j_o} = \frac{2A}{\Sigma_j \sqrt{c_j z_j}} \sqrt{\frac{z_j}{c_j}}$$

Problem 8, at the end of this chapter, requests that the numbers presented in the previous section be used with the Lagrangian solutions for x_j, subject to constraints on N and A.

Perpetual Inventory Systems

The economic lot size model and the economic order quantity model are based on the assumption that there will be no variability in demand. In most practical instances this assumption cannot be sustained. As a result, a class of inventory models has been designed to cope with situations where the demand level fluctuates.

Many companies use perpetual inventory systems wherein withdrawal quantities are entered on the item's stock card each and every time that a unit is withdrawn from stock. The withdrawal quantity is subtracted from the previous stock level to determine the present quantity of stock on hand. A minimum level is designated as the *reorder level* for each item. This *reorder point* quantity is marked on the respective stock card. When the minimum level has been reached, then an order is placed for the economic order quantity, x_o. The level of stock represented by the reorder point is equal to the expected demand in the lead time plus what is called the reserve stock or buffer stock. This buffer has been designed to absorb a certain percentage of the fluctuations in demand that are likely to occur for each particular item. The reserve stock is geared to provide some chosen level of protection against stock outages. The level that is chosen is based on the balance of out-of-stock costs and carrying costs associated with the reserve stock. Figure 12.14 illustrates the way in which a perpetual inventory system operates.

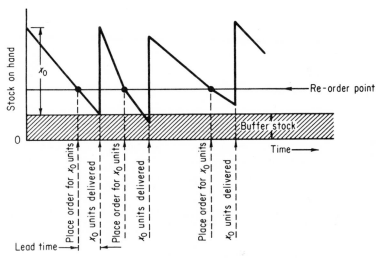

Figure 12.14

A perpetual inventory system.

The calculation of the reorder point is not difficult to accomplish. First, as has been noted, stock must be provided to cover the expected demand *in the lead time period*, $\bar{z}_{LT}$. Then, buffer is to be provided, which gives some specified level of protection ($k\sigma$'s) against going out of stock in the same lead time interval. Figure 12.15 depicts the situation.

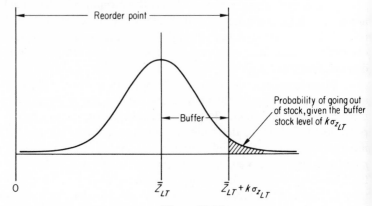

Figure 12.15

The reserve stock and order size values can be determined by minimizing a total cost equation, such as the following:

$$TC(x_o) = \frac{z}{x} C_r + \frac{cx}{2} C_c + (k\sigma_{z_{LT}})cC_c + \frac{z}{x} C_o \int_{\mu}^{\infty} f(y)\, dy.$$

Here, C_o is a fixed shortage cost, $f(y)$ is the demand distribution in the lead time interval and $\mu = \bar{z}_{LT} + k\sigma_{z_{LT}}$. We must minimize the equation, $TC(x_o)$, with respect to x and with respect to $(k\sigma_{z_{LT}})$, so we set the appropriate partial derivatives equal to zero, as follows:

$$\frac{\partial TC(x)}{\partial x} = -\frac{zC_r}{x^2} + \frac{cC_c}{2} - \frac{zC_o[1 - F(\mu)]}{x^2} = 0$$

$$\frac{\partial TC(x)}{\partial (k\sigma_{z_{LT}})} = cC_c - \frac{zC_o}{x} f(\mu) = 0$$

These two equations cannot be solved explicitly. First, solve each equation for x and equate the results, thus:

$$[f(\mu)]^2 = \frac{2cC_c}{zC_o^2} \{C_r + C_o[1 - F(\mu)]\}$$

The answer will be found by iteration for the particular functions that prevail.[19] The value of x can be obtained by substitution and the value of k from the ordinate measure, $f(\mu)$.

[19] See Martin K. Starr and David W. Miller, *Inventory Control: Theory and Practice* (Englewood Cliffs, N.J.: Prentice-Hall, Inc., 1962), pp. 122–24.

The so-called two-bin system provides a clever way of continuously monitoring the reorder point in a perpetual inventory system. Figure 12.16 is almost self-explanatory in this regard.

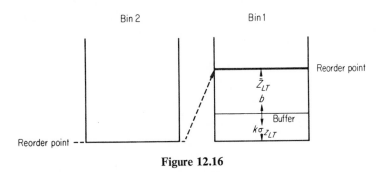

Bin 2   Bin 1

$\bar{z}_{LT}$

b

Buffer

$k\sigma_{z_{LT}}$

Reorder point

Reorder point --

Figure 12.16

A two-bin perpetual inventory system.

When a replenishment order is received, Bin 1 is filled to the reorder point level. The remainder of the order is placed in Bin 2. Obviously, if Bin 1 is at the reorder point level, all the incoming items are placed in Bin 2. When Bin 2 is emptied, a new order is placed. The two-bin system is not feasible for all items, but when it is, a great deal of clerical work is bypassed.

When a computer is used for determining the stock on hand in a perpetual inventory system, it is desirable to utilize a *real time* computer system. This means that as withdrawals are made from stock, then immediately (or relatively so) this information is fed to the computer, which subtracts the amount of the withdrawal and records the quantity that remains on hand. Only in this way can the stock card be kept up to date. When the stock on hand falls below, or is equal to, the reorder level, an order is placed for x_o units. If delay occurs in recognizing the need to place an order, then the item is far more likely to go out of stock. The *age of information* in a perpetual inventory system is crucial.

Periodic Inventory Systems

Periodic systems are based on the determination of a *fixed* and regular review period. Some items may be reviewed once a week, others once a month, semiannually, or yearly. The optimal period is determined by $x_o/z = t_o$. Usually, certain items have shorter review periods than others. These would be items where, although the demand level is relatively high, the average stock

level is kept low, because, for example, the cost per unit is high. At each review, the stock on hand is determined. An order is then placed for a *variable*
quantity. This quantity is larger than usual when demand has been greater
than expectation. It is smaller than usual when demand has been less than
expectation. Thus, in the case of the periodic inventory model, the review
period is fixed, but the order quantity is variable. Figure 12.17 illustrates the
way in which a periodic ordering system functions.

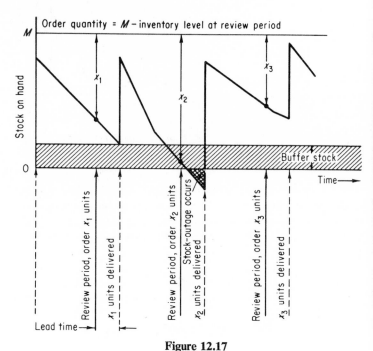

Figure 12.17

A periodic inventory system.

The target level M is determined by first calculating the expected de-
mand in the lead time plus one review period, t_o, i.e., $\bar{z}_{(LT+t_o)}$. To this is added
the buffer or reserve stock that must offer protection against excessive de-
mand in a lead time plus a review period, i.e., $k\sigma_{z_{(LT+t_o)}}$. Thus, $M = \bar{z}_{(LT+t_o)} +$
$k\sigma_{z_{(LT+t_o)}}$. The buffer stock for the periodic model is larger than it is for the
perpetual inventory model. On the other hand, its clerical costs are lower.
The clerical cost advantage disappears, however, when on-line, real-time
computer systems operate the perpetual model's calculation requirements.
As a result, there is a distinct trend toward perpetual systems and away from
periodic ones.

PROBLEMS

1. For the spare part failure model (p. 335), assume that a salvage cost of $2 now exists. Would this alter the solution to the problem? Use opportunity costs as well as total costs to analyze this situation.

2. If, in a dynamic inventory problem under certainty the costs are:

$$c = \$10 \text{ per item.}$$
$$C_c = 16 \text{ per cent per year.}$$
$$z = 5000 \text{ units per year.}$$
$$C_r = \$10 \text{ per order.}$$

What is the optimal order quantity? Now, assume that you are going to make this same item with equipment that is estimated to produce $p = 30$ units per day. Also, c then equals $6 per item and $C_s = \$150$ per setup. How has your answer changed? What would you do?

3. For a serial ELS model (see pp. 348–349) the following data hold:

i	z_i	C_{s_i}	c_i	p_i
1	200	100	6	10
2	400	50	10	12
3	600	20	15	14
4	800	80	9	20

Also $C_c = .24$ per year. The sequence (predetermined) that should be followed is 1, 2, 3, 4. What run lengths would be recommended?

4. A quantity discount schedule has been offered for the situation discussed in Problem 2. It is:

c	x_i
10	up to 300
9	300 — 4 9 9
8	500 and up

Should either of these discounts be taken?

5. A multiple item inventory problem is based on the following A-type units.

i	z_i	c_i
1	20	6
2	40	10
3	60	15
4	80	9

The costs of carrying and ordering are unknown. How should we proceed?

6. For the example in the text, p. 353, locate the appropriate point on the curve $A \times N = K$ for $C_r = 48$ and $C_c = 0.24$.

7. The lead time is one week. Demand per week is normally distributed with mean of one hundred and standard deviation of twenty-five. Fifty weeks are used in the computation of a working year. Other costs are $c = \$10$ per item, $C_c = 16$ per cent per year and $C_r = \$10$ per order.
   (a) Set up a reasonable perpetual inventory system.
   (b) Devise the appropriate periodic inventory system.
   (c) Compare the two approaches and discuss your choice.

8. Apply the Lagrangian approach to the aggregate inventory problem described on pp. 352–356 of the text. Obtain solutions for x_i with the constraint, $A = \$2000$. Then derive the x_i values for the constraint, $N = 10$. (Note: the "optimal" value, $A = \$2600$, is explained in the text, but the "optimal" value for N is not treated. It can be derived as follows: $A \times N = \frac{1}{2}(260)^2 = 33{,}800$. When $A = 2600$, $N = 13$.)

Product and service quality has become a matter of great social concern in the last half of the twentieth century. This was predictable once technological benefits provided by new industry were taken for granted. Law courts establish increasingly stiffer penalties for damages inflicted by defective products. Insurance companies require complete documentation indicating that all safety factors were considered by the manufacturers before allowing insurance protection against damage suits. Consumer groups have actively fought for higher quality standards and greater quality consistency. Government agencies get involved at all levels. Standards are changing, and the effects will be significant.

Quality
Management 13

The inspection of both incoming and outgoing materials is essential for quality management. Raw materials and subcontracted parts must be of expected quality if the finished goods are to meet standards. A stable process must exist so that inputs of accepted qualities can be transformed to satisfactory outputs. Telephone services, transport, and other services can be subjected to similar concepts concerning their quality.

The Nature of Quality

Quality and cost are critical dimensions of operations management. The interaction between quality and cost is extremely complex. In general:

Product and service quality[1] = f (fixed and variable production system costs).

Selling price = f (production system costs, sales promotion costs).

Sales volume = f (selling price, product and service quality).

Dollar volume = (selling price)(sales volume).

Profit = dollar volume − total costs.

It is usually a safe bet that both dollar volume and total costs will increase with improved quality. Therefore, there is a level of quality as defined *explicitly* that will maximize profits. Such a relationship is suggested in Figure 13.1. The curve of dollar volume is a decelerating, monotonically increasing function because of market saturation. No matter how high the quality, there is an upper limit to the level of quality that can be achieved within a given technological framework.

We often talk about quality in terms that coincide with the consumer's evaluation of quality. To the consumer, quality and "high quality" are the

[1] A satisfactory definition of quality may not be possible without considering quality to be measured relative to competitive qualities.

364

same thing. The manager has a quandary here. As an individual he seeks "high quality," but he must deliver an output of *specified quality* that is commensurate with the investment in the process and his budget for operating costs. In this latter sense, *quality is an agreed-upon set of standards and tolerance limits.* These specifications are operational terms—not value judgments. But in order to consider quality in operational terms, it is an absolute necessity that the dimensions of quality be expressed in measurable terms.

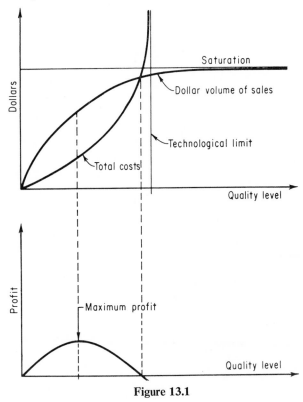

Figure 13.1

There is a level of quality that will maximize profits.

The manager would like to minimize costs and maximize "high quality." These objectives cannot be achieved simultaneously. They are conflicting, multiple objectives; therefore, it is necessary to specify quality constraints. Then, subject to these constraints, cost is to be minimized. A linear programming format—known as the diet problem—models this situation quite well. The activity level, x_j, $(j = 1, 2, \ldots)$ is the amount (or number of units) of ingredient j that is to be used in a mixture having specified minimum qualities, q_i, $(i = 1, 2, \ldots)$. Each unit of x_j contributes an amount a_{ij} of quality i to the final mixture. Thus, the quality constraints are $\sum_j a_{ij}x_j \geq q_i$ for all i. Further, there is a cost c_j for each unit of ingredient j consumed. The objective is to minimize total cost, that is, Min $\sum_j c_j x_j$. Of course, for feasibility all $x_j \geq 0$.

The matrix below illustrates a diet problem:

Qualities	Ingredients			Minimum Qualities
	x_1 lbs.	x_2 gals.	x_3 feet	
Vitamin A	a_{11}	a_{12}	a_{13}	q_1
Phosphorus	a_{21}	a_{22}	a_{23}	q_2
Protein	a_{31}	a_{32}	a_{33}	q_3
Cost per unit of ingredient	c_1	c_2	c_3	

The matrix entry, a_{11}, for example, represents the number of units of vitamin A in a pound of the first ingredient.

Let us examine now the major attributes of quality for *both* inputs to and outputs from the system.

I. Functional Qualities
  1. Purpose utilities
  2. Functional reliability
    a. Deterioration of use function, failure characteristics, and expected lifetime
    b. Cost of maintenance and repair
    c. Supportive guarantees and warranties
  3. Human factors
    a. Safety
    b. Comfort
    c. Convenience

II. Nonfunctional Qualities
  1. Style and appearance
  2. Self-image of user
    a. Price
    b. Prestige
  3. Timeliness of design
  4. Variety

Functional Qualities

In most instances, purpose utility is the most fundamental quality of the output. It is associated with a specific, functional class of uses. Sometimes, purpose is relatively clear, but at other times it is intrinsically difficult to state. In either case, the measurement that counts is how well a product or service performs its intended function. There are physical evaluations and consumer evaluations. Can we measure how good a food product tastes, how comfortable a chair is, or how convenient a hammer is to use? We can measure the sweetness of the food, the number of springs used in the chair, and the hardness of the steel head. There is an assumption about the way in which the measurable, physical factors relate to the consumer's evaluation of the utility of function.

Reliability concerns the variance of performance (according to specifications) over a given period of time. This attribute category raises some interesting problems. Management is responsible for controlling the quality of the product during its manufacture; thereafter, each unit has a history of its own. Observations, measurements, and specifications of quality must include the variety of possible histories for each unit that is sold. When we discuss product reliability, we are referring to the fact that the functional attributes will continue to perform within some set of limits over a given period of time. The width of the limits represents an important aspect of the definition of quality for the design. We expect that parts of the product will become worn with use, whereas other characteristics will age independently of use. Chance events can occur that will affect performance characteristics. Generally, the expected performance will exhibit increasing deviation from the intial design standard over a period of time, as shown in Figure 13.2. We call this phenom-

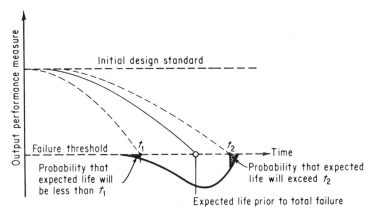

Figure 13.2

Expected performance exhibits increasing deviation from the initial design standard as a function of time.

enon *drift*. It is characteristic of many functional attributes of mechanical, chemical, and electric products, e.g., a light bulb. When first used, it will generate some given number of lumens. Then, as it ages and as a function of both hours of use and the number of times that it is turned on and off, the output of the bulb will vary. It will produce less and less light. At some point, the bulb will fail entirely.

Total failure is easy to define. However, if we can no longer use our light source once its output falls below a certain threshold, then for functional

purposes the light bulb has failed and must be replaced. An ordinary definition of failure for the light bulb specifies a zero output threshold. A more
sophisticated definition requires the specification of a given level of light below
which the unit cannot be said to be performing satisfactorily. A unit can have
erratic performance within the acceptable limits; for example, the light bulb
might get alternately brighter and dimmer. Thus, another measure of reliability is the specification of allowable variability of performance. Both reliability and failure can be described successfully only by using statistical
terms because, we can make a prediction, at best, of how long the unit can
be expected to continue to function satisfactorily.

There are many reasons why failure and reliability, as definitions of
quality, play an important role. Some types of failure do not permit repair,
whereas others do. Some types of failure carry large penalties; others do not.
The definition and specification of quality is concerned with ease of maintenance and the cost of replacement parts. A multi-component unit usually has
different replacement characteristics for each of its parts. Generally, there
are some parts that, when they fail, represent an irremedial breakdown.
Should the manager accept a unit designed in this way, or should he encourage
the development of replacement parts and the service function that is offered
with it? He is concerned with how good the sales engineering service function
is and how accessible it is to customers. Automobile manufacturers stress
this aspect of their product's quality. The manager is also concerned with the
specification of a guarantee period. How long should this period be; what
terms are reasonable; how many different components should be covered?
It is only scratching the surface to measure the length of a rod, to observe
the number of rpm's of a motor, and so forth without tying such measurements into the complete evaluation of product quality and performance.

Human Factors

Man lives in an environment conditioned by his own inputs and outputs. Over time he has become increasingly responsible for the quality of his
environment. The study of how human form and behavior is affected by the
qualities of the environment and its management is called by a number
of different names, e.g., "human factors," "human engineering," "bio-
mechanics," or a British term, "ergonomics."

The human factors area treats both the physiological and psychological
characteristics of people. It attempts to provide high levels of safety and then
comfort. It is concerned first with the way things fit, but also with "the appearances of things," and, consequently, sensory appeals. See for example,
Figure 13.3, which illustrates the design of a foot pedal.

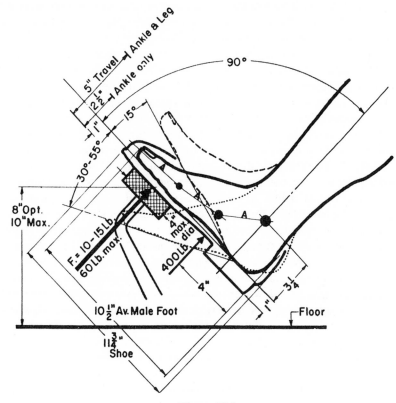

Figure 13.3

Detailed studies and drawings were made of the foot pedal to determine its final placement. The Henry Dreyfuss design group believes that the foot pedal should serve as an extension of the foot. Foot pressure studies were extremely important for the early development of Monotrol Control. [From William F. H. Purcell, A.S.I.D., *Designing for Heavy Duty* (Philadelphia: Automotive Industries Chilton Company, 1962).]

Nonfunctional Qualities

Intangible characteristics, known to play an important part in the individual's judgment of quality, are difficult to measure. Here, we are dealing with intangible qualities of inputs and outputs. This involves us with the sociological, psychological, and physiological implications of quality. There has always been a belief in the marketing field that the consumer is motivated, to some extent, by symbolic relationships of the product to his own personal life. One can find references to Freud, Adler, Jung, and other schools of symbolic analysis in the literature of the motivational market researcher. In theory, at any rate, the industrial designer is able to communicate with the individual on the different levels of his needs whether he is a worker using a machine or a consumer using a product.

These factors taken together establish a frame of reference that is sufficiently psychoanalytic to make the average production man wonder how he can possibly specify quality. Typical of these difficulties are questions concerning the qualities inherent in the visual appearance and styling of a design. Style changes are a function of time. What is in style today can be out of style tomorrow. The way in which one style replaces a previous style should follow some logical pattern—although not necessarily a predictable one with respect to time. In fact, various studies serve to confirm the fact that some form of stability does exist concerning changes in style. Consumer acceptance turns out to be not as erratic as one might suppose at first glance. In some cases, style cycles have been found, for example, in the clothing industry, in hair styles, and in millinery styles.[2] Architects play a primary role in influencing the accepted styles of a particular culture at any point in time. This relationship intrigued many designers and architects.[3] To the extent that product design follows architecture, reasonable predictions can be made about the evaluation of nonfunctional design characteristics. At the same time, we should not lose sight of the basic principles that, because they underlie all matters of shape and form, relate architecture, engineering, and industrial design.[4]

The Quality of Variety

Variety plays an important role as an intangible quality factor. At the input end, workers prefer to have their jobs comprise many different operations and the use of various materials. This recognition has led management to try to provide *job enlargement* (a term that will be heard with increasing

[2] See, for example, Agnes Brook Young, *Recurring Cycles of Fashion (1760–1937)* (New York: Harper & Row, Publishers, 1937).

[3] See, for example: Henry Dreyfuss, *Designing for People* (New York: Simon and Schuster, Inc., 1955); Frederick J. Kiesler, "Architecture as a Biotechnique," *Architectural Record* (September, 1939); Le Corbusier, *Toward a New Architecture* (London: Architectural Press, 1948); Raymond Loewy, *Never Leave Well Enough Alone* (New York: Simon and Schuster, Inc., 1951); Eliel Sarrinen, *Search for Form* (New York: Reinhold Publishing Corp., 1948); Walter Dorwin Teague, *Design This Day* (New York: Harcourt, Brace & World, Inc., 1940).

[4] See for example: George D. Birkhoff, *Aesthetic Measure* (Cambridge, Mass.: Harvard University Press, 1933); Samuel Coleman, *Nature's Harmonic Unity* (New York: The Knickerbocker Press, 1912); *Proportional Form* (New York: The Knickerbocker Press, 1920); Ozenfant, *Foundations of Modern Art*, trans. J. Rodker (New York: Dover Publications, Inc., 1952); J. Schillinger, *The Mathematical Basis of the Arts* (New York: Philosophical Library, 1948); D'Arcy W. Thompson, *On Growth and Form*, Vols. 1 and 2, 2nd ed. (Cambridge, England: University Press, 1959, reprint); L. L. Whyte, ed., *Aspects of Form* (Bloomington, Ind.: Indiana University Press, 1961).

frequency). With respect to outputs, consumers have let it be known that they like *variety*.[5] It is clear that industry could provide more variety if it were so organized.[6] For example, the following tableau provides information critical to increasing the variety level of a product-line.[7]

Table of Specifications for the Kind and Number of Parts to be Combined for Each of a Given Number of Different End Products

Variety of Parts	Variety of Products							
	PR_1	PR_2	PR_3	PR_4	...	PR_j	...	PR_M
PA_1	1	0	1	1	..:	0	...	0
PA_2	0	1	1	2	...	0	...	0
PA_3	0	0	0	0	...	1	...	0
PA_4	0	0	1	0	...	0	...	0
.	.	.	.	.		.		.
.	.	.	.	.		.		.
.	.	.	.	.		.		.
PA_i	0	0	1	0	...	2	...	0
.	.	.	.	.		.		.
.	.	.	.	.		.		.
PA_N	0	0	0	1	...	1	...	1

NOTES: PA_i denotes the part identified by the stock number i. $(i = 1, 2, \ldots N)$.

PR_j denotes the product variation listed in the finished goods catalog as j. $(j = 1, 2, \ldots M)$.

We see that with N different kinds of materials or parts a total of M different output configurations is derived. Some of these products require several units of a single part; for instance, PR_j requires two of PA_i. The maximum possible variety, i.e., maximum M, that can be obtained with N different parts may be very large.[8] How to design parts that can combine to produce the greatest number of products is the issue. It is a problem widely recognized

[5] M. K. Starr, "Modular Production—A New Concept," *Harvard Business Review*, 43: 6 (November–December, 1965), 131–42.

[6] M. K. Starr, "Product Planning from the Top (Variety and Diversity)," *University of Illinois Bulletin*, 65: 144, Proceedings, *Systems: Research and Applications for Marketing* (July 26, 1968), 71–77.

[7] *Op. cit.*, p. 138. Also, see pp. 32–33.

[8] If each part can be used zero, one, or two times (i.e., three options), then the maximum variety that can be derived with N parts will be $3^N - 1$ (one is subtracted because there will be one configuration in which none of the parts appears). With only ten parts $(N = 10)$, the maximum variety is a somewhat astonishing 59,048. Then, if, in addition, the ways and sequences with which the parts can be combined also add variety, then the number of possibilities rises even faster.

and respected by industry. Two major fields, those of computers and auto-mobiles, have made large strides to increase their product-lines with the addition of a minimum number of new rows.

One of the most important quality management functions is to inspect incoming materials to make certain that they conform to quality specifications. Input standards must be stated explicitly, according to the needs of the process for workable materials and to *insure* that process outputs will satisfy market expectations. Inferior materials create many kinds of costs. For example:

Cost of Unusable Items (generally refunded).

Cost of Not Having a Part When It Is Needed.   The item is thought to be in stock, but in actuality it is not. Only a *"stock phantom"* is on hand that cannot do the required job. This cost can be severe. For example, assume that a generator part, known to fail occasionally, is carried in stock at a quantity level in excess of expected usage. The high inventory level is geared to the fact that if no spare is on hand, then the generator is shut down. So a large buffer stock is maintained. Then, a failure of this part occurs. The repair team discovers that all the spares are faulty and cannot be used. They should have been inspected when they were received. In the same way, if a company manufactures a product that requires a raw material or a subcontracted subassembly, which is found to be unusable when it is needed, then production is stopped until a new and usable supply can be obtained.

Cost of Disgruntled Customers.   In this case, we assume that the quality of the purchased items does not affect the production process but does affect the final unit. It is the consumer who perceives the difference in quality. It is the producer of the final unit who receives and deserves full blame—with consequent losses—for having passed the inferior material along to the consumer. The vendor of the inferior items enjoys relative anonymity. Inspection of the purchased item could have avoided this cost, but then, in turn, there is an *inspection cost.*

Proper management of the inspection function is based on the need to balance various costs. We spend as much on the inspection process as would be required to offset penalties of the types described above. If it were possible to set down the total description of the enterprise in equational form, then materials inspection costs would be comprised as some of the terms. As it is, the best that we can do is to isolate this subsystem and attempt to minimize its characteristic total costs.

100 Per Cent Inspection

Total, or 100 per cent inspection, has the highest inspection costs. Such costs might be justified if increased accuracy were derived as a result of using 100 per cent inspection and the penalty for being inaccurate were high. However, total inspection is seldom the most accurate method that can be followed. It has been found that 100 per cent inspection can produce *carelessness* and error due to *fatigue*. The inspector's human debilities become apparent when there are many items to be totally inspected. Furthermore, 100 per cent inspection is out of the question where *destructive testing* is required. A manufacturer of fire crackers, bullets, a food product, or soap flakes cannot destroy his total shipment in order to find out if each item comes up to the standards that he has set. In any case, 100 per cent inspection, whether done by man or machine, is slow, costly, and frequently unreliable—even when it is possible. On the other hand, for a few truly critical items, 200 or 300 per cent inspection might be insufficient. Especially in the project shop (e.g., moon shots), repeated inspection with cross-checks is essential.

Sampling Inspection

In the 1920s, at the Western Electric Company, a growing body of statistical theory was used to develop *sampling plans* that could be employed as substitutes for 100 per cent inspection. These sampling inspection techniques were applied to purchased and subcontracted parts, raw materials, office supplies, and maintenance parts; and they could also be used by a producer to conduct sample tests of his own output.[9] The only sampling procedures used before this work were *proportional sampling methods*, and these were *wrong in concept*. Before we can explain why, let us develop the variables necessary for discussing sampling plans.

1. N = the lot size.

This is usually the total number of items developed by the vendor within a single shipment. More generally, it can be the total production run of the producer for which the conditions of the system remained essentially un-

---

[9] At about the same time, the sequential test methods of statistical quality control were being developed. These are more frequently used by a producer to evaluate and control his output. See pp. 390–399.

changed. Thus, it is hypothesized that the *quality of items within a lot is homogeneous*. This means that the process average for defectives produced does not change from the beginning to the end of the run.

2. n = the sample size.

The items to be inspected should be a representative sample drawn at random from the lot. We don't just inspect material that happens to be at the top of the box.[10]

3. c = the sample criterion.

This criterion is defined so that when n items are drawn from a lot size of N and k items are found to be defective, then if $k > c$, we reject the entire lot. If $k \leq c$, we accept the lot. Therefore, c is sometimes called the acceptance number of the sampling plan.

Proportional sampling was based on the assumption that if we had two lots, A and B, and A was twice as large as B, then we should draw twice as large a sample from A as from B. In effect, the per cent of a lot to be inspected was fixed, say at $\frac{n}{N} = K$. If any rejects were found, then the total lot was to be rejected, that is, $c = 0$ was the acceptance number that was used.

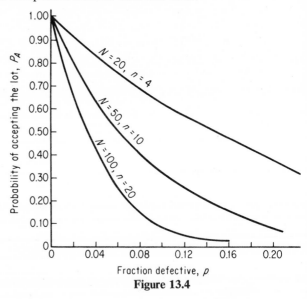

Figure 13.4

Operating Characteristic (*OC*) curves for several proportional sampling plans. In all these cases, $c = 0$ and the proportion sampled is 20 percent.

[10] Housewives have always known this when they buy strawberries.

The operating characteristic curves, called OC curves, shown in Figure 13.4, point out that the proportional sampling scheme is fallacious. The x-axis is the *actual fraction defective* in the lot, called *p*. The OC curve shows how P_A, the probability of accepting the lot, changes with respect to *p* for a number of different sampling plans, all of which utilize the same sampling proportion of $n/N = 0.20$ and the same acceptance number, $c = 0$. Thus, these plans, all of which are based on the *policy* of proportional sampling, produce significantly different results. The probability of accepting a lot of twenty items is much higher than the probability of accepting a lot of fifty items and more so for one hundred items—when proportional sampling is used.

What sampling method should be used then? The answer is that by choosing appropriate values for *n* and *c*, we can develop an OC curve that should be acceptable. What is acceptable is not likely to be the decision of a single company's management. The situation calls for compromise and *negotiation* between the vendor and the purchaser. Reference to Figure 13.5 shows what is involved.

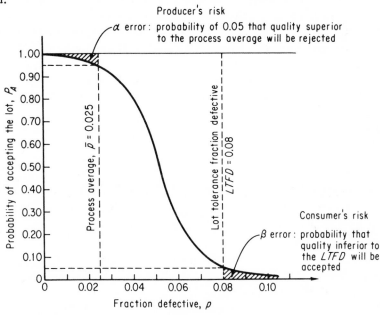

Figure 13.5

Consumer's and producer's risks.

Producer's and Consumer's Risks

The two shaded areas marked α and β are two different kinds of risks. The α area is called the *producer's risk*. It gives the probability that acceptable lots will be rejected. Specifically, it gives the probability that lots having a lower fraction of defectives than are normally produced by the process $\bar{p}$ will be rejected by the sampling plan that is shown. It is the average process rate that we have called $\bar{p}$. On the other hand, the β area represents the probability that unacceptable levels of lot quality will be accepted by the sampling plan. This is called, reasonably enough, the *consumer's risk*. The limiting value, defined by the consumer, is called the lot tolerance fraction defective, *LTFD*.[11] It is the upper limit of fraction defectives that the consumer is willing to tolerate in each lot. Above this point, he would like to reject all lots. But, he knows that this is impossible if he wishes to utilize inspection by sampling methods. Therefore, he compromises by saying that no more than β per cent of the time does he wish to allow such quality to get through his *sampling filter*.

Given a certain process average, $\bar{p}$, and the consumer's specification of *LTFD* and β, then a sampling plan can be found that *minimizes the cost of inspection*. In this cost, we include the expense of *detailing*, which is the operation of totally inspecting (100 per cent) all *rejected lots* to remove the defective pieces. Such a sampling plan imputes a dollar value to α. If the producer wishes to decrease his risk, he can do so by improving the process average, $\bar{p}$. An improvement of this kind may be costly. The consumer would be forced to accept part of this increased cost in the form of higher prices. Whether it is the producer or the consumer who bears the cost of inspection—or if they share it—they must agree that the only rational procedure to be followed is to minimize inspection costs and negotiate about the values for *LTFD* and β. Under some circumstances, they might also consider improvements that can be made in $\bar{p}$.

It is important to observe that any sampling plan, of a specific c and n, completely specifies the α and β risks for given levels of $\bar{p}$ and *LTFD*. In turn, the sampling plan requires n inspections for every lot. If the process average, $\bar{p}$, is the true state of affairs, then α per cent of the time the remainder of the lot will be inspected. Thus, the average number of pieces inspected will be: $n + (N - n)\alpha$.

As n gets large and approaches N, all other factors remaining constant, then the plan becomes increasingly discriminating and α approaches one. The effect is illustrated in Figure 13.6.

This results in the average number of pieces to be inspected approximating N. On the other hand, we observe that as n gets small, approaching one, β increases rapidly and approaches one, while α tends to become zero. In this case, the average number of pieces that will be inspected will be negligible, but the consumer's risk will be high. In between these extremes, there exist appropriate values of c and n that will minimize the average number of pieces to be inspected for some specified level of consumer protection. Thus, in

---

[11] If per cent defective is used instead of fraction defective, the limit is called *LTPD*.

Figure 13.6, plan A requires $[20 + 80(.06)] = 24.8$ pieces to be inspected, on the average; plan B requires $[10 + 90(.21)] = 28.9$ pieces to be inspected. Both plans provide the same consumer risk.

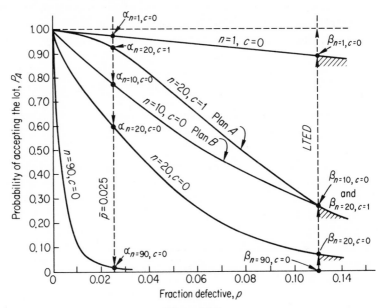

Figure 13.6

As the sample size increases, all other factors remaining constant, the plan becomes increasingly discriminating from the point of view of the consumer, that is, β approaches zero, but the cost of inspection increases rapidly as α approaches one. For a given level of β protection there is a sampling plan that minimizes the cost of inspection. Thus, for $LTFD = 0.12$ and $\beta = 0.26$, plan A has a lower cost of inspection than plan B.

Constructing Acceptance Sampling Plans

How are the kinds of plans that we have been discussing contructed? One of the most direct approaches is to utilize tables that have been designed for this purpose.[12] On the other hand, OC curves can be derived directly from the appropriate mathematical statements. In particular, it will be noted that for sampling without replacement, the *Hypergeometric* distribution should be used. The reason we cannot assume that each item drawn for the sample of size n is then replaced before the next unit is drawn is that the lot size, N, is finite and small enough to allow such an assumption to affect the results.

Assume that the number of defectives in the lot is specified as the vari-

---

[12] Harold F. Dodge and Harry G. Romig, *Sampling Inspection Tables, Single and Double Sampling* (New York: John Wiley & Sons, Inc., 1951).

able x. Then, x/N is the *actual* fraction defective of the lot. When we draw the first unit for the sample, the probability of drawing a defective will be x/N. We do not replace this unit after recording its state, and, therefore, when the second unit of the sample is drawn—no matter what happened with the first sample drawn—the probabilities are a function of $(N - 1)$.

Thus, when the difference between N and $(N - 1)$ is significant, we use the combinatorial formulation:

$$P_j = C_{n-j}^{N-x} C_j^x / C_n^N = \frac{(N-x)!x!n!(N-n)!}{(n-j)!(N-x-n+j)!j!(x-j)!N!}$$

(All variables are described above except j, which equals the number of defectives in the sample.)

Example of the Determination[13] of OC Curves for $c = 0$ and $c = 1$

$$N = 50; n = 10$$

Abscissa Value	For $c = 0$ $j = 0$	$j = 1$	For $c = 1$ $j = 0 + 1$
$p = \dfrac{x}{N} = 0; \quad x = 0$	$P_{A,j=0} = \dfrac{50!10!40!}{10!40!50!}$ $= 1.000$	$P_{A,j=1} = 0.000$	$P_{A,j=0+1} = 1.000$
$p = \dfrac{x}{N} = 0.04; x = 2$	$P_{A,j=0} = \dfrac{48!2!10!40!}{10!38!2!50!}$ $= 0.637$	$P_{A,j=1} = \dfrac{48!2!10!40!}{9!39!50!}$ $= 0.326$	$P_{A,j=0+1} = 0.963$
$p = \dfrac{x}{N} = 0.10; x = 5$	$P_{A,j=0} = \dfrac{45!5!10!40!}{10!35!5!50!}$ $= 0.311$	$P_{A,j=1} = \dfrac{45!5!10!40!}{9!36!4!50!}$ $= 0.432$	$P_{A,j=0+1} = 0.743$
$p = \dfrac{x}{N} = 0.20; x = 10$	$P_{A,j=0} = \dfrac{40!10!10!40!}{10!30!10!50!}$ $= 0.083$	$P_{A,j=1} = \dfrac{40!10!10!40!}{9!31!9!50!}$ $= 0.268$	$P_{A,j=0+1} = 0.351$

[13] NOTE: These computations can be facilitated by using a log table of factorials, for example, E. L. Grant, *Statistical Quality Control*, 3rd ed. (New York: McGraw-Hill Book Company, Inc., 1964), pp. 572–76.

The curves are drawn, in Figure 13.7, for both of the Hypergeometric plans derived above.

When the notion that N is finite and that the system is sensitive to lot size can be discarded, then the Binomial distribution or the Poisson distribution can be used. Both express the condition that the lot size is *infinite*, and they are far easier to use than the Hypergeometric distribution. Figure 13.8 illustrates the fact that as soon as N gets reasonably large (say, approximately one thousand), the assumption of an infinite N does not introduce great inaccuracy into the sampling plan.[14] Consequently, it is frequently quite sensible

[14] In many applications, when $N = 100$, the infinite assumption is satisfactory.

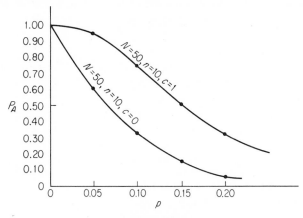

Figure 13.7

to use either the Binomial distribution or the Poisson approximation to the Binomial for such cases.

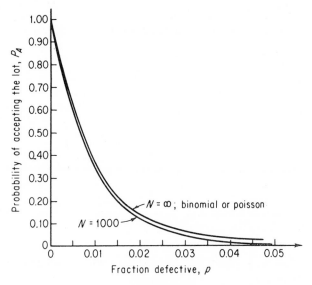

Figure 13.8

When the lot size, N, is reasonably large, say approximately one thousand, the assumption of an infinite lot size does not introduce great inaccuracy into the sampling plan.

For sampling with replacement where the assumption of infinite N seems reasonable, we can use the Binomial distribution. That is,

$$\text{Prob }(k; n, p) = \left[\frac{n!}{k!(n-k)!} \right] p^k q^{n-k}$$

Let $k = 0$ which is equivalent to $c = 0$ and let $n = 100$. Then:

$$\text{Prob } (0; 100, p) = q^{100} = (1 - p)^{100}$$

Fraction Defective, p	1 − p	$(1 - p)^{100} = P_A$
$p = 0.00$	1.00	1.000
$p = 0.01$	0.99	0.367
$p = 0.02$	0.98	0.133
$p = 0.04$	0.96	0.017

For the acceptance number $c = 1$, we require the same kind of addition as was the case for the Hypergeometric. Thus, obtain the sum: Prob $(0; 100, p) +$ Prob $(1; 100, p)$ for all values of p.

Even simpler to use is the Poisson distribution. It also assumes sampling with replacement (i.e., N can be treated as infinite) and the fact that p is small over the range that is of interest.

$$\text{Prob } (k; m) = \frac{m^k e^{-m}}{k!}$$

Let $k = 0$ which is equivalent to $c = 0$, and let $n = 100$; thus, since $m = np$ we have $m = 100p$.

$$\text{Prob } (0; np) = e^{-np}$$

Fraction Defective, p	np = m	Prob (k; m) = P_A
$p = 0.00$	0	1.000
$p = 0.01$	1	0.368
$p = 0.02$	2	0.135
$p = 0.04$	4	0.018

We observe that this result is essentially the same as that obtained by using the Binomial distribution. It should be remembered that a sampling plan where $c = 1$ requires computations of P_A for $k = 0$, which are then added to those of P_A for $k = 1$ to obtain the sampling plan for $c = 1$.

Average Outgoing Quality Limit (AOQL)

In some systems, quality management is assisted by the idea of an averaging outgoing quality (AOQ). This is a measure of the average or expected percentage of defective items that the producer will ship to the consumer under different conditions of per cent defectives.

First, every sampled lot is divided into n and $(N - n)$. The probable number of defectives in the unsampled portion $(N - n)$ is $\bar{p}(N - n)$. Out of every one hundred samples, we expect that P_A will be the fraction that is passed without any further examination. These are the only units that cannot be tagged as defectives and replaced (in the sense of detailing). Then, $P_A\bar{p}(N - n)$ is the expected number of defectives that will be passed without having been identified for every N units processed. The percentage $P_A p(N - n)/N$ is called the AOQ, which changes value as a function of p. It is the expected value of the per cent defectives that would be passed *if* the process is operating at p. This measure reaches a maximum value for some particular value of p. The maximum value is termed the "average outgoing quality limit" (AOQL).

Note, for example, the results obtained from the Hypergeometric distribution, pp. 377–379.

p	$P_A(c = 0)$	$(N - n)/N$	$p[P_A(c = 0)]\left(\dfrac{N - n}{N}\right) =$ AOQ
.00	1.000	.8	0
.04	0.637	.8	0.02038
.10	0.311	.8	0.02488
.11	0.242	.8	0.02130
.20	0.083	.8	0.01328
.	.	.	.
.	.	.	.
.	.	.	.

The maximum value of AOQ has been calculated as 0.02488. It is the AOQL also shown in Figure 13.9.

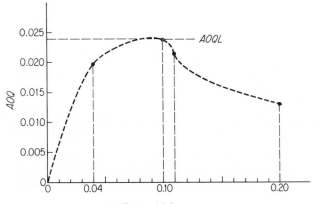

Figure 13.9

Multiple Sampling

Other types of sampling plans are utilized when the amount of inspection required by the single sampling plan appears to be too great. With double sampling, inspection costs can be lowered. The double sampling plan requires two acceptance numbers, c_1 and c_2, such that $c_2 > c_1$. Then, if the observed number of rejects in the first sample of size n_1 is k_1:

1. We accept the lot if $k_1 \leq c_1$;
2. We reject the lot if $k_1 > c_2$.
3. If $c_1 < k_1 \leq c_2$, then we draw an additional sample of size n_2. The total sample is now of size $n_1 + n_2$. If the observed number of rejects in the total sample is $k_1 + k_2$, then:
4. We accept the lot if $(k_1 + k_2) \leq c_2$;
5. We reject the lot if $(k_1 + k_2) > c_2$.

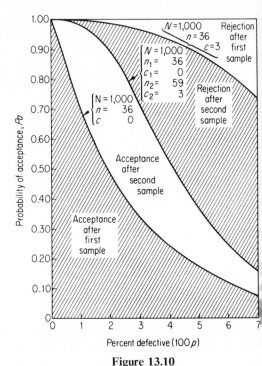

Figure 13.10

Characteristics of a double sampling plan. (From Eugene L. Grant, *Statistical Quality Control*, 3rd ed. (New York: McGraw-Hill Book Co., 1964), p. 364.

Figure 13.10 illustrates the way in which double sampling divides the graph space into unique acceptance and rejection regions.

There are also multiple sampling plans and sequential sampling plans. The criterion for choosing a plan has been implicit throughout our discussion. That is, there is some inspection cost per piece that can vary greatly, depending upon the nature of the item and the *definition of a reject*. The definition of a reject is unlikely to be a straightforward matter.[15] Given such a definition, it might require days of testing to determine whether an item is acceptable. For example, a reject might be defined as a unit possessing any three flaws where one hundred different kinds of flaws could occur.

It is both instructive and fascinating to see how so many different factors come together in a discussion of this kind. We observe that the process average, the quality expectations, the inspection costs, and the market's acceptance of the output are tightly interwoven and that any approach to decision making that bypasses *synthesis* is bound to be absurd.

The Shewhart Output Quality Monitor

Walter Shewhart[16] developed a control monitor that has completely altered the nature of quality control. The primary purpose of this monitor is to determine whether or not a stable system exists. The Shewhart model *monitors* a process to determine whether or not the system is regularly meeting expectations, delivering the specified outcome within the expected range of variation, and achieving the manager's objectives of maintaining a stable process. We must note the meaning of the term control when it is used in this context. If disturbances arise that shift the system off its course (they are called *assignable causes of variation*), something must be done about them. The Shewhart control monitor does not tell what to do; how to do it; when or where to do it. It does not exercise control in this sense. It does tell us that something seems to be changing—that the system no longer appears to be following an established (stable) pattern. This is very vital information. Figure 13.11 locates the Shewhart monitor within the flows of the control system.

For the type of systems to which the Shewhart method is applicable, the objectives must be clearly and explicitly stated. (For example, part *PT* 2 should be cut three inches ± .05 inches in length.) *Assignable causes of variation* are disturbances that might enter the system and remain undetected. The Shewhart control monitor is designed to recognize that such a disturbance has occurred. The reason this monitor is of such fundamental importance is that other causes of variation exist in almost all systems and nothing can be done about them. They are called *chance causes of variation*. It is vital that the manager be able to *separate* the two types of causes of variation and not confuse or lump them together. It is true that chance causes of variation are

---

[15] Note previous discussions concerning quality.

[16] W. A. Shewhart, *Statistical Method from the Viewpoint of Quality Control*, W. E. Deming, ed. (Washington, D.C.: Department of Agriculture, 1939).

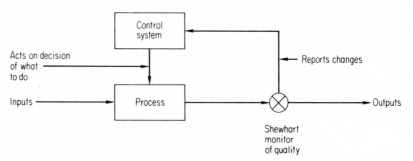

Figure 13.11

disturbances to the system, but these causes can be neither discerned nor removed. There are literally millions of such chance causes, including the behavior of particles at subatomic levels. Because of the conglomeration of chance causes, the machine cannot produce a part that is consistently three inches in length. Instead, we obtain a distribution of lengths like the normal distribution shown in Figure 13.12. The Shewhart model establishes a proce-

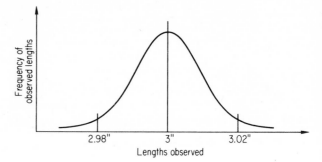

Figure 13.12

A determinate mechanism produces a distribution of values because of chance *causes.*

dure for determining whether or not the variation that is observed is as small as it can be: that is, whether the observed variability is the result of chance cause factors only, or whether there is trouble in the system about which something can be done. This control monitor provides differentiation between types of disturbances. It is expected that the output of a well-designed machine will produce a stable set of characteristics in the product. But various things can happen. A tool can shift position. The quality of material that is being worked on can change.

Shewhart proposed the notion that by measuring a *sequence* of outputs in terms of a specified characteristic, it would be possible to derive control limits that describe the range of process behaviors that *should* be expected *if* the process were stable. (See Figure 13.13.)

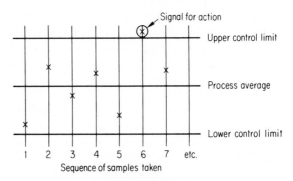

Figure 13.13

Observations are made of the process. As long as the observed values fall within the control limits and do so *without discernible patterns*, no disturbance to the system is believed to have occurred. Thus, as long as the measurements of outputs produced by the system fall between the limits and give evidence of purely random behavior, the process is called stable. When the observed results no longer appear to be random—one test of which is that they fall outside the limits—then the system is termed *out of control* and managerial action is called for.

A pertinent aspect is the fact that *many* production systems, when they are first translated from design to practice and monitored by the Shewhart control model, are revealed to be out of control. By making judicious changes in the system's design, the process can be brought gradually under control. Thereafter, it can be monitored for new disturbances that might enter the system.

Inspection

There is a technology of inspection that is no more appropriate to our present discussion than are the specific technologies of production processes. The manager is primarily involved with the *concept of specifications*, although, in practice, this will be translated into a large variety of detailed technical specifications such as hardness, tensile strength, color, and surface finish. To measure these characteristics he must provide his departments with appropriate instruments such as gauges, micrometers, optical comparators, and devices for measuring hardness, tensile strength, and surface finish. These physical outputs are visible and can be measured. It is expected that they will conform to some set of specifications such as are communicated by a blueprint.

In some areas, however, the specification of output quality is a far more elusive matter than can be dealt with by blueprints; e.g., the tastes of foods or the odors of perfumes. In such areas, the specification of measurable quality is exceedingly difficult.[17] The derivation of a standard against which quality can be measured is the goal in every case. Only if standards can be found is it possible to measure quality. Thus, for example, the Food and Drug Administration (FDA) is required to develop and enforce standards that protect the consumer from hazards that he could not otherwise perceive. Setting such standards is not an easy matter, but once they are set, food and drug samples can then be tested to see whether they meet the selected standards. In a different sense, we have standard yards, standard meters, standard footcandles, and standard colors. Standard intervals between standardized maintenance procedures are specified by the Federal Aviation Administration (FAA) for aircraft. Company C can use a bolt manufactured by Company A and a nut manufactured by Company B because of the accepted conventions of the American Standard. Similarly, standard designs for gauges have been generally accepted and are described as American Gauge Design Standards. We could go on at length discussing various kinds of standards and the methods and scales that have been adopted to measure quality.[18]

Acceptance sampling procedures required a complete definition of what qualities a reject had. Reject v. nonreject would sometimes be a matter of a straightforward "go—no go" test. The acceptance sampling methods were applied, for the most part, to materials obtained from an outside vendor where the quality of the shipment had to be checked. Now, however, we shall introduce the imperative question: How should we monitor *and control* our own output? We have already introduced the Shewhart monitor. Now we must find out how it is used in the areas that statistical quality control is designed to handle.

We do not draw samples at random from a homogeneous lot, as we did for acceptance sampling. Instead, it is essential to monitor the *sequence* of the output. For acceptance sampling, the assumption of homogeneity of the vendor's output was assumed. For our own production process, we no longer can make this assumption. On the contrary, we ask ourselves: Does our process exhibit homogeneity? If the answer is yes, we then ask: How can we guarantee that it will continue to perform in the same way?

Quality control, or quality assurance, is an on-going process inspection procedure. It is a sequential sampling method that is more powerful in many

---

[17] For an interesting discussion with respect to these problems of taste and smell, see *Flavor Research and Food Acceptance*, sponsored by Arthur D. Little, Inc. (New York: Rhinehold Publishing Corp., 1958).

[18] See pp. 371 concerning modular design to maximize variety.

ways than 100 per cent inspection. To insure control, the feedback link shown in Figure 13.11 is required. The inspection operation costs money, and the gain to be derived from this expense at least must offset the costs incurred.

There are two basically different types of inspection.

Classification by Attributes.   This is achieved by sorting the output by type. Thus, for example, we might divide our output into rejects and nonrejects, good and bad, "go" or "no go," or some other binary division. We followed this procedure with acceptance sampling. The definition used to define a defective unit of output may be very complex; nevertheless, the eventual label placed on each unit is limited to either accepted or defective.

Classification by Variables.   In this case, exact scaled measurements are made of particular variables such as length, hardness, weight, thermal conductivity, thermal expansion, electrical resistivity, dielectrical strength, melting point, modulus of elasticity, impact strength, creep strength, and a variety of other physically measurable quantities for which some standard measure and measuring device is available.

SQC Calculations

No matter how well-designed a system is, there will always be some variation from a standard level of performance. Consequently, it is only logical to set the standard as a range. That is why, on blueprints, one sees tolerance ranges stated for specific dimensions, for example, 2.41 ± 0.03. It is expected that the actual (and observed) quality of the item will fall within the specified range. Confusion frequently exists regarding the relationship of the engineer's specifications of tolerance and the characteristics of the production process that is used to produce the part. The engineer's specifications cannot demand more than the process is able to deliver. To be reasonable, tolerance limits must be adjusted to the abilities of the facility. Every facility has a characteristic output variability that can be translated into a range. Thus, if it is desired to cut a steel bar to a given length, then it is expected that variation evidenced as a distribution of observed values will occur around that specified central point. An engineer can specify tolerances from now until doomsday. Unless there is a machine or facility capable of providing parts that fall within this tolerance range, the objective cannot be achieved. Only by means of a new technological development can such specifications be met.

Previously, we mentioned two kinds of factors responsible for variation. These are: (1) *chance cause factors*, which are fundamental to all processes; and (2) *assignable cause factors*, which can be isolated and removed from the process. Statistical quality control, or SQC, is able to differentiate between these causes of variation. Thus, it is possible to determine when a facility is experiencing only the fundamental and inherent variations to which it is always susceptible.

A *control chart* such as the one in Figure 13.13 is the monitor of the control system. The control chart can be used for several purposes. First, to determine the fundamental or inherent variation level of a process. Second, to determine whether the process is stable and continues to be so during the production process. Stability is defined as the condition of a process in which only inherent, *chance cause factors* are at work.

Statistical control procedure is based on the fact that the observed variation within each of a set of samples of size *n* can be directly related to the variation between the means of each sample in the set. Thus, for example, consider the following set of five samples. Each sample is composed of four observations.

Table 13.1

Subgroup Sample Number	Observation Number				Sample Mean $\bar{x}$	Sample Range R
	1	2	3	4		
1	21	31	39	25	29	18
2	17	44	54	13	32	41
3	36	48	19	41	36	29
4	25	31	38	30	31	13
5	35	21	20	34	27.5	15
					155.5	116

Process Average: $\bar{\bar{x}} = \dfrac{155.5}{5} = 31.1$

Average Range: $\bar{R} = \dfrac{116}{5} = 23.2$

It is to be understood that these samples represent a *sequence* of observations made over a period of time (see Figure 13.14). Each sample is called a subgroup; each subgroup, composed of four observations, is obtained by securing four measures in successive order without permitting intervening periods to occur. Then an interval of time is allowed to elapse.

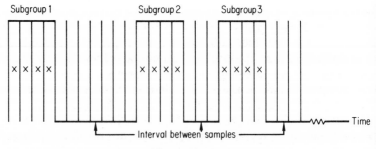

Figure 13.14

The next subgroup sample is taken at a later point in time. It is vital that we preserve the order of the samples although observations can be mixed within samples. Thus, observations taken for subgroup 2 must not be confused with observations taken for subgroup 3. The *preservation of order*, in this sense, is crucial to the use of statistical control.

Sample Design

How is the subgroup size chosen? (Why did $n = 4$ in the example above?) How does the interval between samples get set? This much we can say, usually the interval between samples is fixed and unchanging—although methods do exist that decrease the between-sample-interval when the value of the subgroup mean approaches one of the control limits. Similarly, if a run of a particular pattern other than the expected one seems to be developing, the interval would decrease (see p. 393). The point is that in the face of evidence that the system may be running out of control, the subgroup size should increase and the interval between would decrease until 100 per cent inspection would be used during the emergency. Cost balance is involved in reaching such decisions and so are specific system properties. Referring to cost, let us examine Figure 13.15.

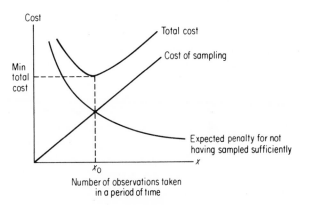

Figure 13.15

There is a point x_0 at which minimum total cost occurs. In general, as more observations are taken (say, in a day), there is an almost linearly increasing cost. As fewer observations are taken, there is a greater chance that the system will go out of control and start producing defective items without it being noticed so that immediate remedial action can be taken. The expected penalty for defective output decreases as x gets larger because the expected length of time that the system will be malfunctioning is decreased.

The question still remains: How to choose subgroup sizes and intervals between samples? Thus, if x is selected at twenty observations per day should this be $n = 2$ repeated ten times with appropriate intervals between or $n = 4$ repeated five times or $n = 10$ once in the AM and once in the PM. The fundamental criterion is that the successive observations within the subgroup should be close enough together to insure that they are relatively *homogeneous* and that no change is likely to have occurred in the process. We then space successive subgroups in such a way that any lack of homogeneity that might occur over time is likely to be picked up. In general practice, subgroup sizes of 4, 5, and 6 can be readily used. The spacing between subgroups will depend on the production rate and the inertial characteristics of the process.

Another important question concerns *how many values are required* before it is possible to set up a control chart. That is, how many subgroups should be collected? In the previous example, we utilized only five subgroup samples. Ordinarily, this is far too few. It is desirable to have at least twenty-five subgroup observations before attempting to draw up *and interpret* the control chart.

Statistical Quality Control Theory

It will be noted that for each subgroup, using the observations in Table 13.1, we have calculated the sample average, or mean value, $\bar{x}$. We can assume equally well that the observations are measurements of the length of a bar, the inside diameter of a pipe, the number of air bubbles in a piece of glass, or the temperature of a water-cooled, moving part. In addition to the *mean value*, we have obtained for each subgroup the difference between the largest observation and the smallest observation. This is the measure of the *range*, called R. Thus, we have obtained the expected value for each subgroup as well as a convenient measure of the variation that appeared in the subgroup.

The variance of sample means for subgroups of size n_1, $\sigma_{\bar{x}_1}^2$, can be compared to the variance of sample means for subgroups of size n_2, $\sigma_{\bar{x}_2}^2$, by a simple relationship. The same statement can then be made for the respective standard deviations.

$$\sigma_{\bar{x}_1}\sqrt{n_1} = \sigma_{\bar{x}_2}\sqrt{n_2}$$

The $\sigma_{\bar{x}_i}$'s are called the *standard error of the mean*. These standard deviations are parameters of their respective distributions of subgroup averages, based on the particular sample size that is involved.

Figure 13.16 illustrates several distributions, each of which is based on a different sample subgroup size, and compares these distributions of means to the population distribution. The population distribution can be thought of as a distribution of sample means for which the subgroup size is one. Let us

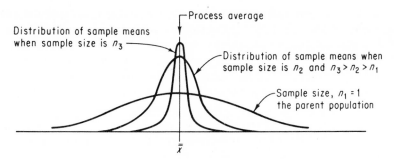

Figure 13.16

The standard deviation of sample means (measured from the process average) decreases in inverse proportion to the square root of the sample size.

denote the population standard deviation by σ_x. Now, if we set the subgroup size of n_1 to be equal to one, we obtain the relationship:

$$\sigma_{\bar{x}_2}\sqrt{n_2} = \sigma_x$$

This expresses the fact that the standard deviation of the population is equal to the square root of the subgroup sample size times the standard deviation of the distribution of means for that subgroup size. We can rewrite this, for any n, as follows:

$$\sigma_{\bar{x}_n} = \frac{\sigma_x}{\sqrt{n}}$$

Thus, the standard deviation of the distribution of means associated with subgroup size n is equal to the population's standard deviation divided by the square root of n.

It is frequently more convenient to measure the *range* than to go through the calculation of the standard deviation. Tables have been prepared that give the relationship of the *expected range* to the population standard deviation for different sample sizes assumed to be drawn from a Normal universe.[19] This ratio factor is designated as d_2.

$$d_2 = \frac{\bar{R}}{\sigma_x}$$

Let us introduce this relationship into our previous equation for the standard error of the mean, and thereby derive:

$$\sigma_{\bar{x}_n} = \frac{\bar{R}}{d_2\sqrt{n}}$$

It is usual to position control limits as some specified number of standard

[19] See the tables in Grant, *op. cit.*, p. 561.

deviations away from the expected value of the process. We shall use 3σ control limits, which is the value most commonly selected for industrial systems. Consequently, we can then write:

$$3\sigma_{\bar{x}_n} = \frac{3\overline{R}}{d_2\sqrt{n}} = A_2\overline{R}$$

The A_2 factor is available in table form (see p. 395) where $A_2 = \dfrac{3}{d_2\sqrt{n}}$. The upper control limit and the lower control limit, where the process average is $\bar{\bar{x}}$, would be given by:

upper control limit for $\bar{x}$: $UCL_{\bar{x}} = \bar{\bar{x}} + A_2\overline{R}$
lower control limit for $\bar{x}$: $LCL_{\bar{x}} = \bar{\bar{x}} - A_2\overline{R}$

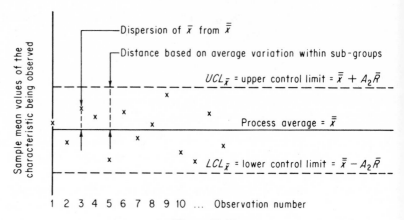

Figure 13.17

Control chart for variables—$\bar{x}$.

Figure 13.17 shows a control chart on which we have marked the upper limit, the lower limit, and the grand process average, which is the mean value of the sample means, called $\bar{\bar{x}}$. We observe that the distance between the process average and the upper or lower control limit is a function of $\overline{R}$. The value $\overline{R}$, in turn, is the average range obtained for the subgroup samples of size n. Thus, the distance between the process average and the control limits is a function of the average variability associated with subgroups of size n.

On our control chart, in proper sequence, we enter the $\bar{x}$ values that are the subgroup averages. Statistical theory tells us that if the process is stable, then the successive values of the sample means will fall between the control limits 99.7 per cent of the time. This is true because 3σ limits were used. If we had utilized limits other than 3σ, we would obtain different probabilities of exceeding the control limits.

If the character of the parent population changes because assignable causes enter the system, then, this should become apparent when some value or values of $\bar{x}$ will fall outside the control limits. Another characteristic of an unstable system is that a *run* of values all above or all below the process average may occur. Runs are usually symptomatic that a process is *trending* in a particular direction. Let us examine the probabilities with which control emergency signals will appear when the process is stable. First, the probability of a point falling outside the 3σ limits is approximately $1/380$. Second, the probability that nine points in a row will lie on one side of the process average is about $1/256$; that ten points in a row will fall on a particular side of the grand mean is about $1/512$.

For most manufacturing processes it is assumed that the parent populations of the various output dimensions conform to the Normal distribution. SQC, as described by Shewhart, is based on this assumption. An important question arises then as to what happens when the population is not normally distributed. Ideally, we would like the control system to operate in much the same way. That is, as long as the population remains stable, no matter what shape it has, we would like to be able to use the control criterion to tell us that no change has occurred in the process. It is a delightful gift of nature that distributions of sample means will tend to be Normal even though the population from which the samples are drawn is not normally distributed. Shewhart had shown that even though samples are drawn from rectangular, triangular, and other types of distributions, the distributions of the sample means tend to be Normal. It is sufficiently true so that, in general, we need not concern ourselves with this problem.

Monitoring Variables

We shall proceed to derive two different charts that are used when scaled measurements of the variables to be controlled have been obtained. In Table 13.1, we found that the grand mean of the process was 31.1 and that the average range of the five subgroups of size four was 23.2. Although five subgroups do not constitute a sufficient sample for actual intentions of monitoring a process, nevertheless, it is sufficient for illustrative purposes. Figure 13.18 shows the $\bar{x}$ chart.

It has been constructed by means of the formulations previously given for both the upper and lower control limits of the $\bar{x}$ chart. The A_2 factor is obtained from the table that follows. A_2 when $n = 4$ is equal to 0.73. This is multiplied by $\bar{R}$, which is equal to 23.2. Then, the product, which is approximately 16.9, is added to $\bar{x}$ for the upper control limit and subtracted from $\bar{x}$ for the lower control limit. Our control chart indicates no lack of stability. The same procedures are followed when the number of subgroups is much larger than five.

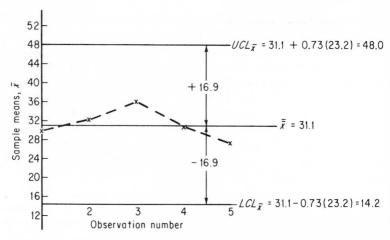

Figure 13.18

Control chart for variables, $\bar{x}$, for data given in Table 13.1. [A_2 (when $n = 4$) = 0.73.]

The $\bar{x}$ chart is intended to monitor the process average. When measurements of variables are used, it is also possible to construct a chart to monitor the process dispersion. This chart is called an R chart. It is based on the range measures that had to be derived for the $\bar{x}$ chart. We will not investigate the detailed reasoning involved in the development of the upper and lower control limits for the R chart because it closely parallels our previous discussion for the $\bar{x}$ chart. Table 13.2 presents the appropriate equations, as well as the respective D values that, like A_2, must be used for the determination of R chart control limits. Utilizing the D factors obtained from the table, we construct the appropriate R chart for our example. This is shown in Figure 13.19.

Symptoms and Diagnosis

The construction of the R chart is straightforward, as was the construction of the $\bar{x}$ chart. It is the interpretation of the charts that is of crucial importance. If there is a shift in the population character, then it can be of the following types: (1) The process average may change; (2) the process dispersion may change; or (3) both of these changes may take place. If only the average changes, this fact will probably be picked up by the $\bar{x}$ chart and not by the R chart. The situation might occur, for example, if the machine setting shifts permanently; that is, the change is of a *sustained* type. In certain cases, the population mean or process average will remain unchanged, but the dispersion of the process will shift. For example, an operator may be able to control his output at the mean level, but he does this by working fast at cer-

Table 13.2 Factors for Determining from $\bar{R}$ the 3-sigma Control Limits for $\bar{x}$ and R Charts

Number of Observations in Subgroup *n*	Factor for $\bar{x}$ Chart A_2	Factors for R Chart	
		Lower Control Limit D_3	*Upper Control Limit* D_4
2	1.88	0	3.27
3	1.02	0	2.57
4	0.73	0	2.28
5	0.58	0	2.11
6	0.48	0	2.00
7	0.42	0.08	1.92
8	0.37	0.14	1.86
9	0.34	0.18	1.82
10	0.31	0.22	1.78
11	0.29	0.26	1.74
12	0.27	0.28	1.72
13	0.25	0.31	1.69
14	0.24	0.33	1.67
15	0.22	0.35	1.65
16	0.21	0.36	1.64
17	0.20	0.38	1.62
18	0.19	0.39	1.61
19	0.19	0.40	1.60
20	0.18	0.41	1.59

Upper Control Limit for $\bar{x}$ = $UCL_{\bar{x}} = \bar{\bar{x}} + A_2\bar{R}$
Lower Control Limit for $\bar{x}$ = $LCL_{\bar{x}} = \bar{\bar{x}} - A_2\bar{R}$
Upper Control Limit for R = $UCL_R = D_4\bar{R}$
Lower Control Limit for R = $LCL_R = D_3\bar{R}$

Source: E. L. Grant, *Statistical Quality Control*, 3rd ed. (New York: McGraw-Hill Book Co., Inc., 1964), p. 562. All factors in this table are based on the Normal distribution.

tain times and slow at other times to compensate. Such performance should create a pattern of instability that is likely to be detected on the R chart and not on the $\bar{x}$ chart.

A variety of change combinations can occur when *sporadic* elements enter and leave the system in some unknown fashion. These assignable causes are more difficult to detect than the sustained types that were discussed above. Other types of changes can also occur. For example, a gradual shift in the mean. Tool wear could account for such *trend* shifts. Worker carelessness can produce the kind of sporadic behavior in which both limits may be repeatedly violated. Runs will appear for a variety of reasons and can usually be associated with trend factors, such as tool or gauge wear. It should be noted that the process is not always the guilty party. The inspectors and/or their tools might account for a signal of instability. To assist management, the entire relevant system must be isolated so that meaningful process conclusions can be drawn.[20]

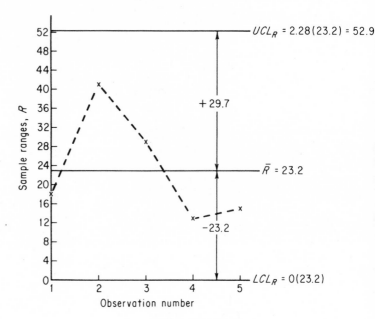

Figure 13.19

Control chart for range variable, R—data given in Table 13.1. [D_3 factor for lower control limit (when $n = 4$) = 0.00. D_4 factor for upper control limit (when $n = 4$) = 2.28.]

The use of the $\bar{x}$ and the R chart is one of the most powerful methods available for monitoring the behavior of a process. It is likely that a newly established process will not be stable at the outset. It will require attention, refinement, and consideration before it can be brought into control. The process behavior must then be checked against the engineering specifications. The result will influence both the design of the process and the redesign of the output. Figure 13.19 indicates the way in which output tolerance limits and statistical process control limits might be related to each other. We have modified the control limits for Figure 13.20 so that they apply to the parent population. This modification was accomplished by means of the equation

---

[20] 100 per cent inspection does not provide such analytic assistance for the diagnosis of causes of change. The "zero-defects" programs, urged by many companies on their employees, should be interpreted in the light of control theory as being unobtainable goals set for psychological reasons rather than for strictly technological ones.

for the *standard error of the mean*. The tolerance limits do not require alteration because they already apply to the parent population distribution.

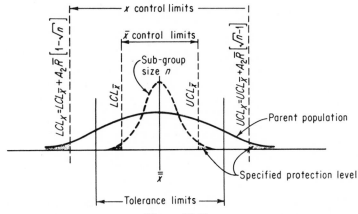

Figure 13.20

The relationship of tolerance limits and control limits. ($\bar{x}$ values can fall within tolerance limits although x values will fall outside with greater frequency than the specified level of protection.)

Monitoring Attributes

We shall now consider a less elaborate control device, called the *p*-chart. The *p*-chart is less expensive to utilize than the $\bar{x}$ and R charts because only a single chart is used, and the required computations are less onerous than those required for the $\bar{x}$ and R charts. The *p*-chart is called the control chart for *fraction defectives*. It is based on sampling by attributes, which was previously described. The key, as was the case for acceptance sampling, is the ability to define a defective. As might be suspected, because the *p*-chart is less expensive to use than control charts for variables, it is not as sensitive as the combination of the $\bar{x}$ and the R charts. It is not as good a diagnostic tool because it loses information; even the $\bar{x}$ chart used alone is a more powerful tool. However, the *p*-chart will indicate the existence of assignable causes when they occur, and it does this at a lower cost.

The data must be collected in the same way as was previously explained for monitoring variables. That is to say, homogeneous subgroups are chosen and a period of time is allowed to elapse between the subgroup observations. The same reasoning applies to subgroup sizes and between sample intervals. The sequential character of the control chart is as much in evidence as it was before, and the preservation of the order of observation is as crucial. Let us consider an example of a *p*-chart. Table 13.3 presents data for six consecutive

Table 13.3

| Subgroup Sample | Observations | | Computations | | | Plot |
	Number Inspected, n	Number Defective	σ	UCL $\bar{p} + \sigma$	LCL $\bar{p} - \sigma$	Fraction Defective
1	25	1	0.053	0.128	0.022	0.040
2	25	2	0.053	0.128	0.022	0.080
3	36	3	0.044	0.119	0.031	0.083
4	64	4	0.033	0.108	0.042	0.063
5	25	3	0.053	0.128	0.022	0.120
6	25	2	0.053	0.128	0.022	0.080
	$\overline{200}$	$\overline{15}$				

$$\bar{p} = \frac{15}{200} = 0.075$$

$$\sigma = \sqrt{\frac{\bar{p}(1 - \bar{p})}{n}} = \sqrt{\frac{(.075)(.925)}{n}} = 0.263 \sqrt{\frac{1}{n}}$$

subgroup samples. However, we note that the number of observations made for each subgroup varies in this particular case. It is still possible to construct appropriate control limits, but for the example we have chosen they will vary, as shown in Figure 13.21.

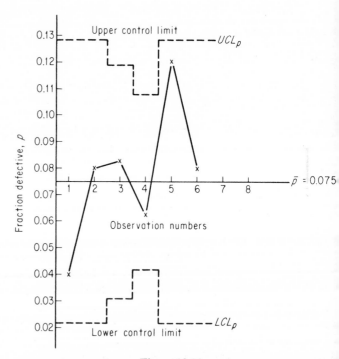

Figure 13.21

Control chart for attributes, p—data given in Table 13.3.

The number of observed defectives is recorded for each subgroup. The total number of inspected items is now divided *into* the total number of observed defectives. This gives the process average, $\bar{p}$. For our example, $\bar{p}$ is equal to 0.075. To determine the control limits we utilize the Binomial description of the *standard error of the mean*, that is,

$$\sigma = \sqrt{\frac{\bar{p}(1 - \bar{p})}{n}}$$

This is a function of the subgroup sample size n. Because the upper and lower control limits are specified in terms of σ, the limits vary as a function of n. For this example we have chosen 1σ limits.

The complete computations are shown in Table 13.3, and are represented in Figure 13.21. When the subgroup size is constant, then the computations are even further simplified. Only one upper and one lower control limit need be drawn on the p-chart. The advantage of illustrating variable subgroup sizes is that, in practice, it is not always possible to draw samples of constant size. Our sample values fall into the pattern of a stable process. Figure 13.22 illustrates a system in which a lack of control exists. We observe

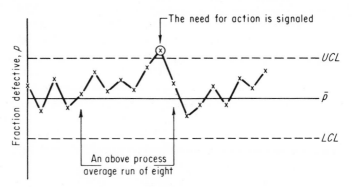

Figure 13.22

The control chart indicates that the system is unstable.

that a point has gone out of control. This usually is taken as a signal that something is awry and that corrective action should be taken. It is always possible, but improbable, that the "out" point occurred by chance. The run lends credence to the contention that a change is taking place and provides sufficient supporting evidence to the belief that our observation is not spurious.

For previous examples we chose 3σ and later 1σ limits. *The choice of $k\sigma$ control limits,* as to whether they are 1σ, 2σ, or 3σ, or some value in between, *is a management policy decision.* It is hard to defend a choice of one or another control limit, but the characteristics of the decision are such that if the penalty is high for not recognizing when the process is out of control, then it becomes more desirable to utilize *less than* 3σ limits. The distance between the limits decreases as the size of k decreases. This means that more events are likely to fall outside the control limits. The choice of k is a matter of balancing costs. Pertinent costs include the expense that occurs when a signal is received upon which *action* will be taken. The system must be examined in an attempt to track down assignable causes whether or not they exist in reality. An opposing cost is that of *inaction* when instability actually exists but is not recognized. Such a state of affairs can penalize the process heavily. With this guide in mind, the manager should choose those control-limit values that promise to balance the penalties.

Control-chart values must be regularly reviewed. This includes, $\bar{x}$, $\overline{R}$, and $\overline{p}$ for the fraction defectives chart. Changes detected in averages can, in turn, affect the σ value that is computed and utilized. In all control technology, it is essential to *review* and *update the system's parameters* so that decisions can be based on "what is" and not on "what was." Particularly, after an assignable cause has been detected and removed from the system, it is necessary to readjust the control parameters; sometimes another twenty-five subgroup observations are required before it is again possible to apply the control criterion.

Another control chart, occasionally used by industry, is called the *c*-chart. This control chart can be applied to situations where it is desirable to record the frequency of occurrence of a *number of different types of defects* that are found for a particular item. For example, we can examine telescope lenses for different kinds of defects and flaws. Then, we might list the observed frequency of the different kinds of defects that occur in every inspected unit. When using the *c*-chart, it is most usual to have a subgroup size of one— although this is not a requirement. It *is* necessary, however, that the defects of different types occur at random with respect to each other. Otherwise the underlying assumptions of the *c*-chart will not be met.

New applications for statistical control systems are constantly being developed. It is even possible to learn something about behavioral systems and worker productivity by means of *SQC*.[21] It is a requisite that basic processes should be demonstrated analytically to be stable, and if not, made so before synthesis is undertaken. Thus, the values of λ and μ should be known to be stable before they are utilized for stochastic line-balancing systems. Similarly, the parameters of inventory formulations or of sequencing models must be tested for stability before being employed. Otherwise, it is quite possible to derive a solution for a system that is shifting out from under you and that no longer exists at the time of implementation.

[21] See S. B. Littauer, "Technological Stability in Industrial Operations," *Transactions of the New York Academy of Sciences*, Series II, 13:2 (Dec., 1950), 67–72.

The Quality Control Decision Matrix

Shewhart control can be expressed in decision theory terms. Once this is recognized, we are able to construct a decision matrix where outcomes are substituted for environments. Further, to complete the transformation we measure a set of new outcomes p_{ij} that are the probabilities that the outcome O_j will occur when the strategy S_i is used. Thus, for five outcome levels and three strategies, we have:

		Outcomes				
		O_1	O_2	O_3	O_4	O_5
	S_1	p_{11}	p_{12}	p_{13}	p_{14}	p_{15}
Strategies	S_2	p_{21}	p_{22}	p_{23}	p_{24}	p_{25}
	S_3	p_{31}	p_{32}	p_{33}	p_{34}	p_{35}

In many instances, the environments are unknown. This must be the case when only chance causes produce variation in the system. We cannot enumerate the relevant environments that account for the fact that a milling machine produces a distribution of part sizes rather than an *exact* duplicate each time.

Because we cannot list all relevant environments, our decision matrix is based on the substitution of outcomes for environments. In the cells of the matrix we have entered the probability that a specific strategy will produce a given outcome. According to Shewhart, if the system is stable, we would expect these probabilities to remain unchanged. Frequently, the probabilities for any given strategy row would be described by a Normal distribution.

Let us take a specific case. Assume that a pipe is to be manufactured where the OD (outside diameter) is a critical factor. Further, we shall assume that any one of three different machines—M_1, M_2, M_3—can do this job. The outcomes range across the conceivable dimensions that each type of machine might produce when the job is properly set up to produce an OD of 5.04: for example, with M_1, a hand lathe; M_2, a turret lathe; and M_3, an automatic screw machine:

Measure of Outside Diameter (in Inches)							
5.01	5.02	5.03	5.04	5.05	5.06	5.07	EV
M_1	0.03	0.07	0.10	0.60	0.10	0.07	0.03	5.04
M_2	0.02	0.05	0.08	0.70	0.08	0.05	0.02	5.04
M_3	0.01	0.03	0.06	0.80	0.06	0.03	0.01	5.04

All machines produce the same expected value for the OD. But much greater control is available with M_3 than with M_2, and M_2 is better than M_1. (Control is greater when variability is less.) The expected OD value can be obtained for each strategy by multiplying the outcome probability by the outcome value (j) and then summing them. Thus: $EV_i = \Sigma_j\ p_{ij}O_j$; ($i = 1, 2, 3$). Assuming that these probability distributions are stable and that the probability estimates are believable, then it is required that we use the expected value criterion. This was previously discussed in Chapter 3, where it was explained that the only criterion for reaching decisions under conditions of risk was the expected value.

Let us consider a different example for the purpose of illustrating some additional points about quality management.

	\multicolumn{6}{c}{(*pH*) Outcomes}
	5.8	5.9	6.0	6.1	6.2	EV
S_1	0.0	0.2	0.6	0.2	0.0	6.00
S_2	0.2	0.2	0.2	0.2	0.2	6.00
S_3	0.1	0.3	0.2	0.3	0.1	6.00
S_4	0.1	0.2	0.3	0.2	0.2	6.02

Four different processes are available for producing a soft drink. The pH[22] is to be kept as close to 6.0 as possible. A series of experiments and tests is run, and the results have been organized in a control matrix form. We observe that strategies one, two, and three have the same expected values. Again, their distributions are quite dissimilar. Strategy four has a higher expected value than is desired. Strategy three produces a bimodal distribution.[23] This frequently indicates that at least one assignable cause of variation exists. Such cause enters and leaves the system from time to time, giving rise to two kinds of happenings and bimodality. Generally, the Shewhart criterion would produce evidence of the fact that the S_3 strategy does not conform to a stable system.

We observe that the expected value is not a sufficient guide. The utility obtained from these outcomes gets progressively worse as we move further away—in either direction—from the objective value of 6.0. But, given equal expected values, we will always prefer a process that has minimum variance. So quality is a function of the expected value's closeness to the objective value and the strategy's performance variance as well.

Let us use the measure R_i to determine the degree of control for each strategy.[24]

---

[22] The symbol pH is commonly used in expressing hydrogen ion concentration. The neutral point is pH 7. Above 7 alkalinity increases; below 7 acidity increases.

[23] Two peaks of maximum probability occur with a valley in between, unlike the Normal or the Poisson distributions that are unimodal.

[24] This measure is equivalent to the redundancy measure of information theory.

$$R_i = \frac{\log N + \sum_j p_{ij} \log p_{ij}}{\log N}; \quad i = 1, 2, 3 \ldots$$

N equals the number of outcome classes and the p_{ij}'s are the matrix entries previously described. The most direct explanation of this formula can be had by example. Returning to the pH example, we get:

$$R_1 = \frac{\log 5 + 0 + 0.2 \log 0.2 + 0.6 \log 0.6 + 0.2 \log 0.2 + 0}{\log 5} = 0.41$$

$$R_2 = \frac{\log 5 + 5(0.2) \log 0.2}{\log 5} = 0.00$$

$$R_3 = \frac{\log 5 + 2(0.1) \log 0.1 + 2(0.3) \log 0.3 + 0.2 \log 0.2}{\log 5} = 0.06$$

$$R_4 = \frac{\log 5 + 0.1 \log 0.1 + 3(0.2) \log 0.2 + 0.3 \log 0.3}{\log 5} = 0.03$$

The measure that we have used will always be equal to 0.00 when all possible outcomes are equally likely. This is equivalent to a chaotic system with no organization and, therefore, no control. The second strategy is like this, and it would never be used if there were another strategy that yielded the same expected value but a better control measure. The first strategy produces the highest control measure, $R_1 = 0.41$, though it may not be as high as we might like. Thus, if a new strategy were found that produced the outcome 6.00 with 100 per cent certainty, it would have a control measure $R = 1.00$, or perfect control.

We should note that the scale divisions used will directly influence the control measure. If we were able to measure pH only to the closest 0.5, then we would have quite a different control matrix, namely:

	5.5	6.0	6.5
S_1	0.000	1.000	0.000
S_2	0.000	1.000	0.000
S_3	0.000	1.000	0.000
S_4	0.000	1.000	0.000

Perfect control would be indicated for all four strategies. The expected values would also be identical. This is an important point. Management, to be effective, must understand the measurement problem that underlies all decision making and control. Knowledge of the process leads to the specification of appropriate measuring instruments and scale divisions. If *too-fine* vernier scales are employed, then lack of control will frequently appear, requiring time and attention when such emphasis is unwarranted. Conversely, *too-crude* scales will make a situation appear to be invariant to the strategic alternatives when, in fact, the degree of attainment of the system's objectives will be affected.

Assuming proper measurement and scaling, the production manager must decide for himself what to do when, for example, the objective is 6.00 and two strategies exist such that:

	Outcome	Control Measure
S_1	5.08	0.92
S_2	6.00	0.20

We can suppose that a function[25] such as

$$(\Delta EV_i)^\alpha/(R_i)^\beta = V_i$$

exists. ΔEV_i is the measured deviation of the expected value from the quality objective; R_i is the control measure for the ith strategy[26] α and β are weights that describe the relative importance of deviation from objective (α) and degree of control that can be exercised (β). Assuming that we could estimate α and β, then we would choose the strategy that has the lowest value of V_i. For our example, assuming that $\alpha = 2$ and $\beta = -1$, we select V_2.

$$V_1 = \frac{(6.00 - 5.08)^2}{(0.92)} = 0.92; \quad V_2 = \frac{\epsilon}{(0.20)} = 5\epsilon$$

Since ϵ is very small, 5ϵ is also negligible.

PROBLEMS

1. Omega Electronics is a small company that manufactures a vacuum tube that is highly resistant to vibration and heat. Only destructive testing can be used to check the acceptability of a tube. Each tube is costly. The application of the tube is such that a failure endangers many lives. What inspection procedure would you use?

2. The Yukon Company requires a destructive test to determine the quality of the firecrackers that it manufactures. Assume that five giant firecrackers compose a lot. The company tests one and ships four, if the

---

[25] In the next chapter, we shall again encounter such a function. It should be noted that the inventory formulation $AN = K$ also could have been written, $A^\alpha N^{-\beta} = K$ where $\alpha = 1$, $\beta = -1$. There is a great deal more generality for such functions than might be supposed.

[26] We require that $\Delta EV_i > 0$ and $R_i > 0$. This can be accomplished by substituting $(\Delta EV_i + \epsilon)$ and $(R_i + \epsilon)$, ϵ being very small, when $\Delta EV_i = 0$ or $R_i = 0$.

test is successful. If the test is not successful, the remaining four are sold as seconds.

(a) Specify the characteristics of this single sampling plan and derive the OC curve.

(b) What do you think of this plan?

3. Can quality control exist without feedback? How about quantity control? Explain your answer.

4. A shampoo manufacturer specifies that the contents of a bottle of shampoo should weigh 6 ± 0.10 ounces net. A statistical quality control operation is established and the following data are obtained:

Sample Number				
1	6.06	6.20	6.04	6.10
2	6.10	5.95	5.98	6.05
3	6.03	5.90	5.95	6.00
4	6.03	6.05	6.10	5.94
5	6.12	6.40	6.20	6.00

(a) Construct an $\bar{x}$ chart based on these five samples.

(b) Construct an R chart based on these five samples.

(c) What points, if any, have gone out of control?

(d) Comment on your results and briefly discuss the role of SQC in operations management. Include such factors as management's choice of tolerance limits, subgroup size, and sample size.

5. A food processor specified that the contents of a jar of jam should weigh 14 ± 0.10 ounces net. A statistical quality control operation is set up, and the following data are obtained:

Sample Number				
1	14.02	14.04	14.08	14.06
2	14.10	14.24	14.00	14.90
3	14.80	14.75	14.70	14.51
4	14.59	14.90	14.01	14.02
5	14.96	14.26	14.81	14.17
6	14.40	14.83	14.68	14.93
7	14.86	14.32	14.90	14.04
8	14.56	14.96	14.69	14.63
9	14.85	14.71	14.05	14.91
10	14.75	14.19	14.05	14.09

(a) Construct an $\bar{x}$ chart based on these ten samples.

(b) Construct an R chart based on these ten samples.

(c) What points, if any, have gone out of control?

(d) What reasons could be given for the appearance of an assignable cause at some time in the future?

(e) What can be surmised from the shapes of the curves on these charts?

6. On p. 401, a control matrix is presented to represent the performance of three different machines, viz., a hand lathe, a turret lathe, and an automatic screw machine. All three machines assure the same expected value for the OD of a pipe that is to be made. Use these data to determine the degree of control that can be obtained with each machine. Comment on your results.

The investment in plant and equipment is generally so large that it is surprising how little effort has been spent on rationalizing facility management. Surprising, that is, until one realizes how resistant these major decision areas are to normative modeling and quantitative description. Evaluatory approaches that measure return on investment (ROI) are among the most advanced techniques in use. Still, some structural approaches have been developed, and we will discuss these here. First, we will treat the plant location problem, then the plant layout problem, and finally, the facilities maintenance problem.

Facilities

Management 14

The foundation underlying all operations decisions has been set up by design decisions. But how do these design decisions get made? For example, why is the company making the particular products that it produces? Changes in product-line, we have previously discussed (pp. 117–120), but it is also clear that an organization develops experience along certain lines and its management and workers have a natural tendency to do what they understand. The "human" component of decision making always is more in evidence as the problems being studied become more global and less amenable to any analysis that cannot cope with the requirement for total, large system synthesis.

Plant Location

It isn't that management doesn't study the plant location problem, carefully and in detail. It is just that too many factors operate to permit plant location decisions to be made by a formal model. The decision is a major commitment; reversal can only be accomplished under severe and sometimes catastrophic penalty. So, an important step is classification of the right information. Here are some of the factors to consider:

1. *Location Dependent Upon the Nature of the Process Inputs.* This is typically the case where bulky or heavy raw materials are required for the production process. As a general rule, analytic-type industries (see p. 144) are likely to locate near the source of their materials. In addition to materials that are process inputs, we also have labor inputs, which are discussed in Chapter 15. Labor costs are one of the most important factors in the determination of a suitable plant location for certain labor-heavy industries. Service industries are particularly sensitive to this factor. Companies that employ large labor forces have been known to change their locations to take advantage of a lower wage scale. This motive impelled New England textile firms to close up shop in the North and move South. However, with increasing mechanization, the labor problem has been alleviated to an extent for all

industries. There has also been a reduction in differential wage rates by regions of the country. Taken together, these changes have reduced the dependency of the location decision on the cost of labor.[1]

In addition to the advantage of lower wage rates for similar skills, there are more subtle costs of labor. Foremost is the availability of manpower and, in particular, of various skill levels within a particular region. Movement from a high skill, high wage rate area to a low skill, low wage rate area can only be accomplished when sufficient process mechanization is achieved. The computer has altered the skill requirements and availabilities of white collar functions. Technological progress and computer data processing permit a company to trade-off higher machine investments for lower wages and for less manpower and skill. A trade-off potential is created between manpower and machine power, which tends to make the location decision less dependent on the expense of both indirect and direct labor. Labor cost evaluation also includes consideration of turnover rates, absenteeism, and employee reliability, as well as costs of hiring and training workers. These considerations were essential in Chapter 9 where aggregate scheduling was treated. Different schedules will arise according to the nature of the costs we have just discussed. So we see that the plant location (system's design-type problem) interacts specifically with the management of operations. The size of a labor market and the attitudes of labor and labor unions can also figure heavily in some plant location decisions. These considerations are likely to affect location decisions with respect to urban labor markets as compared to suburban and rural markets. From various sources, demographic information by areas— such as population size, education, and income—can be pooled with industrial data concerning hourly earnings, right-to-work laws, and so forth. Such a data base, at least, allows the manager to be a well-informed decision-maker.

2. *Location Dependent Upon the Process Outputs.*   The location of the company's markets can be significant under certain circumstances, e.g., characteristic of service industries. Because the facility specializes in service, it is only reasonable that locations should be selected near those individuals who require the service. Synthetic industries (p. 143) are frequently oriented in terms of locating near the market, because many raw materials must be gathered together from diverse locations and assembled into single units.

3. *Location Dependent Upon Process Requirements.*   Many processes require special environments. When the technology of the process requires large amounts of water, then only a location where such water resources are available can be considered. Another common process requirement concerns

---

[1] International wage differentials present something of an illusion. Tariffs, cost of materials, international exchange rates, taxes, and other factors tend to balance out what might otherwise appear to be substantial advantages.

the need for substantial amounts of power. There are not too many locations that could meet an extremely heavy demand. Accordingly, the size of the location problem is immediately cut down. Certain processes pollute the environment. For such cases, both urban and suburban locations are automatically ruled out. Sometimes, a process is responsive to factors such as temperature, humidity, high salinity, and weather conditions in general. An additonal aspect of weather that is frequently overlooked can be noted. If a process requires highly skilled individuals to perform certain operations, then absenteeism can be a significant detrimental factor. For such cases, it might be desirable to locate in a region where the common cold would be a less virile destroyer of time. Circumstances can occur where process requirements with respect to environment can override all other considerations.

4. *Location Dependent Upon Personal Preferences.*   Occasionally, the entrepreneurs or chief executives prefer a given location for entirely personal reasons. Not infrequently, having decided to relocate an operating facility, strong monetary incentives must be used to encourage company personnel to relocate with the company. The cost of moving personnel and inducing them to do so must be balanced against the costs of building a new group with the same level of skills and company loyalty in the new location. Often, the preferences of the firm's top executives to remain where they are will take precedence over considerations that otherwise might be considered more important.

5. *Location Dependent Upon Tax and Legal Factors.*   Because of severe taxes on the corporation, as well as personal income taxes, sales taxes, etc., locations that are desirable with respect to other variables will be bypassed. In fact, a favorable local tax structure provides such basic motivation that many decisions are made to locate a new plant or to relocate a going operation solely for this reason. In addition to tax advantages, communities attempt to attract industries by providing industrial parks or properly zoned land at advantageous rates. Although some communities desire any kind of industrial growth, most attempt to attract only certain types of industries. Others have been reluctant and even hostile toward any industrial development.

6. *Location Dependent Upon Site and Plant Availabilities.*   There is a complex "deferred choice" problem that exists. At any point in time there is a list of available sites. Some sites already have a plant built on them that can either be purchased or rented. Other sites require building. Assume that each site could be evaluated with a single measure and that a ranked order list of such measures is developed. Figure 14.1 illustrates a list, where λ_{E_k} is the arrival rate of new list entries of quality E_k.

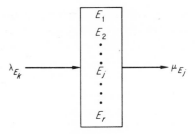

Figure 14.1

The list also suffers departures, i.e., μ_{E_i}. Then the question is: When is E_1 good enough so that it can be chosen as a location? If the manager waits, his best choice may disappear; if he doesn't wait, the day after he commits the company to a new location, a preferred one may appear. The problem has striking similarities to the dynamic programming formulation of the commodity buying situation described on pp. 331–333. In this case, the rank order of the evaluation measure is substituted for the commodity price, and similar probabilistic information must be collected.

The criterion of quality, E_j, is complex and difficult to conceive, let alone measure. The manager must be able to define the type of shelter that is needed to house the operations facility and the issues involved in making a plant location decision. Sometimes these matters are related—and sometimes they are not. Each process requires its own kind of protection. An oil refinery can be exposed to the elements. An automobile factory must be enclosed to protect equipment and in-process inventories that would be vulnerable to weather. When renting, building, or buying, a great many factors must be considered. Expert assistance from architects and building engineers should be obtained to insure the proper evaluation of an existing structure or in order to plan a new structure. Among the elements to be considered are:

1. *Is there enough floor space?*

2. *Is the space open with wide bays so that machines, men, and materials handling equipment can be effectively arranged and utilized?*

3. *How many stories are there?*   Early factories were multistoried. With the development of improved transportation, particularly the automobile, plants could be located outside the central city on less expensive land. The one-story building followed from this. It is usually preferred unless sufficient reasons can be found to justify multistory buildings that are more expensive to construct. In certain industries, gravity feed conveyers are used. In such cases, multiple storied buildings are likely to be preferred.

4. *What kind of roof is used?*   This was an important question at one time, not any longer. Roof shapes permit a degree of control over illumination,

temperature, and ventilation,[2] but technological advances have reduced the significance of roof design with respect to these factors. On the other hand, if the process requires hoists and cranes, then high roofs and ceilings remain a relevant constraint.

5. *What type of construction should be used?*   The answer given will in large measure determine the feasibility of converting an old building to conform to a new set of specifications. This answer will be the major determinant of both new construction costs and the speed of construction. Even insurance rates will be dependent upon the type of construction that is used. Building codes must be observed. Industrial parks usually require a degree of conformity with respect to construction and appearance.

6. *What kind of maintenance requirements will there be?*   Older buildings have greater costs for maintaining the structure. The resale value of a structure may be an important determinant. In general, *special purpose buildings* designed for a unique process make special structural demands and create a lower resale value than *general purpose buildings*. The latter have process requirements that are not unique but fit a pattern that is generally acceptable for many different kinds of processes.

7. *Should we rent, buy, or build?*   The answer to this question depends upon what is available. If a suitable building exists, then its cost can be compared with costs that would be incurred if a new building were constructed. Rent or buy alternatives depend upon what is offered, i.e., the list problem previously discussed. If no suitable structure exists, then an appropriate facility must be constructed. Airline terminals are built for this reason. In the communications field, radio and TV stations are built to specifications. Power generating plants are seldom found in unused, rentable condition. So, clearly, when there is nothing available to meet the need, it must be built. On the other hand, when the process requirements are not unique, many suitable facilities usually can be found. This would apply to office space which is commonly rented. *Job shop* operations generally can be suitably located in a variety of types of plants that can be rented and/or purchased. *Flow shop* operations are not that flexible. The problem of buying, renting, or building should be resolved by means of a comparison of costs based on present worth analysis. To accomplish this we make use of the discounting procedures that were explained on pp. 105–113.

8. *What conveniences should the building have?*   There must be adequate rest rooms. If the building is located at a distance from the city, it might be

---

[2] For example, the saw-tooth roof construction was extensively used to provide even illumination of work spaces; irrigation of roof tops was used for temperature control.

essential to provide a parking lot as well as cafeteria facilities. Many companies require a medical room or a plant hospital on the premises. In some instances an auditorium is included in the plans. In a different sense, railroad sidings or ship docking facilities may be of major importance. If this is the case, the construction plan must take such factors into account.

9. *What appearance should the building have?* Different architectural styles appear at different points in time. Attitudes and policies of management will strongly influence these decisions. Some executives consider appearance to be a frill whereas others take it so seriously that they insist on illumination of the building at night and the provision for an impressive view from the air. There is no question that a beautiful building increases employee pride in their company and can influence the consumer's evaluation of the company. On the other hand, how these truisms affect productivity and profit is reserved for personal judgment at the moment.

Location Cost Analysis

A refinery can be located at the oil fields close to its raw material sources. It could also be located adjacent to its market. An automobile factory can be located close to its source of process inputs. The heavy manufacturing operations can be separated from the required assembly operations. Then, the latter can be located close to the markets that desire the process outputs. Although the problem is complex, we know that there is some optimal locational arrangement of facilities. The question is: How do we go about determining this optimal arrangement? We have discussed many variables that affect plant location decisions. It is unreasonable to attempt to consider all such factors that might be relevant in one case or another. However, let us examine the location problem in another light. *A location decision represents an attempt to minimize costs,* including opportunity costs, for example, the cost of staying put and not moving to a new location. The location investigation has a cost all its own that should be considered before undertaking a location analysis.

The plant location problem is of the long-term, nonrepetitive type. The many relevant risk factors are seldom able to be analyzed properly. The plant location decision requires a sizable investment and creates heavy sunk costs. It involves other costs as well. Let us consider two kinds of fundamental cost factors; namely, tangible costs and intangible costs. The latter are distinguished by the fact that it is almost impossible to *measure* them. They can only be judged intuitively. Although it is difficult to measure many of the tangible costs; nevertheless, to some extent, they can all be measured. Among the tangible costs are:

1. The cost of land;
2. The cost of renting, buying, or building;

3. Transportation costs of raw materials and fuels;
4. Transportation costs of moving finished goods to the market;
5. Power and water costs;
6. The cost of taxes and insurance;
7. Labor costs;
8. The cost of moving, including production stoppage costs incurred during relocation.

In determining an optimal location, it is the significance of intangible costs that places the most severe burden on the manager. Let us consider a few of these.

1. *Competition for labor* within a restricted labor market introduces a cost that changes over time. It will vary as a function of the attractiveness of a particular region for all industries. The situation is dynamic. When an attractive general location exists, a number of companies begin to move to this area in order to take advantage of its opportunities. Saturation must occur, and at some point competition for the available labor resources can become significant; paradise is transformed to limbo.

2. *Union attitudes* are exceedingly important but difficult to evaluate. It is seldom possible to do more than intuitively assess such conditions. Militant unions develop reputations that are widely known. But a change of leadership or policy within the union can significantly alter the stereotype. Shifts in the economy and changes in the welfare and fortune of a particular industry will bring about rapid shifts in union attitudes.

3. *Community attitudes* are not measurable. Small conclaves of resistance to industrial developments must not be overlooked, particularly when such groups are led by a few individuals who are influential members of the community. It is possible to document specific instances where companies have fully developed plans to move into a new community only to discover that a strong and militant group exists that is prepared to resist the incursion. Because of its investment in the decision that has been made, and because some executives become outraged at being pariahs, some companies will occasionally attempt to fight this battle. Even if the company legally succeeds in installing itself, the enmity that has been aroused will, in all likelihood, prove to be a lasting penalty.

4. *Local and state ordinances* must be taken into account. There is no direct way to attach a cost to such rulings. Knowledgeable legal assistance is required to interpret the situation so that it can be evaluated. Each location possibility poses its own economic considerations in terms of such costs as workmen's compensation payments, unemployment insurance, waste disposal laws, pollution and smoke control requirements, noise abatement rules, and other nuisance regulations.

5. *The costs of weather* and other natural phenomena should not be overlooked. Such events as hurricanes, earthquakes, and floods can produce

heavy penalties. These are acts of nature but, at the same time, they are less unexpected in certain areas than in others. Companies locating in the North must be prepared to pay for heating equipment and fuel bills. Industries locating in the South may require air-conditioning expenses. Other costs related to weather concern the maintenance of plant and the deterioration of equipment.

How can all these factors be related? Assuming that we could measure all the costs, we might then write an equation of the general form:

Total costs $= f$(tangible, intangible, and opportunity cost factors)

and we would minimize the equation. All matters that might interact with the location decision such as plant layout, output productivity and costs, maintenance and machine replacement costs, market demand, transportation costs, and competitive actions would be included. Because we can't do this, the method outlined in the next section at least offers an approach.

Facility Selection Using Dimensional Analysis

Decisions related to intangible cost systems present great difficulties. Several means of resolving these problems can be suggested.

1. Entirely subjective decisions can be made.
2. A quasi-objective approach can be utilized, which requires that *preference measures* be stated for various factors that describe different aspects of the system's performance. Weights or index numbers can be used to express preference. These measures are then compared in some objective manner.
3. Methods of decision making under uncertainty can be used (see pp. 69–73).

The major difficulty in evaluating alternative plant and facility designs is the fact that conflicting objectives having quite different dimensions must be somehow combined to provide a reasonable basis for evaluation. Let us develop an example so that we can view this kind of problem in specific terms.

Assume that in searching for a new plant location, two plans have been developed. (The discussion could easily include many more of the factors we have previously discussed without changing, in any way, the significance of what we are about to say.) Let plan 1 specify building a plant in Denver, while plan 2 specifies building a plant in Atlanta. The proposals might have been *hypothetically* evaluated as shown in Table 14.1.

Table 14.1

Outcomes	Plan 1	Plan 2	Weight[3]
Building costs and equipment costs—yearly depreciated value	$500,000	$300,000	4
Taxes (per year)	$ 50,000	$ 20,000	4
Power cost (per year)	$ 20,000	$ 30,000	4
Community attitude	1	2	1
Product quality as a function of worker morale and skill	2	3	5
Flexibility to adapt to situations that are likely to occur	1	6	3

Dollars must be added together. Using discounting (pp. 107–108), the dollar expenses are made to apply to the same period of time. Also, companies will have different measures for the relative importance of dollars, depending upon their assets. If such factors as community attitude, product quality, and flexibility could be associated with a dollar value, there would not be a dimensional problem to resolve. However, it must be recognized that these latter elements represent *intangible costs*. The attempt to estimate such costs would prove arduous with little conviction that the results are satisfactory. On the other hand, it is possible for the manager to rank the relative merits of the two plans for each intangible factor.

The example utilizes a scale from one to ten, where the value of one represents the "best possible" result and the value of ten would be the least desirable. This is because the table is written in terms of costs. (The value ten would be optimal if the table had been constructed in terms of profit.) Thus, with respect to community attitude, plan 1 is preferred to plan 2 although, on the whole, both of them seem to be considered desirable. With respect to flexibility, plan 2 is apparently quite inferior to plan 1. Let us turn to the third column in the table—headed "Weight." These weighting factors (or index numbers) represent the relative importances of the set of outcome objectives that are being analyzed. According to the weights that have been assigned, product quality is the most important consideration whereas community attitude is least important. Flexibility is rated as being slightly more important than costs. This arrangement of weighting values would undoubtedly change if the company's capitalization were altered or if the planning objectives were modified. The numbers that we have used represent assignments for a particular set of individuals and circumstances.

Various approaches can be used for obtaining the weights. These include:

1. Using the estimates of that individual who is responsible for this decision.
2. Using an average value, obtained by pooling the opinions of a number of individuals who have different responsibilities with respect to the project.

---

[3] The larger the weight the more important the dimension is considered to be, relative to the other dimensions.

3. Employing an informal blending of the opinions of a number of individuals to develop a set of estimates and weights that are agreeable to all concerned parties.

A noteworthy characteristic of the third approach is that it creates an opportunity for the project participants to *communicate* with each other about the facility decision.

First, with respect to which factors are likely to be critical determinants of the decision.

Second, concerning the estimates for each of the outcomes, a set of which must be supplied for each of the alternative plans.

Third, the weighting factors that indicate the relative importance in each individual's mind for the critical factors required to evaluate the system.

A multiplication method of evaluating alternatives by means of weighting factors is frequently used.[4]

The approach we will employ, which is particularly suitable for dealing with intangible factors, requires that preference be expressed as the products of the outcomes raised to powers for each plan. We can then compare the plans in ratio with each other. This is:

$$R = \frac{\text{Preference for plan 1}}{\text{Preference for plan 2}}$$

$$= \left(\frac{O_{11}}{O_{21}}\right)^{w_1} \left(\frac{O_{12}}{O_{22}}\right)^{w_2} (\cdots) \left(\frac{O_{1j}}{O_{2j}}\right)^{w_i} (\cdots) \left(\frac{O_{1n}}{O_{2n}}\right)^{w_n}$$

where estimates are supplied to describe the values of the various outcomes that each plan will produce. For the ith alternative we would have O_{i1}, O_{i2}, $\ldots$, O_{ij}, $\ldots$, O_{in}. Each outcome objective is then weighted for its relative importance. Let us call the weighting factors w_1, w_2, $\ldots$, w_j, $\ldots$, w_n. It will be noted that the ratio R is a pure number that has no dimensional involvement.[5] Of course, this would be no advantage in a case where evaluation in terms of a single dimension was possible so that distance measures would also be available to discriminate between the plans.

Let us return to the numerical example. All costs are based on a one-year period, so we add them together yielding \$570,000 and \$350,000, respectively, for plans 1 and 2. Accordingly,

[4] See, for example, the use of this method to evaluate alternative aircraft designs as used by a major aircraft manufacturer, L. Ivan Epstein, "A Proposed Measure for Determining the Value of a Design," *The Journal of the Operations Research Society of America*, 5: 2 (April, 1957), 297–99. Also, C. Radhakrishna Rao, *Advanced Statistical Methods in Biometric Research* (New York: John Wiley & Sons, Inc., 1952), p. 103; also, see Walter R. Stahl, "Similarity and Dimensional Methods in Biology," *Science*, 137: 20 (July, 1962), 205–12, and P. W. Bridgman, *Dimensional Analysis* (New Haven: Yale University Press, 1922). This is also available in paperbound edition, 1963.

[5] Thus, for example, $\dfrac{(x\text{'s \$})^{w_1}(x\text{'s quality})^{w_2}}{(y\text{'s \$})^{w_1}(y\text{'s quality})^{w_2}}$ = pure number.

$$R = \frac{\text{Preference for plan 1}}{\text{Preference for plan 2}} = \left(\frac{570,000}{350,000}\right)^4 \left(\frac{1}{2}\right)^1 \left(\frac{2}{3}\right)^5 \left(\frac{1}{6}\right)^3 = 0.002$$

We will choose plan 1 because the ratio is less than one. That is, the costs in the denominator are greater than the costs in the numerator. Accordingly, we choose the plan in the numerator. The method of evaluation that we have employed is useful for a wide range of project-type decisions. It would be appropriate for product design decisions, process design decisions, equipment selection, and plant location plans. When we find that one location factor dominates all others, special methods can be used. The next section considers such a situation. In general, however, plant selection and location involve many variables. Problem resolution is begun by eliminating possibilities that violate initial constraints, thereby reducing the number of real alternatives to manageable proportions.

Locating Multiple Facilities

When transportation costs dominate the plant location problem (either of raw materials to the plant or of finished goods from the plant to warehouses), then a relatively straightforward model exists for analyzing this situation. The problem we are tackling is trivial if only one market and one raw material source exists. This is illustrated in Figure 14.2.

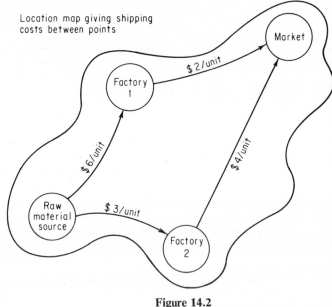

Figure 14.2

Plant location problem—factory 1 or factory 2? (Where only one market and one raw material source exists.)

The raw materials required for one unit would cost $6.00 if shipped to factory 1, called F_1. The cost is $3.00 if shipped to factory 2, called F_2. On the other hand, the cost of shipping a finished unit to the market from F_1 is $2.00; from F_2 it is $4.00. Total transportation costs for the factory location F_1 are $8.00 per unit. This is one dollar more than total transport costs for F_2. Therefore, we would choose F_2—if transportation costs are the dominating factor with respect to the choice of location. Now, let us complicate the problem by creating two markets and by allowing the possibility of multiple facilities. Figure 14.3 illustrates this situation, which fits the pattern of a very

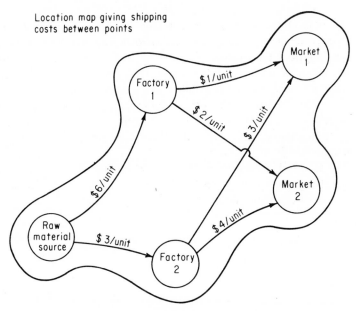

Location map giving shipping costs between points

Figure 14.3

Plant location problem—factory 1, factory 2, or both? (Where two markets and one raw material source exist.)

simple distribution problem. It can be resolved by means of the transportation algorithm.[6] Therefore, of course, the problem can also be solved by means of linear programming. (If alternative raw material sources existed as well as alternative markets, or if shipments between plants could play an important role, then the transshipment form of network model can be used.[7])

[6] The algorithm was previously described for the resolution of machine loading and aggregate scheduling problems, see pp. 278–287, 240–248, respectively.
[7] See Harvey M. Wagner, *Principles of Management Science* (Englewood Cliffs, N.J.: Prentice-Hall, Inc., 1970), pp. 140–45.

Using the costs specified in Figure 14.3, we can prepare a transportation matrix, as follows:

Finished Goods Transport Costs

Raw Material Transport Costs	Factory	M_1	M_2	Supply
$6	F_1	$1/unit	$2/unit	90 units/day
$3	F_2	$3/unit	$4/unit	90 units/day
Demand		40 units/day	40 units/day	

We have added the description of *supply* and *demand*. In other words, each market demands forty units per day to be shipped from either F_1 or F_2 or a combination. Both factories would be designed to have a maximum productive capacity of ninety units per day. Which location should be chosen for our factory? We allow the possibility of choosing both.

First, we note that total daily supply, given both plants, exceeds total daily demand by one hundred units, assuming that the two factories operate at full capacity. To correct the theoretical imbalance between supply and demand we create a dummy market M_D to absorb one hundred units per day. The M_D market does not really exist. Whichever factory is assigned the job of supplying the dummy market is, in effect, eliminated as a location. For example, a possible shipment pattern might be:

Factory	Market M_1	M_2	M_D	Supply
F_1			90	90
F_2	40	40	10	90
Demand	40	40	100	180

It will be found that this allocation is the optimal one. Therefore, we interpret the matrix as stating that F_2 is the best location and that F_1 should be eliminated because it has been assigned the task of supplying the dummy market, which doesn't exist. We also note that the excess capacity of F_2 has been allocated to the dummy, which is as it should be.

The transportation procedure (see pp. 240–247) consists of evaluating the difference in costs that would result from alternative shipping patterns. If a savings could be made by shifting a unit, then we would put as many units as possible into the preferred shipment pattern. The best solution will result in minimum total transportation costs, and we will have tested to find out if there is any better arrangement. For the previous example, the matrix of total transportation costs would be determined as follows:

Total Transport Costs per Unit
Market

Factory	M_1	M_2	M_D
F_1	$6 + 1 = \$7$	$6 + 2 = \$8$	$\$0$
F_2	$3 + 3 = \$6$	$3 + 4 = \$7$	$\$0$

The raw material transportation costs have been added to the finished goods transportation costs. Any shipments to the dummy market cost $0 because it doesn't exist.

Now, let us consider a more elaborate example.

		Market		
Factory	M_1	M_2	M_D	Supply
F_1	\$7/unit	\$8/unit	\$0/unit	50 units/day
F_2	\$6/unit	\$7/unit	\$0/unit	90 units/day
F_3	\$8/unit	\$10/unit	\$0/unit	90 units/day
Demand	40 units per day	40 units per day	150 units per day	230 units per day

The cost entries in the matrix are total transportation costs per unit. The company has an actual *operating factory*, F_1, which has a maximum capacity of fifty units per day. The demand for the product is greater than the supply, viz., eighty units per day. The locations F_2 and F_3 are under serious consideration. Whichever is chosen, it has been decided to install a new unit with a production capacity of ninety units per day. As before, transportation costs dominate the plant location decision. We make a first allocation, using the Northwest Corner Method.[8]

		Market		
Factory	M_1	M_2	M_D	Supply
F_1	40	10		50
F_2		30	60	90
F_3			90	90
Demand	40	40	150	230

We must now test to find out whether a cost reduction can be achieved. There are four possible changes that could be made.

1. We could shift ten units from F_1, M_2 to F_1, M_D. Thus:

[8] In this case, the number of shipments used should never exceed $N + M - 1$, where: $N + M - 1 =$ the number of markets (N) + the number of factories $(M) - 1 = 3 + 3 - 1 = 5$.

| Factory | Market | | | Supply |
	M_1	M_2	M_D	
F_1	40		10	50
F_2		40	50	90
F_3			90	90
Demand	40	40	150	230

If more than ten units were shifted, this would create a negative shipment at the intersection of F_1, M_2, which is a situation that could not be tolerated. Similar restrictions exist with respect to other changes.

2. We can shift thirty units from F_2, M_2 to F_2, M_1.
3. We can shift thirty units from F_2, M_2 to F_3, M_1.
4. We can shift thirty units from F_2, M_2 to F_3, M_2.

Let us evaluate the marginal change in cost that will result from shipping one unit from F_1 to M_D.

1. Ship one unit from F_1 to M_D: $+\$0$
2. Ship one less unit from F_1 to M_2: $-\$8$
3. Ship one more unit from F_2 to M_2: $+\$7$
4. Ship one less unit from F_2 to M_D: $-\$0$
   Total $\overline{-\$1}$

The total cost can be reduced one dollar by making this change. Each of ten units can be shipped for \$1.00 less per unit. This is a total cost reduction of \$10.00. Proceeding in the same fashion we find:

1. Shipping one unit from F_2 to M_1 produces zero change.
2. Shipping one unit from F_3 to M_1 would result in extra expense of \$2.00 per unit.
3. Shipping one unit from F_3 to M_2 would result in extra expense of \$3.00 per unit.

Accordingly, we shift ten units from F_1, M_2 to F_1, M_D. The resulting transportation matrix is now tested to determine whether by modifying this

| Factory | Market | | | Supply |
	M_1	M_2	M_D	
F_1	40	$+1$	10	50
F_2	-1	40	50	90
F_3	$+1$	$+3$	90	90
Demand	40	40	150	230

arrangement any other savings could be made. The marginal cost changes that would result from further modification of the shipping pattern are shown in the circles of the above matrix. Additional improvement is possible. Forty units can be shifted from F_1, M_1 to F_2, M_1. We would then have:

Factory	M_1	M_2	M_D	Supply
F_1	(+1)	(+1)	50	50
F_2	40	40	10	90
F_3	(+2)	(+3)	90	90
Demand	40	40	150	230

The marginal cost analysis shows that no further improvements can be obtained. Because factories 1 and 3 ship only to the dummy, they will be eliminated. The solution also states that factory 2 will operate at 89 per cent of capacity.

The limitations and strengths of the transportation procedure are apparent. An optimal plant location can be determined based on relevant cost data. On the other hand, we know that many other factors are usually required to properly evaluate alternative locations. The intangible factors have been totally ignored by this method. When the intangibles are critical, then perhaps a method similar to dimensional analysis should be utilized in conjunction with managerial intuition.

Programming Approaches to Location

A variety of mathematical models have been developed to assist in the analysis of location opportunities. For the most part, they represent extensions of the transportation algorithm previously described. As soon as other factors are added, the simple transportation model no longer suffices. Complex integer programming considerations hold. Consequently, branch and bound algorithms become appealing.[9] A computer program, developed in conjunction with a so-called FLP (facility location planner) procedure, has been cited for its helpfulness. The material that follows explains this approach.[10]

... Illustration of How FLP Works

Shown on the map are five customer demand centers (C_1, C_2, C_3, C_4, C_5) and four potential warehouse sites (W_1, W_2, W_3, W_4). The table on page 424 shows the warehouse and distribution costs for this hypothetical problem. The fixed warehouse costs include all costs associated with opening each warehouse. This might include the

[9] See, for example, M. A. Efroymson and T. L. Ray, "A Branch and Bound Algorithm for Plant Location," *Operations Research*, Vol. 14, No. 3 (May–June, 1966), 361–68.

[10] Robert J. Atkins and Richard H. Shriver, "New Approach to Facilities Location," *Harvard Business Review*, Vol. 46, No. 3 (May–June, 1968), 75.

Fixed Warehouse Cost and Distribution Costs from Warehouse to Each of Five Different Customers

	Fixed Cost per Year	Distribution Costs from Warehouse to Customer				
		C_1	C_2	C_3	C_4	C_5
W_1	$4,500	$ 3,000	$10,000	$ 8,000	$18,000	$14,000
W_2	6,000	9,000	4,000	6,000	5,000	5,000
W_3	6,000	12,000	6,000	10,000	4,000	8,000
W_4	8,000	8,000	6,000	5,000	12,000	9,000

amortized cost of building the warehouse and/or the additional inventory cost associated with adding the warehouse to the distribution system. The warehouse-to-customer costs include FOB cost at the warehouse, the warehouse handling cost, and the warehouse-to-customer transportation costs.

[From: Robert J. Atkins and Richard H. Shriver, "New approach to facilities location," HARVARD BUSINESS REVIEW, May-June 1968, page 75.]

Steps in solving this problem.

1. The *minimum* variable cost saving associated with opening each warehouse are calculated (Concept 1). If for any warehouse this minimum cost saving is greater than the fixed cost associated with opening the warehouse, that warehouse is opened. In this problem it is clear that for customer C_1, opening warehouse W_1 will save at least $5,000 per year ($8,000 − $3,000); and since the fixed cost of W_1 is only $4,500 per year, W_1 will be in the optimal solution. As the reader may verify, no other warehouses can be fixed open at this point.

2. The *maximum* possible variable cost savings associated with opening each of the other warehouses are calculated. Any warehouse where this maximum saving is less than the fixed cost of the warehouse is fixed closed (Concept 2). In the sample problem, since W_1 is the only warehouse fixed open, we could save $30,000 per year (i.e., $10,000 − $4,000 for C_2 plus $8,000 − $6,000 for C_3, plus $18,000 − $5,000 for C_4 plus $14,000 − $5,000 for C_5) if warehouse W_2 is open, and thus W_2 cannot

be fixed closed at this point. Similarly, warehouses W_3 and W_4 cannot be closed yet. Thus, the effect of the first application of Concepts 1 and 2 is that W_1 will be in the optimal solution, and warehouses W_2, W_3, and W_4 are still in an undecided state.

3. Now apply Concept 3, which simply involves applying well-defined "rules of search" for evaluating the remaining warehouse alternatives. For example, let us arbitrarily open warehouse W_2. (The actual rules used for deciding which warehouse to open or close are not critical to understanding the procedure.) After opening W_2, check to see if any warehouses can now be fixed closed (using Concept 2 again). In this case, since W_1 and W_2 are fixed open at this point, the maximum saving associated with opening W_3 is $1,000 per year (i.e., $5,000 − $4,000 for C_4), and the maximum saving for W_4 is $1,000 per year (i.e., $6,000 − $5,000 for C_3). Therefore W_3 and W_4 can be closed at this point since the maximum possible savings for each ($1,000 and $1,000) are less than their respective fixed costs ($6,000 and $8,000). Thus, assuming W_2 is open, the minimum distribution cost for the system is $23,000 per year variable cost ($3,000 for C_1 plus $4,000 for C_2 plus $6,000 for C_3 plus $5,000 for C_4 plus $5,000 for C_5) and $10,500 fixed costs for warehouses W_1 and W_2. Thus the total cost, assuming W_2 open, is $33,500 per year; this is a complete solution, since every warehouse has been either opened or closed.

4. Assume warehouse W_2 is closed. (Remember that W_1 was fixed open at the beginning and W_3 and W_4 are still undecided.) With W_2 fixed closed, W_3 must now be open, because at least $8,000 ($12,000 − $4,000) can be saved for C_4, and this exceeds the fixed cost for W_3. Thus, the total variable cost for the system must be at least $26,000 ($3,000 for C_1 plus $6,000 for C_2 plus $5,000 for C_3 plus $4,000 for C_4 plus $8,000 for C_5) plus the fixed cost $4,500 for W_1, and $6,000 for W_3 for a total cost of $36,500 per year. However, we now have an incomplete solution (i.e., W_3 and W_4 are still free) which has a higher cost than a previous complete solution. If we proceed to a complete solution, by setting warehouses W_3 and W_4 either opened or closed, the cost can only increase.

5. The minimum cost solution. We have shown that the optimal solution to the sample problem is to open warehouses W_1 and W_2 and close warehouses W_3 and W_4. Furthermore, customer C_1 should be supplied from warehouse W_1 and all other customers from W_2.

Many other techniques have been suggested including the use of elaborate simulation analyses. A great deal more study is required, however, to determine whether formal methodology has captured a sufficient part of the real problem (especially, the intangibles) to warrant substantial investments by organizations faced with real problems.

The Layout Problem

Once the process has been specified and the appropriate types of equipment have been selected, it is then necessary to arrange all the systems' components into an *optimal layout*. In some cases, the plant has been selected; in others, that choice is yet to be made. Generally, consideration has been given to the selection of specific machines, the number of such machines needed to provide a balanced system, the connections for material flows between the machines, and the placement of operators and the number of operators. Usually, however, alternatives exist. The list of alternatives is maintained and interacts with layout decisions. This is not easy to show, because the layout problem *with fixed equipment selections* is still extremely complex.

Decisions regarding the arrangement of specific elements are what we refer to as the layout problem. Often, the specific elements are grouped into machine centers. Although physical models of the plant floor and the selected equipment are frequently helpful in guiding arrangement, intuition underlies their use. Models can be two or three dimensional. Often, two dimensional floor plans with cut-outs, or templates, representing the various pieces of equipment are used. When conveyers are employed, overhead space requirements may be important and three dimensional models are preferred.

Can an optimal layout really be found? At the present time, it is non-operational to talk about an optimal arrangement. There are too many possible variations and usually no way to search through them all. As the production process approaches total mechanization and, ultimately, complete automation, then technological constraints operate. The flow shop configuration warrants large study investments. The notion of an optimal layout becomes more tenable. For the general case it is desirable to talk about a satisfactory layout.

What is a satisfactory layout? Some of the possible measures of a layout's effectiveness would be:

1. The capacity of the system under different arrangements;
2. The costs of various systems arrangements; and
3. The flexibility to change a layout as required.

One thing is clear; for flow and project shops it is essential to balance the output rates of consecutive operations. This is the line-balancing problem that we have previously discussed.

The layout problem is complicated by the question of whether we will make do with an existing plant or build a new one to our specifications. Frequently, when a plant rental arrangement is used, basic structural changes either are prohibited or are not economically sensible. When an existing structure has been purchased, it may not be economically feasible to knock down walls, add sections, or make other structural changes. Such alterations require investment in plant, and such investments must be justified in terms of alternative uses of these funds. The relative permanency desired for any physical arrangement of components is a matter that arises here. If a continuous production line is to be set up, it obviously presents different conditions than would be encountered with a job shop system.

Various common approaches to the plant layout problem include:

1. The use of intuition, know-how, and common sense in conjunction with consideration of psychological factors, human factors, and human engineering.
2. The use of schematics, such as flow process diagrams, flow process charts, and both two- and three-dimensional models, all clearly dominated by intuition. (See Figures 14.4, 14.5, and 14.6.)

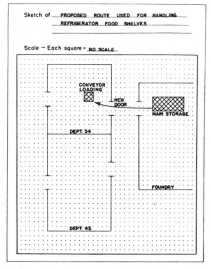

Figure 14.4

Flow diagram for original method of handling refrigerator food shelves from bulk storage to plating department. [From Marvin E. Mundel, *Motion and Time Study*, 4th ed. (Englewood Cliffs, N.J.: Prentice-Hall, Inc., 1967), p. 60.]

3. The use of queueing theory for line balancing, with men, materials handling equipment, in-process storage arrangements, and machines.
4. The use of network theory including variants of the assignment method for arranging components so as either to maximize production throughput or to minimize time through the network.
5. The simulation of various layout arrangements to test the interrelationships of facilities and materials handling equipment.
6. The use of programming techniques that are more elaborate and demanding than the assignment algorithm.

A Layout Assignment Model

The problem we are treating is surprisingly large and complex when put into quantitative terms. The strictly intuitive approach dismisses billions or trillions of alternatives for what seem like logical reasons. It is always possible

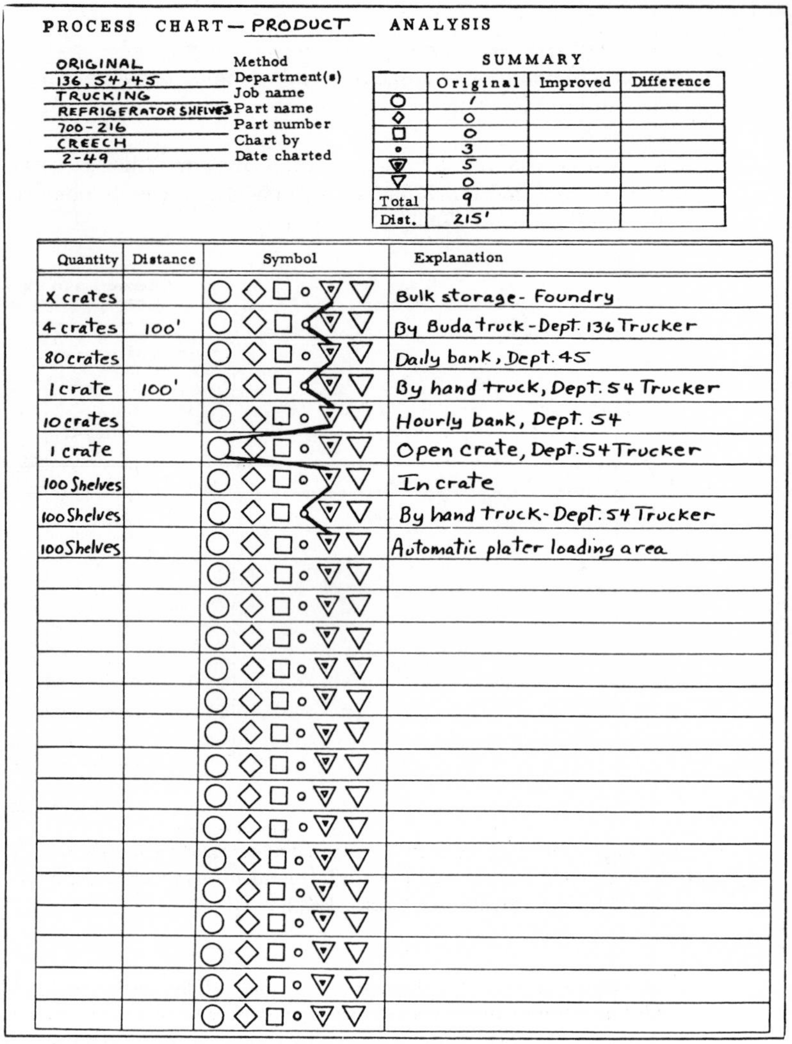

PROCESS CHART — PRODUCT ANALYSIS

ORIGINAL
136, 54, 45 .... Method
TRUCKING .... Department(s)
REFRIGERATOR SHELVES .... Job name
700-216 .... Part name
CREECH .... Part number
2-49 .... Chart by
.... Date charted

	SUMMARY		
	Original	Improved	Difference
◯	1		
◇	0		
□	0		
•	3		
▽ (filled)	5		
▽	0		
Total	9		
Dist.	215'		

Quantity	Distance	Symbol	Explanation
X crates		◯ ◇ □ ∘ ▽ ▽	Bulk storage - Foundry
4 crates	100'	◯ ◇ □ ∘ ▽ ▽	By Buda truck - Dept. 136 Trucker
80 crates		◯ ◇ □ ∘ ▽ ▽	Daily bank, Dept. 45
1 crate	100'	◯ ◇ □ ∘ ▽ ▽	By hand truck, Dept. 54 Trucker
10 crates		◯ ◇ □ ∘ ▽ ▽	Hourly bank, Dept. 54
1 crate		◯ ◇ □ ∘ ▽ ▽	Open crate, Dept. 54 Trucker
100 Shelves		◯ ◇ □ ∘ ▽ ▽	In crate
100 Shelves		◯ ◇ □ ∘ ▽ ▽	By hand truck - Dept. 54 Trucker
100 Shelves		◯ ◇ □ ∘ ▽ ▽	Automatic plater loading area

Figure 14.5

Process chart-product analysis for original method of handling refrigerator food shelves from bulk storage to plating department. [From Marvin E. Mundel, *Motion and Time Study*, 4th ed. (Englewood Cliffs, N.J.: Prentice-Hall, Inc., 1967), p. 59.]

that an excellent (unsuspected) solution is ignored in this way. But one thing is certain, while optimality may be missed by the manager, an illogical and inappropriate solution will not be accepted by him.

Let us define the *job shop* as consisting of *n machine centers*, MC_j ($j = 1, 2, \ldots, n$). Each machine center has a fundamentally different activity. We shall choose, as our objective: Minimize materials handling costs. If we have a plant, its configuration will constrain the way in which we can assign

428

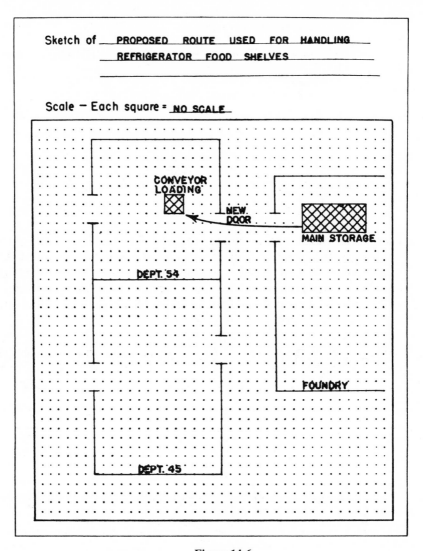

Figure 14.6

Flow diagram for proposed method of handling refrigerator food shelves from bulk storage to plating department. [From Marvin E. Mundel, *Motion and Time Study*, 4th ed. (Englewood Cliffs, N.J.: Prentice-Hall, Inc., 1967), p. 67.]

machine centers to plant areas.[11] For an example, assume that five plant areas are designated, and the question is: How to assign five machine centers to these areas?

[11] For example, heavy machinery can only be assigned to certain areas. Cranes may require special height clearance; upper floors are needed for gravity conveyers; press shops cannot be located near offices because of noise; receiving and shipping should logically be close to truck docks and rail spurs, etc.

Figure 14.7 portrays a floor layout with five "location hubs."

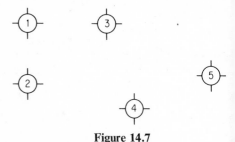

Figure 14.7

In some sense, these conform to the floor plan of the plant.

Clearly, the layout problem of a flow shop or a project shop would be different from a job shop. The layout, in the case of the first two shop configurations, would interact with the line balance solutions and project trade-off solutions that we previously derived in earlier chapters. So, it is most often the job shop layout problem to which we address ourselves. The job shop can have many different flow patterns. The layout problem is complicated when a common set of facilities that must be shared by multiple products requires different flow paths and sequences through the system. For example, Figure 14.8 portrays a shop where alternate routes must be followed by

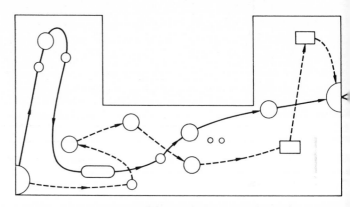

Figure 14.8

several products in the company's product-mix. It is unreasonable to expect that intuition can find layout plans that are reasonably close to optimal for such cases. As a rule of thumb, the product that contributes the greatest percentage to total profit is given preferential treatment and the others less so in accordance with their value to the company. At least, this heuristic simplifies the problem. With one major product being processed (flow shop configuration), it is reasonable to route the product on some kind of *a minimum cost path*.

A First Approach

Divide the plant floor into sections. Next, we measure either the time or distance required to transport an item from each plant section to all other plant sections. It is then possible to construct a matrix that shows the appropriate cost factor for transporting between any two positions on the plant floor. An example of such a matrix would be:

Matrix of Traverse Distances Between
Plant Sections (in feet)

		To position			
		A	B	C	D
From position	A	.	10	20	32
	B	10	.	16	16
	C	20	16	.	12
	D	32	16	12	.

The diagonal of the matrix is blocked, because such transport has no meaning. Also, as a general rule, the matrix will be symmetrical, that is, the distance from A to B will be equal to the distance from B to A. This is not always the case, especially if unidirectional (e.g., gravity) conveyer systems connect some of the plant sections. In order to determine an optimum layout plan we must discover a closed loop that will result in the minimum traverse path. The steps to be taken are identical with those used for resolving the traveling salesman assignment problem. There are two minimum-time tours (each having a value of thirty-eight). One of the satisfactory closed-loop solutions looks like this:

		To position			
		A	B	C	D
From position	A	.	x		
	B		.	x	
	C			.	x
	D				.

We have assumed that A is the receiving point and D is shipping. Usually, in these problems, there will be constrained input (receiving) and output (shipping) portals. The various network combinations are explored between these portals. For a large matrix, *the branch and bound algorithm* can be used to provide the solution for the minimum tour.

A Second Approach

Another way to proceed *heuristically* is to *minimize nonadjacent* assignments. Adjacency has to be represented by some kind of distance function, e.g., where $d_{kl} > C$ is defined as nonadjacency for the floor locations, k and l. In Figure 14.9, let us assume that d_{13} and d_{31} (being symmetric and $> C$) are nonadjacent by our criterion.

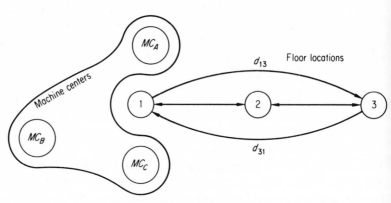

Figure 14.9

We would try to place our machine centers, MC_A, MC_B, MC_C, at the locations L_1, L_2, L_3 in such a way as to minimize the flow of materials between L_1 and L_3. This leads to the obvious requirement for a definition of flows between machine centers. The matrix $[F_{ij}]$ does this, where F_{ij} is the volume of flow per unit time *between machine centers i and j* (not floor locations, k and l).

$$[F_{ij}] = \begin{bmatrix} \rightarrow & MC_1 & MC_2 & \ldots & MC_n \\ MC_1 & F_{11} & F_{12} & \ldots & F_{1n} \\ MC_2 & F_{21} & F_{22} & \ldots & F_{2n} \\ \vdots & \vdots & \vdots & & \vdots \\ MC_n & F_{n1} & F_{n2} & \ldots & F_{nn} \end{bmatrix}$$

We can augment the matrix $[F_{ij}]$ with a cost matrix $[C_{ij}]$, where C_{ij} is the cost per unit of flow per unit of distance moved. Then, $[F_{ij}] [C_{ij}] = [FC_{ij}]$, where FC_{ij} is the total *flow cost per unit of distance moved* for machine centers i and j. (If the cost C_{ij} is the same as the cost C_{ji}, then the total work flow between centers can be obtained by addition, i.e., $FC'_{ij} = FC_{ij} + FC_{ji}$. We will not make this assumption.)

Because of the concept of adjacency in this second approach, exact measures of distance are not used; instead, the two classes of distance are defined—those that are adjacent (1, 2 and 2, 3) and those that are non-adjacent (1, 3).

Assume that the matrix FC_{ij} is nonsymmetric as follows:

$$FC_{ij}$$

	A	B	C
A	—	2	5
B	1	—	3
C	6	4	—

Let the first pairing be $A1$, $B2$ and $C3$. Then, Figure 14.10 results.

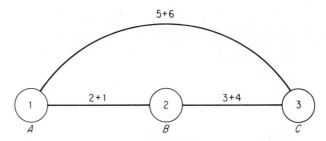

Figure 14.10

This does not minimize nonadjacent flows, as would $A1$, $C2$, $B3$, for which the nonadjacent flows equal $2 + 1 = 3$, so we make the change. In larger problems, a sequence of such interchanges might be required before a satisfactory arrangement develops. The "minimum-nonadjacent" heuristic is useful but hardly satisfactory for a large layout problem where a great deal of materials handling expense is required.

A Third Approach

To resolve this assignment problem in terms of *all* the obvious factors that are relevant, we must note that the flow cost matrix $[FC_{ij}]$ has to be matched against a *distance function* matrix $[d_{kl}]$,[12] thus:

---

[12] The first approach missed the existence of the FC_{ij} matrix; the second approach categorizes distance measures, d_{kl}, as either/or.

	Machine Centers				Locations		
	A	B	C		1	2	3
A	FC_{AA}	FC_{AB}	FC_{AC}	1	d_{11}	d_{12}	d_{13}
B	FC_{BA}	FC_{BB}	FC_{BC}	2	d_{21}	d_{22}	d_{23}
C	FC_{CA}	FC_{CB}	FC_{CC}	3	d_{31}	d_{32}	d_{33}

When multiplied together, a total cost matrix $[TC_{ij}]$ results. But multiplication requires a matching (assignment) of the distance function matrix with the matrix describing flows between machine centers. How do we know which arrangement should be used?

$A1, B2, C3$
$A2, B1, C3$
$A3, B2, C1$, etc.?

There are $n!$ arrangements. As n increases, this number rapidly grows to inadmissible proportions for calculation and evaluation. Returning to our 3×3 example, assume that the two matrices are:

$[FC_{ij}]$				$[d_{kl}]$				$[TC_{ij}]$		
	A	B	C		1	2	3		$A1$	$B2$	$C3$
A	—	2	5	1	—	25	40	$A1$	—	50	200
B	1	—	3	2	25	—	10	$B2$	25	—	30
C	6	4	—	3	40	10	—	$C3$	240	40	—

(Note: the matrices are joined by $\cdot$ and $=$ signs: $[FC_{ij}] \cdot [d_{kl}] = [TC_{ij}]$)

Here, the distances are symmetric, i.e., $d_{kl} = d_{lk}$. We obtain the flow diagram shown in Figure 14.11, for the assignment $A1, B2, C3$.

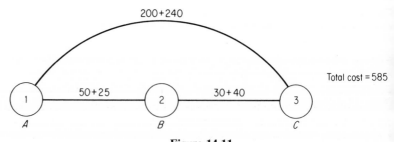

Figure 14.11

The minimum cost, obtained by using our second approach based on the nonadjacency of one and three would be:

$[FC_{ij}]$				$[d_{kl}]$				$[TC_{ij}]$		
	A	B	C		1	3	2		A1	B3	C2
A	—	2	5	1	—	40	25	A1	—	80	125
B	1	—	3	3	40	—	10	B3	40	—	30
C	6	4	—	2	25	10	—	C2	150	40	—

The middle and right tables are joined by $\cdot$ and $=$.

The total cost $= \Sigma \Sigma TC_{ij} = (125 + 150) + (40 + 30) + (80 + 40) = 465.$

But a better result is available; in fact, it is the optimum. Namely, for $A3$, $B1$, $C2$, the total cost equals 405. Figure 14.12 shows why the nonadjacency heuristic can only take one so far in achieving the best possible layout.

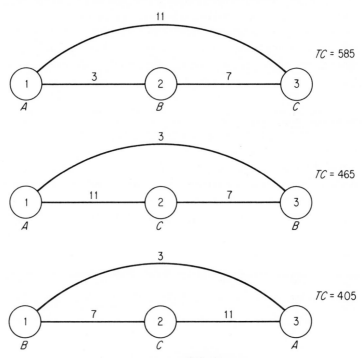

Figure 14.12

The problem of this third approach can be stated explicitly:

$$\text{Minimize } \Sigma \Sigma \Sigma \Sigma d_{kl}FC_{ij}x_{ik}x_{jl}$$
$$\quad\quad\quad\quad i\ j\ l\ k$$

where the x_{ik}'s are either 0 or 1. $x_{ik} = 0$ if MC_i is not assigned to location k. $x_{ik} = 1$ if MC_i is assigned to location k.

The constraints that apply are: $\Sigma_i x_{ik} = 1$ and $\Sigma_k x_{ik} = 1$ for all $i, j, \ldots$

and for all $k, l, \ldots$ This insures that only one machine center is assigned to a location and that each location has only one machine center assigned to it. This is a quadratic integer programming problem for which no simple solution procedure exists.

The nonadjacency heuristic is not sufficiently powerful to cope with a big problem. Total enumeration is out of the question for a big problem. However, a strong heuristic approach exists. It was developed by G. C. Armour and E. S. Buffa, and called CRAFT (Computerized Relative Allocation of Facilities Technique).[13] The improvement algorithm is based on exchanging the locations of pairs of machine centers, and for each exchange computing the alteration in materials handling costs. There are $n(n-1)/2$ such pairs starting with any one machine center. The best exchange is made and then the procedure continues starting with a different machine center. As an upper limit $n^2/2$ computations are required with each of n iterations (which also is a reasonable upper limit) whereas total enumeration requires $n!$ computations.[14] As reported in the articles cited in the footnote, the algorithm is effective and provides substantial savings over an intuition-based layout.

A Fourth Approach

It seems reasonable to note that under certain restricted conditions we can find a value C_{ik} for assigning the ith machine center to the kth location. If such costs exist independently, i.e., without being affected by ij's and kl's, then the problem becomes a regular, linear assignment problem. Thus:

$$\text{Minimize } \sum_i \sum_k c_{ik}x_{ik}$$

with the constraints $\sum_k x_{ik} = 1$ and $\sum_i x_{ik} = 1$. In matrix form, we would have

Matrix of Costs

		Locations		
		1	2	3
	A	6	5	4
Machine centers	B	5	8	9
	C	7	10	8

which is readily resolved in the fashion of the network assignment algorithm.

[13] Gordon C. Armour and Elwood S. Buffa, "A Heuristic Algorithm and Simulation Approach to the Relative Location of Facilities," *Management Science*, 9: 2 (January, 1963), 294–309. Also, see, Elwood S. Buffa, Gordon C. Armour, and Thomas E. Vollmann, "Allocating Facilities with 'CRAFT,'" *Harvard Business Review*, 42: 2 (March–April, 1964), 136–58.

[14] At $n = 4$, the BEP is reached; thereafter $n!$ grows far more rapidly than $n[n(n-1)/2]$.

Replacement of Facilities

The choice and arrangement of facilities can be critical, interacting with plant layout. Over time, a process ages. It must be constantly renewed and updated. Otherwise, there is increasing risk that it will become obsolete. As an expression of this fact, accounting practice attempts to design and apply a depreciation procedure that captures the essence of the way in which the value of a company's facilities changes with *use* and *age* over a period of time.

We must understand the relevance of alternative methods of depreciation with respect to machine replacement. In Figure 14.13, three different methods for calculating depreciation are illustrated. Each of these has its own characteristic advantages and disadvantages.

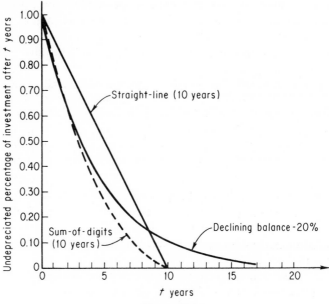

Figure 14.13

Three alternative depreciation methods.

Straight-line depreciation, in this case, is applied to a ten-year period. This linear function has the property of decreasing by the same amount each year. That amount is simply N/T, where N is the initial facility cost and T is the facility lifetime over which it will amortized. Thus, at any time t the undepreciated portion will be $N - tN/T$.

The method called *declining balance* involves nonlinear change that is achieved by taking a fixed percentage, p, of the undepreciated balance every year. Thus, at any time t the undepreciated portion will be $N(1 - p)^t$. For example, consider a machine costing $1,000 with $p = 0.20$. After three years, the undepreciated portion will be $512. At the end of ten years it will still be approximately $107. Therefore, the declining-balance method does not fully write-off the investment by the end of the ten-year period. Instead, it approaches the full write-off asymptotically but never reaches it.

The third method is called the *sum-of-digits method*. In this case, for a ten-year period we obtain the sum of $10 + 9 + 8 + 7 + 6 + 5 + 4 + 3 + 2 + 1$, which equals fifty-five. At the end of the first year we depreciate the principal N by an amount $(10/55)N$. For the second year's depreciation we use $(9/55)N$; third-year depreciation equals $(8/55)N$. The total amount depreciated over the ten-year period will be $(10/55)N + (9/55)N + \ldots + (1/55)N$. This is equal to $(55/55)N$, that is, full depreciation. We observe that for each succeeding year the fraction used decreases. In order to determine the denominator value for the sum-of-digits method for a period of T years, we can utilize the formula, $T(T + 1)/2$. Thus, we obtain for $T = 10$ years, $10(11)/2 = 55$.

The straight-line method should be used when the facility is used up in equal amounts over a period of time. This method doesn't penalize any one year in particular. The remaining two methods penalize the initial years more than the latter ones. The declining-balance method leaves some amount of undepreciated value at the time of intended replacement, which can be associated with salvage value. Depreciation methods are usually designed to reflect the funding policies of the company for facility replacement, as well as the company's tax situation. The Machinery and Allied Products Institute of Washington, D.C. has done a great deal to comprehensively organize the data requirements and to design a method of analysis for the machine replacement problem. Their approach, called the MAPI method, is widely utilized by industry. A requirement of this method is that costs should be based on the process and system performance. Conversely, costs should not be measured for the individual facility in isolation from the system.

Let us look first at the MAPI chart entitled Summary of Analysis. We observe that Figure 14.14 on p. 440 comprises three major divisions.

1. Required investment;
2. Next-year advantage from the project—where the project can be interpreted as the investment in a new facility;
3. Computation of MAPI urgency rating, which is a relative measure of the return on investment.

Let us go through the required steps with an example in mind, introducing the necessary data as we proceed.

1. We wish to evaluate the replacement of machine B with two smaller machines, B_1. The installed cost of the new machines is $50,000 apiece, or $100,000.

2. The disposal value of machine B is $20,000.
3. No capital additions are required or contemplated if the proposed change is not made. For some cases, extensive repairs might be necessitated if a replacement is not made; but we are not considering ourselves to be faced with such a situation.
4. The investment that is released or avoided by the contemplated replacement is the sum of $2 + 3$. This equals $20,000.
5. The net investment, then, is $80,000.

We now calculate the next-year advantage to be gained. First, we determine the operating advantage, and then we consider the nonoperating advantage, so that the total advantage can be determined. We begin by considering the effect of the equipment change on revenue.

6. Assuming one shift, 35 operating hours per week, and 50 weeks per year for the new equipment, we obtain 1750 operating hours per year.
7. The new equipment will improve output quality. We *estimate* that this will be worth $10,000 per year.
8. The volume of output will remain the same.
9. The total shows a $10,000 increase—no decrease.

We now move to the consideration of the facility change on operating costs. These are steps ten through twenty-five. For our example, there has been a decrease of $4000 in direct labor and an increase in indirect labor of $1500. Maintenance costs are decreased by $1000, and downtime is decreased by $1000. We charge ourselves for increased floor space requirements, *estimating* this increase to be $1500.

26. The total increase in operating costs is $3000; total decrease is $6000.
27. The net increase in revenue is *estimated* at $10,000.
28. The net decrease in operating costs is $3000.
29. The resultant next-year operating advantage is $13,000.

With respect to nonoperating advantage:

30. If we delay in replacing facility B, the salvage value will decrease by $5000. No additional investments will be required for facility B.
31. Then, total advantage will be $18,000.

All this is straightforward. Now we look at Chart III, called the Computation of MAPI Ugency Rating. Available investment funds can be used in many different ways. There is competition between alternative facilities, dividends to stockholders, increased salaries or wages, improvement studies, and so forth. If we can obtain a measure of the relative urgency (or desirability) of alternative investments, then we can determine a reasonable guide for action. This is what the MAPI urgency rating is intended to do.

PROJECT NO. **1B vs 2B₁·'s**   SHEET I

SUMMARY OF ANALYSIS
(SEE ACCOMPANYING WORK SHEETS FOR DETAIL)

I. REQUIRED INVESTMENT

1	INSTALLED COST OF PROJECT	$ 100,000	1
2	DISPOSAL VALUE OF ASSETS TO BE RETIRED BY PROJECT	$ 20,000	2
3	CAPITAL ADDITIONS REQUIRED IN ABSENCE OF PROJECT	$	3
4	INVESTMENT RELEASED OR AVOIDED BY PROJECT (2+3)	$ 20,000	4
5	NET INVESTMENT REQUIRED (1−4)	$ 80,000	5

II. NEXT-YEAR ADVANTAGE FROM PROJECT

A. OPERATING ADVANTAGE
(USE FIRST YEAR OF PROJECT OPERATION)*

6	ASSUMED OPERATING RATE OF PROJECT (HOURS PER YEAR)	1,750	6

	EFFECT OF PROJECT ON REVENUE	Increase	Decrease	
7	FROM CHANGE IN QUALITY OF PRODUCTS	$ 10,000	$	7
8	FROM CHANGE IN VOLUME OF OUTPUT			8
9	TOTAL	$ 10,000 A	$ B	9

	EFFECT OF PROJECT ON OPERATING COSTS			
10	DIRECT LABOR	$	$ 4,000	10
11	INDIRECT LABOR	1,500		11
12	FRINGE BENEFITS			12
13	MAINTENANCE		1,000	13
14	TOOLING			14
15	SUPPLIES			15
16	SCRAP AND REWORK			16
17	DOWN TIME		1,000	17
18	POWER			18
19	FLOOR SPACE	1,500		19
20	PROPERTY TAXES AND INSURANCE			20
21	SUBCONTRACTING			21
22	INVENTORY			22
23	SAFETY			23
24	FLEXIBILITY			24
25	OTHER			25
26	TOTAL	$ 3,000 A	$ 6,000 B	26

27	NET INCREASE IN REVENUE (9A−9B)	$ 10,000	27
28	NET DECREASE IN OPERATING COST (26B−26A)	$ 3,000	28
29	NEXT-YEAR OPERATING ADVANTAGE (27+28)	$ 13,000	29

B. NON-OPERATING ADVANTAGE
(USE ONLY IF THERE IS AN ENTRY IN LINE 4)

30	NEXT-YEAR CAPITAL CONSUMPTION AVOIDED BY PROJECT:			30
	A DECLINE OF DISPOSAL VALUE DURING THE YEAR		$ 5,000	A
	B NEXT-YEAR ALLOCATION OF CAPITAL ADDITIONS		$	B
		TOTAL	$ 5,000	

C. TOTAL ADVANTAGE

31	TOTAL NEXT-YEAR ADVANTAGE FROM PROJECT (29+30)	$ 18,000	31

* For projects with a significant break-in period, use performance after break-in.

Figure 14.14

MAPI replacement analysis form. Courtesy Machinery and Allied Products Institute.

32. We subtract the tax from the gross dollar gain shown in the prior step. The tax for this example is calculated at 50 per cent. Therefore, the next-year advantage after income tax will be $9000. Tax consideration is an important strength of the MAPI procedure. All too frequently, taxes are overlooked in the investment decision process.

33. The MAPI chart allowance is determined by using columns A through F of Chart III. We also require the use of Figure 14.15, which gives us a

PROJECT NO. 1B vs 2B₁'s

III. COMPUTATION OF MAPI URGENCY RATING

32 TOTAL NEXT-YEAR ADVANTAGE AFTER INCOME TAX (31 − TAX) $ 9,000

33 MAPI CHART ALLOWANCE FOR PROJECT (TOTAL OF COLUMN F, BELOW) $ 8,000 *

(ENTER DEPRECIABLE ASSETS ONLY)

Item or Group	Installed Cost of Item or Group A	Estimated Service Life (Years) B	Estimated Terminal Salvage (Percent of Cost) C	MAPI Chart Number D	Chart Percent- age E	Chart Percent- age × Cost (E × A) F
2 Machines B₁ (straight-line depreciation)	$100000	8	10	1	8.0	$ 8,000
					TOTAL	$ 8,000

34 AMOUNT AVAILABLE FOR RETURN ON INVESTMENT (32 − 33) $ 1,000

35 **MAPI URGENCY RATING** (34 ÷ 5) · 100   % 1.25

* Since the chart allowance does not cover future capital additions to project assets, add an annual proration of such additions, if any, to the figure in Line 33.

Figure 14.14 (cont.)

percentage to apply to the required investment based on depreciation, machine wear,[15] and salvage value.

Column A: Installed cost of two B_1 facilities—$100,000.
Column B: *Estimated* service life in years—eight years.
Column C: *Estimated* salvage value after eight years—$10,000, which is 10 per cent of the initial investment.

[15] This refers to the way in which the facility declines as a profit producer because of technological factors. See Figure 14.16.

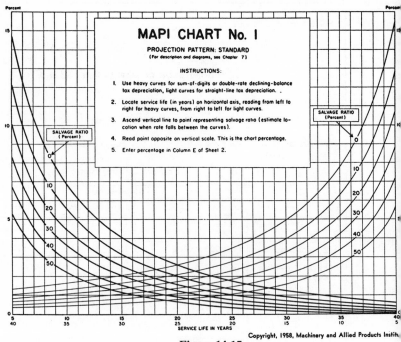

Figure 14.15

MAPI chart to be used on equipment with a standard projection pattern. Courtesy Machinery and Allied Products Institute.

Column D: We must now use the most appropriate MAPI chart. Three different kinds are available. We have only illustrated the *standard* projection chart, which we will apply to our example. The difference between the available charts is illustrated in Figure 14.16.

   MAPI Chart 1 is the standard projection indicating that the value of the facility as a profit producer declines linearly over its lifetime. We shall

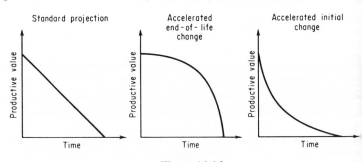

Figure 14.16

Three different patterns that describe the way in which the productive value of a facility can change over time.

assume that straight-line depreciation applies, and, consequently, referring to Figure 14.15, we use the light lines that are associated with the scale running from right to left on the abscissa.

Column E: For our assumptions, we obtain a chart percentage of 8 per cent, or the decimal fraction 0.08.

Column F: This is $100,000(0.08) = $8000, which is the TOTAL.[16]

34.   The amount available for return on investment is $9000 − $8000 = $1000.

35.   Therefore, the MAPI urgency rating will be: $\dfrac{\$1,000}{\$80,000}(100) = 1.25$ per cent.

Based on this figure, it is unlikely that the operations manager will replace the present facility B.

The MAPI urgency rating expresses the first year, after-tax returns as a percentage of the required investment. By using this measure of effectiveness, or modifications of it, the various process alternatives can be examined in a reasonable manner. Rational policies will dominate the design and control of the process.

In summary, the major advantage of the MAPI method is that it permits a simple and consistent method to be applied for evaluating all company facilities—and this in terms of an appropriate measure of effectiveness, viz., return on investment. If, however, a one-year planning horizon is insufficient to adequately portray the situation, then other steps must be taken.

Preventive and Remedial Maintenance of Facilities

Another vital aspect of facilities management concerns the way in which the process is serviced, repaired, and maintained. We observed that in various ways maintenance costs entered the replacement computations that we have just completed. Of frequent concern is the basic question: Should we repair and maintain the facilities regularly on a scheduled basis, or should we wait for equipment and facility failures? The answer must be dictated by the characteristics of the facilities and the relevant costs. Replacement models are varied in nature. They must be so in order to cope with the great variety of situations that can arise. We shall introduce a rather fundamental model for comparing *preventive* maintenance strategies with *remedial* maintenance strategies. But it should be clear that the circumstances of each situation will dictate the construction of a suitable model.

Assume that M identical machines are used for a particular production process. Let:

---

[16] It will be noted that column F is obtained by $E \times A \div 100$.

K_1 = The cost of providing preventive maintenance for one machine;

and,

K_2 = The average cost of servicing a breakdown.

In general, $K_2 > K_1$; when this does not hold, preventive maintenance would not be used. Next, we observe the frequencies with which machine breakdowns occur (additional information can usually be obtained from the equipment manufacturer). Let:

p_j = The probability that a machine will break down in the jth month after it has been serviced.

To begin, calculate the cost of not providing any preventive maintenance. This will be equal to the number of machines, M, divided by the expected period between breakdowns for these machines, $\sum\limits_{j} jp_j$, and multiplied by the cost, K_2. Thus:

$$TC \text{ (no preventive maintenance)} = \frac{MK_2}{\sum\limits_{j} jp_j}$$

As an example, assume that $M = 50$ machines and that the probability distribution is as follows:

(a) jth Month After Maintenance	(b) Probability of Failure in the jth Month p_j	($a \times b$)
1	0.30	0.30
2	0.10	0.20
3	0.10	0.30
4	0.20	Expected 0.80
5	0.30	Period 1.50
	$\sum\limits_{j} p_j = 1.00$	Between = 3.10 months Breakdowns

The expected period between breakdowns is shown as the total of the column marked ($a \times b$). Then, if the average cost, K_2, per machine breakdown is $60.00, we would obtain:

$$TC \text{ (no preventive maintenance)} = \frac{(50)(\$60)}{3.1} = \$967.74 \text{ per month}$$

The next logical step is to determine the total cost of the maintenance policy that calls for preventive maintenance at the end of every month. The charge, in this case, is K_1 per machine. Meanwhile, random breakdowns will be serviced at the K_2 rate. The number of breakdowns by the end of the first month will be designated F_1. Then:

$$F_1 = Mp_1$$

This will cost K_2F_1 or K_2Mp_1; and, in addition, all M machines will be serviced at the K_1 rate. Thus:

$$TC \text{ (monthly preventive maintenance)} = K_1M + K_2Mp_1 = K_1M + K_2F_1$$

For our example, letting $K_1 = \$10$ per machine, the total cost will be:

$$TC \text{ (monthly preventive maintenance)} = \$10(50) + \$60(50)(0.30)$$
$$= \$1400 \text{ per month}$$

Because the total cost for monthly maintenance is higher than for pure remedial maintenance, we will determine the total cost for preventive maintenance used every two months. The total number of breakdowns occurring by the end of the second month will be called F_2. Then:

$$F_2 = M(p_1 + p_2) + F_1p_1$$

We observe that some of the machines that failed and were repaired in the first month contribute to breakdowns in the second month, that is, F_1p_1. The total cost for this policy will be:

$$TC \text{ (preventive maintenance every two months)} = K_1M + K_2F_2$$
$$= K_1M + K_2[M(p_1 + p_2) + F_1p_1]$$
$$= \$10(50) + \$60[50(0.40) + 15(0.30)] = \$1970 \text{ per two months}$$

The total cost we have just determined is a two-month bill. Therefore, we divide this result by two in order to obtain an average monthly total cost. The result is $985, which is far better than the average monthly total cost of the monthly preventive maintenance policy, viz., $1400, but not better than the policy of providing no preventive maintenance at all, which was $967.74.
In general, then,

$$TC \text{ (for preventive maintenance every } j \text{ months)} = K_1M + K_2F_j$$

where

$$F_j = M(p_1 + p_2 + p_3 + \ldots + p_j) + F_1p_{j-1} + F_2p_{j-2} + \ldots + F_{j-1}p_1$$

Our comparison is made on the basis of $TC(j)/j$ = average monthly total cost.

The following table lists the results for our example, where $j = 0$ represents the policy of using no preventive maintenance.

Month j Policy	F_j	$TC(j) = 500 + 60F_j$	Average Monthly Total Cost
0			$ 967.74
1	15.00	$1400	1400.00
2	24.50	1970	985.00
3	33.85	2531	843.67
4	49.11	3447	861.65
5	73.57	4914	982.84
6	etc.		

We observe that the minimum cost policy calls for preventive maintenance every three months. Periods longer and shorter than that result in greater average monthly costs. The approach we have just utilized can be applied to a variety of situations.[17] Suitable process control is obtained by means of line-balancing, replacement, and repair and maintenance strategies. The development of optimal systems can only be achieved when the inter-relationships between all these areas are taken into account. Each aspect of the process affects the kinds of decision that must be made in the others. Isolation into problem-type compartments cannot help but create serious process and systems suboptimizations.

Multiple Facilities

The determination of optimal sizes for several interacting facilities is a problem that can be viewed on a national scale (i.e., between sectors), on a corporate scale (i.e., between subsidiaries), and even on a departmental scale. The flows of materials between the interacting facilities represent both constraints and opportunities. This significant problem in facilities management has been treated at great length by Wassily Leontieff's Input-Output Analysis.[18] Such input-output analysis is easily accomplished with linear programming. The three matrices shown below describe the essential elements:

A = the bill of goods matrix (in this case, we have illustrated three outputs and three inputs).

B = the technological matrix (the coefficients are usually obtained empirically).

C = the activity level matrix ($x_j \geq 0, j = 1, 2, \ldots, n$).

---

[17] For example, see: M. Sasieni, A. Yaspan, and L. Friedman, *Operations Research: Methods and Problems* (New York: John Wiley & Sons, Inc., 1959), pp. 108–12.

[18] See Robert Dorfman, Paul A. Samuelson, and Robert M. Solow, *Linear Programming and Economic Analysis* (New York: McGraw-Hill Book Company, Inc., 1958).

$$
\begin{array}{ccc}
A & B & C
\end{array}
$$

$$
\begin{array}{l}
\text{Output} \left\{
\begin{bmatrix} y_1 \\ y_2 \\ y_3 \end{bmatrix}
\right.
\\
\begin{array}{l}
\text{Negative} \\
\text{outputs} \\
\text{are inputs}
\end{array}
\left.
\begin{bmatrix} y_4 \\ y_5 \\ y_6 \end{bmatrix}
\right.
\end{array}
\begin{bmatrix}
a_{11} & a_{12} & \cdots & a_{1n} \\
a_{21} & a_{22} & \cdots & a_{2n} \\
a_{31} & a_{32} & \cdots & a_{3n} \\
a_{41} & a_{42} & \cdots & a_{4n} \\
a_{51} & a_{52} & \cdots & a_{5n} \\
a_{61} & a_{62} & \cdots & a_{6n}
\end{bmatrix}
\begin{bmatrix}
x_1 \\ x_2 \\ x_3 \\ \cdot \\ \cdot \\ x_n
\end{bmatrix}
$$

The system of equations that results is as follows:

$$
\begin{aligned}
y_1 &= a_{11}x_1 + a_{12}x_2 + \ldots + a_{1n}x_n \\
y_2 &= a_{21}x_1 + a_{22}x_2 + \ldots + a_{2n}x_n \\
&\quad \cdot \qquad \cdot \qquad \qquad \cdot \\
&\quad \cdot \qquad \cdot \qquad \qquad \cdot \\
&\quad \cdot \qquad \cdot \qquad \qquad \cdot \\
y_6 &= a_{61}x_1 + a_{62}x_2 + \ldots + a_{6n}x_n
\end{aligned}
$$

Let us consider a specific problem, where our objective is to determine how much of the total company's operating budget should be allocated to each of two subsidiaries, which produce complimentary commodities, called 1 and 2. We arrange our data, letting x_j = number of units produced by the jth subsidiary.

| | | | | Productivity Measures | |
				Subsidiary 1 x_1	Subsidiary 2 x_2
y_1	Selling	\$1/#	Chemical A	10#/hr/unit	−5#/hr/unit[19]
y_2	price	\$5/#	Chemical B	20#/hr/unit	0
y_3		\$12/#	Chemical C	12#/hr/unit	10#/hr/unit
y_4		\$10/#	Chemical D	−6/hr/unit	+8#/hr/unit
y_5	Cost	\$6/mh	Labor	−10 mh/hr/unit	−5 mh/hr/unit

Figure 14.17 portrays the flow patterns that relate these two facilities. It is simple enough to write the specific equations that apply to this example.

$$
\begin{aligned}
A: y_1 &= 10x_1 - 5x_2 \quad (\#/\text{hr}) \\
B: y_2 &= 20x_1 \quad (\#/\text{hr}) \\
C: y_3 &= 12x_1 + 10x_2 \quad (\#/\text{hr}) \\
D: y_4 &= -6x_1 + 8x_2 \quad (\#/\text{hr}) \\
L: y_5 &= -10x_1 - 5x_2 \quad \left(\frac{\text{manhours}}{\text{hour}}\right)
\end{aligned}
$$

[19] Subsidiary 2 requires Chemical A for its output; 5 pounds (#) per hour per unit of capacity. Similarly, note that Subsidiary 1 requires Chemical D. Both subsidiaries require inputs of manhours (mh) per hour per unit of capacity.

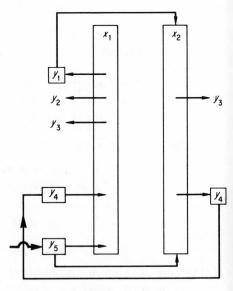

Figure 14.17

Maximize $[z = (1)y_1 + 5y_2 + 12y_3 + 10y_4 + 6y_5]$

where z is profit in dollars per hour.

Then, by substitution, we obtain:

$$z = \left.\begin{array}{r} 10x_1 - 5x_2 \\ + 100x_1 \\ + 144x_1 + 120x_2 \\ - 60x_1 + 80x_2 \\ - 60x_1 - 30x_2 \end{array}\right\} = 134x_1 + 165x_2$$

Assume the constraints are as follows:

$$y_1 \geq 5\#/\text{hr}, \ y_4 \geq 6\#/\text{hr}$$
$$y_5 \geq -30 \text{ mh/hr}$$

The y_5 constraint fixes company size. These constraints become:

$$10x_1 - 5x_2 \geq 5$$
$$-6x_1 + 8x_2 \geq 6$$
$$-10x_1 - 5x_2 \geq -30$$
$$\text{or} \quad 10x_1 + 5x_2 \geq 30$$

We show the graphical solution in Figure 14.18.

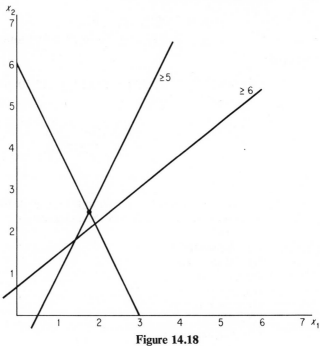

Figure 14.18

The optimal point occurs where the two constraint lines cross, that is,

$$10x_1 - 5x_2 = 5$$
$$10x_1 + 5x_2 = 30$$
$$\overline{ 10x_2 = 25}$$

Thus, $x_2 = 2.5$ units

And, solving for x_1, we obtain: $10x_1 - 12.5 = 5$

$$10x_1 \qquad = 17.5$$
$$x_1 \qquad\quad = 1.75 \text{ units}$$

The ratio of units produced by the first and second subsidiaries is:

$$\frac{x_1}{x_2} = \frac{1.75}{2.50} = \frac{\frac{7}{4}}{\frac{5}{2}} = 0.7.$$

Thus, the sizes of subsidiary 1 and subsidiary 2 should be in the ratio of 7 to 10. Then the flows are fixed:

$$y_1 = \quad 17.5 - 12.5 = 5; \quad y_1 \geq 5$$
$$y_2 = \quad 35$$
$$y_3 = \quad 46$$

$$y_4 = 30.5; \quad y_4 \geq 6$$
$$y_5 = -30; \quad y_5 \geq -30 \text{ (See footnote }[20])$$

and profit;

$$z = 134(1.75) + 165(2.5) = 234.50 + 412.50 = \$647/\text{hr}.$$

PROBLEMS

1. The industries listed below tend to form high-density clusters in specific geographic areas. Is there a rational explanation?
   (a) Steel
   (b) Automobiles
   (c) Stock yards
   (d) Textiles
   (e) Electronics
   (f) Aircraft
   (g) Rubber
   (h) Motion pictures
   (i) Books
   (j) Cigarettes
2. The Omicron Company has two factories, A and B, located in Wilmington, Delaware and San Francisco, California, respectively. Each has a production capacity of 550 units per week. Omicron's markets are Los Angeles, Chicago, and New York. The demands of these markets are for 150, 350, and 400 units, respectively, in the coming week. A matrix of shipping distances is prepared, and the shipping schedule is determined to minimize total shipping distance. Estimate the distances and solve this problem on that basis.
3. Omicron decides to build a third plant. The strongest contenders are Chicago, Illinois and Cleveland, Ohio. The new plant would have a productive capacity of 400 units. Keeping the market demands unchanged from Problem 2 above, what should Omicron do?
4. Complete the total enumeration of all possible iterations for the 3×3 layout problem described in the text (pp. 434–435). This much has been completed already:

A	B	C	TC_{ij}
1	2	3	585
1	3	2	465
3	1	2	405

[20] This fixes the size of the system.

5. Use the various approaches to the layout problem to resolve the following situation:

	F_{ij}					C_{ij}					d_{kl}			
	A	B	C	D		A	B	C	D		1	2	3	4
A	—	10	6	12	A	—	4	5	3	1	—	15	5	10
B	5	—	9	8	B	4	—	5	3	2	15	—	5	10
C	14	15	—	3	C	3	4	—	6	3	5	5	—	25
D	10	8	16	—	D	5	3	2	—	4	10	15	25	—

6. Using the matrix below, determine the best layout for the system.

		Locations					
		1	2	3	4	5	6
	A	16	25	9	16	7	14
	B	12	22	5	14	9	32
Machine	C	35	41	13	8	14	8
centers	D	26	14	24	10	31	14
	E	40	15	15	26	16	18
	F	28	11	6	18	19	22

Matrix of costs for each assignment

7. Explain why:
   (a) In a job shop, the matrix $[F_{ij}]$ might have few zero entries whereas, in a flow shop, the matrix might have one entry per row;
   (b) Why, in almost all cases, is there a tendency for the matrix to be loaded above the diagonal, i.e., $F_{ij} >> F_{ji}$

8. Compare straight-line depreciation (twenty years) with the equivalent sum of digits result. What salvage value would remain after twenty years with a 10 per cent rate for the declining balance method? Assume an investment of $10,000.

9. For replacement of facilities, use the example of the MAPI approach given in the text, pages 438–443, but make the following change:
   (a) Column B—estimated service life—fifteen years.
      How does this alteration affect the urgency rating? Discuss.
   Now, go back to the original example and make the following changes:
   (b) Use declining balance depreciation instead of the straight-line determination.
      How has this modification affected the observed result? Discuss.
   (c) Finally, going back to the original problem statement, alter step thirty-two.

Change the tax rate from 50 to 40 per cent. What effect does this have? Discuss.

10. Study the preventive versus remedial maintenance of facilities problem described in the text, where the appropriate failure distribution might be variant A, described below:

jth Month After Maintenance	Variant A Probability of Failure in the jth Month	Variant B Probability of Failure in the jth Month
1	0.10	0.10
2	0.20	0.15
3	0.40	0.20
4	0.20	0.25
5	0.10	0.30
	1.00	1.00

(a) Compare your results obtained under the variant A assumption with that described in the text.

(b) Use the variant B distribution, and compare your answers with the previous results.

(c) For the original example, let $K_2 = \$50$ per machine. What effect does this have?

(d) For the original example, let $K_1 = \$20$ per machine. What effect does this have?

Undoubtedly, the most trying problem that management has faced over the years has been the question of how to deal with the man in the system. Job evaluation, productivity analysis, and labor cost determination have proven to be elusive, both for definition and for measurement. The contribution of manpower to the total cost of the output is usually sizable. This explains why the problem of measuring manpower costs has received continuous attention over many years. In this area there has been a continual improvement of measurement methods, but no sudden illumination or discovery of a panacea. By and large, the problem is still quite critical for industry.

Manpower *Management* 15

A startling case history was obtained in the 1930s by a study group from Harvard at the Western Electric Company in Chicago. The study concerned such questions as whether levels of illumination have some effect on productivity. It was discovered that whether or not the illumination was raised or lowered, productivity was improved. The key discovery was that employees responded positively to management's interest and attention.

Wage Plans and Incentives

An area of great importance to the manager concerns the motivational forces that affect man's productivity. Behavior can be influenced by various inducements (for example, monetary incentives) whereas machines cannot be (a major difference at the man-machine interface). Motivation can be positive or negative. We associate the latter with poor employee morale. On the face of it, one would suppose that an average level of morale existed from which positive and negative deviations could be measured. Of course, there is no standard to use in this way. With discussions of incentives and motivation, the major difficulty is the measurement problem. Nevertheless, accepting the lack of precision involved, we recognize that motivation exists as a real causal factor in a man-machine system.

Many factors affect the level of motivation of an employee. These include prestige, social standing, and importance of the job. Also included are vacations, leisure time, and freedom of hours. For the most part, these categories represent intangibles that defy definition and measurement. We speak of leadership—knowing that an undefinable characteristic is involved that is intimately connected with the subject of motivation and incentive. We lack a yardstick by which to measure it. One of the few ways to set an objective standard for the control of incentives is through wage plans.

What is an equitable wage? Do we measure real wages in terms of the cost of living, or do we compare monetary wages as they are found in different parts of the country? Is it reasonable to compare, for a given industry, rural with urban wages? There has been a continuing attempt to relate monetary

454

wages to real wages. For this reason the minimum wage as fixed by law has been steadily increased over the years in order to keep pace with a rising cost of living. From each company's point of view there is some level of wages that is optimal. High wages remove dollars that could otherwise be invested in expansion possibilities. Dollars are withheld from stockholders. This action produces unpredictable results on the stock market. It generally lowers the credit ratings that banks will offer. Low wages, on the other hand, discourage highly skilled and able personnel, produce negative motivation, increase turnover rates, and increase recruitment costs. From the company's point of view, therefore, neither high nor low wages are desirable. Rather, a wage rate that produces a balanced system of costs is desired.

To determine wage rates, we must separate two questions: What constitutes a reasonable output for a day of work? and What wages should be paid for reasonable amounts of different kinds of outputs? Job evaluation is at the core of the second question.

There are many different but reasonable approaches to the problem of job evaluation. The first requires purely qualitative evaluations. A second possibility calls for the ranking of jobs. A third approach is based upon a point system that we will describe. The purely qualitative approach is susceptible to personal bias. Because of this, it is disappearing from use. Ranking does not indicate how much one job differs from another. Let us, therefore, consider the most elaborate of the named approaches—the point system. A job is classified in terms of a number of factors, such as:

1. Intelligence required for the job;
2. Physical skill required for the job;
3. Physical effort required for the job;
4. Responsibility that must be assumed in order to accomplish the job;
5. Working conditions, including the environment and other human factors relevant to job accomplishment.

Any job can be described in terms of these variables. Each task requires a varying amount of each factor. By assigning point values to each factor, it is possible to derive a total score for any job. The score is equivalent to a monetary wage rate. It is intended to reflect the requirements of the job in terms of the significant factors. Presumably, in this way an approach is made to the problem of determining true worth to the company. After all, the real issue is: What is a particular job, or set of operations, worth to the company? For machines, the costs are easily derived, but for men, the problem has never been resolved.

To convert job point levels into appropriate wage rates, the *key-job concept* can be used. Certain key positions exist that are *commonly found* in the industry. These key jobs might include the position of secretary, foreman, and skilled tool and die-makers. Such jobs tend to have high interchangeability within an industry and often between different industries as well. The key jobs are carefully studied in terms of the relevant factors, then a job rating is assigned to each key job based upon an industry-wide, geographic analysis of the going wage rates for key positions. A curve can then be drawn such as is shown in Figure 15.1. First, key jobs representing a broad range of

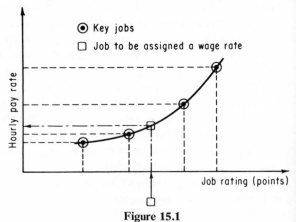

Figure 15.1
The key-job concept.

job ratings and hourly pay rates are located on this graph. Then, a curve is put through the key job points. It follows that all other jobs can be assigned appropriate wage rates by using interpolation between the key job points and extrapolation from the end points.

Additional factors intervene. These include the use of incentive plans, merit rating systems, the importance of seniority, the effect of cost of living factors, the supply and demand both regionally and nationally for certain skills, and the notion of a guaranteed annual wage. Before proceeding further, let us recapitulate the steps required to establish a rate structure:

1. Develop relevant job factors;
2. Classify jobs in terms of the relevant factors;
3. Select key jobs and determine appropriate wage rates;
4. Assign wage rates to nonkey jobs by interpolation and extrapolation;[1]
5. Take special factors into account such as seniority, merit ratings, and incentive plans.

Various models suitable for the analysis of employee motivation have been developed.[2] We shall only mention a few. They are concerned with the

[1] Many jobs can only be assigned a wage according to the expected contributions of the worker. This is characteristic of executive and administrative positions. It is also true of creative and research jobs.

[2] Historically, there has been great interest in this subject regarding the development of incentive plans. Frederick W. Taylor, Henry Towne, Henri Fayol, and others were concerned with incentive, profit-sharing, work definition, work division, authority and responsibility, and the question of satisfactory pay.

methods used to obtain maximum worker participation. They are designed, on the one hand, to provide equitable distinction between workers who expend different amounts of energy and contribute different benefits to the company. On the other hand, they are intended to provide a balanced system of wages for the company.

1. Straight Piece-Work Model:

$$W = HA \left(\frac{O_A}{O_S}\right)$$

where:

H = Hourly rate in dollars per hour.
A = Actual time worked in hours per week.
O_A = Actual output per hour in pieces per hour.
O_S = Standard output per hour in expected number of pieces per hour.
W = Weekly wage rate in dollars per week.

H/O_S is the rate in dollars per piece of completed work and is derived in terms of an output standard (from time studies) and a wage standard (from job evaluation). The worker, however, has no security with this fundamental wage plan. His weekly wage decreases proportionally as his actual work output falls.

2. Piece-Work Model with a Guaranteed Base:

$$\text{for } O_A \leq O_S \quad W = HA$$

$$\text{for } O_A > O_S \quad W = HA \left(\frac{O_A}{O_S}\right)$$

In this case, the worker is guaranteed at least a weekly wage rate of $W = HA$. As his actual output becomes greater than standard output, he can take home additional money.

3. General Incentive Model:

$$\text{for } O_A \leq O_S \quad W = HA$$

$$\text{for } O_A > O_S \quad W = HA \left[1 + k \left(\frac{O_A}{O_S} - 1\right)\right]$$

Here again, the minimum is established at $W = HA$. Now, however, we observe that the incentive given is proportional to the size of the coefficient k. For O_A greater than O_S, some fraction of the value of the extra production of the worker is paid to him as both reward and incentive. The value of k

depends upon the plan that is used. For example, there is the Halsey 50-50 plan where $k = \frac{1}{2}$. In the 100 per cent bonus plan,[3] $k = 1$. In the Bedaux plan, $k = \frac{3}{4}$.

Productivity

In the previous section, which dealt with wage plans, we pointed out that the problem of determining labor costs has two parts. First: What is a fair or a reasonable output? That is: How many pieces should be expected per unit of time? The second part deals with the question: What is fair wage for fair output? The difficulty of answering these questions is underscored by such further queries as: How can we equate the work done by a secretary and a punch press operator? What is a reasonable salary for the research director as compared to the production manager? If two men work equally hard, but one turns out ten pieces while the second turns out twenty pieces, should we pay them equal salaries? Should a man be paid for time or for physical output?

All these questions seem to hinge on two rational points. First, what value does the company derive from its manpower component? Second, considering the factor of supply and demand for the kind of services that the company requires, how much should it pay? It is the search for a measure of value that has led to *production standards*. These standards state specifically what the expected productivity is for a particular job. But, the output rate for any one worker is variable. Furthermore, differences exist between workers. How, then, are these standards established? Because manpower is variable, which individual is the standard man?

Time Studies

Jobs differ from one another and so do men. In order to find a common ground for setting standards and for evaluating the efforts and outputs of men, it was necessary to begin the analysis on a very elementary level. Originally, *production studies* were used. These represented situations where the worker was constantly observed over a long period of time. The approach can be compared to *100 per cent inspection*. Both the job and the worker were studied with patient detail. This method has such shortcomings that it is now almost a historical curiosity. The primary weaknesses are high cost, unreliable results, and belligerent subjects. The 100 per cent sample gave way to sampling procedures. Present-day time studies are based on sampling methods derived from developments begun in the 1920s. Instead of tracking the worker

---

[3] This is equivalent to the piece-work model with a guaranteed base.

continuously for long periods of time, time study methods—by obtaining a sufficient sample of observations—attempted to answer such questions as: How long does it take to do a job, and what is the expected daily output of a worker?

First, the time study man observes the overall job. Next, he breaks the job down into basic elements. These, when added together, form the job cycle. This cycle should be relatively short and repetitively used. It will constitute the major portion of the worker's job. For long-cycle jobs, time study methods are difficult to apply.

A stop watch is employed to time the cycle elements. Usually, the stop watch is attached to a time study board that holds an observation or time study sheet. Such a time study sheet is shown in Figure 15.2. on page 460. In this case, the job we are considering has been broken down into two elements. Observations for element one in the first cycle are entered in the appropriate column These are followed by the observations for element two in the first cycle. Then, cycle two begins, and so forth. It can be seen that these element values are *continuously* timed. The sample size is thirty cycles, all of which are listed on our sheet. After the observations have been made, the time study man goes to his desk and begins to compute. The initial cycle takes 0.20 minutes. Of this, element one consumed 0.14 minutes and element two took the remaining 0.06 minutes.[4] The second cycle ends at 0.36 minutes. This means that the second cycle consumed $0.36 - 0.20 = 0.16$ minutes. For the second cycle, element one required 0.11 minutes and element two used the remaining 0.05 minutes. The rest of the values are obtained in the same way, by subtraction.

In addition to the basic cycle, the time sheet lists *extraneous elements*. These are operations which must be done every now and then. Extraneous elements will break into the short-cycle system regularly. Therefore, when we include them, the total job is not really short cycle, but of longer duration. Elements one and two constitute a *major subcycle* within this system.

The element which has the longest cycle (between its appearances in the job) seems to be *D*, occurring in this sample only after twenty-two cycles of elements 1 and 2. It is the shortest, common cycle for *all* elements in the system. This point is significant; repetitive jobs usually include very long-cycle, extraneous elements. As the time study man observes the way in which the job is being handled he must catch these longer-cycle elements and include them in his study.

Now, we must obtain a summary of what has been observed. A typical summary form is shown in Figure 15.3. All the elements, *one, two, A, B, C,* and *D* are listed. Total times are collected for each element as they appeared in the thirty cycle period. Those are the column sums for each element, including the extraneous factors.

---

[4] The stop watch used is a decimal-minute type. It is read directly in hundredths of a minute.

Name of Job
Name of Worker
Name of Observer
Date

Observations (all times in hundredths of a minute)

Cycle	Cycle Elements				Extraneous Job Elements							
Cycle	1	Δ	2	Δ	A	Δ	B	Δ	C	Δ	D	Δ
1	14	14	20	6								
2	31	11	36	5								
3	48	12	53	5								
4	65	12	70	5								
5	83	13	86	3								
6	97	11	104	7								
7	117	13	122	5								
8	134	12	139	5								
9	151	12	156	5								
10	167	11	171	4								
11	184	13	207	4	203	19						
12	218	11	222	4								
13	233	11	237	4								
14	249	12	256	7								
15	269	13	289	6			283	14				
16	301	12	306	5								
17	318	12	338	6					332	14		
18	350	12	355	5								
19	368	13	376	8								
20	389	13	394	5								
21	406	12	410	4								
22	423	13	429	6							448	19
23	461	13	467	6								
24	478	11	482	4								
25	493	11	497	4								
26	507	10	510	3								
27	520	10	526	6								
28	537	11	542	5								
29	554	12	560	6								
30	573	13	579	6								
Total		359		154		19		14		14		19

Figure 15.2

Continuous timing is used; Δ represents subtraction to get element times.

The *total time* for element one is 359; for element two it is 154; and it is 19, 14, 14, and 19, respectively, for the extraneous elements *A*, *B*, *C*, and *D*. The number of observations for each element is recorded. There are thirty observations for elements one and two. By chance, during this period of time,

Element	1	2	A	B	C	D	Σ
Total time	359	154	19	14	14	19	579
Number of observations	30	30	1	1	1	1	64
Expected cycles per occurrence*	1	1	100	50	50	500	
Average time or selected time	11.97	5.13	0.19	0.28	0.28	0.04	17.89
Allowances or leveling factors	0.95	1.00	1.00	1.00	1.00	1.00	
Adjusted time or normal time	11.37	5.13	0.19	0.28	0.28	0.04	17.29
R & D correction	110%	110%	110%	110%	110%	110%	
Standard time	12.51	5.64	0.21	0.31	0.31	0.04	19.02

Standard: $\dfrac{60 \text{ minutes}}{\text{hour}} \times \dfrac{100}{19.02} \dfrac{\text{boxes}}{\text{minutes}} \cong 316$ boxes per hour

* By job design specifications.

Figure 15.3

Time study summary form.

each extraneous element occurs once. The third row of our summary sheet lists the number of cycles designed to occur between elements. We divide the first row by the product of rows two and three. In this way, an *average time*, or *selected time*, is developed for each of the operations that constitute the job. For example, dividing 359 by (30 × 1), we obtain 11.97 hundredths of a minute, or 0.1197 minutes, for element one, 0.0513 minutes for element two, and so forth.

Now we come to one of the most disagreeable jobs in the time study system. This is the choice of an *allowance* or *leveling factor*. Any effort for precision that we may have been striving for up to this point might just as well be discarded as having been a waste of time. We will not bandy words. Time study permits a meaningful and useful *rough* fix to be made on the system's manpower output and costs. However, because leveling must be used, real precision can never be obtained. The issue is concerned with the following. Who should the time study man observe? Generally, he chooses an average worker, operating under standard conditions, who presumably uses a routinized method. But if the subject appears to work at something more or less than an average rate, a leveling factor, or allowance, must be applied. For the normal worker the leveling factor is 100 per cent. This leaves the resulting system of numbers unchanged. On what basis does the time study man decide whether a worker is performing above, below, or exactly at the normal level? The answer is that time study men, after much practice, can exhibit far more agreement among themselves than would occur by chance, even though the concept of a standard basis for allowances is vague, undefined, and subjective. Training in leveling is accomplished in many ways. One of the most successful is by means of motion pictures, where the projector has a variable speed control.

The *allowance* is applied to *average time*, from which we obtain *adjusted time*, or *normal time*. This is simply the product of the average time and the allowance. Thus, if the leveling factor is 110 per cent, meaning that the observed worker is faster than normal, then the adjusted time will be larger than the average time, meaning that the normal (slower) worker can be expected to take a longer than observed time. In the case of the operator who is working at 95 per cent of normal, in the judgment of the time study man, multiplication produces a normal time that is smaller than the selected time, meaning that the average worker can go faster.

Even if we could accept leveling with equanimity, we must now add an additional *rough* correction. This is the rest and delay correction factor. Usually, it is assigned values that range from 5 per cent to 15 per cent, depending upon the character of the job, the degree of personal needs, and so on. The adjusted, or normal time, is multiplied by the R & D (rest and delay, in this context) factor. In this way we derive the *standard time* that is the basis of the production standard. We note that the standard times are listed along the bottom row of the summary box. Each element, including the extraneous elements, have their standard times. The sum of all the elemental standard times is the standard time of the operation. In our example this is 0.1902 minutes. We can divide 60 minutes per hour by the operation's total standard time. This tells us that approximately 316 boxes per hour is the expected output rate for the job. That is, 60/0.1902 equals 316 boxes per hour. If the wage rate for this class of job is $2.00 per hour, then the labor cost component for the operation would be $2.00/316 = $0.006, or a little more than a half-cent apiece. This would be the expected cost of the operation.

Primary weaknesses of time study are: the definition of an average worker, applying the leveling factor, applying the R & D correction, and not recognizing influential extraneous elements. Ingenious answers have been found for some of these problems. Time study is a skill. To begin with, the use of the stop watch requires training and practice. The same applies to leveling. Skilled practitioners of this art seldom break down elements into less than 0.04 minutes because less than this interval is exceedingly difficult to observe. The major criticism of time study centers around leveling, but another problem worthy of consideration is the fact that the worker's performance may not be stable in the Shewhart sense. Also, the fact that the worker is not necessarily interested in participating in the study and may have no desire to provide an accurate production standard of performance is another criticism. The expert time study man is supposed to sense this and make appropriate changes in the leveling factor. One can question who will win such a contest—the worker or the time study man?

Time Study Samples

In spite of these objections, some form of time study must be used. Therefore, an issue of importance to the time study field is: How many cycles should be observed? That is, how large a sample should be taken? The statistical formula given below is predicated on the assumption of a degree of accuracy in time studies that is not warranted by the circumstances. Nevertheless, some means must be found for setting a proper sample size. We have:

$$N' = \left[\frac{40\sqrt{N \sum\limits_{i=1}^{i=N} x_i^2 - (\sum\limits_{i=1}^{i=N} x_i)^2}}{\sum\limits_{i=1}^{i=N} x_i} \right]^2$$

where x_i is the ith observation for a particular element; N is the number of cycles observed up to this point; and N' is the number of cycles that *should be* observed, that is, specifically the required number of cycles to be observed so that we obtain 95 per cent confidence that the true element time lies within the range $x \pm 0.05x$, which is ± 5 per cent of the observed average time.

Because the job can comprise many different elements, we must use the element that will dominate the sample size by requiring the largest value[5] of N'. Having completed a partial study, the time study man will check to find out how much further he should go. If he obtains a value for N' that is larger than N, he must continue to take observations. This sample size evaluation procedure is repeated until the value of N' is equal to or less than the actual number of observations made, that is, $N' \leq N$. Let us examine the following example.

| | | | Element | |
| Reading | 1 | 2 | 1 | 2 |
i	$x_i(1)$	$x_i(2)$	$x_i^2(1)$	$x_i^2(2)$
1	14	6	196	36
2	11	5	121	25
3	12	5	144	25
4	12	5	144	25
5	13	3	169	9
	62	24	774	120

$$N'(1) = \left(\frac{40\sqrt{5(774) - (62)^2}}{62} \right)^2 = 10.9$$

$$N'(2) = \left(\frac{40\sqrt{5(120) - (24)^2}}{24} \right)^2 = 6.6$$

[5] This will be associated with elements exhibiting great measurement variability, and, because of the nature of this formulation, with elements having small average values.

We begin with $N = 5$ observations of the two elements and find that N' for element one dominates the sample size. It specifies 10.9 readings. Because we have taken only five readings, we must enlarge the sample size. We might take another five or six readings and then test again. In this way, we keep collecting observations until we find that N' is equal to or less than N.

The methods of time study, in spite of the inherent problems, are widely used by industry. The need for this kind of information is fundamental. At the same time, for many applications, such as long-cycle systems and for preestimating jobs that do not yet exist, other methods had to be developed. We shall now consider these.

Work Sampling

The ideas fundamental to materials acceptance sampling plans were extended to encompass *work*, that is, operations and activities of the man in the system. In the 1930s, Tippett reported on his experiments with work sampling in English textile factories; and at about the same time, Morrow was utilizing this type of technique in factories in the U.S.A. Just as in the case of materials sampling, the observations to be made represent less than a 100 per cent study. Therefore, the observations must be random and of sufficient number so that an accurate picture can be constructed of what is going on in the system. Consider the following. We will divide the day into 450 intervals, each of which is a working minute. On a purely random basis, we will select 54 of these 450 intervals; these will constitute the sample. Thus, if 450 numbered chips were thrown into a bowl—where the chips are numbered consecutively from 1 to 450—then by drawing 54 chips at random from the bowl, we could determine a set of observation assignments for that day.

A method simpler to use than the bowl of chips requires tables of random numbers[6] and Monte Carlo number assignments. We know that a random number table has no pattern whatever for the numbers listed in the table. The Monte Carlo assignments could be made as follows. We wish to sample 54 out of 450 minute intervals. This is 0.12 of the total number of daily intervals. Then, let the Monte Carlo numbers 00-11 stand for: Take an observation; and the Monte Carlo numbers 12-99 stand for: No observation is to be taken. We now draw 450 pairs of random numbers in succession. As we read successive numbers from the table, we check to find out whether we are supposed to take an observation. Thus, assume the following random numbers:

62831   04609   83826   57106   38640

---

[6] See p. 203 for a table of random numbers.

Reading these off in pairs from left to right, we find:

Time Interval	Random Number	Monte Carlo Interpretation	Working	Idle
1	62	No observation		
2	83	No observation		
3	10	Observation	x	
4	46	No observation		
5	09	Observation	x	
6	83	No observation		
7	82	No observation		
8	65	No observation		
9	71	No observation		
10	06	Observation		x
	etc.			

Because all random numbers are equally likely, on the average, 1.2 out of ten random numbers will signify that an observation should be made. The sample that we have drawn has delivered three out of ten, but this is in the nature of statistical systems. Sometimes they will be high, sometimes low; in the long run, the results will average out. Our purpose is to insure that a good sample is drawn; and one that no one, neither observer nor worker, can anticipate. Only in this way can the observations be unexpected and the situation that is observed be known to be unstaged, unpremeditated, and representative. Following the directives of the random numbers, the observer makes his appearance at the work place at the third, fifth, tenth, and so on intervals. He makes his observations, records them, and departs.

The purpose of the observations, for the above example, has been to determine whether the worker was engaged or idle. If a particular project or operation was the observation base, then categories of what was being done might be used. When a sufficient sample has been taken, ratios can be formed as descriptive measures of what goes on in the system. For example, assume that for a particular day, forty-five observations have been made. Forty times the individual was found to be busy. Then 40/45, or 8/9, of the time the operator can be assumed to have been engaged in a productive task.

The idea of work sampling is not to catch the worker off guard. Rather, it is to map out his activities and to help him utilize his time more fully. A more elaborate study than the one we have just described will help to make this point more apparent.

	Filing	Phoning	Typing	Other	Total
Number of times observed	60	30	182	28	300
Per cent of total	20	10	61	9	100

Designing a study that will reveal *needed* information with measurable reliability that cannot be obtained in a less expensive way is the essence of the work sampling, or operations sampling, technique. But how large a sample is needed? The same question was asked previously with respect to time studies. We have:

$$N = \left(\frac{k^2}{s}\right) p(1 - p)$$

where

$N =$ The number of observations to be taken to provide a sufficient sample. A sufficient sample is defined by management in terms of the two parameters, k and s.

$k =$ The number of normal standard deviations required to give a confidence measure of α. When $k = 1$, $\alpha = 68$ per cent; when $k = 2$, $\alpha = 95$ per cent; when $k = 3$, $\alpha = 99.7$ per cent.

$\alpha =$ The likelihood that the true value of p falls within the range $p \pm s$.

$s =$ The accuracy range specified by management such that the true value of p falls within the range $p \pm s$.

$p =$ The fraction of total observations that an activity is observed to occur. When using this formula, we need only compute N for the one activity that dominates the sample size requirements.[7] This will be the activity whose observed p is closest to $\frac{1}{2}$.

As an example we shall use the office sampling figures that were previously given. The typing activity has a value of p that is closest to $\frac{1}{2}$, viz., $p = 0.61$. Let $k = 2$ and $s = 0.05$. Then,

$$N = \left(\frac{2}{0.05}\right)^2 (0.61)(0.39) = 381$$

Because only three hundred observations were made, it is necessary that an addition be made to the sample. We will presume that one hundred more observations are taken and that $p(\text{typing}) = \frac{240}{400} = 0.60$. Then,

$$N = \left(\frac{2}{0.05}\right)^2 (0.6)(0.4) = 384$$

which is smaller than the actual sample, so the sample size is sufficient and we can stop.

---

[7] It should be noted that the sample formula given for time study samples, p. 463, was based on an interval of the type $p \pm sp$. If we had used that relationship here, our sample size formula would be:

$$N = \left(\frac{k}{s}\right)^2 \left(\frac{1-p}{p}\right)$$

The dominating activity, in this case, will be the one with the smallest p value.

Predetermined Time Standards

It is difficult to obtain accurate measures of a fair day's output under most circumstances. There is also the problem of preparing estimates for jobs that have not been physically actualized. Both of these motives led to the development of synthetic or predetermined time standards. Casting about for some way of categorizing the work measurement field, we can generalize, as follows:

1. Time study is applicable for short-cycle, repetitive operations that are presently being performed and can, therefore, be observed.
2. Work sampling can be used for long-cycle, repetitive operations that are presently being performed so they can be observed. The cycle must be stable or else the sample has no meaning.
3. Predetermined (or synthetic) time studies can treat nonrepetitive, non-cyclical jobs and jobs that are not being performed so they cannot be observed.

The basis of synthetic time standards is the fact that every job is composed of a set of elements that are common to all jobs. The unique feature of a particular job is the way in which this common alphabet of elements is used and the way in which the elements are arranged. Frank Gilbreth was one of the first management pioneers to describe such an alphabet of job elements or modules. He called these modules *therbligs* and named seventeen of them. For example,[8]

Grasp: Begins when hand or body member touches an object. Consists of gaining control of an object. Ends when control is gained.

Position: Begins when hand or body member causes part to begin to line up or locate. Consists of hand or body member causing part to line up, orient, or change position.

Assemble: Begins when the hand or body member causes parts to begin to go together. Consists of actual assembly of parts. Ends when hand or body member has caused parts to go together.

Hold: Begins when movement of part or object, which hand or body member has under control, ceases. Consists of holding an object in a fixed position and location. Ends with any movement.

Once the standard modules, or work elements, were named, then it was possible to study thousands of different operations in which each of these elements appeared. Motion pictures were made of many different kinds of jobs; and these in turn were analyzed to determine the appropriate statistical

[8] Marvin E. Mundel, *Motion and Time Study, Principles and Practices*, 4th ed. (Englewood Cliffs, N.J.: Prentice-Hall, Inc., 1970), pp. 242–63.

distribution of element times. Expected standard times were obtained in this way. Tables of such standard times for various work elements are available. For example, there is the system of synthetic standards known as MTM, the methods-time-measurement system. Another well-known system is that of *Work-Factor*, for which tables of standards are also available.[9] Using predetermined standards, it is possible to derive a standard time for a job. First, describe the job completely and isolate the work elements. Then, determine the appropriate times for each element as specified by the system that is being used. Finally, add the times together. Some advantages of synthetic time standards, when they can be applied, are:

1. The leveling factor problem is bypassed. It is already included in the synthetic time standard, because rating differences are averaged out across many jobs and many operators. In short, no rating factor is required with these systems.
2. Distortions that arise because of observer bias and interaction between the observer and the worker can be controlled and removed from the synthetic times, which is not the case for time studies.
3. Time studies are normally based upon an established job. For all new jobs there is a learning period for the worker.[10] During this period, observations are unreliable. The problem is bypassed through the use of predetermined time standards.
4. The cost of determining production standards is reduced.
5. The synthetic production standard is founded upon element times derived from very large samples of observations. This increased reliability of the standard time cannot be obtained with time studies, because it is out of the question to utilize such large samples for studying any one particular job.
6. The speed of preparing cost estimates, as well as their reliability, for new jobs, new products, and so on, is greatly improved. Production schedules can be quickly determined and modified. Product-mix analyses can be similarly expedited.

Work Simplification

This was the core from which modern production management evolved. Taylor, Gantt, Gilbreth, and others recognized that intuitive and judgmental methods of managing could be assisted by "scientific" analysis. The form that the analysis took was based on the premise that *if the parts were im-*

---

[9] Harold B. Maynard, G. J. Stegemerten, and John L. Schwab, *Methods-Time-Measurement* (New York: McGraw-Hill Book Co., Inc., 1948). J. H. Quick, J. H. Duncan, and J. A. Malcolm, Jr., *Work-Factor Time Standards, Measurement of Manual and Mental Work* (New York: McGraw-Hill Book Co., Inc., 1962), pp. 435–46.

[10] See pp. 472–73.

proved, then the whole must be better. We now know that analysis can go just so far, and that, in fact, it can mislead us. We talk about the system, and wherever we use analysis we subsequently require synthesis. We reject efficiency without the simultaneous consideration of effectiveness.

None of this, however, reduces the utility of work simplification when properly applied. After all, efforts to improve efficiency represent investments. Like all investment alternatives, the burden of proof that an efficiency study is the best possible way to proceed falls upon those who would use it. But it must also be remembered that diminishing utility is likely to set in when what is already quite efficient is asked to be more so. The desire for efficiency and perfection is frequently more a matter of personal values than of systems rationality.

A familiar work simplification problem is concerned with the operating characteristics of the man-machine system. The *man-machine time chart* encourages visual analysis of the way in which man-machine operations are coordinated. In Figure 15.4 we observe that both the operator and his

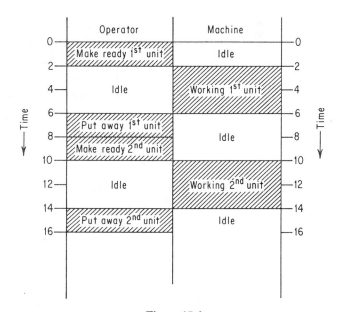

Figure 15.4

Man-machine time chart—machine A, plan 1.

machine are idle 50 per cent of the time. The problem seems to stem from the fact that the machine cannot be used during the *make ready* or the *put away* operations. In other words, the primary machine function must be interrupted, both to prepare and to remove successive parts. *If this were not true,*

*then the more efficient arrangement shown in Figure 15.5 could be used. Here,
after the first cycle, both man and machine are 100 per cent utilized.*

Let us, now, assume that a different facility, machine B, can be used
where make ready and put away idle the facility but can be simultaneously
performed. Then, if a helper is supplied to the operator, the machine utilization can be increased from $\frac{1}{2}$ to $\frac{2}{3}$. Both the operator and the helper have only
$\frac{1}{3}$ utilization factors. This is shown in Figure 15.6.

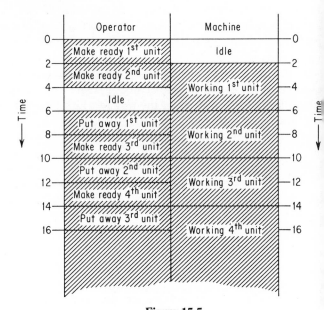

Figure 15.5

Man-machine time chart—machine Q.

We shall complete this discussion by assuming that the data below are
descriptive of the situation:

> Operator's wage = \$3.00 per hour
> Helper's wage = \$1.50 per hour
> Machine A's cost = \$10.00 per hour
> Machine B's cost = \$14.50 per hour
> Value of output = \$2.00 per piece

We can analyze the situation in the following way:

Plan 1. Machine A is utilized 50 per cent of the time. It takes four minutes
to make a part, therefore, 7.5 parts are made per hour. These are valued at
\$15.00. From this we subtract the sum of machine A's hourly cost and the

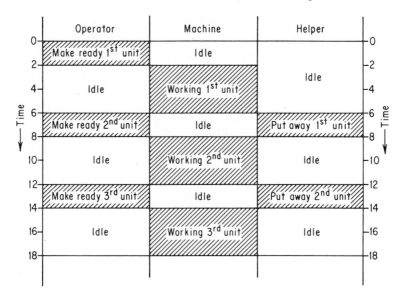

Figure 15.6

Man-machine time chart—machine B, plan 2.

hourly wage of the operator, that is, $15.00 − $13.00 = $2.00, which is the measure of profit per hour for plan 1.

Plan 2.   Machine B is utilized $66\frac{2}{3}$ per cent of the time. Therefore, 10 parts can be made per hour. These are valued at $20.00. We subtract machine B's hourly cost and the hourly wages of both the operator and his helper. This gives $20.00 − $19.00 = $1.00 of profit per hour. Therefore, we prefer plan 1.

For what value of output would these plans be equal? This is easily answered by solving the following equation:

$$7.5p − 13.00 = 10p − 19.00$$

whence, $p = $2.40, satisfies the conditions.

We can see how closely related work simplification is to time study analysis. Before output standards are set, jobs should be studied and brought to a point where common sense and good judgment can no longer be readily used to improve the operations. Nevertheless, at a particular moment in time, an individual may get a sudden insight as to how a well-studied job can be further improved. Generally, there has been deemphasis on work simplification because: Product life is getting shorter and line changeovers to new and modified output designs are becoming more frequent; high-level mechanization and automation of the flow shop require intense preplanning so that little need exists for on-going improvement of operations; more elaborate methodologies have appeared that compete for investment study dollars with the older work simplification methods. These newer methodologies are generally capable of producing greater returns on investments than the older approaches.

The Learning Phenomenon

The worker seldom has a fixed productivity rate. Generally, he improves with practice, and his rates of output deteriorate between practice intervals. Learning is held responsible for the observed improvement, and after a while, such learning reaches a productivity plateau where the rate of increase is slow enough to be considered negligible. This is shown in Figure 15.7.

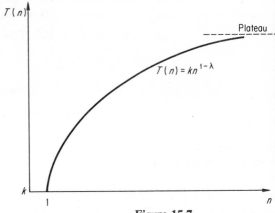

Figure 15.7

The equation, $T(n) = kn^{1-\lambda}$ is read as follows:

$T(n) = $ *cumulative* time to make n units, consecutively;
$k = $ time required to make the *first* unit $n = 1$;
$n = $ trial number, i.e., the number of units made; and
$\lambda = $ the learning coefficient, $0 \leq \lambda < 1$.

We observe that when $\lambda = 0$, the cumulative time $T(n)$ increases linearly (kn), and there is no plateau. As $\lambda \to 1$, the "plateau effect" becomes accentuated. Leveling-off is always expected to occur. The value of λ, therefore, reflects the speed with which the "plateau effect" is felt.

Often, average time measures are used to describe learning. Thus,

$$\bar{T}(n) = \frac{T(n)}{n} = kn^{-\lambda}$$

The same terms apply, as before. When $\lambda = 0$, $\bar{T}(n) = k$, which is the condition for linear learning. Figure 15.8 illustrates $\bar{T}(n)$.

Attempts such as these to describe one of the most complex of all human phenomena in quantitative terms has been shown to work with some reasonable level of predictive success.[11] Especially, in labor intensive situations, the results can be useful. Many refinements exist including *S*-curves and learning functions that include variables to describe the character of the job to be done.[12]

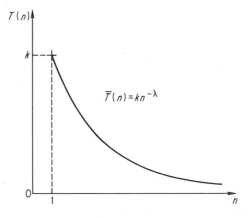

Figure 15.8

At the same time, all learning models suffer from serious flaws. The learning function used must be matched to the particulars of the specific situation. Empirical knowledge is essential.[13] Forgetting as a function of the pattern of intervals between trials deserves serious attention, and little is known about this aspect of the problem. Still, in project planning, as Norden has shown (pp. 216–217), the learning model has introduced a great deal more predictive ability than had previously existed. And it is clear that we need to understand more about the learning situation. Does job enlargement have any effect on learning rates? What is the significance, in time studies, of the assumption that a worker can be tested at a stable point of "normal" activity?

Yet, despite its liabilities, there is general agreement that learning models bring the *behavioral* and the *quantitative* together. This is critical if synthesis is ever to be achieved.

[11] C. C. Pegels, "On Startup or Learning Curves: An Expanded View," *Management of Production*, edited by Martin K. Starr (London, England: Penguin Books Ltd., 1970), pp. 183–95.

[12] Martin K. Starr, *Management: A Modern Approach* (New York: Harcourt Brace Jovanovich, Inc., 1971), pp. 236–39.

[13] Nicholas Baloff, "Estimating the Parameters of the Startup Model—An Empirical Approach," *The Journal of Industrial Engineering*, 18: 4 (April, 1967), 248–53.

The nature of *synthesis*, which is the putting together of complex segmented components, is not entirely a mystery. As it is better understood, so will a "true" systems theory come to exist. At issue are such difficult behavioral problems as the one illustrated in Figure 15.9.

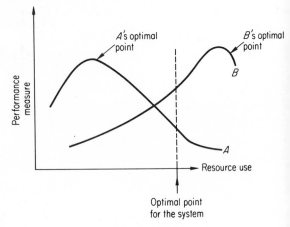

Figure 15.9

A does poorly in individual performance at the system's optimal, but the team of *A + B* wins. Even *B* is not doing as well in his personal performance as he could if he were "a loner." Yet the issue is not completely described in terms of compromise, because there is also the lack of compromise that must be considered. If *A* attempts to work at his optimal and *B* tries to operate at his optimal, then a competitive situation develops. The result is likely to be that entirely different system's performance functions apply. *A* and *B* in competition may produce a system's function that is everywhere inferior to what might have occurred if either one of them has succeeded in dominating the system, or if compromise had been obtained. But, reverse effects have also been known. So, much needs to be done to understand how the individual can be made to benefit by doing what is good for the system as a whole.

PROBLEMS

1. The Ficus Company is a fig packer. The imported figs are weighed out in lots of one pound. There are twelve figs to the pound, on the average. The figs must be inserted in a jar to which a portion of fig syrup is added. Then the jar is sealed with a twist cap.

(a) Analyze the job. Develop what you consider to be a good sequence of work elements.

(b) Sketch the process flow and layout (see pp. 427–430).

(c) Use a process chart to detail the work involved (see p. 428).

(d) Prepare a time sheet.

(e) Assume that the time study has been taken and supply your own hypothetical data for these observations. Then determine the standard time for the job. (Use at least ten cycles.)

(f) Check to see if the sample size is sufficient. If it is, stop. If not, supply additional hypothetical data until an acceptable size is achieved.

2. The President of Ficus learns about predetermined time standards. He calls you in and asks for a report on the applicability of synthetic time methods to check the above times. Develop the appropriate report.

3. Assume that the man-machine situation on pp. 469–471 is now as follows: Both *make ready* and *put away* can only be accomplished when the machine is idle. These operations cannot be performed simultaneously. Two machines are used and are to be tended by a single operator. The element times are unchanged. Use a man-machine time chart to find the best way of handling this situation.

4. Develop a work sampling schedule where the objective is to determine how the personnel in a research laboratory spend their time.

5. What factors would ordinarily be considered when a proposed plan calls for replacing a man with a machine? What criteria would apply to the decision?

6. Company X is about to undertake a program to encourage its employees to suggest new products and revisions of present design. A strong incentive is provided. The company employs 5,000 workers, and it is expected that the number of suggestions per year will average about one per man. Assuming that the average working year is 250 days, there will be about twenty suggestions per day to be screened. The suggestions are to be sorted by the sales division. Only marketable ideas will be forwarded to operations management. It is decided that production will use an initial screening process in order to quickly eliminate the unworkable suggestions. Those ideas that pass the screening will then be subjected to a more intensive feasibility study.

(a) Develop a logical procedure that operations management can follow in order to achieve its objectives. Make sure you include all questions required by the decision process.

(b) Estimate the number of employees required to administer such a program.

7. With respect to the learning models of pp. 472–473, let $k = 10$ minutes and $n = 2$. What values would $T(n)$ and $\overline{T}(n)$ have? Develop appropriate curves for $T(n)$ and $\overline{T}(n)$ given $k = 10$. Discuss your results.

8. Synthesis and coordination clearly have a great deal to do with each other. Do we learn anything more about the system's problem of synthesis by examining the character of coordination? For example, examine what coordination is essential for line balancing, product-mix decisions and the trim problem (pp. 148–150, 119–120, 290–291, respectively).

Bibliography

Baumol, William J., *Economic Theory and Operations Analysis* (2nd ed.). Englewood Cliffs, N.J.: Prentice-Hall, Inc., 1965.

Bowman, Edward H., and Robert B. Fetter, *Analysis for Production and Operations Management* (3rd ed.). Homewood, Illinois: Richard D. Irwin, Inc., 1967.

Brown, R. G., *Smoothing, Forecasting and Prediction*. Englewood Cliffs, N.J.: Prentice-Hall, Inc., 1962.

Brown, Robert G., *Statistical Forecasting for Inventory Control*. New York: McGraw-Hill Book Co., Inc., 1961.

Buffa, Elwood S., *Modern Production Management* (3rd ed.). New York: John Wiley & Sons, Inc., 1969.

Buffa, Elwood S., ed., *Readings in Production and Operations Management*. New York: John Wiley & Sons, Inc., 1969.

————, *Operations Management: Problems and Models* (2nd ed.). New York: John Wiley & Sons, Inc., 1968.

Conway, Richard W., William L. Maxwell, and Louis W. Miller, *Theory of Scheduling*. Reading, Mass.: Addison-Wesley Publishing Company, 1967.

Cox, D. R., and W. L. Smith, *Queues*. New York: John Wiley & Sons, Inc., 1961.

Dorfman, Robert, Paul A. Samuelson, and Robert M. Solow, *Linear Programming and Economic Analysis*. New York: McGraw-Hill, Inc., 1958.

Eilon, Samuel, *Elements of Production Planning and Control*. New York: The Macmillan Co., 1962.

Elmaghraby, S. E., *The Design of Production Systems*. New York: Reinhold Publishing Corporation, 1966.

Feller, William, *Introduction to Probability Theory and Its Applications* (3rd ed.), Vol. I. New York: John Wiley & Sons, Inc., 1957.

Ferguson, Robert O., and Lauren F. Sargent, *Linear Programming: Fundamentals and Applications*. New York: McGraw-Hill Book Co., Inc., 1958.

Forrester, J. W., *Industrial Dynamics*. New York: John Wiley & Sons, Inc., 1961.

Garrett, Leonard J., and Milton Silver, *Production Management Analysis*. New York: Harcourt, Brace & World, Inc., 1966.

476

Gavett, J. William, *Production and Operations Management*. New York: Harcourt, Brace & World, Inc., 1968.

Grant, E. L., *Statistical Quality Control* (2nd ed.). New York: McGraw-Hill Book Co., Inc., 1953.

Hare, Van Court, Jr., *Systems Analysis: A Diagnostic Approach*. New York: Harcourt, Brace & World, Inc., 1967.

Hottenstein, Michael P., *Models and Analysis for Production Management*. Scranton, Pennsylvania: International Textbook Company, 1968.

Magee, J. F., and D. M. Boodman, *Production Planning and Inventory Control*. New York: McGraw-Hill Book Co., Inc., 1967.

Massé, Pierre, *Optimal Investment Decisions*. Englewood Cliffs, N.J.: Prentice-Hall, Inc., 1962.

McMillan, Jr., Claude and Richard F. Gonzalez, *Systems Analysis: A Computer Approach to Decision Models* (revised edition). Homewood, Illinois: Richard D. Irwin, Inc., 1968.

Miller, David W., and Martin K. Starr, *Executive Decisions and Operations Research* (2nd ed.). Englewood Cliffs, N.J.: Prentice-Hall, Inc., 1969.

Miller, Richard B., *Plant Location Factors United States, 1966*. Monograph, Noyes Development Corporation, 118 Mill Road, Park Ridge, N.J.

Miller, Robert W., *Schedule, Cost, and Profit Control with PERT*. New York: McGraw-Hill Book Co., Inc., 1963.

Mize, Joe H., and J. Grady Cox, *Essentials of Simulation*. Englewood Cliffs, N.J.: Prentice-Hall, Inc., 1968.

Morse, P. M., *Queues, Inventories, and Maintenance*. New York: John Wiley & Sons, Inc., 1958.

Muth, John F., and Gerald L. Thompson, eds., *Industrial Scheduling*. Englewood Cliffs, N.J.: Prentice-Hall, Inc., 1963.

Naylor, T. H., J. L. Balintfy, D. S. Burdick, and K. Chu, *Computer Simulation Techniques*. New York: John Wiley & Sons, Inc., 1966.

Progress in Operations Research, Vol. I, Russell L. Ackoff, ed., 1961; *Progress in Operations Research*, Vol. II, David B. Hertz and Robert T. Eddison, eds., 1964; *Progress in Operations Research*, Vol. III, Julius Aronofsky, ed., 1968. New York: John Wiley & Sons, Inc.

Saaty, T. L., *Elements of Queuing Theory*. New York: McGraw-Hill Book Co., Inc., 1961.

Sasieni, M., A. Yaspan, and L. Friedman, *Operations Research, Methods and Problems*. New York: John Wiley & Sons, Inc., 1959.

Shewhart, Walter A., *Economic Control of Quality of Manufactured Product*. Princeton, N.J.: D. Van Nostrand Co., Inc., 1931.

Siu, R. G. H., *The Tao of Science*. New York: John Wiley & Sons, Inc., 1957.

Starr, Martin K., ed., *Management of Production*. England: Penguin Books Ltd., 1970.

——, *Management: A Modern Approach*. New York: Harcourt Brace Jovanovich, 1970.

——, and David W. Miller, *Inventory Control—Theory and Practice*. Englewood Cliffs, N.J.: Prentice-Hall, Inc., 1962.

Stockton, R. Stansbury, *Introduction to PERT*. Boston: Allyn and Bacon, Inc., 1964.

Terborgh, George, *An Introduction to Business Investment Analysis*. Washington, D.C.: Machinery & Allied Products Institute, 1958.

————, *Business Investment Management*. Washington, D.C.: Machinery and Allied Products Institute, 1967.

Wagner, Harvey M., *Principles of Management Science*. Englewood Cliffs, N.J.: Prentice-Hall, Inc., 1970.

Wilde, Douglass J., *Optimum Seeking Methods*. Englewood Cliffs, N.J.: Prentice-Hall, Inc., 1963.

Wiest, J. D., and F. K. Levy, *A Management Guide to PERT/CPM*. Englewood Cliffs, N.J.: Prentice-Hall, Inc., 1969.

Appendix

$$\phi(z) = \frac{1}{\sqrt{2\pi}}\, e^{-\frac{1}{2}z^2}$$

To Four Decimal Places

z	.00	.01	.02	.03	.04	.05	.06	.07	.08	.09
.0	.3989	.3989	.3989	.3988	.3986	.3984	.3982	.3980	.3977	.3973
.1	.3970	.3965	.3961	.3956	.3951	.3945	.3939	.3932	.3925	.3918
.2	.3910	.3902	.3894	.3885	.3876	.3867	.3857	.3847	.3836	.3825
.3	.3814	.3802	.3790	.3778	.3765	.3752	.3739	.3725	.3712	.3697
.4	.3683	.3668	.3653	.3637	.3621	.3605	.3589	.3572	.3555	.3538
.5	.3521	.3503	.3485	.3407	.3448	.3429	.3410	.3391	.3372	.3352
.6	.3332	.3312	.3292	.3271	.3251	.3230	.3209	.3187	.3166	.3144
.7	.3123	.3101	.3079	.3056	.3034	.3011	.2989	.2966	.2943	.2920
.8	.2897	.2874	.2850	.2827	.2803	.2780	.2756	.2732	.2709	.2685
.9	.2661	.2637	.2613	.2589	.2565	.2541	.2516	.2492	.2468	.2444
1.0	.2420	.2396	.2371	.2347	.2323	.2299	.2275	.2251	.2227	.2203
1.1	.2179	.2155	.2131	.2107	.2083	.2059	.2036	.2012	.1989	.1965
1.2	.1942	.1919	.1895	.1872	.1849	.1826	.1804	.1781	.1758	.1736
1.3	.1714	.1691	.1669	.1647	.1626	.1604	.1582	.1561	.1539	.1518
1.4	.1497	.1476	.1456	.1435	.1415	.1394	.1374	.1354	.1334	.1315
1.5	.1295	.1276	.1257	.1238	.1219	.1200	.1182	.1163	.1145	.1127
1.6	.1109	.1092	.1074	.1057	.1040	.1023	.1006	.0989	.0973	.0957
1.7	.0940	.0925	.0909	.0893	.0878	.0863	.0848	.0833	.0818	.0804
1.8	.0790	.0775	.0761	.0748	.0734	.0721	.0707	.0694	.0681	.0669
1.9	.0656	.0644	.0632	.0620	.0608	.0596	.0584	.0573	.0562	.0551
2.0	.0540	.0529	.0519	.0508	.0498	.0488	.0478	.0468	.0459	.0449
2.1	.0440	.0431	.0422	.0413	.0404	.0396	.0387	.0379	.0371	.0363
2.2	.0355	.0347	.0339	.0332	.0325	.0317	.0310	.0303	.0297	.0290
2.3	.0283	.0277	.0270	.0264	.0258	.0252	.0246	.0241	.0235	.0229
2.4	.0224	.0219	.0213	.0208	.0203	.0198	.0194	.0189	.0184	.0180
2.5	.0175	.0171	.0167	.0163	.0158	.0154	.0151	.0147	.0143	.0139
2.6	.0136	.0132	.0129	.0126	.0122	.0119	.0116	.0113	.0110	.0107
2.7	.0104	.0101	.0099	.0096	.0093	.0091	.0088	.0086	.0084	.0081
2.8	.0079	.0077	.0075	.0073	.0071	.0069	.0067	.0065	.0063	.0061
2.9	.0060	.0058	.0056	.0055	.0053	.0051	.0050	.0048	.0047	.0046
3.0	.0044	.0043	.0042	.0040	.0039	.0038	.0037	.0036	.0035	.0034
3.1	.0033	.0032	.0031	.0030	.0029	.0028	.0027	.0026	.0025	.0025
3.2	.0024	.0023	.0022	.0022	.0021	.0020	.0020	.0019	.0018	.0018
3.3	.0017	.0017	.0016	.0016	.0015	.0015	.0014	.0014	.0013	.0013
3.4	.0012	.0012	.0012	.0011	.0011	.0010	.0010	.0010	.0009	.0009
3.5	.0009	.0008	.0008.	.0008	.0008	.0007	.0007	.0007	.0007	.0006
3.6	.0006	.0006	.0006	.0005	.0005	.0005	.0005	.0005	.0005	.0004
3.7	.0004	.0004	.0004	.0004	.0004	.0004	.0003	.0003	.0003	.0003
3.8	.0003	.0003	.0003	.0003	.0003	.0002	.0002	.0002	.0002	.0002
3.9	.0002	.0002	.0002	.0002	.0002	.0002	.0002	.0002	.0001	.0001
4.0	.0001	.0001	.0001	.0001	.0001	.0001	.0001	.0001	.0001	.0001
z	.00	.01	.02	.03	.04	.05	.06	.07	.08	.09

$$A = \int_z^\infty \phi(z)\, dz$$

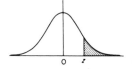

z	.00	.01	.02	.03	.04	.05	.06	.07	.08	.09
.0	.5000	.4960	.4920	.4880	.4840	.4801	.4761	.4721	.4681	.4641
.1	.4602	.4562	.4522	.4483	.4443	.4404	.4364	.4325	.4286	.4247
.2	.4207	.4168	.4129	.4090	.4052	.4013	.3974	.3936	.3897	.3859
.3	.3821	.3783	.3745	.3707	.3669	.3632	.3594	.3557	.3520	.3483
.4	.3446	.3409	.3372	.3336	.3300	.3264	.3228	.3192	.3156	.3121
.5	.3085	.3050	.3015	.2981	.2946	.2912	.2877	.2843	.2810	.2776
.6	.2743	.2709	.2676	.2643	.2611	.2578	.2546	.2514	.2483	.2451
.7	.2420	.2389	.2358	.2327	.2296	.2266	.2236	.2206	.2177	.2148
.8	.2119	.2090	.2061	.2033	.2005	.1977	.1949	.1922	.1894	.1867
.9	.1841	.1814	.1788	.1762	.1736	.1711	.1685	.1660	.1635	.1611
1.0	.1587	.1562	.1539	.1515	.1492	.1469	.1446	.1423	.1401	.1379
1.1	.1357	.1335	.1314	.1292	.1271	.1251	.1230	.1210	.1190	.1170
1.2	.1151	.1131	.1112	.1093	.1075	.1056	.1038	.1020	.1003	.0985
1.3	.0968	.0951	.0934	.0918	.0901	.0885	.0869	.0853	.0838	.0823
1.4	.0808	.0793	.0778	.0764	.0749	.0735	.0721	.0708	.0694	.0681
1.5	.0668	.0655	.0643	.0630	.0618	.0606	.0594	.0582	.0571	.0559
1.6	.0548	.0537	.0526	.0516	.0505	.0495	.0485	.0475	.0465	.0455
1.7	.0446	.0436	.0427	.0418	.0409	.0401	.0392	.0384	.0375	.0367
1.8	.0359	.0351	.0344	.0336	.0329	.0322	.0314	.0307	.0301	.0294
1.9	.0287	.0281	.0274	.0268	.0262	.0256	.0250	.0244	.0239	.0233
2.0	.0228	.0222	.0217	.0212	.0207	.0202	.0197	.0192	.0188	.0183
2.1	.0179	.0174	.0170	.0166	.0162	.0158	.0154	.0150	.0146	.0143
2.2	.0139	.0136	.0132	.0129	.0125	.0122	.0119	.0116	.0113	.0110
2.3	.0107	.0104	.0102	.0099	.0096	.0094	.0091	.0089	.0087	.0084
2.4	.0082	.0080	.0078	.0075	.0073	.0071	.0069	.0068	.0066	.0064
2.5	.0062	.0060	.0059	.0057	.0055	.0054	.0052	.0051	.0049	.0048
2.6	.0047	.0045	.0044	.0043	.0041	.0040	.0039	.0038	.0037	.0036
2.7	.0035	.0034	.0033	.0032	.0031	.0030	.0029	.0028	.0027	.0026
2.8	.0026	.0025	.0024	.0023	.0023	.0022	.0021	.0021	.0020	.0019
2.9	.0019	.0018	.0018	.0017	.0016	.0016	.0015	.0015	.0014	.0014
3.0	.0013	.0013	.0013	.0012	.0012	.0011	.0011	.0011	.0010	.0010
3.1	.0010	.0009	.0009	.0009	.0008	.0008	.0008	.0008	.0007	.0007
3.2	.0007	.0007	.0006	.0006	.0006	.0006	.0006	.0005	.0005	.0005
3.3	.0005	.0005	.0005	.0004	.0004	.0004	.0004	.0004	.0004	.0003
3.4	.0003	.0003	.0003	.0003	.0003	.0003	.0003	.0003	.0003	.0002
3.5	.0002	.0002	.0002	.0002	.0002	.0002	.0002	.0002	.0002	.0002
3.6	.0002	.0002	.0001	.0001	.0001	.0001	.0001	.0001	.0001	.0001
3.7	.0001	.0001	.0001	.0001	.0001	.0001	.0001	.0001	.0001	.0001
3.8	.0001	.0001	.0001	.0001	.0001	.0001	.0001	.0001	.0001	.0001
3.9	.0000	.0000	.0000	.0000	.0000	.0000	.0000	.0000	.0000	.0000
z	.00	.01	.02	.03	.04	.05	.06	.07	.08	.09

Index

A

Abstract models, 4
Arcs:
  activities on, 187–88
  networks, 188
Assignment method:
  algorithm for relatively continuous loading of production facilities, 269–72
  network version of, 276–78

Assignment method (*cont*):
  rules after row and column subtraction, 272–76
Attributes:
  classification by, 387
  monitoring, 397–400
  systems of, 252
Autocorrelations, 262–64
Average outgoing quality limit (AOQL), 380–81